The Consumer Society Reader

Edited by

Martyn J. Lee

BLACKWELL
Publishers

First published 2000

2 4 6 8 10 9 7 5 3 1

Blackwell Publishers Inc.
350 Main Street
Malden, Massachusetts 02148
USA

Blackwell Publishers Ltd
108 Cowley Road
Oxford OX4 1JF
UK

Library of Congress Cataloging-in-Publication Data

The consumer society reader / edited by Martin J. Lee.
     p.   cm.
Includes bibliographical references and index.
ISBN 0-631-20797-X (hardbound: alk. paper). — ISBN 0-631-20798-8
(pbk.: alk. paper)
   1. Consumer behavior—Social aspects.   2. Consumption (Economics)—
Social aspects.   I. Lee, Martyn J., 1961–   .
   HF5415.32.C6592   2000
   306.3—dc21   99-16939
                                                                         CIP

British Library Cataloguing in Publication Data

A CIP catalogue record for this book is available from the British Library.

Typeset in 10½ on 13 pt Galliard
by Ace Filmsetting Ltd, Frome, Somerset
Printed in Great Britain by T. J. International, Padstow, Cornwall

This book is printed on acid-free paper.

The Consumer Society Reader

For *Christine, Tom,* and *Morgan*

Contents

Contents

Preface

Anyone who has ever found themselves in the position of contemplating an edited collection of previously published material, such as this one, will at some early stage I strongly suspect have entertained the fantasy that the book could in some way emerge as a "definitive statement" of the subject under consideration. A few days of serious work in thinking through the potential material for inclusion and the organization of the thematic content, however, soon reveals this fantasy to be exactly that: a fantasy. So it is with *The Consumer Society Reader*. The sheer breadth and diversity of the potential subject matter, coupled with the vast corpus of literature which addresses this subject matter, makes no such "definitive statement" possible. This is not a book, therefore, that remotely claims to be "all things to all readers." Instead, I have chosen quite deliberately to trace a very particular path through the subject of consumer society, to construct a certain narrative around the particular themes I have decided to concentrate on. The focus of *The Consumer Society Reader*, therefore, can be said broadly to be concerned with an appreciation of *the complex relationship between production and consumption during the twentieth century*. This broad focus I elucidate in the Introduction. In view of this, inevitably some of the potential themes we might typically associate with the consumer society are marginalized, indeed some may have been neglected altogether. This should not be taken as an indication that such themes are in themselves insignificant, or that I think them to be insignificant. It is merely that this book should be read solely with the view that its contents represent a specific "take," and only a specific take, on the subject matter.

I have tried to keep the organization of the material as simple as possible. Each chapter is introduced with some brief notes which indicate the general topic and argument of the chapter, and which say something about the position that is adopted by the author. I have, wherever possible, sought to reproduce the text exactly as it appears in the original, maintaining all headings, sub-headings, and emphases in the form that they appear there, and reproducing the author's notes on the text. I have, unless absolutely unavoidable, resisted the use of ellipsis. Cross-references to works included in the Reader are enclosed in square brackets.

In editing this Reader I should like to thank the following people. For undertaking some of the more mundane tasks, but also for their valuable intellectual contributions, thanks go to Mike Ellis, Sarah Ferguson, Rosie Howard, Christine Lee, and Claire Lapworth. Thanks are also due to Clive Richards, Associate Dean of the School of Art and Design at Coventry University, for his continued support in this project, as well as many helpful and supportive comments from my colleagues in Communication, Culture and Media at Coventry. For their invaluable advice and constructive comments along the way I should also like to thank Sut Jhally, Lawrence Grossberg, Douglas Kellner, John Corner, Jim McGuigan, Don Slater, and Graham Murdock. The staff at Blackwell Publishers have been particularly supportive (and more than a little patient) in seeing this Reader through to completion. I should like to thank in particular Jill Landeryou of Blackwell, Oxford, who commissioned the Reader, and in the USA, Susan Rabinowitz, Ken Provencher, and Beth Remmes.

Finally, while I have of course endeavoured to eradicate all errors, I take full responsibility for any that may remain. Every effort has been made to trace the copyright holders but if any have been inadvertently overlooked both I and the publishers will be pleased to make the necessary arrangements at the first opportunity.

Introduction

Historians looking back at the twentieth century may well conclude that it was the century of the consumer society. Notwithstanding two brutal world wars, a bitter, protracted, and at times near apocalyptic cold war, and the rise (and in most cases) fall of state socialism across large sections of the globe, what has undoubtedly had the most significant impact upon the way of life of ordinary people in industrial societies over the last century has been the mass availability of consumer goods. No aspect of everyday life has been left untouched by the arrival of the consumer society: from the dwellings we inhabit; the modes of transportation and communication we use to travel and converse with others; the foodstuffs we eat; the clothes we wear; the ways in which we spend our leisure-time; indeed, the very structure of daily time itself – all of these changes are not simply the outcome of scientific and technological advancements but in fact reflect a profound and fundamental change in the way that, as societies, we organize our very means to existence.

That this claim, at first glance, might appear somewhat hyperbolic is no doubt due to our thorough and complete inculcation into the "system" of consumer society; we are indeed so immersed in its logic, its modes of address and manners that we can scarcely begin to conceive of a form of social life which is not organized around the consumption of mass-produced commodities. It is precisely this taken-for-granted character, the very "ordinariness" of our consumer society which makes it forgivable that for most of us, most of the time, we are unable to reflect on what is in fact an "extra-ordinary" and quite remarkable form of social organization. This volume, then, is about many of the ways in which we have approached and attempted to make sense of this way of life.

Our grandparents, and if not them then certainly their parents, would without doubt have lived in a world which would have been just about as different from our own as it is possible to imagine. It would not have been simply that their material needs (needs for food, clothing, and shelter, for example) would have been satisfied quite differently to our own, but indeed their very dreams, hopes, and aspirations (for a long and healthy life, to have healthy and successful children, for instance – dreams, hopes, and aspirations perhaps not unlike our own in their essential character) would actually have been sought to have been fulfilled under a very different framework of expectancy. Consumer society, in fact, is not just about the satisfaction of needs, but in many ways it is about the forms through which we view the world and our position within it as well as gauge the progress of our life-trajectories. This is not to imply that our way is somehow an improvement (or for that matter an impoverishment) over that of our grandparents; simply that the arrival of consumer society during the last one hundred years has transformed not only our material existence but also our ontology, our very being itself.

This last assertion clearly prompts a plethora of questions about the ways in which consumer society intersects with our daily lives: how do we manage to negotiate, for example, a material world constructed largely through and by commodities? To what extent does the necessary consumption of these commodities either empower or disempower us as individuals, groups, or larger collectivities? How do these commodities and their symbolic mediation through advertising and other promotional forms reinforce particular patterns of social relations? How are particular social interests "written-into" consumer goods while others are systematically "written-out?" Under what circumstances can those people whose interests are, seemingly, not represented in consumer goods manage to reclaim and rearticulate them as an expression of their own needs and desires?

Beyond such questions, of course, lies a range of more overtly political ones: what are the consequences of consumer society on the earth's natural resources? To what extent has "First World" consumer capitalism come to represent a new form of colonialism, colonizing, either through its systems of production or consumption, or both, the majority of the "Third World?" How have the material infrastructures of consumer society – the shopping complexes, malls, and retail parks – redefined both the character and function of our towns and cities? What are the consequences of the erosion of indigenous, traditional cultures, of either the Third or First Worlds, by the all-pervasive cultures of consumption and promotion?

The questions proliferate. The aim of this volume is to present many of the essential themes that connect with consumer society, as well as indicate something of the variety of response to these themes. In organizing the content I have, however, deliberately avoided, at least in the narrow sense of the term, a "perspectives" approach in which a particular subject may be examined from a number of discrete and often mutually antagonistic disciplinary perspectives. While many of the selections included here clearly hail from recognizable academic disciplinary bases, their inclusion has been determined primarily on the basis of what each piece says about its subject matter and its contribution to our overall understanding of consumer society, rather than because it may represent a good illustration of, say, an anthropological or cultural studies approach to the subject.

The book is in two parts. Part 1 concerns itself primarily with some of the important theoretical and conceptual material through which we have come to appreciate the dominant themes of our consumer society. Part 2 takes a broadly historical view of the century, generally moving chronologically from its outset to the present-day. However, this section should not be read simply as a descriptive history; what I have tried to do is present many, if not all, of the themes indicated in Part 1 as they variously emerged and took political, cultural, social, and economic precedence at particular points in time. Some of the pieces were produced during the period they discuss and represent something of the intellectual character of the debates around consumption which existed at that time; others were written retrospectively and attempt to summarize and place in a broader historical and social context the themes of the period under discussion. The overall aim of both sections, then, is not just to present a number of abstracted theoretical, philosophical, and speculative approaches to consumption, but to demonstrate how such approaches have emerged and connected with real material and historical developments during the last one hundred years or so.

Theoretical and Conceptual Foundations

Given that my primary concern in this book is with the emergence of a consumer society during the twentieth century, it may seem rather odd, at first glance, that the first two contributions deal neither directly with consumption nor were produced within or are "about" this time frame. Of course, it is the particular strength of Marx that he has bequeathed us by far the most systematic and penetrating analysis of capitalism we currently have. It is thus within the specific logic of capitalism, and to no considerably small extent within Marx's analysis of this logic, that many of the debates about consumption have been framed and understood. The pieces included here represent the "two sides" of Marx's work, namely the "philosophical" and the "economic" Marx. Chapter 1, "Estranged Labour," is taken from the Economic and Philosophical Manuscripts and dates from 1844. While the piece, not surprisingly given its author, primarily concerns itself with labor and production, it is clear that consumption is intimately connected with these activities. This connection between labor (production) and consumption, Marx implies, is not to be regarded solely in the narrower economic and political sense, but in the most profound sense of all: that of its relation to human species-being itself. Labor, Marx argues, is essential to our ontological composition; that is, we create and inhabit a material world in our own image and which reflects the unique character of our needs. This material world emerges from and becomes manifest in our products, the products of our labor. Therefore, consumption – the processes of using and employing these products – is simply the *realization* of labor and production, and, therefore, the realization of essential human species-being itself. Consumption, in other words, is the *release*, albeit made possible by labor, of our true characters as human beings and it is this which ultimately separates us from the rest of the animal kingdom. Under capitalism however, Marx continues, this vital relation between labor and consumption is ruptured; workers no longer engage in labor to produce products to satisfy their own needs, but rather sell their labor-power in return for wages. Labor is thus "estranged" from its essential purpose in creating products which reflect the needs of the worker. Likewise, consumption becomes the consumption of products created by another, and whose primary purpose is not the satisfaction of a need but the procurement of profit. Under such a conception, consumption itself therefore becomes estranged or "alienated": we live in a world of phenomenal forms, materials which, in their estrangement from us, may indeed "satisfy" certain material or biological needs but cannot hope to connect with our existential and ontological "essence." As Herbert Marcuse, writing over one hundred years later, but clearly with Marx's words very much in mind, puts it: "The people recognize themselves in their commodities; they find their soul in their automobile, hi-fi set, split-level home, kitchen equipment. The very mechanism which ties the individual to society has changed" (Marcuse, 1986: 9).

Marx's conclusions in chapter 1, reached in abbreviated form and presented somewhat poetically, are given their most systematic and rigorous treatment in *Capital*, volume one of which was published in 1867. The understanding implied by Marx and made explicit in the quotation from Marcuse that commodities represent non-essential dimensions of our species-being is formally captured in the concept of "fetishism." For Marx, the commodity has two aspects: those of use-value and exchange-value. Use-value (the value of a commodity in its use) is simply that property of a commodity which is capable of satisfying human needs and thus, according to Marx, is the expression of a relationship between a person/need and an object/satisfaction. The notion of exchange-value (the value of a commodity in its exchange) by contrast expresses the rate and ratio at which, at a given moment in time, one commodity exchanges with another; that is, its "equivalence" in other commodities. Typically this expression of commodity equivalences is mediated through the money system and becomes apparent in the commodity's price. A commodity's price, therefore, does not reflect some intrinsic economic worth but rather is simply the abstracted expression of it's exchange rate with other commodities which also bear their own price. Unlike use-value, exchange-value, it would seem, expresses a relationship purely between objects and, consequently, if use-value represents the expression of a social relationship between people and objects then exchange-value is the expression of a non-social relationship between one object and another. It is at this point of recognition, however, that Marx explodes the fantasy of this latter aspect of the commodity. Exchange-value may appear to us, he argues, as a straightforward relationship of equivalences between objects, but, as he makes clear elsewhere in *Capital*, the commodity is in fact the expression of a certain amount of human labor in production. If commodities are actually expressions of human labor (and by implication expressions of the social conditions under which that labor was performed), then the relation between different commodities is actually the expression of a relation between different acts of labor. Exchange-value is thus revealed to be the expression of a social, rather than a non-social, relation:

> It is nothing but the definite social relation between men themselves which assumes here, for them, the fantastic form of a relation between things ... I call this the fetishism which attaches itself to the products of labour as soon as they are produced as commodities. (Marx, 1976: 165)

For Marx, then, it is this "mysterious" aspect of the commodity which ultimately prevents us from recognizing the exploitative essence of capitalism. This theme resurfaces almost as a leitmotif among neo-Marxist commentators during the twentieth century. Indeed, in the hands of many commentators fetishism becomes an even more powerful concept when it is used to analyze the role commodities play within the sphere of consumption rather than solely within the sphere of production. For the French critic Jean Baudrillard (see chapters 3 and 19) the very mechanism by which capitalism conceals its exploitative character has shifted its center of gravity during the twentieth century from the field of production to that of consumption. In *For a Critique of the Political Economy of the Sign* (Baudrillard, 1981) Baudrillard extends Marx's original conceptual and theoretical reach by introducing a new conception of the value-form, namely that of "sign-value," while simultaneously attacking Marx for naturalizing, that is, making a fetish himself out of the concept of use-value. To be sure, he argues, commodities are fetishized in exchange. But they perhaps receive their most thorough form of fetishization in use-value. There is nothing "natural" about human needs, he continues; rather, all needs are socially and historically contingent. Commodities of consumption (the satisfiers of these needs), therefore, inevitably possess a significatory capacity, a "sign-value." In the twentieth century this sign-value which attaches to commodities is increasingly determined by the powerful institutions of advertising, motivational research, and commodity promotion generally. These institutions grant consumer goods their cultural meanings within a self-referential system of cultural meanings, calculating and recalculating their "worth" (their cultural meaning) according to the precise conditions of the (symbolic) "market." For Baudrillard, then, this system is as totalitarian as it is impenetrable to resistance: consumers merely assimilate the meanings transferred onto them via advertising's manipulation of the "code" of commodity sign-values.

With Baudrillard we have the clear and unequivocal assertion that consumption is as much a *cultural activity and process* as it is an economic one. Although perhaps lacking the theoretical sophistication of Baudrillard, this general claim was actually made just as forcefully many years earlier by Thorstein Veblen in his now classic account of the leisure class (see chapter 4). In *The Theory of the Leisure Class* Veblen identifies a prescient subclass of contemporary consumer society. This emergent leisure class, defined primarily by their increasing pecuniary strength, feel it incumbent upon themselves to objectify this pecuniary status in manifest display. This, suggests Veblen, takes the form of a conspicuous consumption of goods and leisure, and, indeed, anything that is either ostensibly wasteful or that signals a cultural distance from the world of social necessity (of labor, work, or any activity or object that is remotely useful in its character). While Veblen's ideas in this respect do tend perhaps to collapse consumption into a rather singularly motivated set of activities – consumption is surely more than just the conspicuous display of goods to demonstrate status relations - his ideas form nonetheless an important primary foundation for our understanding of what constitutes a very visible, although by no means exclusive, feature of modern consumption practice.

Veblen, and to the same extent, although perhaps in different contexts, both Marx and Baudrillard, writes against the grain of what was, and arguably still is, the received "common sense" orthodoxy of the conception of consumption, namely that expressed in conservative political economy. It is significant that all three writers are keen to frame their remarks within the context of a systematic rebuttal of such conceptions. Such an orthodoxy simply posits, usually in a rather unreflective manner, a "sovereign consumer," a rational and free-thinking individual who is seen to maximize his (for in such accounts the consumer is invariable male) satisfactions through a wise calculation of the various merits and limitations of the goods on offer against their price. While at one level the naive instrumentalism of this type of "value-for-money" approach to consumer activity hardly requires the effort of a critique, at another level it perhaps deserves the most rigorous and systematic one. For when "real-world" decisions have to be made, usually by government agencies, about consumption matters (how much should governments subsidize certain aspects of consumption, should the free market decide alone what goods should be available, what proportion of tax-payer's money should be spent on the arts, what proportion on popular cultural activities, etc.), then it is more often than not to precisely the naive instrumentalism of the economists that governments turn. In this context, it is arguable that Colin Campbell's systematic demolition of such ideas expressed in chapter 5 becomes required reading for economists and governments alike.

In fact, Campbell's critique is extended beyond the very basic conception of consumer behavior offered by the economists to include derivatives of that approach initiated by Veblen himself. Almost as something of a sop to the very idea that consumers could be motivated by anything other than purely rational, economic, and utilitarian motives, Campbell suggests, economists have been forced to concede that phenomena such as "snob effects" (an attempt to "distance oneself from the Joneses" through the consumption of goods which have an exclusive character) and "bandwagon effects" (an attempt to "keep up with the Joneses" through the consumption of those goods seen to be consumed by the social group to which one aspires) represent aberrant (i.e. cultural) motivations within consumer behavior. That such reduced and feeble derivations of Veblen's ideas, themselves hardly offering the most insightful understanding of consumption, should be virtually the only allowance made by economics to the cultural genesis of consumption is proof indeed of its epistemological impoverishment.

Perhaps the most forceful case in support of the assertion that consumer activities might in fact have cultural, rather than purely economic, origins, is that found in Mary Douglas's and Baron Isherwood's *The World of Goods*, published originally in 1978. The lateness of the date of publication, coupled with the fact that this book is often regarded as one of the first significant and genuinely authoritative statements about the cultural dimensions of consumption, is perhaps indicative of how relatively neglected consumption has been as a serious area for scholarly enquiry. Drawing heavily on empirical anthropological evidence from a variety of non-"Western," premodern cultures, Douglas and Isherwood advance the basic argument that goods in all cultures function first and foremost as concrete manifestations of the social practices and rituals of their users. Goods therefore perform an essentially communicative purpose, "making visible and stable the categories of culture." Notwithstanding the deeply problematical implication that consumer goods and behaviors in advanced capitalist societies are effectively homologous to those found in non-capitalist, premodern cultures, Douglas and Isherwood's contribution to our understanding of the significance of consumption is extremely welcome. It is, however, through the work of Pierre Bourdieu that such an anthropology of consumption receives by far its most thorough-going and detailed treatment.

In its basic premise Bourdieu's work, perhaps best represented in *Distinction*, his monumental account of postwar French culture, owes more than a minor debt to Veblen. Consumption, argues Bourdieu, is motivated first and foremost by the need for social groupings or "class-fractions" to achieve recognized status or "distinction." In this, goods (be they works of art, music, foodstuffs, or items of interior design) present the multiple opportunities for groups to exercise their cultural skills, competences, and knowledge of the particular field in question; that is, to demonstrate something of the stock of "cultural capital" they possess. Through the "art" of knowing what to consume and, more importantly, the "correct" (most erudite) manner or mode in which to consume, groups are able to objectify their status and social standing in the eyes of others, to confirm and reconfirm the boundaries of what properly constitutes the "tasteful" and the "tasteless," and in so doing to situate themselves on the "right" side of such a boundary. In such a schema, and this is perhaps what ultimately separates Bourdieu's work from that of Douglas and Isherwood, consumption comes to represent more than merely the disinterested objectification of cultural practice, but rather it becomes the very site of a class struggle conducted through culture.

This general conclusion is explored in some detail in Mike Featherstone's *Lifestyle and Consumer Culture*. Featherstone uses both Bourdieu's theoretical insight and his particular class-fraction categories to examine the cultural implications of the taste patterns and adopted lifestyles of the "new petit bourgeoisie," a rising class within the social structure composed in no small measure of the "cultural intermediaries" – the image and symbolic specialists who work, for example, in the media professions and the cultural industries generally. The conclusions here are important. For if both Bourdieu and Featherstone are correct in their assertions that, first, consumption among this class of individuals is essentially a political process of symbolic violence and, second, that this class plays an increasingly important role in producing and distributing the symbolic resources used by *everyone*, then it is clear that it is of more than mere "academic" significance that we come to appreciate exactly what the political dimensions of this field of symbolic struggle are.

While anthropological approaches to the study of consumption have been enormously influential and valuable in informing our overall knowledge of the issues involved, even the more sophisticated sociological variants such as that presented in Bourdieu's *Distinction* are not without their problems. Of these, perhaps the most damaging to their reputation is the unwillingness (or even inability) to find a space for the role played by the producers of goods (and by implication their commercial mediators – advertisers, marketers, and other forms of commercial promotion) in fixing the symbolic meanings of those goods *prior* to their arrival in the hands of their eventual consumers. We are forced to conclude, on reading Bourdieu for example, that goods are effectively little other than "symbolic utilities," if not quite blank canvases upon which groups are free to express their cultural competences, then at least infinitely malleable materials in the ways they can be pressed into the service of the "symbolic violence" involved in achieving distinction. While essentially sympathetic to Bourdieu's general approach, Daniel Miller is also keen to emphasize this significant shortcoming. In chapter 9 (taken from his excellent *Material Culture and Mass Consumption* published in 1987) Miller argues that no simple or singular explanation or "theory" of consumption is effectively possible: the character of the sum total of commodities available to us is intrinsically so diverse, the origins of their production so various, the interests invested in them during their stages of conception, production, design, and promotion, for example, so non-uniform, and, finally, the social and cultural contexts of their use and consumption so different from one another, that claims to any generalized and generalizable account of what happens to goods and their consumers in the process of consumption are inevitably fallacious. To demonstrate this Miller draws on a variety of studies involving some very different forms of the commodity. Houses and children's sweets, to choose two examples referred to by Miller, are, to be sure, both subjected to the forces of commodification. But perhaps here is where the similarity ends – we would be naive in the extreme to think that we could arrive at any satisfactory appreciation of the forces at play and the issues at stake in the consumption of these vastly different objects merely by subjecting them to the same process of theoretical abstraction by virtue of the fact that they are both commodities. What is important, argues Miller, is not the commodification process *per se*, but the specific context in which commodification occurs – exactly what is being commodified? Who are the producers? Who are the intended consumers? Who are the actual consumers? For each and every commodity, therefore, the variables will be different. The best response to the complexity of this material culture of commodities, Miller continues, is not so much to develop a plurality of approaches to the subject of consumption, but rather to recognize "a pluralism which already confronts us" (Miller, 1987: 175).

No clearer demonstration of this last point can be found than Dick Hebdige's essay (chapter 10) on the Italian scooter (itself used as illustrative material by Miller). In this extraordinarily detailed and generally exemplary study, Hebdige traces the shifting meanings and uses of the scooter, both in space and in time. The scooter is thus placed on a complex analytical grid which considers the movement of the object from its conception, production, and mediation (its advertising and promotion), to the variety of uses to which it is eventually put. At the same time Hebdige overlays the way in which the scooter also shifted its meanings through its historical lifetime – as a vehicle for women during its early years, as an exemplary manifestation of "Italianate style and taste" and "good design" during the 1950s, its incorporation into British cultural life (through, for example, films such as *Summer Holiday* and *Wonderful Life*) and especially its adoption as an icon of mod culture during the 1960s. If nothing else, the sheer complexity of Hebdige's findings (and here the essay really ought to be allowed to speak for itself) should force us to conclude, once and for all, that there can be no possible "Theory of consumption."

An alternative way to conceptualize the general questions under discussion is to treat the "forces" of production and consumption as a dialectic – as opposing forces, of which production (capital and its functionaries) is unquestionably the dominant while consumption ("the people") is subordinate. Such an approach need not be exclusively Marxist in its origin, however, as Michel de Certeau's contribution here from *The Practice of Everyday Life* attests. If in Baudrillard's schema the "game" between production and consumption is essentially one-sided (consumers become little more than mere pawns in the process of the manipulation of the code of sign-value), then with de Certeau consumption is seen to exact no small measure of revenge. De Certeau's argument revolves around the metaphor of warfare, in particular that of guerrilla warfare in which the dominant "military" force (production) adopts sophisticated *strategies* to (literally) "target" consumption. But as with any large conventional army, it is hampered by the general inflexibility of its size, and, in addition, must contend with the fleet-of-foot maneuvers, the "guileful ruses" or *tactics* employed by the subordinate field of consumption. De Certeau's chapter is in parts deceptively simple and seductive in its metaphorical conception, in other parts decidedly complex – at times to the point of convolution - in its speculative abstraction. In spite of this (or perhaps because of it?) *The Practice of Everyday Life* and the ideas contained in this chapter especially, have attained over recent years, particularly among some writers within the field of cultural studies, a certain exalted status. In such accounts (see, for example, chapter 25 by John Fiske) the previously pacific and obedient domain of consumption is seen to have been liberated from the totalizing domination of ideology and become a subversive, creative, and "empowering" cultural activity.

The Character of the Consumer Society

Moments of genesis are notoriously difficult to discern. Indeed, as Don Slater argues in chapter 12 of part 2, there may be a strong temptation for every genera-tion to see their variant of consumer culture as new and unique. On closer inspec-tion, however, Slater suggests, each "moment" in the history of consumer culture is in fact merely an extension and "working through" of precedents set by an earlier phase. Nonetheless, and notwithstanding Slater's ingenious "unveiling" of an entire history of precedents of consumer society, if we were for a moment to imagine history suspended and forced to reduce the vast edifice of our present-day, twentieth-century consumer society to a single moment of genesis, then that moment would surely have to be the one in 1913 when the first of Henry Ford's Model T automobiles rolled off the assembly line at his plant in Dearborn, Michi-gan. Ford's dual revolution in car production, the wholesale implementation of "Taylorist" labor practices to replace an older craft production, coupled with the introduction of single-purpose, dedicated machinery, had, of course, the effect of increasing vastly the scale of production while simultaneously lowering unit costs. If, however, we were to consider the matter of the genesis of consumer society more carefully we might in fact, as David Harvey indeed does, concede that the true moment of its birth came one year later in 1914, when Ford introduced his five-dollar, eight-hour day for workers (Harvey, 1989: 125). Behind this unprecedentedly high wage for production work lay a recognition (although, we might conclude, merely at this point symbolic) that for mass production to suc-ceed as a generalized schema for capitalist wealth creation it required a corre-sponding "system" of *mass consumption*, a system which would necessarily be underpinned by a social average wage that was sufficient ultimately to absorb pro-duction's output.

Thus we arrive at the simple and inescapable imperative of twentieth-century capitalism: to ensure both the sufficient material means and the cultural desire within the population in general to enable this population to consume that pro-portion of goods that is roughly equivalent to the total net output of goods. It is perhaps arguable that, today, we may take for granted the second aspect of this imperative – the cultural desire to consume – as having already been achieved; within 1920s USA, as Stuart Ewen demonstrates forcefully in his book *Captains of Consciousness*, it is precisely this aspect of consumption which is perceived to be the major hurdle that mass-production capitalism must overcome if it is to succeed. The establishment of a mass-production/mass-consumption economy was therefore never just about a routine and technological reorganization of productive resources or, for that matter, the provision of material infrastructures and an adequate financial fund for consumption; it was, to no small degree, underwritten by a definite ideological crusade waged by, in particular, a burgeoning advertising industry on behalf of productive capital. Accordingly, as far as the history of contemporary capitalism goes, the 1920s (and we might add every decade since) was a period in which a primary function of capital was no less than one of social planning and engineering.

Historians seem genuinely divided on exactly how effective this prewar ideological assault on potential consumers actually was. There is a suggestion that established and traditional cultural patterns which were, as Ewen himself suggests, based on "an agglomeration of self-sufficiency, communitarianism, localized popular culture, thrift and subjective social bonds and experiences" (ibid.: 58), were also extremely resilient to erosion from the sort of cultural modernity inscribed within an emerging consumer society. Indeed, one would perhaps imagine that whatever the various ideological seductions and temptations offered to people during the 1920s, the massive privations of the Depression years of the 1930s would see an inevitable reassertion of a traditional cultural sensibility which eschewed mass consumption in favor of the more "ontologically wholesome" practices of home production and simply "making do." However, the picture that actually emerges in the 1930s, at least according to Gary Cross (chapter 14), reveals an altogether different narrative: in both the US and Britain, according to the various evidences marshaled by Cross, ordinary people had to a large extent already assumed the "prejudices of consumption," were prepared to forsake certain material necessities in order to maintain some semblance of luxury consumption, and, when extreme poverty banished even this, hid themselves away until such a time of affluence enabled them once again to join the ranks of mass consumers.

By the 1940s, and certainly by the 1950s, the transition from what might be called a traditional, pre-Fordist way of life to a decidedly modern one organized around the dictates of the Fordist mass-consumer marketplace was, while not fully completed, then certainly well under way. It is one, seldom explored, facet of this transition that is considered by Sharon Zukin in chapter 15. Zukin examines the changing character of the notion of the "local neighborhood" through the role played by shops and shopping within this constructed space. Indeed, this geographical, social, and cultural construction is in many respects the epitome of the sort of traditionalism described by Ewen. Drawing upon her own childhood memories, as well as the reflections of other writers on their similar experiences, the local neighborhood shopping street is revealed as a place infused with strong interpersonal social relations: a place where gossip is exchanged, a place where shopkeepers and customers all know each other by name, and where information about the goods being sold is often mediated publically by certain well-known local customers, a practice tacitly sanctioned by some store owners. The context for this concrete expression of the "local community," at least in Zukin's US experience of it, is that articulated primarily by the variables of race and ethnicity (Zukin's locale is predominantly Jewish). Thus the shifting racial and ethnic populations in the US, and the break-up of many racially and ethnically concentrated locales, is bound up with, although not necessarily a direct result of, the emergence during the postwar years of a fully-fledged Fordist consumer society and culture.

The "move downtown," the shift away from the local shopping street to the new urban shopping complexes of department stores and malls which was well underway by the late 1950s in the US, was also the moment at which we arrive in the "affluent society." For many working in the employ of industry, business, advertising, or indeed within the government, this is the very moment of the long-awaited delivery of the "American dream." The mass-consumer market, it seemed, had created a new world of wealth and opportunity, social democracy, and individual freedom; who – aside from perhaps a few "misguided" radical intellectual thinkers and "aberrant" economists – could possibly complain?

One such aberrant economist was John Kenneth Galbraith who, through a substantial corpus of writings over many years, became one of a select band of people who, in effect, represented America's liberal conscience. The essence of Galbraith's polemical broadside against the rationale for the justification of the whole productive apparatus was that the claim, so often made by those in industry and business, that mass production was simply in existence to satisfy a greater and greater proportion of our individual and social needs, was spurious in the extreme. The fact is, Galbraith concluded, many of the needs and wants that business and industry claim to be satisfying have been brought into existence in the first place by the system of mass production itself. Hence, the very *raison d'être* of the consumer society is thus revealed to be nothing other than the realization of a self-fulfilling prophecy: production creates a plethora of desires, wants, and needs, primarily through advertising and salesmanship, only then to appear as the savior of society by providing the wherewithal to satisfy those desires, wants, and needs. As Galbraith concludes: "so it is that if production creates the wants it seeks to satisfy . . . then the urgency of the wants can no longer be used to defend the urgency of the production. Production only fills a void that it has itself created" (Galbraith, 1958: 127). Very similar concerns to those expressed by Galbraith are also made in the populist writings of Vance Packard who, in chapter 17 for example, argues that the US has become so self-obsessed with the issue of its own economic growth that it cannot see that there is in fact no reasonable or justifiable purpose for such growth, especially when its essential product, through phenomena such as the material and aesthetic obsolescence of goods, is that of waste.

The alternative critical stance to that represented here by Galbraith and Packard exists within a primarily European tradition of intellectual radical Marxism.[1] This is represented here (chapter 20) by a brief extract from Haug's *Critique of Commodity Aesthetics*, which takes a critical view of the fetishized "phenomenal forms," originally described by Marx, within the context of 1960s consumer society; and to a very large extent by chapter 19, an extract from Baudrillard's early work *The System of Objects*. In this piece Baudrillard is keen to explore the proposition that the new world of consumer goods represents a new form of language in which brand names, in particular, are said to stand in place of and signify quite complex social meanings. For Baudrillard, however, it is arguable that, in the technical sense at least, this does form a new language; if it does, then it is "undoubtedly the most impoverished of languages: full of signification and empty meaning. It is a language of signals. And the 'loyalty' to a brand name is nothing more than the conditioned reflex of a controlled affect."

Baudrillard is in fact responding in many ways to the then extremely fashionable "science" of "motivation research," of which Ernest Dichter's contribution here (chapter 18) is a typical example. Motivation research actually amounts to little more than a mixture of a rather basic form of "pop" anthropology and psychology. Nonetheless, we should not underestimate its importance, especially in the way that advertisers of the period adopted its findings with relish. Motivation research seemed to offer something in the way of a "scientific" explanation of the associational qualities and attributes of particular goods; that is, why certain goods and products come to mean what they do to consumers. From this basis advertisers, marketers, and product designers claimed to be addressing what appear as essentially non-rational motivations in consumers, such as those of "desires" and "wants," in a completely new and rational way, a development confirmed in Leiss, Kline, and Jhally's summary of the evolution of the modern advertising industry (chapter 21).

The dominant image of the postwar consumer society that emerged in both liberal and radical critiques is that of a society managed and administered totally in all its respects. While capitalism had for many years seemingly known how best to organize the material variables of mass production (labor, technology, material resources, and the like), by the early 1960s it seemed also to have developed techniques for the appropriate organization and control of those far more volatile cultural variables of desire and wanting. It had, to borrow the title of Dichter's book, created a "strategy of desire."

This commensurability between production and consumption, not only in a quantitative sense but also in the sense of matching cultural attitudes towards consumption to those required by production, is captured in Michel Aglietta's concept of a "regime of accumulation" (chapter 22). The neo-Marxist political economy of "Regulation School" writers such as Aglietta[2] stresses that it was precisely this close correspondence between production and consumption over a number of years which made Fordism such an effective and successful (in capitalist terms) regime. Nowhere is this close correspondence more clearly seen than in the area of product design. The "functional aesthetic" of Fordism is thus an aesthetic clearly determined by the technical engineering demands of a mass-production system, but it is also culturally resonant with the ideological climate of the times: products were functionally adapted, although increasingly only in a symbolic manner, to reflect the values of scientific objectivity, faith in the future, and a belief in a social progress made possible through rationalistic planning.[3]

Given the seemingly unshakable foundations which underpinned Fordism during the postwar years, should we register surprise at the way in which not only its economic basis but also its cultural hegemony collapsed so spectacularly during the 1970s? For David Harvey (chapter 23) the answer is an unequivocal "no." Following Marx's prognosis for capitalism in general, he argues that any regime of accumulation – however permanent its appearance, however stable and efficient its infrastructures of social and economic regulation present themselves – always conceals an inevitable drift towards some form of crisis of "overaccumulation." For Harvey, Aglietta, and other socioeconomic commentators (including many writing from a non-Marxist position) it was ultimately Fordism's inflexibility in adapting and responding to changing market circumstances that lay at the heart of the crisis of the 1970s. It was, in essence, generally too costly to readapt or alter, at least on any significant scale, plant, machinery, and labor practices so as to accommodate the production of new forms of commodities once the old staple markets had reached saturation point. In the sphere of consumption directly, this structural weakness was exacerbated, in spite of the professed new knowledge about consumer motivations described above, by precisely *a lack of any real or economically useful knowledge* of consumption. Thus, throughout the period of Fordism, consumption was more often than not regarded simply as a socially unstratified agglomeration of buyers who, it was perceived, were more than content with the standardized and uniform character of the goods available to them.

In the face of the sudden and dramatic economic shifts of the 1970s, of which the 1973 oil crisis was perhaps the most obvious manifestation, and, in addition, the break-up of the postwar cultural and political consensus (in part triggered by the radicalism and "politicization" of culture during the late 1960s seen, for example, in the rise of feminism, student activism, civil rights movements, anti-war campaigns, etc.), Fordism seemed petrified.

As the 1970s wore on, and certainly by the early 1980s, it was clear to many, especially but by no means exclusively within the radical conservativism of the New Right, that the time was long overdue for a systematic and total restructuring of advanced capitalist economies. Starting with production, but quickly extending to both the spheres of distribution and consumption, notions of flexibility, adaptability, multi-tasking, diversity, and choice, backed by a computer-driven technological revolution, soon established themselves as the new orthodoxies of this emergent "post-Fordism."[4] By the late 1980s the Fordist schema of production, while not entirely dead, certainly had a more than competent rival in post-Fordist economic practice. More startling than the growing strength of post-Fordism in production, however, was the rebirth of consumer culture (Lee, 1993). As Frank Mort (chapter 24) argues, consumption has moved center stage, not only in the battle to establish the economic high ground of the period, but also as a primary means through which individuals come to express their cultural identities. Mort's piece in fact forms part of the "New Times" manifesto, an attempt by several liberal thinkers on the British Left to realign socialist politics in general, and the British Labour Party in particular, towards the dramatically reconstituted economic, political, social, and cultural landscape of the period.[5] Mort argues that at the heart of this realignment should be an attempt by the Left to reclaim the category of consumption; to recognize the real significance it has on most people's lives and to appreciate it as a source of genuine pleasure and symbolic creativity.

If the party-political Left, particularly in Britain, was being urged to consider seriously the positive, creative, and liberating merits of contemporary consumption, then for some sections of the intellectual Left, especially within the increasingly influential field of cultural studies, no such exhortations were necessary. Following some of the insights gleaned into the "active reading processes" involved in the "consumption" of media texts based on the "encoding/decoding" model (see, in particular, Hall, 1980; Morley, 1980), and drawing strongly on the theoretical legacies of such intellectual heavyweights as Bourdieu and, especially, de Certeau, writers such as John Fiske, in a string of books and essays published during the late 1980s and early 1990s (chapter 25, this volume; Fiske, 1987; 1993), stressed the transformative powers and subversive pleasures involved in consumption. Fiske argued that while producers of mass-consumption artifacts might inscribe within those artifacts certain dominant or preferred meanings (through advertising, for example), it could be by no means assured that those meanings would be activated or realized, at least in the ways producers wanted them to be, by consumers. Consumers bring to bear on their consumption practices their subjective experiences of the world, which Fiske suggested are typically ones of subordination and disempowerment. Yet most consumers are also extremely semiotically literate and tactically astute; rather than being merely the terrain upon which consumers' subordination is reproduced, consumption is a site of positive resistance. In consuming, we engage in creative acts of willful textual subversion, distorting preferred meanings and using goods in a whole range of ways for which they were not "intended." This is where Fiske's ideas represent the polar-opposite of those held by thinkers such as Baudrillard (who even in his later "postmodernist" writings still insists on the passive, uncritical status of consumption). Ultimately, according to Fiske, the sphere of consumption becomes simply the space of a "semiotic democracy": "All the cultural industries can do is produce a repertoire of texts or cultural resources for the various formations of the people to use or reject in the ongoing process of producing their popular culture" (Fiske, 1989: 23–4).

Assaults on Fiske's ideas have been legion. Of these, two particular positions are included here. The first, represented by John Clarke (chapter 26), re-emphasizes the role and significance of production within the broader relationship it shares with consumption. There is a genuine danger, warns Clarke, that in the clamor to unearth resistant and oppositional uses of mass-produced commodities we may lose sight of the significance of the fact that commodities are in the first instance economic phenomena and thus (as many writers – notably Marx – have long re-minded us) already conceal an entire history of exploitation (of people and, in-creasingly, natural resources). The second critique of Fiske's ideas, expressed here by Jim McGuigan (chapter 27), is perhaps the most damning. The overemphasis on notions of "semiotic democracy" and "creative" and "active" consumption practices is taken to its logical conclusion. In spite of the left-wing rhetoric and quasi-revolutionary conceptions of "the people" within Fiske's work, we are forced to conclude, argues McGuigan, that the construction of such an autonomous con-sumer ultimately differs very little in reality to the similarly autonomous variant of the consumer found within neo-classical economics, and which was so enthusias-tically adopted by the New Right during the 1980s. Semiotic democracy thus becomes a mere pseudonym for consumer sovereignty, and is therefore the point at which an exaggerated cultural populism of a supposedly radical Left meets the sort of populism commonly espoused by the New Right.

The Consumer Society Reader concludes with Andrew Wernick's sobering reflec-tions on our current "promotional culture" (chapter 28). In essence, Wernick suggests that it is now no longer possible to speak of a range of discrete categories of promotion (for example, "advertising," "marketing," and "public relations"). Rather, these things are now so interconnected and interdependent that the bounda-ries between them have been all but erased. Moreover, the generalized category of promotion has become all-pervasive, articulating not only commodities in the "tra-ditional" or proper sense of the term, but virtually all available goods and all forms of institutions, regardless of whether they are privately or publically owned. To paraphrase Frederic Jameson, promotion itself has become "the condition of con-temporary culture." All discourse, argues Wernick, is so saturated with the rhetori-cal devices of promotion that, in our public lives and perhaps increasingly in our private lives, we are unable to think and act outside of a promotional frame of reference.

Whatever their primary focus, all the selections chosen for *The Consumer Society Reader* ultimately emphasize that consumption is first and foremost a *political* category that touches our lives in the most profound ways. The project for all of us, not just for intellectuals or those engaged "professionally" with consumer society, is to understand this politics of consumption so that we may begin to harness and redirect its enormous powers towards some form of better collective future. I hope *The Consumer Society Reader* is a positive contribution to this project.

Notes

1 Of this tradition perhaps the most obvious names are those writers associated with the Frankfurt School, such as Theodor Adorno, Max Horkheimer, and Herbert Marcuse, who actually took up residence in the US, an experience which in itself was to have a profound impact on their writings.
2 See also in particular the work of Alain Lipietz.
3 For an elaboration of how this functionalist aesthetic of Fordism emerged and was developed, initially through the design principles of "streamlining," see Dick Hebdige's essay "Towards a cartography of taste" (Hebdige, 1988).
4 One of the earliest systematic accounts of how this new post-Fordism (or in their terms "flexible specialization") should be constituted in production can be found in Piore and Sabel (1984).
5 The "New Times project" which appeared throughout the period 1987–9 was associated with the now defunct British journal *Marxism Today* (see in particular Hall and Jacques, 1989). It is interesting to compare the striking similarities between some of the "consumptionist" and "youth-oriented" rhetoric of the Labour government which came to power in 1997 and the rhetoric often found in the New Times writing. Whether "credit," in the laudatory sense of the term, should go to the New Times project for its role in reinventing the British Labour Party is, perhaps, something of a moot point.

References

Baudrillard, J. (1981) *For a Critique of the Political Economy of the Sign*, St Louis MO: Telos.
Ewen, S. (1976) *Captains of Consciousness*, New York: McGraw-Hill.
Fiske, J. (1987) *Television Culture*, London: Methuen.
Fiske, J. (1989) *Understanding Popular Culture*, London: Unwin Hyman.
Fiske, J. (1993) *Power Plays, Power Works*, New York and London: Verso.
Galbraith, J. K. (1958) *The Affluent Society*, London: Hamish Hamilton.
Hall, S. (1980) "Encoding/decoding", in Hall, S., Hobson, D., Lowe, A., and Willis, P. (eds) *Culture, Media, Language*, London: Hutchinson.
Hall, S. and Jacques, M. (eds) (1989) *New Times: The Changing Face of Politics in the 1990s*, London: Lawrence and Wishart.
Harvey, D. (1989) *The Condition of Postmodernity*, Oxford: Blackwell Publishers.
Hebdige, D. (1988) *Hiding in the Light*, London: Routledge.
Lee, M. J. (1993) *Consumer Culture Reborn: The Cultural Politics of Consumption*, London: Routledge.

Marcuse, H. (1986) *One Dimensional Man*, London: Ark.

Marx, K. (1976) *Capital*, vol. 1, Harmondsworth: Penguin Books.

Miller, D. (1987) *Material Culture and Mass Consumption*, Oxford: Blackwell Publishers.

Morley, D. (1980) *The Nationwide Audience*, London: BFI.

Piore, M. J. and Sabel, C. F. (1984) *The Second Industrial Divide: Possibilities for Prosperity*, New York: Basic Books.

Part I
Theoretical and Conceptual Foundations

1

Estranged Labour

Karl Marx

In one of the few places in which consumption is explicitly discussed in his work,[1] Marx emphasizes its deep ontological importance to human beings. In "organic" human societies, he argues, consumption constitutes a dynamic relation with production in which essential human species-being comes to be fulfilled or "realized." Under capitalism and the system of wage-labor, however, where workers neither see nor consume directly the fruits of their labor, this relation is ruptured and humans are disconnected or "alienated" from their ideal life circumstance.

We have started out from the premise of political economy. We have accepted its language and its laws. We presupposed private property; the separation of labour, capital and land, and likewise of wages, profit and capital; the division of labour; competition; the concept of exchange value, etc. From political economy itself, using its own words, we have shown that the worker sinks to the level of a commodity, and moreover the most wretched commodity of all; that the misery of the worker is in inverse proportion to the power and volume of his production; that the necessary consequence of competition is the accumulation of capital in a few hands and hence the restoration of monopoly in a more terrible form; and finally the distinction between capitalist and landlord, between agricultural worker and industrial worker, disappears and the whole of society must split into the two classes of *property owners* and *propertyless workers*.

Political economy proceeds from the fact of private property. It does not explain it. It grasps the *material* process of private property, the process through which it actually passes, in general and abstract formulae which it then takes as *laws*. It does not *comprehend* these laws, i.e. it does not show how they arise from the nature of private property. Political economy fails to explain the reason for the division between labour and capital, between capital and land. For example, when it defines the relation of wages to profit it takes the interests of the capitalists as the basis of

From "The Economic and Political Manuscripts" in *Early Writings* (London: Verso, 1975), pp. 322–30. Reprinted by permission of the publishers.

its analysis; i.e. it assumes what it is supposed to explain. Similarly, competition is frequently brought into the argument and explained in terms of external circumstances. Political economy teaches us nothing about the extent to which these external and apparently accidental circumstances are only the expression of a necessary development. We have seen how exchange itself appears to political economy as an accidental fact. The only wheels which political economy sets in motion are *greed* and the *war of avaricious competition*.

Precisely because political economy fails to grasp the interconnections within the movement, it was possible to oppose, for example, the doctrine of competition to the doctrine of monopoly, the doctrine of craft freedom to the doctrine of the guild and the doctrine of the division of landed property to the doctrine of the great estate; for competition, craft freedom and division of landed property were developed and conceived only as accidental, deliberate, violent consequences of monopoly, of the guilds and of feudal property and not as their necessary, inevitable and natural consequences.

We now have to grasp the essential connection between private property, greed, the separation of labour, capital and landed property, exchange and competition, value and the devaluation [*Entwertung*] of man, monopoly and competition, etc. – the connection between this entire system of estrangement [*Entfremdung*] and the *money* system.

We must avoid repeating the mistake of the political economist, who bases his explanations on some imaginary primordial condition. Such a primordial condition explains nothing. It simply pushes the question into the grey and nebulous distance. It assumes as fact and events what it is supposed to deduce, namely the necessary relationship between two things, between, for example, the division of labour and exchange. Similarly, theology explains the origin of evil by the fall of man, i.e. it assumes as a fact in the form of history what it should explain.

We shall start out from a *present-day* economic fact.

The worker becomes poorer the more wealth he produces, the more his production increases in power and extent. The worker becomes an ever cheaper commodity the more commodities he produces. The *devaluation* of the human world grows in direct proportion to the *increase in value* of the world of things. labour not only produces commodities; it also produces itself and the workers as a *commodity* and it does so in the same proportion in which it produces commodities in general.

This fact simply means that the object that labour produces, its product, stands opposed to it as *something alien*, as a *power independent* of the producer. The product of labour is labour embodied and made material in an object, it is the *objectification* of labour. The realization of labour is its objectification. In the sphere of political economy this realization of labour appears as *loss of and bondage to the object*, and appropriation as *estrangement*, as *alienation* [*Entäusserung*].

So much does the realization of labour appear as loss of reality that the worker loses his reality to the point of dying of starvation. So much does objectification appear as loss of the object that the worker is robbed of the objects he needs most not only for life but also for work. Work itself becomes an object which he can only obtain through an enormous effort and with spasmodic interruptions. So much does the appropriation of the object appear as estrangement that the more objects the worker produces the fewer can he possess and the more he falls under the domination of his product, of capital.

All these consequences are contained in this characteristic, that the worker is related to the *product of his labour* as to an *alien* object. For it is clear that, according to this premise, the more the worker exerts himself in his work, the more powerful the alien, objective world becomes which he brings into being over against himself, the poorer he and his inner world become, and the less they belong to him. It is the same in religion. The more man puts into God, the less he retains within himself. The worker places his life in the object; but now it no longer belongs to him, but to the object. The greater his activity, therefore, the fewer objects the worker possesses. What the product of his labour is, he is not. Therefore, the greater this product, the less he is himself. The externalization [*Entäusserung*] of the worker in his product means not only that his labour becomes an object, an *external* existence, but that it exists *outside him*, independently of him and alien to him, and begins to confront him as an autonomous power; that the life which he has bestowed on the object confronts him as hostile and alien.

Let us now take a closer look at *objectification*, at the production of the worker, and the *estrangement*, the *loss* of the object, of his product, that this entails.

The worker can create nothing without *nature*, without the *sensuous external world*. It is the material in which his labour realizes itself, in which it is active and from which and by means of which it produces.

But just as nature provides labour with the *means of life* in the sense that labour cannot *live* without objects on which to exercise itself, so also it provides the *means of life* in the narrower sense, namely the means of physical subsistence of the *worker*.

The more the worker *appropriates* the external world, sensuous nature, through his labour, the more he deprives himself of the *means to life* in two respects: firstly, the sensuous external world becomes less and less an object belonging to his labour, a *means of life* of his labour; and secondly, it becomes less and less a *means of life* in the immediate sense, a means for the physical subsistence of the worker.

In these two respects, then, the worker becomes a slave of his object; firstly in that he receives an *object of labour*, i.e. he receives work, and secondly in that he receives *means of subsistence*. Firstly, then, so that he can exist as a *worker*, and secondly as a *physical subject*. The culmination of this slavery is that it is only as a *worker* that he can maintain himself as a *physical subject* and only as a *physical subject* that he is a worker.

5

(The estrangement of the worker in his object is expressed according to the laws of political economy in the following way: the more the worker produces, the less he has to consume; the more value he creates, the more worthless he becomes; the more his product is shaped, the more misshapen the worker; the more civilized his object, the more barbarous the worker; the more powerful the work, the more powerless the worker; the more intelligent the work, the duller the worker and the more he becomes a slave of nature.)

Political economy conceals the estrangement in the nature of labour by ignoring the **direct** *relationship between the* **worker** *(labour)* **and production**. It is true that labour produces marvels for the rich, but it produces privation for the worker. It produces palaces, but hovels for the worker. It produces beauty, but deformity for the worker. It replaces labour by machines, but it casts some of the workers back into barbarous forms of labour and turns others into machines. It produces intelligence, but produces idiocy and cretinism for the worker.

The direct relationship of labour to its products is the relationship of the worker to the objects of his production. The relationship of the rich man to the objects of production and to production itself is only a *consequence* of this first relationship, and confirms it. ... Therefore when we ask what is the essential relationship of labour, we are asking about the relationship of the worker to production.

Up to now we have considered the estrangement, the alienation of the worker only from one aspect, i.e. his *relationship to the products of his labour*. But estrangement manifests itself not only in the result, but also in the *act of production*, within the *activity of production* itself. How could the product of the worker's activity confront him as something alien if it were not for the fact that in the act of production he was estranging himself from himself? After all the product is simply the résumé of the activity of production. So if the product of labour is alienation, the alienation of activity, the activity of alienation. The estrangement of the object of labour merely summarizes the estrangement, the alienation in the activity of labour itself.

What constitutes the alienation of labour?

Firstly, the fact that labour is *external* to the worker, i.e. it does not belong to his essential being; that he therefore does not confirm himself in his work, but denies himself, feels miserable and not happy, does not develop free mental and physical energy, but mortifies his flesh and ruins his mind. Hence the worker feels himself only when he is not working. His labour is therefore not voluntary but forced, it is *forced labour*. It is therefore not the satisfaction of a need but a mere *means* to satisfy means outside itself. Its alien character is clearly demonstrated by the fact that as soon as no physical or other compulsion exists it is shunned like the plague. External labour, labour in which man alienates himself, is a labour of self-sacrifice, of mortification. Finally the external character of labour for the worker is demonstrated by the fact that it belongs not to him but to another. Just as in religion the spontaneous activity of the human imagination, the human brain and the human heart detaches itself from the individual and reappears as the alien activity of a god or of a devil, so the activity of the worker is not his own spontaneous activity. It belongs to another, it is a loss of his self.

The result is that man (the worker) feels that he is acting freely only in his animal functions – eating, drinking and procreating, or at most in his dwelling and adornment – while in his human functions he his nothing more than an animal.

It is true that eating, drinking and procreating, etc., are also genuine human functions. However, when abstracted from other aspects of human activity and turned into final and exclusive ends, they are animal.

We have considered the act of the estrangement of practical human activity, of labour, from two aspects: (1) the relationship of the worker to the *product of labour* as an alien object that has power over him. This relationship is at the same time the relationship to the sensuous external world, to natural objects, as an alien world confronting him in hostile opposition. (2) The relationship of labour to the *act of production* within *labour*. This relationship is the relationship of the worker to his own activity as something which is alien and does not belong to him, activity as passivity [*Leiden*], power as impotence, procreation as emasculation, the worker's *own* physical and mental energy, his personal life – for what is life but activity? – as an activity directed against himself, which is independent of him and does not belong to him. *Self-estrangement*, as compared with the estrangement of the *object* [*Sache*] mentioned above.

We now have to derive a third feature of *estranged labour* from the two we have already looked at.

Man is a species-being, not only because he practically and theoretically makes the species – both his own and those of other things – his object, but also – and this is simply another way of saying the same thing – because he looks upon himself as the present, living species, because he looks upon himself as a *universal* and therefore free being.

Species-life, both for man and animals, consists physically in the fact that man, like animals, lives from inorganic nature; and because man is more universal than animals, so too is the area of inorganic nature from which he lives more universal. Just as plants, animals, stones, air, light, etc., theoretically form a part of human consciousness, partly as objects of science and partly as objects of art – his spiritual inorganic nature, his spiritual means of life, which he must first prepare before he can enjoy and digest them – so too in practice they form a part of human life and human activity. In a physical sense man lives only from these natural products, whether in the form of nourishment, heating, clothing, shelter, etc. The universality of man manifests itself in practice in the universality which makes the whole of nature his *inorganic* body, (1) as a direct means of life and (2) as the matter, the object and the tool of his life activity. Nature is man's *inorganic* body, that is to say nature in so far as it is not the human body. Man *lives* from nature, i.e. nature is his *body*, and he must maintain a continuing dialogue with it if he is not to die. To say that man's physical and mental life is linked to nature simply means that nature is linked to itself, for man is part of nature.

Estranged labour not only (1) estranges nature from man and (2) estranges man from himself, from his own active function, from his vital activity; because of this it also estranges man from his *species*. It turns his *species-life* into a means for his individual life, and secondly it turns the latter, in its abstract form, into the purpose of the former, also in its abstract and estranged form.

For in the first place labour, *life activity, productive life* itself appears to man only as a *means* for the satisfaction of a need, the need to preserve physical existence. But productive life is species-life. It is life-producing life. The whole character of a species, its species-character, resides in the nature of its life activity, and free conscious activity constitutes the species-character of man. Life itself appears only as a *means of life*.

The animal is immediately one with its life activity. It is not distinct from that activity; it *is* that activity. Man makes his life activity itself an object of his will and consciousness. He has conscious life activity. It is not a determination with which he directly merges. Conscious life activity directly distinguishes man from animal life activity. Only because of that is he a species-being. Or rather, he is a conscious being, i.e. his own life is an object for him, only because he is a species-being. Only because of that is his activity free activity. Estranged labour reverses the relationship so that man, just because he is a conscious being, makes his life activity, his *being* [*Wesen*], a mere means for his *existence*.

The practical creation of an *objective world*, the *fashioning* of inorganic nature, is proof that man is a conscious species-being, i.e. a being which treats the species as its own essential being or itself as a species-being. It is true that animals also produce. They build nests and dwellings, like the bee, the beaver, the ant, etc. But they produce only their own immediate needs or those of their young; they produce one-sidedly, while man produces universally; they produce only when immediate physical need compels them to do so, while man produces even when he is free from physical need and truly produces only in freedom from such need; they produce only themselves, while man reproduces the whole of nature; their products belong only immediately to their physical bodies, while man freely confronts his own product. Animals produce only according to the standards and needs of the species to which they belong, while man is capable of producing according to the standards of every species and of applying to each object its inherent standard; hence man also produces in accordance with the laws of beauty.

It is therefore in his fashioning of the objective that man really proves himself to be a *species-being*. Such production is his active species-being. Through it nature appears as *his* work and his reality. The object of labour is therefore the *objectification of the species-life of man*: for man reproduces himself not only intellectually, in his consciousness, but actively and actually, and he can therefore contemplate himself in a world he himself has created. In tearing away the object of his production from man, estranged labour therefore tears away from him his *species-life*, his true species-objectivity, and transforms his advantage over animals into the disadvantage that his inorganic body, nature, is taken from him.

In the same way estranged labour reduces spontaneous and free activity to a means, it makes man's species-life a means of his physical existence.

Consciousness which man has from his species, is transformed through estrangement so that species-life becomes a means for him.

(3) Estranged labour therefore turns *man's species-being* – both nature and his intellectual species-powers – into a being *alien* to him and a *means* of his *individual existence*. It estranges man from his own body, from nature as it exists outside him, from his spiritual essence [*Wesen*], his *human* essence.

(4) An immediate consequence of man's estrangement from the product of his labour, his life activity, his species-being, is the *estrangement of man from man*. When man confronts himself, he also confronts *other* men. What is true of man's relationship to his labour, to the product of his labour and to himself, is also true of his relationship to other men, and to the labour and the object of the labour of other men.

In general, the proposition that man is estranged from his species-being means that each man is estranged from the others and that all are estranged from man's essence.

Man's estrangement, like all relationships of man to himself, is realized and expressed only in man's relationship to other men.

In the relationship of estranged labour each man therefore regards the other in accordance with the standard and the situation in which he as a worker finds himself.

Note

1   Perhaps the most systematic discussion of consumption in Marx's entire work is found in the *Grundrisse* (Harmondsworth: Penguin Books, 1973). See also chapter 3 of D. Miller, *Material Culture and Mass Consumption* (Oxford: Blackwell Publishers, 1987) for a particularly lucid summary of Marx's position on the ontological implications of the rupture between production and consumption under capitalism.

2

The Fetishism of the Commodity and its Secret

Karl Marx

This is Marx's "classic" account of the way in which commodities take on suprahuman and "mysterious" qualities and characteristics. The radical rupture between production and consumption in capitalist societies, discussed in the previous chapter, removes for consumers the possibility of knowing the true status of the social relations of the production of commodities. This leaves commodities open to a "fetishization" and, at least in contemporary capitalist societies, an investment (by advertising, promotion, and the like) with nonessential and imaginary meanings and attributes.[1]

A commodity appears at first sight as an extremely obvious, trivial thing. But its analysis brings out that it is a very strange thing, abounding in metaphysical subtleties and theological niceties. So far as it is a use-value, there is nothing mysterious about it, whether we consider it from the point of view that by its properties it satisfies human needs, or that it first takes on these properties as the products of human labour. It is absolutely clear that, by his activity, man changes the forms of the materials of nature in such a way as to make them useful to him. The form of wood, for instance, is altered if a table is made out of it. Nevertheless the table continues to be wood, an ordinary, sensuous thing. But as soon as it emerges as a commodity, it changes into a thing which transcends sensuousness. It not only stands with its feet on the ground, but, in relation to all other commodities, it stands on its head, and evolves out of its wooden brain grotesque ideas far more wonderful than if it were to begin dancing of its own free will.

The mystical character of the commodity does not therefore arise from its use-value. Just as little does it proceed from the nature of the determinants of value. For in the first place, however varied the useful kinds of labour, or productive activities, it is a physiological fact that they are functions of the human organism, and that each such function, whatever may be its nature or its form, is essentially the expenditure of human brain, nerves, muscles and sense organs. Secondly, with regard to the foundation of the quantitative determination of value, namely the

From *Capital* vol. 1 (London: Verso, 1976), pp. 163–77. Reprinted by permission of the publishers.

duration of that expenditure or the quantity of labour, this is quite palpably different from its quality. In all situations, the labour-time it costs to produce the means of subsistence must necessarily concern mankind, although not to the same degree at different stages of development. And finally, as soon as men start to work for each other in any way, their labour also assumes a social form.

Whence, then, arises the enigmatic character of the product of labour, as soon as it assumes the form of a commodity? Clearly, it arises from this form itself. The equality of the kinds of human labour takes on a physical form in the equal objectivity of the products of labour as values; the measure of the expenditure of human labour-power by its duration takes on the form of the magnitude of the value of the products of labour; and finally the relationship between producers, within which the social characteristics of their labours are manifested, take on the form of a social relation between the products of labour.

The mysterious character of the commodity-form consists therefore simply in the fact that the commodity reflects the social characteristics of men's own labour as objective characteristics of the products of labour themselves, as the socio-natural properties of these things. Hence it also reflects the social relation of the producers to the sum total of labour as a social relation between objects, a relation which exists apart from and outside the producers. Through this substitution, the products of labour become commodities, sensuous things which are at the same time suprasensible or social. In the same way the impression made by a thing on the optic nerve is perceived not as a subjective excitation of that nerve but as the objective form of a thing outside the eye. In the act of seeing, of course, light is really transmitted from one thing, the external object, to another thing, the eye. It is a physical relation between physical things. Against this the commodity-form, and the value relation of the products of labour within which it appears, have absolutely no connection with the physical nature of the commodity and the material [*dinglich*] relations arising out of this. It is nothing but the definite social relation between men themselves which assumes here, for them, the fantastic form of a relation between things. In order, therefore, to find an analogy we must first take flight into the misty realm of religion. There the products of the human brain appear as autonomous figures endowed with a life of their own, which enter into relations both with each other and with the human race. So it is in the world of commodities, and is therefore inseparable from the production of commodities.

As the foregoing analysis has already demonstrated, this fetishism of the world of commodities arises from the peculiar social character of the labour which produces them.

Objects of utility become commodities only because they are the products of labour of private individuals who work independently of each other. The sum total of the labour of all these private individuals forms the aggregate labour of society. Since the producers do not come into social contact until they exchange the products of their labour, the specific social characteristics of their private labours appear only within this exchange. In other words, the labour of the private individual manifests itself as an element of the total labour of society only through the relations which the act of exchange establishes between the products, and, through their mediation, between the producers. To the producers, therefore, the social relations between their private labours appear as what they are, i.e. they do not appear as direct social relations between persons and social relations between things.

It is only by being exchanged that the products of labour acquire a socially uniform objectivity as values, which is distinct from their sensuously varied objectivity as articles of utility. This division of the product of labour into a useful thing and a thing possessing value appears in practice only when exchange has already acquired a sufficient extension and importance to allow useful things to be produced for the purpose of being exchanged, so that their character as values has already to be taken into consideration during production. From this moment on, the labour of the individual producer acquires a twofold social character. On the one hand, it must, as a definite useful kind of labour, satisfy a definite social need, and thus maintain its position as an element of the total labour, as a branch of the social division of labour, which originally sprang up spontaneously. On the other hand, it can satisfy the manifold needs of the individual producer himself only in so far as every particular kind of useful private labour can be exchanged with, i.e. counts as the equal of, every other kind of useful private labour. Equality in the full sense between different kinds of labour can be arrived at only if we abstract from their real inequality, if we reduce them to the characteristic they have in common, that of being the expenditure of human labour-power, of human labour in the abstract. The private producer's brain reflects the twofold social character of his labour only in the forms which appear in practical intercourse, in the exchange of products. Hence the socially useful character of his private labour is reflected in the form that the product of labour has to be useful to others, and the social character of the equality of the various kinds of labour is reflected in the form of the common character, as values, possessed by these materially different things, the products of labour.

Men do not therefore bring the products of their labour into relation with each other as values because they see these objects merely as the material integuments of homogeneous human labour. The reverse is true: by equating their different products to each other in exchange as values, they equate their different kinds of labour as human labour. They do this without being aware of it. Value, therefore, does not have its description branded on its forehead; it rather transforms every product of labour into a social hieroglyphic. Later on, men try to decipher the hieroglyphic, to get behind the secret of their own social product: for the characteristic which objects of utility have of being values is as much men's social product as is their language. The belated scientific discovery that the products of labour, in so far as they are values, are merely the material expressions of the human labour expended to produce them, marks an epoch in the history of mankind's development, but by no means banishes the semblance of objectivity possessed by the social characteristics of labour. Something which is only valid for this particular form of production, the production of commodities, namely the fact that the specific social character of private labours carried on independently of each other consists in their equality as human labour, and, in the product, assumes the form of the existence of value, appears to those caught up in the relations of commodity production (and this is true both before and after the above-mentioned scientific discovery) to be just as ultimately valid as the fact that the scientific dissection of the air into its component parts left the atmosphere itself unaltered in its physical configuration.

What initially concerns producers in practice when they make an exchange is how much of some other product they get for their own; in what proportions can the products be exchanged? As soon as these proportions have attained a certain customary stability, they appear to result from the nature of the products, so that, for instance, one ton of iron and two onces of gold appear to be equal in value, in the same way as a pound of gold and a pound of iron are equal in weight, despite their different physical and chemical properties. The value character of the products of labour become firmly established only when they act as magnitudes of value. These magnitudes vary continually, independently of the will, foreknowledge and actions of the exchangers. Their own moment within society has for them the form of a movement made by things, and these things far from being under their control, in fact control them. The production of commodities must be fully developed before the scientific conviction emerges, from experience itself, that all the different kinds of private labour (which are carried on independently of each other, and yet, as spontaneously developed branches of the social division of labour, are in a situation of all-round dependence on each other) are continually being reduced to the quantitative proportions in which society requires them. The reason for this reduction is that in the midst of the accidental and ever-fluctuating exchange relations between the products, the labour-time socially necessary to produce them asserts itself as a regulative law of nature. In the same way, the law of gravity asserts itself when a person's house collapses on top of him. The determination of the magnitude of value by labour-time is therefore a secret hidden under the apparent movements in the relative values of commodities. Its discovery destroys the semblance of the merely accidental determination of the magnitude of the value of the products of labour, but by no means abolishes that determination's material form.

Reflection on the forms of human life, hence also scientific analysis of those forms, takes a course directly opposite to their real development. Reflection begins *post festum*,[2] and therefore with the results of the process of development ready to hand. The forms which stamp products as commodities and which therefore are the preliminary requirements for the circulation of commodities, already posses the fixed quality of natural forms of social life before man seeks to give an account, not of their historical character, for in his eyes they are immutable, but of their content and meaning. Consequently it was solely the analysis of the prices of commodities which led to the determination of the magnitude of value, and solely the common expression of all commodities in money which led to the establishment of their character as values. It is however precisely this finished form of the world of commodities – the money form – which conceals the social character of private labour and the social relations between the individual workers, by making those relations appear as relations between material objects, instead of revealing them plainly. If I state that coats or boots stand in relation to linen, or with gold or silver (and this makes no difference here), as the universal equivalent, the relation between their own private labour and the collective labour of society appears to them in exactly this absurd form.

The categories of bourgeois economics consist precisely of forms of this kind. They are forms of thought which are socially valid, and therefore objective, for the relations of production, belonging to this historically determined mode of social production, i.e. commodity production. The whole mystery of commodities, all the magic and necromancy that surround the products of labour on the basis of commodity production, vanishes therefore as soon as we come to other forms of production.

As political economists are fond of Robinson Crusoe stories, let us first look at Robinson on his island. Undemanding though he is by nature, he still needs to satisfy, and must therefore perform useful labours of various kinds: he must make tools, knock together furniture, tame llamas, fish, hunt and so on. Of his prayers and the like, we take no account here, since our friend takes pleasure in them and sees them as recreation. Despite the diversity of his productive functions, he knows that they are only different forms of activity of one and the same Robinson, hence only different modes of human labour. Necessity itself compels him to divide his time with precision between his different functions. Whether one function occupies a greater space in his total activity than another depends on the magnitude of the difficulties to be overcome in attaining the useful affect aimed at. Our friend Robinson Crusoe learns this by experience, and having saved a watch, ledger, ink and pen from the shipwreck, he soon begins like a good Englishman, to keep a set of books. His stock book contains a catalogue of the useful objects he possesses, of the various operations necessary for their production, and finally of the labour-time that specific quantities of these products have on average cost to him. All the relations between Robinson and these objects that form his self-created wealth are so simple and transparent that even Mr Sedley Taylor[3] could understand them. And yet those relations contain all the essential determinants of value.

Let us now transport ourselves from Robinson's island, bathed in light, to medieval Europe, shrouded in darkness. Here, instead of the independent man, we find everyone dependent – serfs and lords, vassals and suzerains, laymen and clerics. Personal dependence characterizes the social relations of material production as much as it does the other spheres of life based on that production. But precisely because relations of personal dependence form the given social foundation, there is no need for labour and its products to assume a fantastic form different from their reality. They take the shape, in the transactions of society, of services in kind and payments in kind. The natural form of labour, its particularity – and not, as in a society based on commodity production, its universality – is here its immediate social form.. The *corvée* can be measured by time just as well as the labour which produces commodities, but every serf knows that what he expends in the service of his lord is a specific quantity of his own personal labour-power. The tithe owed to the priest is more clearly apparent than his blessing. Whatever we may think, then, of the different roles in which men confront each other in such a society, the social relations between individuals in the performance of their labour appear at all events as their own personal relations, and are not disguised as social relations between things, between the products of labour.

For an example of labour in common, i.e. directly associated labour, we do not need to go back to the spontaneously developed form which we find at the threshold of the history of all civilized peoples. We have one nearer to hand in the patriarchal rural industry of a peasant family which produces corn, cattle, yarn, linen and clothing for its own use. These things confront the family as so many products of its collective labour, but they do not confront each other as commodities. The different kinds of labour which create these products – such as tilling the fields, tending the cattle, spinning, weaving and making clothes – are already in their natural form social functions; for they are functions of the family, which, just as money as a society based on commodity production, possesses its own spontaneous division of labour. The distribution of labour within the family and the labour-time expended by the individual members of the family, are regulated by differences of sex and age as well as by seasonal variations in the natural conditions of labour. The fact that the expenditure of the individual labour-powers is measured by duration appears here, by its very nature, as a social characteristic of labour itself, because the individual labour powers, by their very nature, act only as instruments of the joint labour-power of the family.

Let us finally imagine, for a change, an association of free men, working with the means of production held in common, and expending their many different forms of labour-power in full self-awareness as one single social labour force. All the characteristics of Robinson's labour are repeated here, but with the difference that they are social instead of individual. All Robinson's products were exclusively the result of his own personal labour and they were therefore directly objects of utility for him personally. The total product of our imagined association is a social product. One part of this product serves as fresh means of production and remains social. But another part is consumed by the members of the association as means of subsistence. This part must therefore be divided amongst them. The way this division is made will vary with the particular kind of social organization of production

15

and the corresponding level of social development attained by the producers. We shall assume, but only for the sake of a parallel with the production of commodities, that the share of each individual producer in the means of subsistence is determined by his labour-time. Labour-time would in that case play a double part. Its apportionment in accordance with a definite social plan maintains the correct proportion between the different functions of labour and the various needs of the associations. On the other hand, labour-time also serves as a measure for the part taken by each individual in the common labour, and of his share in the part of the total product destined for individual consumption. The social relations of the individual producers, both towards their labour and the products of their labour, are here transparent in their simplicity, in production as well as in distribution.

For a society of commodity producers, whose general social relation of production consists in the fact that they treat their products as commodities, hence as values, and in this material [*sachlich*] form bring their individual, private labours into relation with each other as homogeneous human labour, Christianity with its religious cult of man in the abstract, more particularly in its bourgeois development, i.e. in Protestantism, Deism, etc., is the most fitting form of religion. In the ancient Asiatic, Classical-antique, and other such modes of production, the transformation of the product into a commodity, and therefore men's existence as producers of commodities, plays a subordinate role, which however increases in importance as these communities approach nearer and nearer to the stage of their dissolution. Trading nations, properly so called, exist only in the interstices of the ancient world, like the gods of Epicurus in the *intermundia*,[4] or Jews in the pores of Polish society. Those ancient social organisms of production are much more simple and transparent than those of bourgeois society. But they are founded either on the immaturity of man as an individual, when he has not yet torn himself loose from the umbilical cord of his natural species-connection with other men, or on direct relations of dominance and servitude. They are conditioned by a low stage of development of the productive powers of labour and correspondingly limited relations between men within the process of creating and reproducing their material life, hence also limited relations between man and nature. These limitations are reflected in the ancient worship of nature, and in other elements of tribal religions. The religious reflections of the real world can, in any case, vanish only when the practical relations of everyday life between man and man, and man and nature, generally present themselves to him in a transparent and rational form. The veil is not removed from the countenance of the social-life process, i.e. the process of material production, until it becomes production by freely associated men, and stands under their conscious and planned control. This, however, requires that society possess a material foundation, or a series of material conditions of existence, which in their turn are the natural and spontaneous product of a long and tormented historical development.

Political economy has indeed analysed value and its magnitude, however in-

16

completely, and has uncovered the content concealed within these forms. But it has never once asked the question why this content has assumed that particular form, that is to say, why labour is expressed in value, and why the measurement of labour by its duration is expressed in the magnitude of the value of the product. These formulas, which bear the unmistakable stamp of belonging to a social formation in which the process of production has mastery over man, instead of the opposite, appear to the political economists' bourgeois consciousness to be as much a self-evident and nature-imposed necessity as productive labour itself. Hence the pre-bourgeois forms of the social organization of production are treated by political economy in much the same way as the Fathers of the Church treated pre-Christian religions.

The degree to which some economists are misled by the fetishism attached to the world of commodities, or by the objective appearance of the social characteristics of labour, is shown, amongst other things, by the dull and tedious dispute over the part played by nature in the formation of exchange-value. Since exchange-value is a definite social manner of expressing the labour bestowed on a thing, it can have no more natural content than has, for example, the rate of exchange.

As the commodity-form is the most general and the most undeveloped form of bourgeois production, it makes its appearance at an early date, though not in the same predominant and therefore characteristic manner as nowadays. Hence its fetish character is still relatively easy to penetrate. But when we come to more concrete forms, even this appearance of simplicity vanishes. Where did the illusion of the Monetary System come from? The adherents of the Monetary System did not see gold and silver as representing money as a social relation of production, but in the form of natural objects with peculiar social properties. And what of modern political economy, which looks down so disdainfully on the Monetary System? Does not its fetishism become quite palpable when it deals with capital? How long is it since the disappearance of the Physiocratic illusion that ground rent grows out of the soil, not out of society?

But, to avoid anticipating, we will content ourselves here with one more example relating to the commodity-form itself. If commodities could speak, they would say this: our use-value may interest men, but it does not belong to us as objects. What does belong to us as objects, however, is our value. Our own intercourse as commodities proves it. We relate to each other merely as exchange-values. Now listen to how those commodities speak through the mouth of the economist:

'Value (i.e. exchange-value) is a property of things, riches (i.e. use-value) of man. Value, in this sense, necessarily implies exchanges, riches do not.'[5]

'Riches (use-value) are the attribute of man, value is the attribute of commodities. A man or commodity is rich, a pearl or a diamond is valuable. ... A pearl or a diamond is valuable as a pearl or a diamond.'[6]

So far no chemist has ever discovered exchange-value either in a pearl or a diamond. No economists who have discovered this chemical substance, and who lay special claim to critical acumen, nevertheless find that the use-value of material objects belongs to them independently of their material properties, while their value, on the other hand, forms a part of them as objects. What confirms them in this view is the peculiar circumstance that the use-value of a thing is realized without exchange, i.e. in a social process. Who would not call to mind at this point the advice given by the good Dogberry to the night-watchman Seacoal?[7]

'To be a well-favoured man is the gift of fortune; but reading and writing comes by nature.'

Notes

1   See in particular S. Jhally, *The Codes of Advertising* (New York: Francis Pinter, 1987) and J. Williamson, *Decoding Advertisements: Meaning and Ideology in Advertising* (London: Marion Boyars, 1978).
2   "After the feast," i.e. after the events reflected on have taken place.
3   The original German has here "Herr M. Wirth," chosen by Marx as a run-of-the-mill vulgar economist and propagandist familiar to German readers. Engels introduced "Mr Sedley Taylor," a Cambridge don against whom he polemicized in his preface to the fourth German edition.
4   According to the Greek philosopher Epicurus (*c.* 341–270 BC) the gods existed only in the *intermundia,* or spaces between different worlds, and had no influence on the course of human affairs. Very few of the writings of Epicurus have been preserved in the original Greek, and this particular idea survived only by being included in Cicero, *De natura deorum,* Book 1, Section 18.
5   *Observations on Some Verbal Disputes in Pol. Econ., Particularly Relating to Value, and to Supply and Demand* (London, 1821), p.16.
6   S. Bailey, *A Critical Dissertation on the Nature, Measures and Causes of Value: Chiefly in Reference to the Writings of Mr Ricardo and His Followers. By the Author on the Essays of the Formation and Publication of Opinions* (London, 1825).
7   In Shakespeare's comedy *Much Ado About Nothing,* Act 3, Scene 3.

3

Beyond Use Value

Jean Baudrillard

The erstwhile exemplary Marxist Baudrillard is here drawn towards a critique of Marx. Fundamental to a proper understanding of Marx's analysis of the fetishism of commodities, argues Baudrillard, is the notion that a final ontological sanctuary from the exploitation of exchange-value can be found in use-value, for in use-value is revealed the true and essential character of human needs. According to Baudrillard, however, Marx fails to recognize the social, and indeed cultural, character of use-value; that is, that use-value is both a social construct and historically contingent. Marx's "naturalization" of use-value, Baudrillard continues, thus amounts to nothing short of a form of fetishism of use-value under which is concealed the symbolic exploitation of consumers through the tyranny of the "code" of sign-value.

The status of use value in Marxian theory is ambiguous. We know that the commodity is both exchange value and use value. But the latter is always concrete and particular, contingent on its own destiny, whether this is in the process of individual consumption or in the labor process. (In this case, lard is valued as lard, cotton as cotton: they cannot be substituted for each other, nor thus "exchanged.") Exchange value, on the other hand, is abstract and general. To be sure, there could be no exchange value without use value – the two are coupled; but neither is strongly implied by the other:

> In order to define the notion of commodity, it is not important to know its particular content and its exact destination. It suffices that before it is a commodity – in other words, the vehicle (support) of exchange value – the article satisfy a given social need by possessing the corresponding useful property. That is all.[1]

Thus, use value is not implicated in the logic peculiar to exchange value, which is a logic of equivalence. Besides, there can be use value without exchange value (equally for labor power as for products, in the sphere outside the market). Even if it is continually reclaimed by the process of production and exchange, use value is

From "For a critique of the political economy of the sign" in M. Poster (ed.) *Jean Baudrillard: Selected Writings* (Cambridge: Polity Press, 1988), pp. 64–75.

never truly inscribed in the field of the market economy: it has its own finality, albeit restricted. And within it is contained, from this standpoint, the promise of a resurgence beyond the market economy, money and exchange value, in the glorious autonomy of the simple relation of people to their work and their products.

So it appears that commodity fetishism (that is, where social relations are disguised in the qualities and attributes of the commodity itself) is not a function of the commodity defined *simultaneously* as exchange value and use value, but of exchange value alone. Use value, in this restrictive analysis of fetishism, appears neither as a social relation nor hence as the locus of fetishization. Utility as such escapes the historical determination of class. It represents an objective, final relation of intrinsic purpose (*destination propre*), which does not mask itself and whose transparency, as form, defies history (even if its content changes continually with respect to social and cultural determinations). It is here that Marxian idealism goes to work; it is here that we have to be more logical than Marx himself – and more radical, in the true sense of the word. For use value – indeed, utility itself – is a fetishized social relation, just like the abstract equivalence of commodities. Use value is an abstraction. It is an abstraction of the *system of needs* cloaked in the false evidence of a concrete destination and purpose, an intrinsic finality of goods and products. It is just like the abstraction of social labor, which is the basis for the logic of equivalence (exchange value), hiding beneath the "innate" value of commodities.

In effect, our hypothesis is that needs (i.e. the system of needs) are the *equivalent of abstract social labor*: on them is erected the system of use value, just as abstract social labor is the basis for the system of exchange value. This hypothesis also implies that, for there to be a system at all, use value and exchange value must be regulated by an identical abstract logic of equivalence, an identical code. The code of utility is also a code of abstract equivalence of objects and subjects (for each category in itself and for the two taken together in their relation); hence, it is a combinatory code involving potential calculation (we will return to this point). Furthermore, it is in itself, as system, that use value can be "fetishized," and certainly not as a practical operation. It is always the systematic abstraction that is fetishized. The same goes for exchange value. And it is the *two* fetishizations, reunited – that of use value and that of exchange value – that constitutes commodity fetishism.

Marx defines the form of exchange value and of the commodity by the fact that they can be equated on the basis of abstract social labor. Inversely, he posits the "incomparability" of use values. Now, it must be seen that:

1 For there to be economic exchange and exchange value, it is also necessary that the principle of utility has already become the reality principle of the object or product. To be abstractly and generally exchangeable, products must also be thought and rationalized in terms of utility. Where they are not (as in

primitive symbolic exchange), they can have no exchange value. The reduction to the status of utility is the basis of (economic) exchangeability.

2 If the exchange principle and the utility principle have such an affinity (and do not merely coexist in the commodity), it is because utility is already entirely infused with the logic of equivalence, contrary to what Marx says about the "incomparability" of use values. If use value is not quantitative in the strictly arithmetical sense, it still involves equivalence. Considered as useful values, all goods are already comparable among themselves, because they are assigned to the same rational-functional common denominator, the same abstract determination. Only objects or categories of goods cathected in the singular and personal act of symbolic exchange (the gift, the present) are strictly incomparable. The personal relation (noneconomic exchange) renders them absolutely unique. On the other hand, as a useful value, the object attains an abstract universality, an "objectivity" (through the reduction of every symbolic function).

3 What is involved here, then, is an object form whose general equivalent is utility. And this is no mere "analogy" with the formulas of exchange value. The same logical form is involved. Every object is translatable into the general abstract code of equivalence, which is its rationale, its objective law, its meaning – and this is achieved independently of who makes use of it and what purpose it serves. It is functionality which supports it and carries it along as code; and this code, founded on the mere adequation of an object to its (useful) end, subordinates all real or potential objects to itself, without taking anyone into account at all. Here, the economic is born: the economic calculus. The commodity form is only its developed form, and returns to it continually.

4 Now, contrary to the anthropological illusion that claims to exhaust the idea of utility in the simple relation of a human need to a useful property of the object, use value is very much a social relation. Just as, in terms of exchange value, the producer does not appear as a creator, but as abstract social labor power, so in the system of use value, the consumer never appears as desire and enjoyment, but as abstract social need power (one could say *Bedürfniskraft*, *Bedürfnisvermögen*, by analogy with *Arbeitskraft*, *Arbeitsvermögen*).

The abstract social producer is man conceived in terms of exchange value. The abstract social individual (the person with "needs") is man thought of in terms of use value. There is a homology between the "emancipation" in the bourgeois era of the private individual given final form by his or her needs and the functional emancipation of objects as use values. This results from an objective rationalization, the surpassing of old ritual and symbolic constraints. In a radically different type of exchange, objects did not have the status of "objectivity" that we give them at all. But henceforward secularized, functionalized and rationalized in purpose, objects become the promise of an ideal (and idealist) political economy, with its watchword "to each according to his needs."

At the same time, individuals, now disengaged from all collective obligations of a magical or religious order, "liberated" from archaic, symbolic or personal ties, at last private and autonomous, define themselves through an "objective" activity of transforming nature – labor – *and* through the destruction of utility for their benefit: needs, satisfactions, use value.

Utility, needs, use value: none of these ever come to grips with the finality of subjects who face their ambivalent object relations, or with symbolic exchange between subjects. Rather, it describes the relation of individuals to themselves conceived in economic terms – better still, the relation of the subject to the economic system. Far from the individual expressing his or her needs in the economic system, it is the economic system that induces the individual function and the parallel functionality of objects and needs.[2] The individual is an ideological structure, a historical form correlative with the commodity form (exchange value), and the object form (use value). The individual is nothing but the subject thought in economic terms, rethought, simplified, and abstracted by the economy. The entire history of consciousness and ethics (all the categories of occidental psycho-metaphysics) is only the history of the political economy of the subject.

Use value is the expression of a whole metaphysic: that of utility. It registers itself as a kind of *moral law* at the heart of the object – and it is inscribed there as the finality of the "need" of the subject. It is the transcription at the heart of things of the same moral law (Kantian and Christian) inscribed on the heart of the subject, positivizing it in its essence and instituting it in a *final* relation (with God, or to some transcendent reality). In both cases, the circulation of value is regulated by a providential code that watches over the correlation of the object with the needs of the subject, under the rubric of functionality – as it assures, incidentally, the coincidence of the subject with divine law, under the sign of morality.

This is the same teleology that seals the essence of the subject (his or her self-identity through the recognition of this transcendent finality). It establishes the object in its truth, as an essence called use value, transparent to itself and to the subject, under the rational banner of utility. And this moral law effects the same fundamental reduction of all the symbolic virtualities of the subject and the object. A simple finality is substituted for a multiplicity of meanings. And it is still the principle of equivalence that functions here as the reducer of symbolic ambivalence:

1   It establishes the object in a functional equivalence to itself in the single framework of this determined valence: utility. This absolute signification, this rationalization by identity (its equivalence to itself) permits the object to enter the field of political economy as a positive value.
2   The same absolute simplification of the subject as the subject of moral consciousness and needs permits him or her to enter the system of values and practices of political economy as an abstract individual (defined by identity, equivalence to himself or herself).

Thus the functionality of objects, their moral code of utility, is as entirely governed by the logic of equivalence as is their exchange value status. Hence, functionality falls just as squarely under the jurisdiction of political economy. And if we call this abstract equivalence of utilities the object form, we can say that *the object form is only the completed form of the commodity form*. In other words, the same logic (and the same fetishism) plays on the two sides of the commodity specified by Marx: use value and exchange value.

By not submitting use value to this logic of equivalence in radical fashion, by maintaining use value as the category of "incomparability," Marxist analysis has contributed to the mythology (a veritable rationalist mystique) that allows the relation of the individual to objects conceived as use values to pass for a concrete and objective – in sum, "natural" – relation between man's needs and the function proper to the object. This is all seen as the opposite of the abstract, reified, "alienated" relation the subject would have towards products as exchange values. The truth of the subject would lie here, in usage, as a concrete sphere of the private relation, as opposed to the social and abstract sphere of the market.[3] (Marx does provide a radical analysis of the abstraction of the private individual as a social relation in another connection, however.) Against all this seething metaphysic of needs and use values, it must be said that abstraction, reduction, rationalization, and systematization are as profound and as generalized at the level of "needs" as at the level of commodities. Perhaps this was not yet very clear at an anterior stage of political economy, when one could imagine that if individuals where alienated by the system of exchange value, at least they would return to themselves, become themselves again in their needs and in the moment of use value. But it has become possible today, at the present stage of consummative mobilization, to see that needs, far from being articulated around the desire or demand of the subject, find their coherence elsewhere: in a generalized system that is to desire what the system of exchange value is to concrete labor, the source of value. All the drives, symbolic relations, object relations, even perversions – in short, all the subject's *labor* of cathexis – are abstracted and given their general equivalent in utility and the system of needs, as all values and real social labor find their general equivalent in money. Everything surging from the subject, his or her body and desire, is dissociated and catalyzed in terms of needs, more or less specified in advance by objects. All instincts are rationalized, finalized, and objectified in needs – hence symbolically cancelled. *All ambivalence is reduced by equivalence*. And to say that the system of needs is a system of general equivalence is no metaphor: it means that we are completely immersed in political economy. This is why we have spoken of *fetishism of use value*. If needs were the singular, concrete expression of the subject, it would be absurd to speak of fetishism. But when needs erect themselves more and more into an abstract system, regulated by a principle of equivalence and general combinatory, then certainly the same fetishism is in play. For this system is not only homologous to that of exchange value and the commodity; *it expresses the latter in all its depth and perfection.*

Indeed, just as exchange value is not a substantial aspect of the product, but a form that expresses a social relation, so use value can no longer be viewed as an innate function of the object, but as a social determination (at once of the subject, the object, and their relation). In other words, just as the logic of the commodity indifferently extends itself to people and things and makes people (all obedient to the same law) appear only as exchange value – thus the restricted finality of utility imposes itself on people as surely as on the world of objects. It is illogical and naive to hope that, through objects conceived in terms of exchange value, that is, in his needs, humans can fulfil themselves *otherwise than as use value.* However, such is the modern humanist vulgate: through the functionality, the domestic finality of the exterior world, man is supposed to fulfil himself *qua man.* The truth is something else entirely. In an environment of commodities and exchange value, man is no more himself than he is exchange value and commodity. Encompassed by objects that function and serve, man is not so much himself as the most beautiful of these functional and servile objects. It is not only *homo economicus* who is turned entirely into use value during the process of capitalist production. This utilitarian imperative even structures the relation of the individual to himself or herself. In the *process of satisfaction*, individuals valorize and make fruitful their own potentialities for pleasure; they "realize" and manage, to the best of their ability, their own "faculty" of pleasure, treated literally like a productive force. Isn't this what all of humanist ethics is based on: the "proper use" of oneself?

In substance, Marx says: "Production not only produces goods; it produces people to consume them, and the corresponding needs." This proposition is most often twisted in such a way as to yield simplistic ideas like "the manipulation of needs" and denunciations of "artificial needs."[4] It is necessary to grasp that what produces the commodity system in its general form is the *concept* of need itself, as constitutive of the very structure of the individual; that is, the historical concept of social beings who, in the rupture of symbolic exchange, autonomize themselves and rationalize their desire, their relation to others and to objects, in terms of needs, utility, satisfaction, and use value.

Thus, it is not merely such and such a value that reduces symbolic exchange, or emerges from its rupture; it is first the structural opposition of two values: exchange value and use value, whose logical form is the same, and whose dual organization punctuates the economic. We are faced here at a global anthropological level with the same schema of "semiological reduction" analyzed in "Fetishism and ideology."[5] In that study, I tried to demonstrate the way in which this binary oppositive structuration constituted the very matrix of ideological functioning; I started from the fact that this structuration is never purely structural: it always plays to the advantage of one of the two terms. *Structural logic* always redoubles in a strategy (thus masculine–feminine, to the profit of masculinity, conscious–unconscious, to the advantage of consciousness, etc.).

Precisely the same thing is going on here. In the correlation:

$$\frac{EV}{UV} = \frac{Sr}{Sd}$$

use value and signified do not have the same weight as exchange value and signifier respectively. Let us say that they have a tactical value; whereas exchange value has strategic value. The system is organized along the lines of a functional but hierarchized bipolarity. Absolute preeminence redounds to exchange value and the signifier. Use value and needs are only an effect of exchange value. Signified (and referent) are only an effect of the signifier. . . . Neither is an autonomous reality, one that either exchange value or the signifier would express or translate in their code. At bottom, they are only simulation models, produced by the play of exchange value and of signifiers. They provide signifiers with the guarantee of the real, the lived, the concrete; they are the guarantee of an objective reality for which, however, in the same moment, these systems *qua* systems substitute their own total logic. (Even the term "substitute" is misleading, in this context. It implies the existence somewhere of a fundamental reality that the system appropriates or distorts. In fact, there is no reality or principle of reality other than that directly produced by the system as its ideal reference.) Use value and the signified do not constitute an *elsewhere* with respect to the systems of the other two; they are only their alibis.

We have seen, in the first approximation, that the field of political economy generalizes and saturates itself through the system of use value (that is, through the extension of the process of abstraction and productive rationality to the entire domain of consumption through the system of needs as a system of values and productive forces). In this sense, use value appears as the completion and fulfillment of exchange value (of political economy in general). The fetishism of use value redoubles and deepens the fetishism of exchange value.

That is a starting point. But it is necessary to see that the system of use value is *not only* the double transposition, or extension of that of exchange value. It functions simultaneously as the latter's ideological guarantee (and once again, if this is so, it is because it is logically structured in the same way). It is understood, of course, that it is a naturalizing ideology we are concerned with here. Use value is given fundamentally as the instance (i.e. tribunal) before which all people are equal. On this view, need, leaving aside any variation in the means of satisfying it, would be the most equally distributed thing in the world.[6] People are not equal with respect to goods taken as exchange value, but they would be equal as regards goods taken as use value. One may dispose of them or not, according to one's class, income, or disposition; but the *potentiality* for availing oneself of them nevertheless exists for all. Everyone is equally rich in *possibilities* for happiness and satisfaction. This is the secularization of the potential equality of all people before God: the democracy of "needs." Thus use value, reflected back to the anthropological sphere, reconciles in the universal those who are divided socially by exchange value.

Exchange value erases the real labor process at the level of the commodity, such that the commodity appears as an autonomous value. Use value fares even better: it provides the commodity, inhuman as it is in its abstraction, with a "human" finality. In exchange value, social labor disappears. The system of use value, on the other hand, involves the resorption without trace of the entire ideological and historical labor process that leads subjects in the first place to think of themselves as individuals, defined by their needs and satisfaction, and so ideally to integrate themselves into the structure of the commodity.

Thus without ceasing to be a system in historical and logical solidarity with the system of exchange value, the system of use value succeeds in naturalizing exchange value and offers it that universal and atemporal guarantee without which the exchange value system simply couldn't reproduce itself (or doubtless even be produced in its general form).

Use value is thus the crown and scepter of political economy:

1 In its lived reality: it is the immanence of political economy in everyday life, down to the very act in which man believes he has rediscovered himself. People do not rediscover their objects except in what they serve; and they do not rediscover themselves except through the expression and satisfaction of their needs – in what they serve.
2 In its strategic value: ideologically, it seals off the system of production and exchange, thanks to an institution of an idealist anthropology that screens use value and needs from their historical logic in order to inscribe them in a formal eternity: that of utility for objects, that of the useful appropriation of objects by man in need.

This is why use-value fetishism is indeed more profound, more "mysterious" than the fetishism of exchange value. The mystery of exchange value and the commodity can be unmasked, relatively – it has been since Marx – and raised to consciousness as a social relation. But value in the case of use value is enveloped in total mystery, for it is grounded anthropologically in the (self-) "evidence" of a naturalness, an unsurpassable original reference. This is where we discover the real "theology" of value – in the order of finalities: in the "ideal" relation of equivalence, harmony, economy, and equilibrium that the concept of utility implies. It operates at all levels: between man and nature, man and objects, man and his body, the self and others. Value becomes absolutely self-evident, *la chose la plus simple*. Here the mystery and cunning (of history and of reason) are at their most profound and tenacious.

If the system of use value is produced by the system of exchange value as its own ideology – if use value has no autonomy, if it is only the *satellite* and *alibi* of exchange value, though systematically combining with it in the framework of political economy – then it is no longer possible to posit use value as an alternative to exchange value. Nor, therefore, is it possible to posit the "restitution" of use value, at the end of political economy, under the sign of the "liberation of needs" and the "administration of things" as a revolutionary perspective.

Even revolutionary perspective today stands or falls on its ability to reinterrogate radically the repressive, reductive, rationalizing metaphysic of utility. All critical theory depends on the analysis of the object form.[7] This has been absent from Marxist analysis. With all the political and ideological consequences that this implies, the result has been that all illusions converged on use value, idealized by opposition to exchange value, when it was in fact only the latter's naturalized form.

Marx and Crusoe

Marx says in volume I of *Capital* (part 1, section 4):

> So far as [a commodity] is a value in use, there is nothing mysterious about it, whether we consider it from the point of view that by its properties it is capable of satisfying human wants, or from the point that those properties are the product of human labor. It is as clear as noonday that man, by his industry, changes the forms of the materials furnished by Nature, in such a way as to make them useful to him . . .
>
> The mystical character of commodities does not originate, therefore, in their use value . . .
>
> The categories of bourgeois economy consist of . . . forms of thought expressing with social validity the conditions and relations of a definite historically determined mode of production, viz., the production of commodities. The whole mystery of commodities, all the magic and necromancy that surrounds the products of labor as long as they take the form of commodities, vanishes therefore, so soon as we come to other forms of production.
>
> Since Robinson Crusoe's experiences are a favorite theme with political economists, let us take a look at him on his island. . . . All the relations between Robinson and the objects that form this wealth of his own creation are here so simple and clear as to be intelligible without exertion, even to Mr Baudrillard.[8] And yet those relations contain all that is essential to the determination of value.

Having quite justifiably played his joke at the expense of the bourgeois economist and their interminable references to Robinson, Marx would have done well to examine his own use of the Crusoe myth. For by opposing the obscure mysticism of commodity value to the simplicity and transparency of Crusoe's relation to his wealth, he fell into a trap. If one hypothesizes (as Marxists do) that all the ideology of bourgeois political economy is summed up in the myth of Robinson Crusoe, then it must be admitted that everything in the novel itself agrees with the mystical theology and metaphysics of bourgeois thought, including (and above all) this "transparency" in man's relation to the instruments and products of his labor.

This ideal confrontation of man with his labor capacity (*Arbeitsvermögen*) and with his needs is not only abstract because it is separated out from the sphere of political economy and commercial social relations; it is abstract *in itself*: not abstracted from political economy, but abstract because it epitomizes the abstraction of political economy itself; that is, the ascension of exchange value via use value, the apotheosis of the economic in the providential finality of utility.

Robinson Crusoe is the outcome of a total mutation that has been in progress since the dawn of bourgeois society (though only really theorized since the eighteenth century). Man was transformed simultaneously into a productive force and a "man with needs." The manufacturers and the ideologues of Nature divided between him themselves. In his labor, he became a use value for a system of production. Simultaneously, goods and products became use values for him, taking on a meaning as functions of his needs, which were henceforth legalized as "nature." He entered the regime of use value, which was also that of "Nature." But this was by no means according to an original finality rediscovered: all these concepts (needs, nature, utility) were born together, in the historical phase that saw the systematization of both political economy and the ideology that sanctions it.

The myth of Robinson Crusoe is the bourgeois avatar of the myth of terrestrial paradise. Every great social order of production (bourgeois or feudal) maintains an ideal myth, at once a myth of culmination and a myth of origin. Theology supported itself on the myth of the fulfilment of man in the divine law; political economy is sustained on the great myth of human fulfilment according to the natural law of needs. Both deal in the same finality: an ideal relation of man to the world through his needs and the rule of Nature; and an ideal relationship with God through faith and the divine rule of Providence. Of course, this ideal vocation is lived from the outset as lost or compromised. But the finality tarries, and use value, entombed beneath exchange value, like the natural harmony of earthly paradise broken by sin and suffering, remains inscribed as an invulnerable essence to be disinterred at the last stage of History, in a promised future redemption. The logic and ideology are the same: under the sign of a bountiful nature, where the primitive hunting and gathering mode of production, anterior to the feudal mode, is highlighted, and from which serfdom and labor are made to disappear, the myth of earthly paradise describes the ideality of feudal relations (suzerainty and fealty of vassals). Likewise, the Crusoe myth describes, in "transparent" isolation (where the anterior mode of agriculture and craftsmanship reappears, and the laws of the market and exchange disappear), the ideality of bourgeois relations: individual autonomy, to each according to their labor and their needs; moral consciousness bound to nature – and, if possible, some Man Friday, some aboriginal servant (but if Crusoe's relations to his labor and his wealth are so "clear," as Marx insists, what on earth has Friday got to do with this set-up?).

In fact, nothing is clear about this fable. Its evidence of simplicity and transparency is, as that of the commodity for Marx, "abounding in metaphysical subtleties and theological niceties." There is nothing clear and natural in the fact of "transforming nature according to one's needs" or in "rendering oneself useful" as well as things. And there was no need for this moral law of use value to have escaped the critique of political economy: the whole system and its "mystery" were already there with Robinson on his island, and in the fabricated immediacy of his relation to things.

Notes

1   Poster comments: 'I have been unable to find this passage in the exact form Baudrillard cites it. But see Marx's *Grundrisse* (New York: Vintage, 1975), for example at the bottom of p. 404.'

2   By the same token, there is no fundamental difference between "productive" consumption (direct destruction of utility during the process of production) and consumption by persons in general. The individual and his or her "needs" are produced by the economic system like unit cells of its reproduction. We repeat that "needs" are a *social labor*, a productive discipline. Neither the actual subjects nor their desires are addressed in this scheme. It follows that there is only productive consumption at this level.

3   Consumption itself is only apparently a concrete operation (in opposition to the abstraction of exchange). For what is consumed isn't the product itself, but its utility. Here the economists are right: consumption is not the destruction of products, but the destruction of utility. In the economic cycle, at any rate, it is an abstraction that is produced or consumed as *value* (exchangeable in one case, useful in another). Nowhere is the "concrete" object or the "concrete" product concerned in the matter (what do these terms mean, anyway?): but rather, an abstract cycle, a value system engaged in its own production and expanded reproduction. Nor does consumption make sense as a *destruction* (of "concrete" use value). Consumption is a labor of expanded reproduction of use value as an abstraction, a system, a universal code of utility – just as production is no longer in its present finality the production of "concrete" goods, but the expanded reproduction of the exchange value system. Only consummation (*consommation*) escapes recycling in the expanded reproduction of the value system – not because it is the destruction of substance, but because it is a transgression of the law and finality of objects, the abolition of their abstract finality. Where it appears to consume (destroy) products, consumption only consummates their utility. Consumption destroys objects as substance the better to perpetuate this substance as a universal, abstract form – hence, the better to reproduce the value code. *Consummation* (play, gift, destruction as pure loss, symbolic reciprocity) attacks the code itself, breaks it, deconstructs it. The symbolic act is the destruction of the value code (exchange and

use), not the destruction of objects in themselves. Only this act can be termed "concrete" since it alone breaks with and transgresses the abstraction of value.

4   It should be pointed out that Marx's formulation in this domain (and the anthropology that they imply) are so vague as to permit culturalist interpretations of the type: "Needs are functions of the historical and social context." Or in its more radical version: "Needs are produced by the system in order to assure its own expanded reproduction"; that is, the sort of interpretation that takes into account only the multiple *content* of needs, without submitting the concept of need itself and the system of needs as form to a radical critique. [As in Marx's *Grundrisse*, p.527, where both the "culturalist" and "more radical" position are mixed. Trans.]

5   In *For a Critique*.

6   Poster comments: 'Here Baudrillard alludes to the rationalist lineage of anthropological substantialism. See the first paragraph of Descartes' *Discourse on Method* which Baudrillard parodies here.'

7   Critical theory must also take the sign form into account. We shall observe that an identical logic regulates the organization of the sign in the present-day system; it turns the signified (referent) into the *satellite* term, the *alibi* of the signifier, the play of signifiers, and provides the latter with a reality guarantee.

8   Any resemblance to a living person is purely coincidental.

4

Conspicuous Consumption

Thorstein Veblen

The term "conspicuous consumption" has become a part of everyday language. Veblen uses the concept to describe the lifestyle of an emergent late-nineteenth and early twentieth-century leisure class, in which the display of high pecuniary status, manifest in the ostentatious exhibition of primarily socially useless goods, becomes the overriding concern. The real importance of Veblen's work here, however, lies in the fact that he was among the first to stress the cultural significance of consumption for social groups in their attempts to fix and demonstrate to others their place within a social hierarchy. In this respect *The Theory of the Leisure Class* can in some ways be read as an early antecedent of Bourdieu's *Distinction* (see chapter 7, this volume).

In what has been said of the evolution of the vicarious leisure class and its differentiation from the general body of the working classes, reference has been made to a further division of labour, – that between different servant classes. One portion of the servant class, chiefly those persons whose occupation is vicarious leisure, come to undertake a new, subsidiary range of duties – the vicarious consumption of goods. The most obvious form in which this consumption occurs is seen in the wearing of liveries and the occupation of spacious servants' quarters. Another, scarcely less obtrusive or less effective form of vicarious conspicuous consumption, and a much more widely prevalent one, is the consumption of food, clothing, dwelling, and furniture by the lady and the rest of the domestic establishment.

But already at a point in economic evolution far antedating the emergence of the lady, specialized consumption of goods as an evidence of pecuniary strength had begun to work out in a more of less elaborate system. The beginning of a differentiation in consumption even antedates the appearance of anything that can fairly be called pecuniary strength. It is traceable back to the initial phase of predatory culture, and there is even a suggestion that an incipient differentiation in this respect lies back of the beginnings of the predatory life. This most primitive differentiation in the consumption of goods is like the later differentiation with which

From *The Theory of the Leisure Class: An Economic Study of Institutions* (London: Allen and Unwin, 1925), pp. 68–101.[1]

we are all too intimately familiar, in that it is largely of a ceremonial character, but unlike the latter it does not rest on a difference in accumulated wealth. The utility of consumption as an evidence of wealth is to be classed as a derivative growth. It is an adaptation to a new end, by a selective process, of a distinction previously existing and well established in men's habits and thought.

In the earlier phases of the predatory culture the only economic differentiation is a broad distinction between an honourable superior class made up of the able-bodied men on the one side, and a base inferior class of labouring women on the other. According to the ideal scheme of life in force at that time it is the office of the men to consume what the women produce. Such consumption as falls to the women is merely incidental to their work; it is a means to their continued labour, and not a consumption directed to their own comfort and fulness of life. Unproductive consumption of goods is honourable, primarily as a mark of prowess and a perquisite of human dignity; secondarily it becomes substantially honourable in itself, especially the consumption of the more desirable things. The consumption of choice articles of food, and frequently also of rare articles of adornment, becomes tabu to the women and children; and if there is a base (servile) class of men, the tabu holds also for them. With a further advance in culture this tabu may change into simple custom of a more or less rigorous character; but whatever be the theoretical basis of the distinction which is maintained, whether it be a tabu or a larger conventionality, the features of the conventional scheme of consumption do not change easily. When the quasi-peaceable stage of industry is reached, with its fundamental institution of chattel slavery, the general principle, more or less rigorously applied, is that the base, industrious class should consume only what may be necessary to their subsistence. In the nature of things, luxuries and the comforts of life belong to the leisure class. Under the tabu, certain victuals, and more particularly certain beverages, are strictly reserved for the use of the superior class.

The ceremonial differentiation of the dietary is best seen in the use of intoxicating beverages and narcotics. If these articles of consumption are costly, they are felt to be noble and honorific. Therefore, the base classes, primarily the women, practise an enforced continence with respect to these stimulants, except in countries where they are obtainable at a very low cost. From archaic times down through all the length of the patriarchal regime it has been the office of the women to prepare and administer these luxuries, and it has been the perquisite of the men of gentle birth and breeding to consume them. Drunkenness and the other pathological consequences of the free use of stimulants therefore tend in their turn to become honorific, as being a mark, at the second remove, of the superior status of those who are able to afford the indulgence. Infirmities induced by over-indulgence are among some peoples freely recognized as manly attributes. It has even happened that the name for certain diseased conditions of the body arising from such an origin has passed into everyday speech as a synonym for "noble" or "gentle." It is only at a relatively early stage of culture that the symptoms of expensive vice are conventionally accepted as marks of a superior status, and so tend to become virtues and command the deference of the community; but the reputability that attaches to certain expensive vices long retains so much of its force as to appreciably lessen the disapprobation visited upon the men of the wealthy or noble class for any excessive indulgence. The same invidious distinction adds force to the current disapproval of any indulgence of this kind on the part of women, minors, and inferiors. This invidious traditional distinction has not lost its force even among the more advanced peoples of to-day. Where the example set by the leisure class retains its imperative force in the regulation of the conventionalities, it is observable that the women still in great measure practice the same traditional continence with regard to stimulants.

This characterization of the greater continence in the use of stimulants practised by the women of the reputable classes may seem an excessive refinement of logic at the expense of common sense. But facts within easy reach of anyone who cares to know them go to say that the greater abstinence of women is in some part due to an imperative conventionality; and this conventionality is, in a general way, strongest where the patriarchal tradition – the tradition that the woman is a chattel – has retained its hold in greatest vigour. In a sense which has been greatly qualified in scope and rigour, but which has by no means lost its meaning even yet, this tradition says that the woman, being a chattel, should consume only what is necessary to her sustenance, – except so far as her further consumption contributes to the comfort of the good repute of her master. The consumption of luxuries, in the true sense, is a consumption directed to the comfort of the consumer himself, and is, therefore, a mark of the master. Any such consumption by others can take place only on a basis of sufferance. In communities where the popular habits of thought have been profoundly shaped by the patriarchal tradition we may accordingly look for survivals of the tabu on luxuries at least of a conventional depreciation of their use by the unfree and dependent class. This is more particularly true as regards certain luxuries, the use of which by the dependent class would detract sensibly from the comfort or pleasure of their masters, or which are held to be of doubtful legitimacy on other grounds. In the apprehension of the great conservative middle class of Western civilization the use of these various stimulants is obnoxious to at least one, if not both, of these objections; and it is a fact too significant to be passed over that it is precisely among these middle classes of the Germanic culture, with their strong surviving sense of the patriarchal properties, that the women are to the greatest extent subject to a qualified tabu on narcotics and alcoholic beverages. With many qualifications – with more qualifications as the patriarchal tradition has gradually weakened – the general rule is felt to be right and binding that women should consume only for the benefit of their masters. The objection of course presents itself that expenditure on women's dress and household paraphernalia is an obvious exception to this rule; but it will appear in the sequel that this exception is much more obvious than substantial.

33

During the earlier stages of economic development, consumption of goods without stint, especially consumption of the better grades of goods, – ideally all consumption in excess of the subsistence minimum, – pertains normally to the leisure class. This restriction tends to disappear, at least formally, after the later peaceable stage has been reached, with private ownership of goods and an industrial system based on wage labour or on the petty household economy. But during the earlier quasi-peaceable stage, when so many of the traditions through which the institution of a leisure class has affected the economic life of later times were taking form and consistency, this principle has had the force of a conventional law. It has served as the norm to which consumption has tended to conform, and any appreciable departure from it is to be regarded as an aberrant form, sure to be eliminated sooner or later in the further course of development.

The quasi-peaceable gentleman of leisure, then, not only consumes of the stuff of life beyond the minimum required for subsistence and physical efficiency, but his consumption also undergoes a specialization as regards the quality of the goods consumed. He consumes freely and of the best, in food, drink, narcotics, shelter, services, ornaments, apparel, weapons and accoutrements, amusements, amulets, and idols or divinities. In the process of gradual amelioration which takes place in the articles of his consumption, the motive principle and the proximate aim of innovation is no doubt the higher efficiency of the improved and more elaborate products for personal comfort and well-being. But that does not remain the sole purpose of their consumption. The canon of reputability is at hand and seizes upon such innovations as are, according to its standard, fit to survive. Since the consumption of these more excellent goods is an evidence of wealth, it becomes honorific; and conversely, the failure to consume in due quantity and quality becomes a mark of inferiority and demerit.

The growth of punctilious discrimination as to qualitative excellence in eating, drinking, etc., presently affects not only the manner of life, but also the training and intellectual activity of the gentleman of leisure. He is no longer simply the successful, aggressive male, – the man of strength, resource, and intrepidity. In order to avoid stultification he must also cultivate his tastes, for it now becomes incumbent on him to discriminate with some nicety between the noble and the ignoble in consumable goods. He becomes a connoisseur in creditable viands of various degrees of merit, in manly beverages and trinkets, in seemly apparel and architecture, in weapons, games, dancers, and the narcotics. This cultivation of the aesthetic faculty requires time and application, and the demands made upon the gentleman in this direction therefore tend to change his life of leisure into a more or less arduous application to the business of learning how to live a life of ostensible leisure in a becoming way. Closely related to the requirement that the gentleman must consume freely and of the right kinds of goods, there is the requirement that he must know how to consume them in a seemly manner. His life of leisure must be conducted in due form. Hence arise good manners in the way pointed out in an earlier chapter. High-bred manners and ways of living are items of conformity to the norm of conspicuous leisure and conspicuous consumption.

Conspicuous consumption of valuable goods is a means of reputability to the gentleman of leisure. As wealth accumulates on his hands, his own unaided effort will not avail to sufficiently put his opulence in evidence by this method. The aid of friends and competitors is therefore brought in by resorting to the giving of valuable presents and expensive feasts and entertainments. Presents and feasts had probably another origin than that of naive ostentation, but they acquired their utility for this purpose very early, and they have retained that character to the present; so that their utility in this respect has now long been the substantial ground on which these usages rest. Costly entertainments, such as the potlatch or the ball, are peculiarly adapted to serve this end. The competitor with whom the entertainer wishes to institute a comparison is, by this method, made to serve as a means to the end. He consumes vicariously for his host at the same time that he is a witness to the consumption of that excess of good things which his host is unable to dispose of single-handed, and he is also made to witness his host's facility in etiquette.

In the giving of costly entertainments other motives, of a more genial kind, are of course also present. The custom of festive gatherings probably originated in motives of conviviality and religion; these motives are also present in the later development, but they do not continue to be the sole motives. The latter-day leisure class festivities and entertainments may continue in some slight degree to serve the religious need and in a higher degree the needs of recreation and conviviality, but they also serve an invidious purpose; and they serve it none the less effectually for having a colourable non-invidious ground in these more avowable motives. But the economic effect of these social amenities is not therefore lessened, either in the vicarious consumption of goods or in the exhibition of difficult and costly achievements in etiquette.

As wealth accumulates, the leisure class develops further in function and structure, and there arises a differentiation within the class. There is a more or less elaborate system of rank and grades. This differentiation is furthered by the inheritance of wealth and the consequent inheritance of gentility. With the inheritance of gentility goes the inheritance of obligatory leisure; and gentility of a sufficient potency to entail a life of leisure may be inherited without the complement of wealth required to maintain a dignified leisure. Gentle blood may be transmitted without goods enough to afford a reputably free consumption at one's ease. Hence results a class of impecunious gentlemen of leisure, incidentally referred to already. These half-caste gentlemen of leisure fall into a system of hierarchical gradations. Those who stand near the higher and highest grades of the wealthy leisure class, in point of birth, or in point of wealth, or both, outrank the remoter-born and the pecuniarily weaker. These lower grades, especially the impecunious, or marginal, gentlemen of leisure, affiliate themselves by a system of dependence or fealty to the great ones; by so doing they gain an increment of repute, or of the means with which to lead a life of leisure, from their patron. They become his courtiers or retainers, servants; and being fed and countenanced by their patron they are indices of his rank and vicarious consumers of his superfluous wealth. Many of these affiliated gentlemen of leisure are at the same time lesser men of substance in their own right; so that some of them are scarcely at all, others only partially, to be rated as vicarious consumers. So many of them, however, as make up the retainers and hangers-on of the patron may be classed as vicarious consumers without qualification. Many of these again, and also many of the other aristocracy of less degree, have in turn attached to their persons a more or less comprehensive group of vicarious consumers in the persons of their wives and children, their servants, retainers, etc.

Throughout this graduated scheme of vicarious leisure and vicarious consumption the rule holds that these offices must be performed in some such manner, or under some such circumstance or insignia, as shall point plainly to the master to whom this leisure or consumption pertains, and to whom therefore the resulting increment of good repute of right inures. The consumption and leisure executed by these persons for their master or patron represents an investment on his part with a view to an increase of good fame. As regards feasts and largesses this is obvious enough, and the imputation of repute to the host or patron here takes place immediately, on the ground of common notoriety. Where leisure and consumption are performed vicariously by henchmen and retainers, imputations of the resulting repute to the patron are effected by their residing near his person so that it may be plain to all men from what source they draw. As the group whose good esteem is to be secured in this way grows larger, more patent means are required to indicate the imputations of merit for the leisure performed, and to this end uniforms, badges and liveries come into vogue. The wearing of uniforms or liveries implies a considerable degree of dependence, and may even be said to be a mark of servitude, real or ostensible. The wearers of uniforms and liveries may be roughly divided into two classes – the free and the servile, or the noble and the ignoble. The services performed by them are likewise divisible into noble and ignoble. Of course the distinction is not observed with strict consistency in practice; the less debasing of the base services and the less honorific of the noble functions are not infrequently merged in the same person. But the general distinction is not on that account to be overlooked. What may add some perplexity is the fact that this fundamental distinction between noble and ignoble, which rests on the nature of the ostensible service performed, is traversed by a secondary distinction into honorific and humiliating, resting on the rank of the person for whom the service is performed or whose livery is worn. So, those offices which are by right the proper employment of the leisure class are noble; such are government, fighting, hunting, the care of arms and accoutrements, and the like, – in short, those which may be classed as ostensibly predatory employments. On the other hand, those employments which properly fall to the industrious class are ignoble; such as handicraft or other productive labour, menial services, and the like. But a base service performed for a person of very high degree may become a very honorific office; as for instance the office of a Maid of Honour or of a Lady in Waiting to the Queen, or the King's Master of the Horse or his Keeper of the Hounds. The two offices last named suggest a principle of some general bearing. Whenever, as in these cases, the menial service in question has to do directly with the primary leisure employments of fighting and hunting, it easily acquires a reflected honorific character. In this way, great honour may come to attach to an employment which in its own nature belongs to the baser sort.

In the latter development of peaceable industry, the usage of employing an idle corps of uniformed men-at-arms gradually lapses. Vicarious consumption by dependents bearing the insignia of their patron or master narrows down to a corps of liveried menials. In a heightened degree, therefore, the livery comes to be a badge of servitude, or rather of servility. Something of an honorific character always attached to the livery of the armed retainer, but this honorific character disappears when the livery becomes the exclusive badge of the menial. The livery becomes obnoxious to nearly all who are required to wear it. We are yet so little removed from a state of effective slavery as still to be fully sensitive to the sting of any imputation of servility. This antipathy asserts itself even in the case of the liveries or uniforms which some corporations prescribe as the distinctive dress of their employees. In this country the aversion even goes to the length of discrediting – in a mild and uncertain way – those government employments, military and civil, which require the wearing of a livery or uniform.

With the disappearance of servitude, the number of vicarious consumers attached to any one gentleman tends, on the whole, to decrease. The like is of course true, and perhaps in a still higher degree, of the number of dependents who perform vicarious leisure for him. In a general way, though not wholly nor consistently, these two groups coincide. The dependent who was first delegated for these duties was the wife, or the chief wife; and, as would be expected, in the latter development of the institution, when the number of persons by whom these duties are customarily performed gradually narrows, the wife remains the last. In the higher grades of society a large volume of both these kinds of service is required; and here the wife is of course still assisted in the work by a more or less numerous corps of menials. But as we descend the social scale, the point is presently reached where the duties of vicarious leisure and consumption devolve upon the wife alone. In the communities of the Western culture, this point is at present found among the lower middle class.

And here occurs a curious inversion. It is a fact of common observation that in this lower middle class there is no pretence of leisure on the part of the head of the household. Through force of circumstances it has fallen into disuse. But the middle-class wife still carries on the business of vicarious leisure, for the good name of the household and its master. In descending the social scale in any modern industrial community, the primary fact – the conspicuous leisure of the master of the household – disappears at a relatively high point. The head of the middle-class household has been reduced by economic circumstances to turn his hand to gaining a livelihood by occupations which often partake largely of the character of industry, as in the case of the ordinary businessman of today. But the derivative fact – the vicarious leisure and consumption rendered by the wife, and the auxiliary vicarious performance of leisure by menials – remains in vogue as a conventionality which the demands of reputability will not suffer to be sighted. It is by no means an uncommon spectacle to find a man applying himself to work with the utmost assiduity, in order that his wife may in due form render for him that degree of vicarious leisure which the common sense of the time demands.

The leisure rendered by the wife in such cases is, of course, not a simple manifestation of idleness or indolence. It almost invariably occurs disguised under some form of work or household duties or social amenities, which prove on analysis to serve little or no ulterior end beyond showing that she does not and need not occupy herself with anything that is gainful or that is of substantial use. As has already been noticed under the head of manners, the greater part of the customary round of domestic cares to which the middle-class housewife gives her time and effort is of this character. Not that the results of her attention to household matters, of a decorative and mundificatory character, are not pleasing to the sense of men trained in middle-class proprieties; but the tastes to which these effects of household adornment and tidiness appeal is a taste which has been formed under the selective guidance of a canon of propriety that demands just these evidences of wasted effort. The effects are pleasing to us chiefly because we have been taught to find them pleasing. There goes into these domestic duties much solicitude for a proper combination of form and colour, and for other ends that are to be classed as aesthetic in the proper sense of the term; and it is not denied that effects having some substantial aesthetic value are sometimes attained. Pretty much all that is here insisted on is that, as regards these amenities of life, the housewife's efforts are under the guidance of traditions that have been shaped by the law of conspicuously wasteful expenditure of time and substance. If beauty or comfort is achieved, – and it is a more or less fortuitous circumstance if they are, – they must be achieved by means and methods that commend themselves to the great economic law of wasted effort. The more reputable, "presentable" portion of middle-class household paraphernalia are, on the one hand, items of conspicuous consumption, and on the other hand, apparatus for putting in evidence the vicarious leisure rendered by the housewife.

The requirement of vicarious consumption at the hands of the wife continues in force even at a lower point in the pecuniary scale than the requirement of vicarious leisure. At a point below which little if any pretence of wasted effort, in ceremonial cleanness and the like, is observable, and where there is assuredly no conscious attempt at ostensible leisure, decency still requires the wife to consume some goods conspicuously for the reputability of the household and its head. So that, as the latter-day outcome of this evolution of an archaic institution, the wife, who was at the outset the drudge and chattel of the man, both in fact and in theory, – the producer of goods for him to consume, – has become the ceremonial consumer of goods which he produces. But she still quite unmistakably remains his chattel in theory; for the habitual rendering of vicarious leisure and consumption is the abiding mark of the unfree servant.

This vicarious consumption practised by the household of the middle and lower classes cannot be counted as a direct expression of the leisure-class scheme of life, since the household of this pecuniary grade does not belong within the leisure class. It is rather that the leisure-class scheme of life here comes to an expression at the second remove. The leisure class stands at the head of the social structure in a point of reputability; and its manner of life and its standards of worth therefore afford the norm of reputability for the community. The observance of these standards, in some degree of approximation, becomes incumbent upon all classes lower in the scale. In modern civilized communities the lines of demarcation between social classes have grown vague and transient, and wherever this happens the norm of reputability imposed by the upper class extends its coercive influence with but slight hindrance down through the social structure to the lowest strata. The result is that the members of each stratum accept as their ideal of decency the scheme of life in vogue in the next higher stratum, and bend their energies to live up to that ideal. On pain of forfeiting their good name and their self-respect in case of failure, they must conform to the accepted code, at least in appearance.

The basis on which good repute in any highly organized industrial community ultimately rests is pecuniary strength; and the means of showing pecuniary strength, and so of gaining or retaining a good name, are leisure and a conspicuous consumption of goods. Accordingly, both of these methods are in vogue as far down the scale as it remains possible; and in the lower strata in which the two methods are employed, both offices are in great part delegated to the wife and children of the household. Lower still, where any degree of leisure, even ostensible, has become impracticable for the wife, the conspicuous consumption of goods remains and is carried on by the wife and children. The man of the household also can do something in this direction, and, indeed, he commonly does; but with a still lower descent into the levels of indigence – along the margin of the slums – the man, and presently also the children, virtually cease to consume valuable goods for appearances, and the woman remains virtually the sole exponent of the household's pecuniary decency. No class of society, not even the most abjectly poor, forgoes all customary conspicuous consumption. The last items of this category of consumption are not given up except under stress of the direst necessity. Very much of squalor and discomfort will be endured before the last trinket or the last pretence of pecuniary decency is put away. There is no class and no country that has yielded so abjectly before the pressure of physical want as to deny themselves all gratification of this higher or spiritual need.

From the foregoing survey of the growth of conspicuous leisure and consumption, it appears that the utility of both alike for the purposes of reputability lies in the element of waste that is common to both. In the one case it is the waste of time and effort, in the other it is a waste of goods. Both are methods of demonstrating the possession of wealth, and the two are conventionally accepted as equivalents. The choice between them is a question of advertising expediency simply, except so far as it may be affected by other standards of propriety, springing from a different source. On grounds of expediency the preference may be given to the one or the other at different stages of the economic development. The question is, which of the two methods will most effectively reach the persons whose convictions it is desired to affect. Usage has answered this question in different ways under different circumstances.

So long as the community or social group is small enough and compact enough to be effectually reached by common notoriety alone, – that is to say, so long as the human environment to which the individual is required to adapt himself in respect of reputability is comprised within his sphere of personal acquaintance and neighbourhood gossip, – so long the one method is about as effective as the other. Each will therefore serve about equally well during the earlier stages of social growth. But when the differentiation has gone farther and it becomes necessary to reach a wider human environment, consumption begins to hold over leisure as an ordinary means of decency. This is especially true during the later, peaceable economic stage. The means of communication and the mobility of the population now expose the individual to the observation of many persons who have no other means of judging of his reputability than the display of goods (and perhaps of breeding) which he is able to make while he is under their direct observation.

The modern organization of industry works in the same direction also by another line. The exigencies of the modern industrial system frequently place individuals and households in juxtaposition between whom there is little contact in any other sense than that of juxtaposition. One's neighbours, mechanically speaking, often are socially not one's neighbours, or even acquaintances; and still their transient good opinion has a high degree of utility. The only practicable means of impressing one's pecuniary ability on these unsympathetic observers of one's everyday life is an unremitting demonstration of ability to pay. In the modern community there is also a more frequent attendance at large gatherings of people to whom one's everyday life is unknown; in such places as churches, theatres, ballrooms, hotels, parks, shops, and the like. In order to impress these transient observers, and to retain one's self-complacency under their observation, the signature of one's pecuniary strength should be written in characters which he who runs may also read. It is evident, therefore, that the present trend of the development is in the direction of heightening the utility of conspicuous consumption as compared with leisure.

It is also noticeable that the serviceability of consumption is a means of repute, as well as the insistence on it as an element of decency, is at its best in those portions of the community where the human contact of the individual is widest and the mobility of the population is greatest. Conspicuous consumption claims a relatively larger portion of the income of the urban than of the rural population, and the claim is also more imperative. The result is that, in order to keep up a decent appearance, the former habitually live hand-to-mouth to a greater extent than the latter. So it comes, for instance, that the American farmer and his wife and daughters are notoriously less modish in their dress, as well as less urbane in their manners, than the city artisan's family with an equal income. It is not that the city population is by nature much more eager for the peculiar complacency that comes of a conspicuous consumption, nor has the rural population less regard for pecuniary decency. But the provocation for this line of evidence, as well as its transient effectiveness, are more decided in the city. This method is therefore more readily resorted to, and in the struggle to outdo one another the city population push their normal standard of conspicuous consumption to a higher point, with the result that a relatively greater expenditure in this direction is required to indicate a given degree of pecuniary decency in the city. The requirement of conformity to this higher conventional standard becomes mandatory. The standard of decency is higher, class for class, and this requirement of decent appearance must be lived up to on pain of losing caste.

Consumption becomes a larger element in the standard of living in the city than in the country. Among the country population its place is to some extent taken by savings and home comforts known through the medium of neighbourhood gossip sufficiently to serve the like general purpose of pecuniary repute. These home comforts and the leisure indulged in – where the indulgence is found – are of course also in great part to be classed as items of conspicuous consumption; and much the same is to be said of the savings. The smaller amount of the savings laid by the artisan class is no doubt due, in some measure, to the fact that in the case of the artisan the savings are a less effective means of advertisement, relative to the environment in which he is placed, than are the savings of the people living on farms and in the small villages. Among the latter, everybody's affairs, especially everybody's pecuniary status, are known to everybody else. Considered by itself simply – taken in the first degree – this added provocation to which the artisan and the urban labouring classes are exposed may not very seriously decrease the amount of savings; but in its cumulative action, through raising the standard of decent expenditure, its deterrent effect on the tendency to save cannot but be very great.

A felicitous illustration of the manner in which this canon of reputability works out its results is seen in the practice of dram-drinking, "treating," and smoking in public places, which is customary among the labourers and handicraftsmen of the towns, and among the lower middle class of the urban population generally. Journeymen printers may be named as a class among whom this form of conspicuous consumption has a great vogue, and among whom it carries with it certain well-marked consequences that are often depreciated. The peculiar habits of the class in this respect are commonly set down to some kind of an ill-defined moral deficiency with which this class is credited, or to a morally deleterious influence which their occupation is supposed to exert, in some unascertainable way, upon the men employed in it. The state of the case for the men who work in the composition and press rooms of the common run of printing-houses may be summed up as follows. Skill acquired in any printing-house or any city is easily turned to account in almost any other house or city; that is to say, the inertia due to special training is slight. Also, this occupation requires more than the average of intelligence and general information, and the men employed in it are therefore ordinarily more ready than many others to take advantage of any slight variation in the demand for their labour from one place to another. The inertia due to the home feeling is consequently also slight. At the same time the wages in the trade are also high enough to make movement from place to place relatively easy. The result is a great mobility of the labour employed in printing; perhaps greater than any other equally well-defined and considerable body of workmen. These men are constantly thrown in contact with new groups of acquaintances, with whom the relations established are transient or ephemeral, but whose good opinion is valued none the less for the time being. The human proclivity to ostentation, reinforced by sentiments of goodfellowship, leads them to spend freely in those directions which will best serve these needs. Hence as elsewhere prescription seizes upon the custom as soon as it gains a vogue, and incorporates it in the accredited standard of decency. The next step is to make this standard of decency the point of departure for a new move in advance in the same direction, – for there is no merit in simple spiritless conformity to a standard of dissipation that is lived up to as a matter of course by everyone in the trade.

The greater prevalence of dissipation among printers than among the average workmen is accordingly attributable, at least in some measure, to the greater ease of movement and the more transient character of acquaintance and human contact in this trade. But the substantial ground of this high requirement in dissipation is in the last analysis no other than the same propensity for a manifestation of dominance and pecuniary decency which makes the French peasant-proprietor parsimonious and frugal, and induces the American millionaire to found collages, hospitals and museums. If the canon of conspicuous consumption were not offset to a considerable extent by other features of human nature, alien to it, any saving should logically be impossible for a population situated as the artisan and labouring classes of the cities are at present, however high their wages or their income might be.

But there are other standards of repute and other, more or less imperative, canons of conduct, besides wealth and its manifestation, and some of these come in to accentuate or to qualify the broad, fundamental canon of conspicuous waste. Under the simple test of effectiveness for advertising , we should expect to find leisure and the conspicuous consumption of goods dividing the field of pecuniary emulation pretty evenly between them at the outset. Leisure might then be expected gradually to yield ground and tend to obsolescence as the economic development goes forward, and the community increases in size; while the conspicuous consumption of goods should gradually gain in importance, both absolutely and relatively, until it had absorbed all the available product, leaving nothing over beyond a bare livelihood. But the actual course of development has been somewhat different from this ideal scheme. Leisure held the first place at the start, and came to hold a rank very much above wasteful consumption of goods, both as a direct exponent of wealth and as an element in the standard of decency, during the quasi-peaceable culture. From that point onward, consumption has gained ground, until, at present, it unquestionably holds the primacy, though it is still far from absorbing the entire margin of production above the subsistence minimum.

The early ascendency of leisure as a means of reputability is traceable to the archaic distinction between noble and ignoble employments. Leisure is honourable and becomes imperative partly because it shows exemption from ignoble labour. The archaic differentiation into noble and ignoble classes is based on an invidious distinction between employments as honorific or debasing; and this traditional distinction grows into an imperative canon of decency during the early quasi-peaceable stage. Its ascendency is furthered by the fact that leisure is still fully as effective an evidence of wealth as consumption. Indeed, so effective is it in the relatively small and stable human environment to which the individual is exposed at that cultural stage, that, with the aid of the archaic tradition which depreciates all productive labour, it gives rise to a large impecunious leisure class, and it even tends to limit the production of the community's industry to the subsistence minimum. This extreme inhibition of industry is avoided because slave labour, working under a compulsion more rigorous than that of reputability, is forced to turn out a product in excess of the subsistence minimum of the working class. The subsequent relative decline in the use of conspicuous leisure as a basis of repute is due partly to an increasing relative effectiveness of consumption as an evidence of wealth; but in part it is traceable to another force, alien, and in some degree antagonistic, to the usage of conspicuous waste.

This alien factor is the instinct of workmanship. Other circumstances permitting, that instinct disposes men to look with favour upon productive efficiency and on whatever is of human use. It disposes them to depreciate waste of substance or effort. The instinct of workmanship is present in all men, and asserts itself even under very adverse circumstances. So that however wasteful a given expenditure may be in reality, it must at least have some colourable excuse in the way of an ostensible purpose. The manner in which, under special circumstances, the instinct eventuates in a taste for exploit and in an invidious discrimination between noble and ignoble classes has been indicated in an earlier chapter. In so far as it comes into conflict with the law of conspicuous waste, the instinct of workmanship expresses itself not so much in insistence on substantial usefulness as in an abiding sense of the odiousness and aesthetic impossibility of what is obviously futile. Being of the nature of an instinctive affection, its guidance touches chiefly and immediately the obvious and apparent violations of its requirements. It is only less promptly and with less constraining force that it reaches such substantial violations of its requirements as are appreciated only upon reflection.

So long as all labour continues to be performed exclusively or usually by slaves, the baseness of all productive effort is too constantly and deterrently present in the mind of men to allow the instinct of workmanship seriously to take effect in the direction of industrial usefulness; but when the quasi-peaceable stage (with slavery and status) passes into the peaceable stage of industry (with wage labour and cash payment) the instinct comes more effectively into play. It then begins aggressively to shape men's views of what is meritorious, and asserts itself at least as an auxiliary canon of self-complacency. All extraneous considerations apart, those persons (adults) are but a vanishing minority today who harbour no inclination to the accomplishment of some end, or who are not impelled of their own motion to shape some object or fact or relation for human use. The propensity may in large measure be overborne by the more immediately constraining incentive to a reputable leisure and an avoidance of indecorous usefulness, and it may therefore work itself out in make-believe only; as for instance in "social duties," and in quasi-artistic or quasi-scholarly accomplishments, in the care and decoration of the house, in sewing-circle activity or dress reform, in proficiency at dress, cards, yachting, golf, and various sports. But the fact that it may under stress of circumstances eventuate in inanities no more disproves the presence of the instinct than the reality of the brooding instinct is disproved by inducing a hen to sit on a nestful of china eggs.

This latter-day uneasy reaching-out for some form of purposeful activity that shall at the same time not be indecorously productive of either individual or collective gain marks a difference of attitude between the modern leisure class and that of the quasi-peaceable stage. At the earlier stage, as was said above, the all-dominating institution of slavery and status acted resistlessly to discountenance exertion directed to other than naively predatory ends. It was still possible to find some habitual employment for the inclination to action in the way of forcible aggression or repression directed against hostile groups or against the subject classes within the group; and this served to relieve the pressure and draw off the energy of the leisure class without resort to actual useful, or even ostensibly useful employments. The practice of hunting also served the same purpose in some degree. When the community developed into a peaceful industrial organization, and when fuller occupation of the land had reduced the opportunities for the hunt to an inconsiderable residue, the pressure of energy seeking purposeful employment was left to find an outlet in some other direction. The ignominy which attaches to useful effort also entered upon a less acute phase with the disappearance of compulsory labour; and the instinct of workmanship then came to assert itself with more persistence and consistency.

The line of least resistance has changed in some measure, and the energy which formally found a vent in predatory activity, now in part takes the direction of some ostensibly useful end. Ostensibly purposeless leisure has come to be depreciated, especially among that large portion of the leisure class whose plebeian origin acts to set them at variance with the tradition of the *otium cum dignitate*. But that canon of reputability which discountenances all employment that is of the nature of productive effort is still at hand, and will permit nothing beyond the most transient vogue to any employment that is substantially useful or productive. The consequence is that a change has been wrought in the conspicuous leisure practised by the leisure class; not so much in substance as in form. A reconciliation between the two conflicting requirements is effected by a resort to make-believe. Many and intricate polite observances and social duties of a ceremonial nature are developed; many organizations are founded, with some specious object of amelioration embodied in their official style and title; there is much coming and going, and a deal of talk, to the end that the talkers may not have occasion to reflect on what is the effectual economic value of their traffic. And along with the make-believe of purposeful employment, and woven inextricably into its texture, there is commonly, if not invariably, a more or less appreciable element of purposeful effort directed to some serious end.

In the narrower sphere of vicarious leisure a similar change has gone forward. Instead of simply passing her time in visible idleness, as in the best days of the patriarchal regime, the housewife of the advanced peaceable stage applies herself assiduously to household cares. The salient features of this development of domestic service have already been indicated.

Throughout the entire evolution of conspicuous expenditure, whether of goods or of services or human life, runs the obvious implication that in order to effectually mend the consumer's good fame it must be an expenditure of superfluities. In order to be reputable it must be wasteful. No merit would accrue from the consumption of the bare necessaries of life, except by comparison with the abjectly poor who fall short even of the subsistence minimum; and no standard of expenditure could result from such a comparison, except the most prosaic and unattractive level of decency. A standard of life would still be possible which should admit of invidious comparison in other respects than that of opulence; as, for instance, a comparison in various directions in the manifestation of moral, physical, intellectual or aesthetic force. Comparisons in all these directions is in vogue today; and the comparison made in these respects is commonly so inextricably bound up with the pecuniary comparison as to be scarcely distinguishable from the latter. This is especially true as regards the current rating of expressions of intellectual and aesthetic force or proficiency; so that we frequently interpret as aesthetic or intellectual a difference which in substance is pecuniary only.

The use of the term "waste" is in one respect an unfortunate one. As used in the speech of everyday life the word carries an undertone of depreciation. It is here used for want of a better term that will adequately describe the same range of motives and of phenomena, and it is not to be taken in an odious sense, as implying an illegitimate expenditure of human products or of human life. In the view of economic theory the expenditure in question is no more and no less legitimate than any other expenditure. It is here called "waste" because this expenditure does not serve human life or human well-being on the whole, not because it is waste or misdirection of effort or expenditure as viewed from the standpoint of the individual consumer who chooses it. If he chooses it, that disposes of the question of its relative utility to him, as compared with other forms of consumption that would not be depreciated on account of their wastefulness. Whatever form of expenditure the consumer chooses, or whatever end he seeks in making his choice, has utility to him by virtue of his preference. As seen from the point of view of the individual consumer, the question of wastefulness does not arise within the scope of economic theory proper. The use of the word "waste" as a technical term, therefore, implies no depreciation of the motives or of the ends sought by the consumer under this canon of conspicuous waste.

But it is, on other grounds, worth noting that the term "waste" in the language of everyday life implies depreciation in what is characterized as wasteful. This common-sense implication is itself an outcropping of the instinct of workmanship. The popular reprobation of waste goes to say that in order to be at peace with himself the common man must be able to see in any and all human effort and human enjoyment an enhancement of life and well-being on the whole. In order to meet with unqualified approval, any economic fact must approve itself under the test of impersonal usefulness – usefulness as seen from the point of view of the generically human. Relative or competitive advantage of one individual in comparison with another does not satisfy the economic conscience, and therefore competitive expenditure has not the approval of the conscience.

In strict accuracy nothing should be included under the head of conspicuous waste but such expenditure as is incurred on the ground of an invidious pecuniary comparison. But in order to bring any given item or element in under this head it is not necessary that it should be recognized as waste in this sense by the person incurring the expenditure. It frequently happens that an element of the standard of living which set out with being primarily wasteful, ends with becoming, in apprehension of the consumer, a necessary of life; and it may in this way become as indispensable as any other item of the consumer's habitual expenditure. As items which sometimes fall under this head, and are therefore available as illustrations of the manner in which this principle applies, may be cited carpets and tapestries, silver table service, waiter's service, silk hats, starched linen, many articles of jewellery and of dress. The indispensability of these things after the habit and the convention have been formed, however, has little to say in the classification of expenditures as waste or not waste in the technical meaning of the word. The test to which all expenditure must be brought in an attempt to decide that point is the question whether it serves directly to enhance human life on the whole – whether it furthers the life process taken impersonally. For this is the basis of award of the instinct of workmanship, and that instinct is the court of final appeal in any question of economic truth or adequacy. It is a question as to the award rendered by a dispassionate common sense. The question is, therefore, under the existing circumstances of individual habit and social custom, a given expenditure conduces to the particular consumer's gratification or peace of mind; but whether, aside from acquired tastes and from the canons of usage and conventional decency, its result is a net gain in comfort or in the fulness of life. Customary expenditure must be classed under the head of waste in so far as the custom on which it rests is traceable to the habit of making an invidious pecuniary comparison – in so far as it is conceived that it could not have become customary and prescriptive without the backing of this principle of pecuniary reputability or relative economic success.

It is obviously not necessary that a given object of expenditure should be exclusively wasteful in order to come in under the category of conspicuous waste. An article may be useful and wasteful both, and its utility to the consumer may be made up of use and waste in the most varying proportions. Consumable goods, and even productive goods, generally show the two elements in combination, as constituents of their utility; although, in a general way, the element of waste tends to predominate in articles of consumption, while the contrary is true for articles designed for productive use. Even in articles which appear at first glance to serve for pure ostentation only, it is always possible to detect the presence of some, at least ostensible, useful purpose; and on the other hand, even in special machinery and tools contrived for some particular industrial process, as well as in the rudest appliances of human industry, the traces of conspicuous waste, or at least of the habit of ostentation, usually become evident on a close scrutiny. It would be hazardous to assert that a useful purpose is ever absent from the utility of any article or of any service, however obviously its prime purpose and chief element is conspicuous waste; and it would be only less hazardous to assert of any primarily useful product that the element of waste is in no way concerned in its value, immediately or remotely.

Note

1   *The Theory of the Leisure Class* was originally published in 1899, with a revised edition in 1912.

5

The Puzzle of Modern Consumerism

Colin Campbell

In this chapter a range of long-standing "theories" which claim to explain consumer behavior are the targets for the author's clinical attacks. These include the hugely influential notion of "marginal utility theory," "instinctivism," "manipulationism" (represented in this Reader by Galbraith and Packard), and rather crude attempts to apply certain Veblenesque ideas to orthodox economic accounts of consumption.

> In the modern world the production of consumption becomes more important than the consumption of production. (John Lukács)

In exploring the issues raised by attempts to explain the consumer revolution in England in the eighteenth century it has become apparent that the principal difficulty is a theoretical one; that is to say, the conceptual framework employed to account for the origins of the new propensity to consume is simply not adequate for the task. Ideas about increased demand stemming from a new outburst of social emulation, coupled with strenuous attempts at manipulation of consumer wants by producers, do not amount to a logically related set of propositions from which cause might effectively be separated from effect, or even a convincingly meaningful pattern of subjective action constructed. In particular, the central role played by changed values and attitudes is not properly explored, nor integrated with observations concerning intellectual movements which might have served to justify the resulting changes in conduct. The blame for this deficiency should not be placed on the historians, however, for it is a characteristic of those social sciences – principally economics and sociology – upon which they are forced to rely. No satisfactory account of the consumer revolution is possible because no satisfactory account of modern consumer behaviour exists, although, ironically, this is

From *The Romantic Ethic and the Spirit of Modern Consumerism* (Oxford: Blackwell Publishers, 1989), pp. 36–57. Reprinted by permission of the author.

due at least in part to the past failure of historians to appreciate the importance of that revolution.[1] It follows from this that the problem of explaining the conduct of modern consumers – and that of accounting for events in the eighteenth century – is, at root, one and the same, with the heightened propensity of contemporary consumers to want goods no easier to account for than that which first appeared over 200 years ago. This is a fundamental truth which is obscured both by a widespread ethnocentricity and a tendency for social scientists to overlook what are the most characteristic features of modern consumerism.

For the truth is that a mystery surrounds consumer behaviour, or, at least, there is a mystery surrounding the behaviour of consumers in modern industrial societies. It does not concern their choice of products, nor why some groups manifest patterns of consumption different from others. Neither does it involve the question of how much of a product a person is willing to purchase at a given price, nor what kind of subconscious forces might influence that decision. The mystery is more fundamental than any of these, and concerns the very essence of modern consumption itself – its character as an activity which involves an apparently endless pursuit of wants;[2] the most characteristic feature of modern consumption being this insatiability. As Fromm observes, 'Contemporary man has an unlimited hunger for more and more goods' (Fromm, 1964: 179), or, as O'Neill expresses it, the modern consumer must learn 'economic tension', that is, the realization that all his wants and desires will never be satisfied (O'Neill, 1978: 225). This can never happen because of the apparently endless process of replacement which ensures that 'When one want is fulfilled, several more usually pop up to take its place' (Markin Jr, 1974: 195).

This is not to say that insatiability itself is especially hard to understand, or that it is confined to modern society. For there is plenty of evidence to suggest that human beings in all cultures are capable of developing addictions. One could say that the Spanish Conquistadors had an insatiable greed for gold, or that Don Juan was similarly hard to satisfy when it came to women. Such non-satiable appetites, however, typically have a single product focus, as is the case with alcoholism or drug addiction; by contrast, the modern consumer (although not proof against such temptations) is characterized by an insatiability which arises out of a basic inexhaustibility of wants themselves, which forever arise, phoenix-like, from the ashes of their predecessors. Hence no sooner than one is satisfied than another is waiting in line clamouring to be satisfied; when this one is attended to, a third appears, then subsequently a fourth, and so on, apparently without end. The process is ceaseless and unbroken; rarely can an inhabitant of modern society, no matter how privileged or wealthy, declare that there is nothing that they want. That this should be so is a matter of wonder.[3] How is it possible for wants to appear with such constancy, and in such inexhaustible fashion, especially when they typically concern novel products and services?[4]

This endless wanting has been described as arising out of the 'revolution in rising expectations' which occurs when traditional societies undergo the series of changes associated with the process of development or modernization (Lerner, 1958). This revolution appears to have the consequence of causing consumers to develop expectations which consistently outstrip realization, something which has led observers to redescribe the change as a 'revolution in rising frustrations'.[5] Whether frustration exceeds satisfaction or not depends upon what Lerner dubs the 'wants–get ratio'. No matter how limited the feelings of frustration, however, and hence how close this ratio comes to one, it is a central fact of modern consumer behaviour that the gap between wanting and getting never actually closes.

It may be objected that the dynamism characteristic of modern consumerism has its origins in the inventiveness which so typifies modern man; an inventiveness which leads to an endless production of novel products and services. Whilst there is truth in this observation, a crucial gap exists between a new 'invention' and a new 'want'. Without claiming that all inventions arise to meet existing needs, the vast majority could be said to arise as the result of attempts to satisfy present needs more efficiently, and if they fail to do this then no new want will result. This rational, instrumental dynamic may have little effect on the basic pattern of gratifications typical of a consumer, whilst profoundly affecting the economic use of resources. In this respect it is crucial to distinguish between a purely economic and a wider social action conception of what 'consumption' means.

In a purely economic sense, consumption refers to those processes through which economic resources are used up; it is, in this respect, the logical opposite of production. This may not, however, involve any human gratification (as is the case, for example, when referring to objects which are accidentally 'consumed' by fire). Humanly conceived, therefore, consumption refers to the 'use of goods in the satisfaction of human wants' (Kyrk, 1923: 4), and is typically the outcome of consciously motivated behaviour. Human beings may, however, also obtain gratification from activities which do not, in any conventional economic sense, involve the use of resources at all (except those of time and human energy), such as the appreciation of natural beauty or the enjoyment of friendship. Consumption habits may alter as a consequence of either an innovation in the use of resources or a modification to the pattern of gratifications. The position adopted here, as will be seen, is that the latter has a more intimate connection with the insatiability of wants than the former.

The continual extinction of wants is as much of a puzzle as their creation, for a natural corollary of endless wanting is the high rate of product (and hence want) obsolescence. How is it that wants depart as suddenly and as effortlessly as they arrive? How is it that individuals manage to cease to want that which they ardently desired only a little while before? For modern consumer society is symbolized at least as much by the mountains of rubbish, the garage and jumble sales, the columns of advertisements of second-hand goods for sale and the second-hand car lots, as it is by the ubiquitous propaganda on behalf of new goods.

There is a widespread tendency to take such behaviour for granted and to assume that, even though it might not be morally desirable, it is at least a perfectly 'normal' or 'rational' mode of acting. It takes only a little reflection to realize, however, that such a view is neither supported by psychology nor anthropology, but is merely the product of a deep-seated ethnocentricity.[6]

For this is certainly not the traditional pattern. In non-literate and pre-industrial societies, consumption, like other aspects of life, is largely governed by custom and tradition, and these forces specify a fixed rather than an open-ended notion of wants. It is not merely that in such societies habit has gained an encrustation of normative approval, but that an endlessly changeable pattern of consumption is impossible for the individual to contemplate, or for the society as it is constituted to tolerate. Riesman and Lerner have stressed how, for the 'tradition-directed' person, 'what exists . . . is all that can exist' (Riesman and Lerner, 1965: 391). At the same time, the efforts of any one individual to 'better' his condition by striving after new wants are not only seen as threatening to the whole community but as fundamentally immoral. Since peasants typically operate with a notion of the 'limited good', that is with the view 'that [since] all the desired things [in] life such as land, wealth, health, friendship and love . . . [exist] in finite quantity and [are] always in short supply', an apparent improvement in the position of one person threatens the entire community (Foster, 1965: 297). In addition, since the traditional way of life has divine legitimation, such 'self-seeking' is also regarded as blasphemous (Lerner, 1958: 400). Most crucially, however, what separates the traditional consumer from his modern counterpart is his view that the novel is to be feared, if not actually regarded as the embodiment of evil (Simmel, 1957: 546).

Thus it is not consumption in general which poses special problems of explanation, so much as that particular pattern which is characteristic of modern industrial societies.[7] It is, after all, easy enough to appreciate the necessary biological basis of many of the acts of consumption involved in the pattern of life exemplified by non-literate, pre-industrial peoples. What is more, consumption in these societies is not an activity clearly set apart from that of production. Consequently, there are few problems of explanation presented by consumption itself, there is merely a need to understand the way of life as a whole. Thus whatever consumption practices are observed require no separate theory, just a thorough understanding of the culture and traditions of the group. Hence the idea that human beings somehow have a 'natural' tendency to display insatiable wanting does not derive any support from history or anthropology. On the contrary, if there is such a thing as a 'normal' pattern in these matters, it is the traditional one of a fixed, limited and familiar set of wants.

Unfortunately this point tends to have been overlooked by social scientists, who consequently have been tempted to develop universal, ahistorical theories of consumer behaviour. The failure to perceive the truly puzzling nature of modern

consumer behaviour derives in large measure from this absence of a proper historical sense and the ethnocentricity which it naturally produces. Thus instead of contemporary practices being regarded as exceptional, pre-modern peoples are typically
considered to be merely prevented from behaving like us because of the lack of an
industrial economy. In this way, the modern pattern is presented as immanent in
history and its peculiarity given teleological justification.

The approach to the phenomenon of consumption which predominates within
the discipline of economics is that associated with the microeconomic theory of
marginal utility; utility being the name given to that quality intrinsic to the item of
consumption from which the consumer derives satisfaction whilst he, in turn, is
always assumed to behave in such a way as to maximize his utility and hence his
satisfaction. This he will endeavour to do by acting rationally in the market within
those limits set by his disposable income and prevailing prices, his motive in entering the market being the need to satisfy his wants and tastes. These are generally
regarded as originating within the personality of the consumer (or are at least
assumed to do so for the sake of the theory) and are revealed in choice, it being
assumed that actual behaviour is a faithful reflection of underlying preferences. In
the classical formulation of this perspective no explanation is offered for the origin
of wants or tastes, nor of how they might develop or change. In addition, although the theory offers predictions concerning the degree of interest which a
consumer might have in a product depending upon the amount of it that he already possesses, it does not offer any insight into the possible differential preferences which a consumer might have for the satisfaction of various wants. Each
want is, in that sense, assumed to posses an equal urgency.

Although the theory of marginal utility has proved to be a powerful tool for the
analysis of certain aspects of consumer choice it has long been obvious that it does
not constitute a theory of consumer behaviour. The familiar criticisms of utility
theory, such as the dubiousness of the assumptions concerning rationality and the
intention to maximize satisfaction, are less pertinent in this respect than the simple
observation that far too much is omitted. A theory which does not even attempt
to account for the nature or origins of wants and tastes, and offers only the most
attenuated suggestion concerning why people buy goods, hardly deserves to be
called a theory of consumer behaviour.

These deficiencies have long been apparent, to economists as well as others, and
yet little effort has been directed at remedying them.[8] Instead, theoretical perspectives drawn from elsewhere have been attached to marginal utility theory in an
attempt to compensate for the more obvious of these inadequacies, a strategy
which is clearly a poor substitute for the development of a satisfactory overall
theory of consumer behaviour. Before looking at these 'incorporated' perspectives, however, and the extent to which they can be said to serve to fill these gaps,
it will be useful to specify how it is that utility theory is unable to explain exactly
that feature which (with the exception of rationality) is most characteristic of modern

consumption. This, as we have seen, is the preference for new wants and, in particular, their rapid and seemingly endless creation.

Given that marginal utility theory assumes that the consumer is seeking to maximize his satisfactions it is not at all clear how a want for a novel product develops, for this offers unknown and hence unestimable satisfactions to set aside the known ones gained from the products presently consumed. How, rationally, could any consumer justify transferring some of his scarce resources from habitual purchases, when all he could be absolutely sure of would be the loss of current satisfactions? As Henry Waldgrave Stuart outlined the problem as long ago as 1917:

> How are we to understand the acquisition, by an individual, of what are called new economic needs and interests? Except by a fairly obvious fallacy of retrospection we cannot regard this phenomenon as a mere arousal of so-called latent or implicit desires. New products and new means of production afford 'satisfactions' and bring about objective results which are unimaginable and therefore unpredictable, in any descriptive fashion, in advance. (Stuart, 1917: 347)

It follows from this argument that the truly 'rational' consumer, determined to maximize his satisfactions at all costs, would simply not strive to obtain new products or services as this would, as Stuart observes, be more in the nature of an adventure or a gamble than 'calculation' (Stuart, 1917: 309).[9] Thus it is that the very assumptions introduced to account for that 'rationality' which is considered to characterize instrumental consumer action actually have the consequence of making its other dominant characteristic – insatiability for new products – appear as an especially 'irrational' and puzzling form of behaviour.

In order to see how economists (and some other social scientists) characteristically supplement these deficiencies of marginal utility theory in an effort to build up a theory of consumer behaviour, it will be useful to look briefly at Galbraith's discussion of consumption as outlined in chapters 10 and 11 of *The Affluent Society* (Galbraith, 1979) [see chapter 16, this volume]. This book was not intended to supply a fully developed theory of consumer behaviour, the aim of its author being to expose what he regarded as the outdated and unhelpful economic myths of the age. This, nevertheless, is an advantage because it means that the discussion is especially revealing of those assumptions which economists commonly make when called upon to consider consumption as a real phenomenon rather than as an abstract aspect of behaviour.

Galbraith's main concern is to demonstrate how irrational is that view which regards all increases in production – as indicated for example by increases in the Gross National Product – as necessarily good irrespective of the nature of the products which are manufactured or the wants which they satisfy. In order to develop a critique of this assumption he examines the sources of consumer demand for goods in modern society and questions the tendency of classical economic theory not to inquire into the origin of wants, but to assume none the less that their urgency does not diminish appreciably as more of them are satisfied (Galbraith, 1979: 136). Galbraith challenges this position with the argument that:

> If the individual's wants are to be urgent, they must be original with himself. They cannot be urgent if they must be contrived for him. And above all they must not be contrived by the process of production by which they are satisfied. For this means that the whole case for the urgency of production, based upon the urgency of wants, falls to the ground. One cannot defend production as satisfying wants if that production creates the wants. (Galbraith, 1979: 143)

Leaving aside for the moment the question of what arguments might or might not be considered to 'defend' the production of goods in a society, Galbraith's subsequent development of this position is of interest because he simultaneously employs the three main strands of thought which can be found in the social sciences as proffered explanations of the origin of consumer wants.

The first of these is the instinctivist tradition, which by locating wants in the biological inheritance of human beings, attempts to assimilate them to the category of 'needs'. This view is clearly visible in Galbraith's subsequent reference to 'independently established need' and 'independently determined desires' and 'wants' (Galbraith, 1979: 137–45 *passim*). Obviously what these desires are taken to be 'independent' of, are both the activities of others and the constraints of culture. This is clear from his above reference to 'urgency' and his employment of this as a criterion of 'independence', citing the example of a hungry man as one who is subsequently 'immune' to attempts of persuasion (Galbraith, 1979: 147–8). From this perspective wants are pre-programmed into consumers and will manifest themselves when goods are supplied without the benefit of any additional action to 'create' them. The second tradition, by contrast, emphasizes the idea of active want creation. Here the assumption is that a 'want' does not arise from any inherent force within the consumer, but is deliberately manufactured within him through such agencies as advertising and salesmanship. These wants he assumes to be 'non-urgent', and hence in some way not 'really' wanted, observing, 'Is a new breakfast cereal or detergent so much wanted if so much must be spent to compel in the consumer a sense of want?' (Galbraith, 1979: 147).[10] This perspective (echoing the 'compel' in the above sentence) will be called the manipulationist tradition of theorizing about wants. The third, and last strand, which Galbraith refers to as 'passive' want creation, also assumes that wants are manufactured rather than inborn (and hence, in this sense, 'non-urgent') but does attribute a key role to the consumer himself, since he acquires new wants as a consequence of imitating or emulating the behaviour of other consumers. Here Galbraith cites Keynes' observation concerning 'needs of the second class', that is those which follow from efforts to keep ahead or abreast of one's fellow beings

(Galbraith, 1979: 144). This tradition, in view of its heavy indebtedness to the writings of Thorstein Veblen, will be called the Veblenesque perspective on want creation.

Instinctivism

The Instinctivist perspective is built in to economic theorizing about consumption as a result of the very language which is standardly employed, most especially through the use of the concepts 'latent want' and 'latent demand'. In one sense, this usage is unimportant, for, as has been noted, the classical approach does not involve consideration of the origin of wants. To that extent it would make little difference to the theorizing engaged in by economists whether wants were thought to be the product of instinct, the activities of others or the result of divine intervention. This is because the concept of want has a taken-for-granted or axiomatic status within economic theory and is not, in any real sense, the product of empirical investigation. On the other hand, there is a tendency for economists to forget this when discussing the real world of human affairs, as it appears does Galbraith. Whilst for economic historians, who are more especially charged with the task of accounting for actual events, the temptation to fall into this trap is a constant one.

This last point is well illustrated in *The Birth of a Consumer Society* (McKendrick et al., 1982) . . . for there is ample evidence to show that the contributors to that book presuppose that wants are indeed inherent within individuals, merely becoming operative when the circumstances are right. McKendrick, for example, when discussing the increased sales of printed calicoes in the 1670s, refers to an 'unleashing of latent home demand' (McKendrick et al., 1982: 14). He also writes of the 'propensity to spend' having previously been held in check by an inadequate supply of goods, and to the factors which 'released' the 'force of fashion'; whilst in discussing the activities of producers, reference is made to 'the kind of latent demand they were attempting to release' (McKendrick et al., 1982: 35; 63; 28). The instinctivist basis of this kind of emanationist phraseology is best revealed in the early reference to 'the unleashing of acquisitive instincts' (McKendrick 1982: 16). These examples will suffice to indicate the nature of the underlying assumption, which is that consumer behaviour is best understood in terms of inherent forces which pre-date their actual expression in the form of demand for goods.

No doubt some of the appeal of such language is that it manages to provide connotations of intensity and urgency by the suggestion that 'instinctive' agencies are at work, and in this way succeeds in conveying something of the dynamism which accompanied this early explosion in demand. Unfortunately, the evidence suggests that it is not used simply to add colour to what would otherwise be a rather dull description of events but is regarded as possessing some explanatory power. What this might be, however, is hard to determine.

On the one hand, the plausibility of the instinctivist or latency assumption rests upon the obvious fact that human behaviour does have a biological basis in such real needs as those for food and shelter. The behaviour motivated by these drives, however, is unspecific and contrasts sharply with the consumer's determined and sharply defined conduct in pursuit of particular products. It is indeed this very difference between needs and wants which argues against any inherited basis for the latter. If, on the other hand, all that is being implied by the use of the term 'latent' is the observation that all human beings have the potential to become willing consumers of any kind of product or service, then it is precisely because this is true that the idea of want as an inherent category is nonsensical. One is left with the suggestion that consumer behaviour might involve some processes of 'manifestation', that is to say, the 'realization' of something which had previously only been 'potential'. To the extent that this is an accurate description of consumption it derives logically from its definition as motivated action. All purposive human conduct is teleological in form and hence possesses the quality of being a 'manifestation' of something 'latent'. It is, however, the precise nature of these motivating processes which is the key issue under debate.[11]

An associated feature of the instinctivist position is the assumed existence of a 'needs–wants' hierarchy in the structure of human motivation. Needs, being biologically based, must be met before the less-basic 'wants' can be experienced;[12] clearly in this view, the satisfaction of given 'needs' immediately brings certain 'higher-order' wants into being, which when met are then replaced by others even 'higher' in the hierarchy. Markin associates this concept with the work of Abraham Maslow, listing the needs (in ascending order), as first those for oxygen, food, water, relief from pain and others with a physiological basis, then those for safety, such as security, protection and routine, followed by the 'love motives' of affection and affiliation. Next come the 'esteem motives' of self-respect and prestige and finally the self-actualization motive of self-fulfilment (Markin, 1974: 195). Galbraith's subscription to this view is revealed by his observation that 'When man has satisfied his physical needs, then psychologically grounded desires take over' (Galbraith, 1979: 136).

The postulation of such a hierarchy is obviously an attempt to cope with the problem of the non-universality of 'instinctivist' desires, that is, that the fact that the whole of humanity does not display one common set of consumer wants. The absence of those wants which is manifested by modern man is thus accounted for by claiming that traditional peoples are still preoccupied with attempts to 'satisfy' basic needs. Such an argument rests upon dubious foundations, for not only is the evidence in support of the existence of such a hierarchy highly debatable (with plenty of data to show that human beings will override the imperatives of biological urges for the sake of a 'higher-order' need such as love or self-respect)[13] but in addition, the evidence in favour of the 'satisfaction' of a need at one level tends to be the appearance of a 'higher' one, thus giving an aura of tautology to this model.[14]

The presentation of individual consumer wants as the emanation of pre-formed, inherited inclinations makes it extremely difficult to understand either the variation or changeability which characterize human desires. If the diversity of human wants is inherited in origin how is it that individuals change their pattern of wanting over a lifetime? Or if wants are akin to needs why is it that they do not take the same form in all societies? If, in addition, a latent want only becomes manifested once the appropriate product is presented to the consumer, how is it that consumption of the product often appears to extinguish the want altogether? Surely, if it sprang from a genuine biological basis it would continually reassert itself? How is it, indeed, that not-wanting occurs? Do individuals also posses latent non-wants? It should be clear by now that the instinctivist position is quite unsupportable. It is, in any case, based on the fallacy of retrospection, as was noted long ago (Stuart, 1917: 347), for it attempts to invoke as evidence in support of the existence of the concept of latent want exactly that behaviour (the presence of demand for a product) which the latent want is supposed to explain.

Manipulationism

The second of the two perspectives employed by Galbraith in an effort to compensate for the inability of economic theory to account for the origin of wants is that of manipulationism, or the view that consumers are 'compelled' to want products as a consequence of the actions of outside agencies; an argument which, as was noted, figures prominently in the standard accounts of the eighteenth-century revolution. Interestingly, it contrasts sharply with instinctivism since it tends to treat individuals as lacking any pre-formed tendencies to act in pursuit of particular goals, regarding them as motivationally 'empty' until 'injected' with wants through the medium of advertising. As this metaphor suggests, this perspective derives from what has been called the 'hypodermic' model of the workings of the mass media, one which implies that the various media of modern society – such as film, television and newspapers – each function like a hypodermic needle to inject a given message into their audience. In this case, what is introduced into the 'blood stream' of consumers is the 'want' for a particular product or service. Clearly, this theory attributes a passive role to the consumer, whilst the onerous task of ensuring that the endless and continuous creation of new wants occurs is attributed to such agents of the producers as advertisers and market researchers.

There are different versions of this manipulationist position with the variations concerning the degree to which the consumer is a willing, if naive, participant in the process, and the specificity of the intentions implanted in him. At one extreme, there is the claim that consumers have their buying habits directly controlled through subliminal techniques, which was Vance Packard's sensational thesis in *The Hidden Persuaders* (Packard, 1957). This view has little empirical support and need not been taken too seriously. At the other extreme there is the idea that mere exposure to information and exhortation is sufficient to generate wants in consumers.[15] Although it is necessary to recognize the obvious fact that consumers are influenced in their actions by the information which they receive from producers it is only the most hypersuggestive of individuals who are likely to rush out and buy products merely because they have been brought to their attention. Hence the fact that advertising exerts an influence on consumers' demand for goods neither helps to explain the origin of wants nor proves that manipulation has taken place. In between the extremes of suggesting that consumers are subject to subliminal control, or prone to hypersuggestibility when presented with such simple injunctions as 'Buy Blogg's Biscuits', are those theories which imply that consumers are persuaded or even 'forced' in some way or other, through processes of which they are conscious, to act in a manner which is either against their inclinations or contrary to their best interests, but which is in the interests of the producers.[16]

Naturally many of the criticisms of this view are the same as those which have long been levelled against the hypodermic model in general. Firstly, there is the obvious fact that advertisements (and other product-promoting material) only constitutes one part of the total set of cultural influences at work on consumers.[17] Among the rest are those which represent the outlook of groups and agencies with very different interests, such as unions, churches, professions and government agencies.[18] Secondly, the market for goods, like the audience for any one medium, is not homogeneous and hence the effect of a message will vary considerably depending upon who receives it. Thirdly and lastly, there is plenty of evidence to show that consumers do not simply 'accept' or 'ingest' commercial messages in an unthinking or unselective fashion, but respond, if only to a degree, in a discriminatory and purposeful manner.[19] This last point is, after all, hardly surprising, for 'manipulation' can only be attempted if there is indeed something to manipulate, and this in turn necessitates some accommodation to whatever might constitute the existing motives of consumers. To be successful in making others act in accordance with one's wishes, therefore, it is necessary to know something about their motives, for only then can one hope to turn their dispositions to one's own advantage. The central importance of this fact for those who would seek to 'manipulate' consumers is revealed by the development of motivation research as an integral feature of modern marketing and advertising. Activity under this heading is largely directed at discovering the dreams, desires and wishes of consumers so that advertisers may build upon these when devising product 'messages'. The common desire to be attractive to the opposite sex, for example, may be used in this way to help sell anything from spot-cream and cigarettes to aperitifs, and it is in this sense that it is often claimed that peoples' 'wants' for products are the result of 'manipulation'.

It is crucial to note two things, however, about this position. Firstly, it is not the basic motivational structure of individuals which is being 'manipulated'. On the contrary, that is precisely what the 'manipulation' is being accommodated to take into account. Thus, although one might argue that the desires and dreams of consumers are 'exploited' in this way, one cannot claim they are simply constructed by the actions of advertisers. Secondly, what the producers of goods and services actually manipulate, through their agents, are not consumers or their wants but, in the first instance at least, the symbolic meanings which are attached to products. They, in effect, manipulate messages. The crucial question then becomes: how does receipt of a message lead to the creation of a want in the consumer? Instead of focusing upon the problematic issues raised by this question and those related ones concerning the consumer's regular and endless wanting, social scientists have become overly preoccupied with the issues of 'manipulation' and 'exploitation', something which appears to be due to the predominant influence of utilitarianism and the two central assumptions which it generates.

The first of these is the idea that only genuine gratification which consumers can obtain from products and services is that provided by their intrinsic utility. Hence, if consumers are persuaded to buy products for 'other' reasons (that is to say, for reasons to do with messages relating to non-utilitarian aspects of the product) then they are being duped in some way. This is the basis of the frequent objection levelled against 'non-informative' advertising of the kind which merely tries to associate a product with a desirable image. It should be obvious, however, that the gratification obtained from the use of a product cannot be separated from the images and ideas with which it is linked, in the way, for example, that eating caviare or drinking champagne is popularly associated with luxurious living. To concentrate the advertising of such products upon their associations (whilst ignoring the presentation of such information about their 'utility' as calorific or alcoholic content) is, therefore, not to mislead the consumer but to stress information directly relevant to potential gratification. In other words, images and symbolic meanings are as much a 'real' part of the product as its constituent ingredients.[20]

The second, and closely related assumption, is that in so far as emotion and imagination, rather than rational calculation, enter into the processes through which the consumer chooses and purchases goods and services, then 'manipulation' or 'exploitation' is involved. This view is predicated on the axiom that consumption is, by definition, a rational process and should approximate to one in practice. If, therefore, advertising and marketing strategies can be seen to bypass these, being patently aimed at influencing the feelings and imagination of the consumer, then, in this sense too, 'manipulation' if not 'exploitation' is involved. Here too, however, the assumption is invalid, for consumer behaviour is just as much a matter of emotion and feeling as it is of cognition, as the centrality of issues of liking and disliking clearly reveal. In fact, the dimension of affective attachment can be said to be more basic to consumption than any issue of rational calculation. There is, therefore, no good reason whatsoever for assuming that the emotional nature of many advertising 'messages' is indicative of the existence of 'manipulation' (or at least, no more than is true of all messages about the product).[21]

This discussion of the issue of manipulation tends to divert attention from the crucial questions concerning how it is that wants come to be formed in consumers. It is quite possible, for example, to accept that the agents of producers, in the form of advertisers, do indeed attempt to manipulate the symbolic meanings or 'messages' which are attached to products in an effort to induce consumers to want them, and that they seek to do this by trying to identify their product with people's general desires. This still leaves open the issue of how this is actually accomplished (in some cases, if not in others) and what part the individual consumer plays in that process. There is also the outstanding question of the regular and continuing sequence of want-creation to be accounted for, together with the problem of disposal or not-wanting.

The Veblenesque Perspective

The last of Galbraith's three strands of consumer theorizing is the one in which the consumer is seen as actively engaged in the creation of his own wants. This he accomplishes, however, in a somewhat incidental fashion, as a byproduct of an overriding concern with the maintenance and enhancement of social status; a perspective which derives almost entirely from the writings of Thorstein Veblen. Once again, the centrality of this argument to the standard historical account of the consumer revolution has already been noted, where it occupies an even more important position than claims concerning the manipulationist creation of wants.

Veblen's theory of consumer behaviour rests upon an insight which had long been familiar to anthropologists but had become obscured by the influence of utilitarianism as far as the behaviour of modern man was concerned. This is the simple fact that the act of consumption has profound socio-cultural significance, and should not be viewed in simple economic terms; commodities have importance as signs or symbols and not merely for the intrinsic satisfaction which they might bring. Consequently, as Diggins (1978: 100) observes, Veblen suggests that the ultimate problem in understanding industrial societies is not how goods come to be made but how they take on meaning. Such an observation is a very necessary corrective to the naive materialism of the utilitarian tradition, and promises to provide a more realistic basis from which to tackle the problem of accounting for the characteristics of modern consumer behaviour.

Unfortunately, Veblen was a little too single-minded in his consideration of the kind of meanings which consumption might signify, concentrating almost exclusively upon issues of social status. His view, as outlined in *The Theory of the Leisure Class* (Veblen, 1957) [see chapter 4, this volume], stressed that the consumption of goods serves, in addition to the conventionally accepted function of satisfying needs, to indicate a person's level of wealth or 'pecuniary strength', and that this is, in turn, a primary index of social status. This function of consumption is well understood by the consumer, and may indeed rival the direct satisfaction of needs in importance, as Veblen explains:

> No class of society, not even the most abjectly poor, forgoes all customary conspicuous consumption. The last items of this category of consumption are not given up except under stress of the direst necessity. Very much of squalor and discomfort will be endured before the last trinket or the last pretence of pecuniary decency is put away. (Veblen, 1957: 85)

This view is based upon certain key assumptions concerning both human motivation and the nature of societies. Veblen assumes, for example, that the motive behind much human activity is emulation and that since 'the possession of wealth confers honour' (Veblen, 1957: 25), the 'end sought by accumulation is to rank high in comparison with the rest of the community in point of pecuniary strength' (Veblen, 1957: 31), a view which would appear to make pride and its companion, envy, the root causes of human action. Clearly, if consumption is regarded essentially as a manifestation of a competitive striving for the scarce commodity of high status, then it would indeed appear as if one had at last provided an answer to the problem of the source of its dynamic. Not surprisingly, therefore, economists have come to employ the term 'Veblen effects' to refer to phenomena which are not explicable within the parameters of marginal utility theory (see Seckler, 1975).

Economists typically employ Veblen's name in making two kinds of modification to their essentially individualistic and utilitarian model of consumer behaviour. The first, which is more specifically called *the* Veblen effect, involves recognizing that the price of a commodity is a culturally significant symbol in its own right, and not merely an index of economic worth or utility. Following Veblen's argument, therefore, they accept that demand for goods may increase with price where the function of consumption is to manifest pecuniary strength. The second, which embraces what are called the 'bandwagon' and 'snob' effects, involve recognition of the fact that an individual's consumption of goods is affected by the behaviour of other consumers. Either an individual's demand for goods or services is increased by the fact that others are seen to be consuming them (bandwagon), or decreased by the fact that others are consuming them (snob) (see Leibenstein, 1982: 12–30).

These Veblenesque modifications to utility theory are notable for their extreme simplicity, as well as the conception that human motivation which they contain. They are very limited assumptions which patently fail to grasp the full complexity of either the symbolic meanings possessed by consumer products and services, or the communal and associational dimension of the act of consumption. Clearly, the price of a commodity is a cultural symbol of some importance and in purchasing and conspicuously displaying it a consumer conveys a message to those around him; a message which may indeed amount to saying: 'see how rich I am, I can afford this very expensive item'. But products and services are redolent with other cultural meanings, notably those which pertain to the issues of 'taste' and 'style', and the purchase and display of a product or service may thus stem more from a desire to convey messages of this kind. In which case price may be a comparatively irrelevant symbol, and not at all central to either the consumer's decision or the message he wishes to convey. Similarly, the fact that an individual's consumption habits are affected by the actions of others cannot be adequately described by the simple alternatives offered above. It would be more realistic to note that consumers are typically striving to make their consumption conform to the pattern exhibited by one group and deviate from that manifested by another; bandwagon and snob are not therefore alternatives but integral features of one 'other-related' pattern of behaviour. More to the point, however, is the fact that reference group theory shows how complex is the real nature of imitative and emulative behaviour, and that any one person may make use of a variety of positive, negative, comparative and normative reference groups (or role models) when deciding what course of action to take.[22] What this means is that the explanations of consumer behaviour offered under the heading 'Veblen effects' are obviously inadequate and do not deserve to be taken too seriously. At best they constitute no more than an outline of the direction in which social science should develop if an adequate understanding of the social dimension of consumer behaviour is to be obtained.[23]

The interpretation given by economists to 'Veblen effects' is also revealing for the nature of the assumptions about human motivation which they contain, the use of the terms 'bandwagon' and 'snob' being especially indicative. Whilst all that is at issue is the fact that a consumer's behaviour is influenced by the actions of others, the gratuitous assumptions made are that this takes the form of getting 'into the swing of things', wishing to be 'one of the boys', or a desire to 'dissociate oneself from the common herd'; motives generally considered to be amongst the least creditable of those which impel people to act. There is no justification for this (apart from the precedent set by Veblen) and one could equally suggest other accounts of associational and disassociational action which did not carry such disreputable overtones. To emulate others or to seek to disassociate oneself from others is neither praiseworthy nor blameworthy in itself but must be judged by the conduct of the 'others' taken as the point of comparison, and upon the motives for acting. What these accounts therefore illustrate is the widespread bias in social science against luxury consumer behaviour, and its taken-for-granted basis in 'other-directed' patterns of motivation.[24]

Veblen's argument is not without its ambiguities and difficulties, and one of these lies at the very heart of the description of that which drives the consumer to engage in conspicuous consumption. Whilst in some places in *The Theory of the Leisure Class* it appears as if he regards the competitive striving for status as the primary dynamic mechanism, at others it is a desire to aspire to that ideal way of life exemplified by those of superior rank; whilst he uses the same term 'emulation' to refer to both processes. At one point, for example, Veblen observes that the standard of expenditure which guides the efforts of the consumer is not that already achieved but one which is just out of reach, commenting that the motive for straining to reach this higher level is 'emulation – the stimulus of an invidious comparison which prompts us to outdo those with whom we are in the habit of classing ourselves' (Veblen, 1957: 103). This seems to imply that any attempt to compare our standard of life with that of our peers will result in feelings of envy and dissatisfaction followed by renewed efforts to improve our status. Studies in reference group theory have shown, however, that this is by no means the necessary outcome of comparisons made with those whom we consider to be our equals, and that satisfaction with one's position is just as likely an outcome as dissatisfaction (Merton, 1968: 225–386 *passim*). Veblen is, in any case, obviously assuming the prevalence of an 'aggressive' rather than 'defensive' form of conspicuous consumption (see Manson, 1981), since he refers to individuals being prompted to 'outdo' each other. In this sense he can be said to be assuming that social life is like a race in which everyone wants to be first rather than a procession in which the predominant concern is to maintain one's position in a line.[25] At other places in the book he presents a somewhat different account of the reasons why people strive for higher levels of consumption, one which relates more to the predominant influence of the leisure class.

Veblen's claim that social status is intimately linked with wealth is but a variant of a more fundamental argument concerning the centrality of a leisured class. Accepting the logic of the claim that time is money, Veblen argues that wealth and leisure are like being symptoms of privilege and high status, and that conspicuous consumption and conspicuous leisure are both ways of gaining honour through displaying waste. What he calls the leisure class is thus at the pinnacle of the system of social stratification and sets the standards which all below must aspire to:

> The leisure class stands at the head of the social structure in point of reputability; and its manner of life and its standards of worth therefore affords the norm of reputability for the community. The observance of these standards, in some degree of approximation, becomes incumbent upon all classes lower in the scale. In modern civilized communities the lines of demarcation between social classes have grown vague and transient, and wherever this happens the norm of reputability imposed by the upper classes extends its coercive influence with but slight hindrance down through the social structure to the lowest strata. The result is that the members of each stratum accept as their ideal of decency the scheme of life in vogue in the next higher stratum, and bend their energies to live up to their ideal. (Veblen, 1957: 70)

It is clear that this account of status striving differs markedly from the earlier one. Here the motive is the desire to live up to an ideal, rather than to outdo one's peers, an activity which can also be labelled 'emulation'. Although Veblen's use of the term 'ideal' is ambiguous, at times apparently signifying simply that pattern of life which people aspire to (as opposed to that which they exhibit) and at other times that which is considered to embody the highest moral and ethical standards, it would seem to be the latter which he has in mind here. From this perspective, therefore, the dynamic ingredient in status striving derives not from attempts to outdo or upstage others in a context of taken-for-granted competition, so much as the necessarily ceaseless efforts involved in attempting to live up to an ideal way of life. Veblen appears to try and reconcile his two uses of the term 'ideal' by assuming, firstly that the leisure class actually lives up to its own cultural ideals, and secondly by claiming that each class sees the one immediately above it as embodying these values to a higher degree than does their own. In this way, Veblen attempts to assimilate the competitive striving for status with idealistically motivated behaviour. It is clear, none the less, that they need have no necessary relationship with each other. In fact, it seems that Veblen confuses two different types of social situation. One is the kind of close-knit community of peers in which intense rivalry for prestige often occurs, say among athletes or actors; this may well be the sort of context in which there is a concern to out-perform one's rivals. The other is the phenomenon of social mobility in a fairly open society, that is to say, one without clear legal or religious barriers to movements between adjacent strata. Upward social movement in this kind of situation clearly requires the adoption of a new style of life, a process which might reasonably involve imitative 'emulation'. This does not, however, necessarily mean that one is trying to compete with anyone out of envy or pride, as an improved standard of living may simply be regarded as attractive in its own right. This error is closely related to Veblen's mistake in assuming an identity between competition and imitation, arguing as he does that where a contest between individuals or groups for higher status exists, then this will take the form of behaviour which imitates those who already hold the higher status. But this is to overlook two important points: firstly, that individuals may gain success over their competitors through innovation rather than imitation (as many entrepreneurs have shown) and, secondly, that social groups (especially social classes) may actually be in conflict over the very question of the criteria to be employed in defining status.[26] This latter case is more important as it denies Veblen's assumption concerning a consensus of values in modern society and hence the existence of a single agreed status system. A more successful way of improving one's own social position may thus be to deny the moral validity of the claim of those above you, asserting in their place grounds for prestige which favour those like yourself. That Veblen did not consider this alternative appears to follow from his assumption that the leisure class held an unchallenged as well as pre-eminent position in modern societies.

Once one abandons Veblen's insistent emphasis upon the invidious aspects of consumption to concentrate upon the extent to which this feature of life is expressive of basic cultural values then further difficulties are encountered.[27] As we have seen, Veblen considered the cultural significance of consumption to lie in its index of status, something which was measured in terms of wealth and leisure, with all other values being treated as either symptoms or derivatives of these. At the same time, he considered modern societies to possess a single elite leisure class constituting the highest embodiment of these values, with all subordinate classes ranked to the extent to which they lived up to this ideal.

A little reflection will be sufficient to reveal some of the many objections to this view. In the first place, high status in modern societies is clearly associated with values other than wealth and leisure, noble birth being merely the most obvious of these. Secondly, the treatment of wealth and leisure as interchangeable, both signifying the honorific value of 'waste', is unconvincing in the light of the Protestant tradition of applauding the first and deploring the second, and the Bohemian version of this view. Thirdly, the treatment of modern societies as culturally monolithic with one class providing all the cultural leadership does not fit with the considerable evidence suggestive of a more complex picture. As Riesman notes:

> Contrary to the situation described by Veblen, it does not seem to us to be the members of the upper class who dictate life styles, which then filter down; these residual legatees of the past are influenced as much as they influence, and the location of style leadership, is ramified and, to our mind, obscure. (Riesman and Roseborough, 1965: 120)

Other attempts to validate Veblen's thesis have provided further support for this conclusion. The study of Laumann and House, for example, showed that the *nouveaux riches* were the group most likely to engage in conspicuous consumption, largely because of their especially strong need to validate a newly acquired social position (Laumann and House, 1973: 430–40). Groups who felt secure in their social status, or who manifested no particular desire to be upwardly mobile, displayed no such marked tendency to conspicuously consume. At the same time, the *nouveaux riches* were very conscious of the necessity to consume conspicuously with 'taste' if their claim to higher status was to become accepted. Those who they regarded as the 'tastemakers', however, were not members of the traditional elite 'leisure class' but professionals whose job it was to advise on such matters, people like architects, decorators, interior designers and fashion correspondents. In accepting their definition of what was regarded as tasteful, the *nouveaux riches* were in effect rejecting the standards of the more traditional upper class. Apart from supporting the suggestion that the status system of modern societies is more complex than Veblen claimed, this research suggests that the social dimensions of status and taste do not necessarily coincide, and that one cannot simply be subsumed under the other.[28]

Fourthly, Veblen's central assertion that the primary cultural meaning of consumption behaviour is to be found in what it indicates about the consumer's social status cannot go unchallenged, for it is clear that among the many meanings commonly attributed to such behaviour are those which have primary significance for character. Fifthly, Veblen's gratuitous equation of the cultural significance of the act of consumption with inter-peer competition for status meant that he had unnecessarily limited his analysis to socially visible or conspicuous action, thereby giving impetus to the long-standing tendency to assume that consumption is an essentially 'other-directed' pattern of behaviour. There seems to be no reason, however, to assume that private or inconspicuous consumption should be any less culturally meaningful than its public counterpart, nor any less expressive of basic cultural values.[29] Sixthly, Veblen offers no explanation of the mechanism through which individuals manage to achieve changes in their pattern of consumer wants. Once again, the way in which a want is itself generated, only later to be extinguished and supplanted by another, is simply not explicated. Beyond the suggestion that pride or envy might be the predominant motives, and that imitation is implicated in the process, these mechanisms remain a mystery.

Lastly, but most important of all, Veblen does not provide a basis for distinguishing traditional from modern consumer behaviour, and hence does not account for that insatiability and desire for novelty which is such a crucial hallmark of the latter. His theory of conspicuous consumption – which intriguingly seems to have been inspired by a traditional ritual in the first place[30] – applies with equal force to all human communities, members of tribal, non-literate societies being just as prone to engage in intense status-competition as any individual in contemporary society, whilst all communities encourage people to live up to ideals. Why then is it commonly thought that Veblen's theory provides an answer to the problem of the dynamic of modern consumerism? For the truth is that his approach only appears to offer an explanation for the extraordinary insatiability which is such a marked feature of this pattern. In so far as Veblen's theory rests upon the assumption that modern consumers are all committed to a policy of aggressive conspicuous consumption, then one form of insatiability is only 'explained' in terms of the problematic assumption of another; in this case the claim that people are motivated by an overwhelming desire to get the better of their fellows, a psychological reductionism about as useful (and convincing) as the older explanation of insatiable consumption as motivated by greed.[31] If, on the other hand, defensive conspicuous consumption is assumed to be widespread, then some other factor must be invoked to explain how change is introduced into the system.

One can easily understand why, in a society in which patterns of consumption are rapidly changing for other reasons, individuals would constantly need to adjust their consumption habits so as to continue to give the correct signals concerning their social status. This does not have to be seen as a 'defensive' response to someone else's efforts to 'steal a march' in the status rankings so much as a 'corrective' manoeuvre. That is, people might make the wrong assessment of an individual's status if he continued to wear out-of-date clothes or drive an old model of car. The dynamic ingredient here, however, is not status competition or emulation, or even imitation, but the phenomenon of fashion itself, and it is only because this is so closely identified with status emulation that the Veblenesque model gives the appearance of accounting for change.

This combined fashion emulation explanation typically has the following form. Those at the top of the social scale have a need to invent new fashions in order to maintain their superiority over those immediately below who, out of emulative desires, are copying their patterns of consumption. This is equally true for those in the next subordinate stratum, and so on, down to the bottom of the status system. As soon as any one social group looks like catching up with the fashion prevalent among those above, the members of the superordinate group will adopt a new fashion in order to maintain their superiority. In this way, fashions are introduced, spread and replaced all through the power of social emulation.[32] Puzzlingly, however, this makes the introduction of a new fashion a response to emulative behaviour (this is what prompts the elite to innovate) whilst also presenting emulative behaviour as a response to the introduction of a new fashion. Indeed, as Herbert Blumer observes, 'most sociological explanations [of fashion] centre on the idea that fashion is basically an emulation of prestige groups' (Blumer, H.G. in Sills, D. L. (ed.) 1968), a view which ignores the fact that there is no good reason whatever why status competition or emulation should require an institution which functions to supply continuous novelty. In this way, the introduction and spread of any one fashion, which is clearly facilitated – like all innovation – by imitation, is confused with an understanding of the modern Western fashion pattern as a whole. Empirical evidence does not really support this model, for, as we have seen, fashionable innovations are not by any means always introduced by the social elite. Hence, although it is possible to see how both modern fashion, and the desire to emulate one's social superiors, might serve to encourage what appear to be similar patterns of action (to the extent that both are envisaged as imitative behaviour this is bound to be true), it is far from obvious how they came to interact so as to produce insatiable wanting in consumers. For, whilst 'fashion' appears to be precisely the ingredient which, when added to Veblen's emulative theory, provides it with its dynamic, there is no adequate explanation of fashion-orientated behaviour which does not, in turn, rest upon theories of emulation. Obviously, one or more crucial elements are missing from the sought-after theory of modern consumerism.

Notes

1   There has been a tendency to leave the subject of consumption to the discipline of economics, which, in turn, is largely a product of that tradition of utilitarian thought

that began to take shape in the eighteenth century. Since economics is a notoriously ahistorical discipline it has been able to avoid confronting the issues of explaining the consumer revolution which coincided with its birth.

2 It goes without saying that modern consumerism has only been made possible through the introduction of a variety of economic, social and technological innovations. Mass production itself is one of these, as too is advertising and credit selling. None the less, even when all these contributory factors have been identified, it still appears that modern consumerism remains unexplained; unexplained that is as a pattern of meaningful conduct.

3 Interestingly, if, at times like Christmas or prior to a birthday, an individual responds to a query concerning what he would like for a present by intimating that there is nothing he wants, this is treated not only as an infraction of the norm of reciprocity but also as a false report of psychological reality.

4 Obviously some wants relate to products which service recurrent needs like those for food and clothing and hence their cyclical reappearance is understandable. The form taken by a want is, however, independent of the need which gives rise to it. Thus, whilst the need for food will be experienced at regular intervals, this may lead, at different times, to a want for a hamburger, a Chinese meal or merely a bar of chocolate. A specific want thus reflects the expression of a preference within the context of a need and the recurrent nature of needs does not explain the ever-changing nature of wants.

5 See comments in Richard Martin, Steven Chaffee and Fausto Izcaray, 'Media and Consumerism in Venezuela', *Journalism Quarterly*, 56 (1979) 296–304.

6 The fact that modern consumers rarely seem to find their own behaviour bewildering is testimony to the powerful taken-for-granted nature of the values and attitudes upon which it rests. It is just these unquestioned assumptions which should have been the main focus of attention for social scientists. Unfortunately, despite a vast amount of investigation into the socio-demographic preferences of consumers, together with extensive, commercially supported, psychological and psychoanalytic inquiry into buying habits, few comparative and historical studies have been undertaken which could have shed light on the spirit of modern consumerism. Only in social anthropology does one sometimes encounter an awareness of the extent to which modern consumer behaviour remains a mystery. See, in this connection, Douglas and Isherwood (1978) [chapter 6, this volume].

7 A fundamental reason why the insatiable nature of modern consumerism has tended to be ignored by social scientists is because classical economics deemed the origin of consumer wants and tastes to be beyond its sphere of inquiry. This has not only had the unfortunate consequence of diverting attention from this crucial question, but, in presenting the rationality of instrumental action as the typical characteristic of modern consumerism, economics has succeeded in making the endless pursuit of wants appear to be both 'natural' and 'irrational'. As far as understanding the nature of modern consumerism is concerned it would have been better for social science if more attention had been paid to the apparent irrationality of ends and less to the postulated rationality of means. The treatment of the ends of action as effectively random, is, as Parsons observed, both a major characteristic of utilitarian social thought and a principal weakness (Parsons, 1949: 59–60).

8   For early critiques see Stuart (1917) and Kyrk (1923). A contemporary critique can be found in Douglas and Isherwood (1978). A noteworthy exception to the economists' general neglect of these problems and a promising attempt to construct a theory of consumption on more realistic assumptions is to be found in Scitovsky (1976).

9   Whilst it could be argued that it is not irrational to believe others when they inform us that a new product will provide greater satisfaction than one currently consumed, this is to assume some standard for comparing satisfactions provided by different products as well as the idea that the tastes of individuals are equitable. Both of these assumptions are rejected by marginal utility theory. Equally, it could be suggested that it is not irrational for a consumer whose disposable income has grown to employ his surplus in trying a new product since he is not in this way losing any existing gratification. It is still the case, even here however, that a more rational strategy would be to use the new wealth to consume more of what is already known to be satisfying. This is indeed what traditional consumers typically do, as has already been noted.

10 Galbraith seems to overlook the fact that much of this expenditure is incurred in attempts to persuade consumers to want one brand of cereal or detergent rather than another.

11 Although the idea that human beings possess some pre-formed or innate disposition to acquire products, as, for example, jackdaws would seem to be endowed with where shiny objects are concerned, is a popular view, it is clearly untenable. Apart from the fact that what is characteristic of human behaviour is its extreme plasticity, and hence the great variety of goods for which there has been some demand at one time or another, this argument overlooks the equally marked tendency of modern consumers to 'disacquire' or dispose of goods.

12 The idea that human motivation can be understood in terms of needs at all is now considered by some psychologists to be highly doubtful. See, for an instance of this scepticism, Wallach and Wallach (1983: 217–25).

13 For evidence that 'higher' needs such as social status and prestige may displace 'lower' biological ones, see Herskovits' reference to competitive yam-growing among the Ponapean in Micronesia and the observation that 'families of a man aspiring to great prestige may go hungry' (Herskovits, 1960: 462).

14 This hierarchy-of-needs perspective also has strong overtones of an evolutionary ethnocentricism, suggesting, as it appears to, that only in modern society do the 'highest' needs find proper expression.

15 This is merely a restatement of the view encountered earlier which presents demands as a reflex phenomenon with an awareness of an increased supply automatically triggering a consumer response. It is a view which bypasses the critical issue of the origin of wants.

16 The adoption of this position is usually clearly signalled by the designation of consumers' wants as 'false'; see, for one of the many examples of this usage, Featherstone (1982).

17 Even here it is important to note that promoters of rival products commonly seek to undermine each other's influence.

18 To claim, as some writers do, that all groups in society represent the interest of the producers of goods either directly or indirectly is to confuse the aims of individual

manufacturers with the continued existence of a particular form of society, whilst to observe that individual consumers only have the wants they do because of the socialization they have experienced is a self-evident and unhelpful truth which applies in all cultures.

19   For a useful summary discussion of the effects of advertising see Dyer (1982: 72–86 *passim*).

20   The manipulationist position thus gains its strength by ignoring the interest which the consumer has in the symbolic meanings of the product and contrasting an assumed utilitarian outlook with the advertisers' symbolic manipulation.

21   Just as price is no more than a symbolic meaning attached to a product the manipulation of which affects the consumer's willingness to buy, so too is desirability a symbolic meaning attached to a product, the manipulation of which affects a consumer's willingness to buy. To assume that individuals are deceived if they buy a product out of a liking for its image, but not if they buy it out of a liking for its price, is strangely contradictory.

22   For material on reference group theory see Merton (1968: 225–86) and for its use in the examination of consumer behaviour see Cocanougher and Grady (1973: 309–14).

23   The fundamental inadequacy of these explanations is clearly revealed when Leibenstein refers to what he calls 'irrational demand', that is, 'purchases that are neither planned nor calculated but are due to sudden urges, whims, etc., and that serve no rational purpose but that of satisfying sudden whims and desires' (Leibenstein 1982: 14); the explanation of consumer behaviour presented in the Veblen effects hypotheses is only marginally less vacuous than this.

24   It is interesting to speculate upon why, although economists generally look with approval upon the individual who acts rationally in pursuit of his own satisfaction and material self-interest, they tend to look with some disapproval upon the individual who acts rationally in pursuit of prestige or social status.

25   It can be noted at this point that the widespread tendency to use the phrase 'keeping up with the Joneses' to refer to competitive striving for higher status is misguided. If the efforts of consumers were limited to maintaining their social position in this way there would be little change in consumption patterns; 'getting ahead of the Joneses' is clearly what Veblen had in mind.

26   It is pertinent in this respect to observe that envy often includes hostility or dislike, and hence that it is not uncommon for an individual to contest another's claim to superior status by denying its legitimacy.

27   That the failure to perceive the extent to which consumption is expressive in this sense is a main shortcoming of Veblen's work is a point made by Davis (1944: 282–6).

28   For further evidence that the arbiters of taste belong to the upper-middle or lower-upper classes and are not members of the societal elite, see Lynes (1959).

29   It is interesting to speculate on what the motive for inconspicuous consumption might be in Veblen's theory. Although the obvious answer is that it is guided merely by the desire for utility this would be to deny the validity of his insight into the cultural significance of the act of consumption . If, however, it is recognized as having symbolic meaning for the consumer then this opens up the possibility that conspicuous

consumption may also manifest these 'inner-directed' concerns.

30   Diggins (1978: 98) suggests that it was Boas's account of the potlatch which provided Veblen with his inspiration for the theory of conspicuous consumption.

31   Veblen assumes that changes in patterns of visible consumption derive from an attempt to aspire to higher social status simply on the grounds that consumption is a form of behaviour which has significance as an indicator of status, but those who use his theory often write as if he had proved that modern consumers act out emulative motives. Veblen did not, in fact, provide much evidence of people's motives.

32   As we have already seen the evidence does not support this model, as fashionable innovations are not necessarily introduced by the social elite.

References

Blumer, H. G. (1968) 'Fashion' in Sills, D. L. (ed.) *International Encyclopaedia of the Social Sciences*, New York: Macmillan/Free Press.

Cocanougher, A. B. and Grady, B. D. (1973) 'Socially distant reference groups and consumer aspirations' in Kassarjian, H. H. and Robertson, T. S. (eds) *Perspectives in Consumer Behaviour*, Glenview, Ill.: Scott Foresman.

Davis, A. K. (1944) 'Veblen on the decline of the Protestant ethic', *Social Forces*, 22.

Diggins, J. P. (1978) *The Bard of Savagery: Thorstein Veblen and Modern Social Theory*, Brighton: Harvester Press.

Douglas, M. and Isherwood, B. (1978) *The World of Goods: Towards an Anthropology of Consumption*, Harmondsworth: Penguin Books.

Dyer, G. (1982) *Advertising as Communication*, London: Methuen.

Featherstone, M. (1982) 'The body in consumer culture', *Theory, Culture and Society*, 1.

Foster, G. M. (1965) 'Peasant society and the image of limited good', *American Anthropologist*, 67.

Fromm, E. (1964) 'The psychological aspects of the guaranteed income' in Theobald, R. (ed.) *The Guaranteed Income: Next Step in Economic Evolution*, New York: Doubleday.

Galbraith, J. K. (1979) *The Affluent Society*, Harmondsworth: Penguin Books.

Herskovits, M. J. (1960) *Economic Anthropology: A Study of Comparative Economics*, New York: Alfred A. Knopf.

Kyrk, H. (1923) *A Theory of Consumption*, London: Isaac Pitman.

Laumann, E. O. and House, J. S. (1973) 'Living room styles and social attributes: the patterning of material artifacts in a modern urban community' in Kassarjian, H. H. and Robertson, T. S. (eds.) *Perspectives in Consumer Behaviour*, Glenview, Ill.: Scott Foresman.

Leibenstein, H. (1982) 'Bandwagon, snob and Veblen effects in the theory of consumers' demand' in Mansfield, E. (ed.) *Microeconomics: Selected Readings*, 4th edn, New York: Norton.

Lerner, D. (1958) *The Passing of Traditional Society: Modernizing the Middle East*, Glencoe, Ill.: Free Press.

Lynes, R. (1959) *The Tastemakers*, New York: Grosset and Dunlop.

McKendrick, N., Brewer, J. and Plumb, J. H. (1982) *The Birth of the Consumer Society: The Commercialization of Eighteenth-century England*, London: Europa Publications.

Manson, R. S. (1981) *Conspicuous Consumption: A Study of Exceptional Consumer Behaviour*, Farnborough: Gower.

Markin Jr, R. J. (1974) *Consumer Behaviour: A Cognitive Orientation*, New York: Macmillan.

Martin, R., Chaffee, S. and Izcaray, F. (1979) 'Media and consumerism in Venezuela', *Journalism Quarterly*, 56.

Merton, R. K. (1968) *Social Theory and Social Structure*, revd and enlarged edn, Glencoe Ill.: Free Press.

O'Neill, J. (1978) 'The productive body: an essay on the work of consumption', *Queen's Quarterly*, 85 (Summer).

Packard, V. (1957) *The Hidden Persuaders*, London: Longmans.

Parsons, T. (1949) *The Structure of Social Action: A Study in Social Theory with Special Reference to a Group of Recent European Writers*, 2nd edn, Glencoe, Ill.: Free Press.

Riesman, D. and Lerner, D. (1965) 'Self and society: reflections on some Turks in transition' in Riesman, D. *Abundance for What? And Other Essays*, New York: Anchor Books.

Riesman, D. and Roseborough, H. (1965) 'Careers and consumer behaviour' in Riesman, D. *Abundance for What? And Other Essays*, New York: Anchor Books.

Scitovsky, T. (1976) *The Joyless Economy: An Inquiry into Human Satisfaction and Consumer Dissatisfaction*, New York: Oxford University Press.

Seckler, D. (1975) *Thorstein Veblen and the Institutionalists: A Study in the Social Philosophy of Economics*, London, Macmillan.

Simmel, G. (1957) 'Fashion', *American Journal of Sociology*, 62, May.

Stuart, H. W. (1917) 'The phases of the economic interest' in Dewey, J. (ed.) *Creative Intelligence: Essays in the Pragmatic Attitude*, New York: Henry Holt.

Veblen, T. (1957) *The Theory of the Leisure Class: An Economic Study of Institutions*, London: George Allen and Unwin.

Wallach, M. A. and Wallach, L. (1983) *Psychology's Sanction for Selfishness: The Error of Egoism in Theory and Therapy*, San Francisco: W. H. Freeman.

6

The Uses of Goods

Mary Douglas and Baron Isherwood

Since its original publication in 1978 *The World of Goods* has become something of the standard work of reference for anthropological approaches to consumption.[1] In this chapter Douglas and Isherwood, in seeking to overturn the traditional economist's naive conception of consumption as a utilitarian activity, are keen to establish the significance of consumer goods less for what they can "do" for us and more for what they can "say" for us. Goods, they argue, are "communicators" which make "visible and stable the categories of culture."

Redefining Consumption

To make a fresh start on the subject, an anthropological definition of consumption would help. To speak sensibly of consumption here, in industrial society, in terms that also apply without strain to distant tribal societies that have barely seen commerce, still less capitalism, is indeed a challenge. But unless we make the attempt there can be no anthropology of consumption. We need somehow to extract the essence of the term, while ignoring the potentially misleading local effects. One boundary may be drawn by an idea essential to economic theory: that is, that consumption is not compelled; the consumer's choice is his free choice. He can be irrational, superstitious, traditionalist, or experimental: the essence of the economist's concept of the individual consumer is that he exerts a sovereign choice. Another boundary may be drawn by the idea central to national bookkeeping that consumption starts where the market ends. What happens to material objects once they have left the retail outlet and reached the hands of the final purchasers is part of the consumption process. These two boundaries raise various problems and borderline cases for economics and do not make a completely satisfactory definition. Together they assume that consumption is a private matter. Consumption that is provided by government as part of its functioning is not properly part of

From *The World of Goods* (London: Routledge, 1979), pp. 56–70. Reprinted by permission of the publishers.

consumption. Central heating or cups of tea drunk in bureaucratic offices count as part of the cost of administration, in the same way as cups of tea or central heating provided by businesses count as costs of production, not as output, when they make their income tax returns. As to consumption being uncoerced, this is not a straight-forward matter either. When a city is proclaimed a smokeless zone by law, house-holders are not free to burn log fires if they choose; nor are car purchasers free to ignore government regulations as to safety, noise, and so on. But by and large the two boundaries capture the essence of the idea and the detailed tidying-up is a matter of convention. So if we define consumption as a use of material possessions that is beyond commerce and free within the law, we have a concept that travels extremely well, since it fits parallel usages in all those tribes that have no commerce.

Seen under this aspect, consumption decisions become the vital source of the culture of the moment. People who are reared in a particular culture see it change in their lifetime: new words, new ideas, new ways. It evolves and they play a part in the change. Consumption is the very arena in which culture is fought over and licked into shape. The housewife with her shopping basket arrives home: some things in it she reserves for her household, some for the father, some for the chil-dren; others are destined for the special delectation of guests. Whom she invites into her house, what parts of the house she makes available to outsiders, how often, what she offers them for music, food, drink, and conversation, these choices express and generate culture in its general sense. Likewise, her husband's judge-ments as to how much of his wages he allots to her, how much he keeps to spend with his friends, etc., result in the channelling of resources. They vitalize one activ-ity or another. They will be unconstrained if the culture is alive and evolving. Ultimately, they are moral judgements about what a man is, what a woman is, how a man ought to treat his aged parents, how much of a start in life he ought to give his sons and daughters, how he himself should grow old, gracefully or disgrace-fully, and so on. How many of his aunts and uncles and orphaned nephews is he expected to support? Do family obligations stop him from migrating? Should he contribute to his union? Insure against sickness? Insure for his own funeral? These are consumption choices which may well involve heavy costs, and which, when made, may determine the evolution of culture.

In most cultures reported over the world, there are certain things that cannot be sold or bought. One obvious case with us is political advance (which should not be bought); as to selling, a man who is capable of selling his honour, or even of selling his grandmother, is condemned by cliché. Everywhere there is at least a notion of some area of untrammelled individual choice. If any local tyrant could march into your home, turn out your friends or force you to add unchosen names to your visiting list, tell you whom you can see and speak to and whom to ignore, then personal freedom and dignity would be lost. If he did it by passing laws, by threat of guns, by threat of lost livelihood, he would probably be judged more immoral even than the rich man who might seek to buy your support. We have in fact succeeded in defining consumption as an area of behaviour hedged by rules which explicitly demonstrate that neither commerce nor force are being applied to a free relationship.

This is why, no doubt, in our society the line between cash and gift is so carefully drawn. It is all right to send flowers to your aunt in hospital, but never right to send the cash they are worth with a message to "get yourself some flowers"; all right to offer lunch or drinks, but not to offer the price of a lunch or a drink. Hosts may go to extravagant lengths to attract and please guests – short of offering them money to come to the party. Social sanctions protect the boundary. Apparently, some fabled New York hostess in the 1890s, worrying how to surpass her rival who habitually gave each guest a rich jewel, was worried even more by their derision when, her turn having come, she folded a crisp $100 bill in each napkin. The right to give cash is reserved for family intimacy. Here again there are details that could be tidied up. But in general it is true to say that around the field of consumption we have a spontaneous, operative boundary between two kinds of services: professional, paid with money and to be classed with commerce, and personal, recompensed in kind and in no other way. Within the field of personal services, freely given and returned, moral judgement of the worth of people and things is exercised. This establishes the first step in a cultural theory of consumption.

A Universe Constructed from Commodities

Instead of supposing that goods are primarily needed for subsistence plus competitive display, let us assume they are needed for making visible and stable the categories of culture. It is standard ethnographic practice to assume that all material possessions carry social meanings and to concentrate a main part of cultural analysis upon their use as communicators.

In every tribal study an account is given of the material parts of the culture. Like us, the members of a tribe have fixed equipment, houses, gardens, barns, and like us, they have durable and non-durable things. The anthropologist usually devotes some space to marshaling the evidence for deciding, from the vantage point of our technology, whether, for example, the cattle husbandry is efficient, the farmer's knowledge of his soils and seasons accurate, the hygienic precautions and the amount of food taken adequate, etc. The material possessions provide food and covering, and this has to be understood. But at the same time it is apparent that the goods have another important use: they also make and maintain social relationships. This is a long-tried and fruitful approach to the material side of existence which yields a much richer idea of social meanings than mere individual competitiveness.

A well-known case is Evans-Pritchard's account of the place of cattle in Nuer lives:

The network of kinship ties which links members of local communities is brought about by the operation of exogamous rules, often stated in terms of cattle. The union of marriage is brought about by the payment of cattle and every phase of the ritual is marked by their transference or slaughter. The legal status of the partners is defined by cattle rights and obligations.

Cattle are owned by families. When the head of the household is alive he has full rights of disposal over the herd, though his wives have rights of use in the cows and his sons own some of the oxen. As each son, in order of seniority, reaches the age of marriage he marries with cows from the herd. The next son will have to wait till the herd has reached its earlier strength before he can marry in his turn. . . . The bond of cattle between brother is continued long after each has a home and children of his own, for when a daughter of any one of them is married the others receive a large portion of her bride-wealth. Her grandparents, maternal uncles, paternal and maternal aunts, and even more distant relatives also receive a portion. Kinship is customarily defined by reference to these payments, being most clearly pointed at marriage, when movements of cattle from kraal to kraal are equivalent to lines in a genealogical chart. It is also emphasized by division of sacrificial meat among agnatic and cognatic relatives. . . . Nuer tend to define all social processes and relationships in terms of cattle. Their social idiom is a bovine idiom.[2]

This approach to goods, emphasizing their double role in providing subsistence and in drawing the lines of social relationships, is agreed upon, practically axiomatic among anthropologists, as the way to a proper understanding of why people need goods. But there are some problems about transferring the insight to our own ethnography of ourselves.

Each brand of the social sciences has been bogged down until it has drawn a distinctive line between the level of human behaviour that its techniques are adapted to analyse and all other levels. Durkheim, for example, required the identification of "social facts" by his rules of method.[3] Each such isolation of a part or layer of the social process is a self-denying ordinance, an austerity, practised for the sake of learning not to pose unanswerable questions. Of course there is always a loss of richness, which the gains in clarity have to justify. Long before Durkheim, economists had carved out a sphere of "economic facts" by disregarding the ends of human activity and concentrating on the problems of choice. The history of anthropology has been one of continual disengagement of theoretical fields from the intrusive assumptions from common sense. In each case enlightenment has followed a decision to ignore the physiological levels of existence which sustain the behaviour in question. For interpreting bizarre kinship terminologies it was at first assumed that the clue to the uses of the terms "Father" and "Mother" would lie in some long-abandoned arrangements for marriage and procreation. No advance was made until kinship terms were cut free from their obvious biological meanings and seen as constituting a system for organizing social relations – a system based on the metaphors of engendering and rearing. In turn, Lévi-Strauss made a similar stand when he ridiculed the idea that the origin of totemism was some gastro-nomic criterion that reserved the most delicious foods to privileged persons. Ani-mals which are tabooed are chosen, he said, because they are good to think, not because they are good to eat. So he was able to reveal a systematic relation be-tween natural and human species as the typical basis of primitive thought.[4] Again, as another example, in nineteenth-century comparative religion, medical material-ism blocked the interpretation of ideas about the contagiousness of magic. Schol-ars were sidetracked by occasional signs of medical benefit following rites of purification. But it can be argued that these rites are better understood as being concerned with making visible the boundaries between cognitive categories than with pathogenicity in the strict medical sense.[5] Now we are trying the same exer-cise with consumption goods, bracketing away for the moment their practical uses. If it is said that the essential function of language is its capacity for poetry, we shall assume that the essential function of consumption is its capacity to make sense. Forget the idea of consumer irrationality. Forget that commodities are good for eating, clothing, and shelter; forget their usefulness and try instead the idea that commodities are good for thinking; treat them as a non-verbal medium for the human creative faculty.

Theoretical Individualism

The time is ripe for this new approach. Individualist theories of knowledge and behaviour have had their day and run their course. Here and there the outposts are still manned. Perhaps Peter Blau is one of the most forceful exponents of the eighteenth-century tradition (to which economics as a whole is heir). The Benthamite view of human psychology starts and ends with the individual agent. Other people appear only insofar as they may help or hinder his life project. He can use or be used by them, but they lurk always in a shadow cast by his egocentric awareness. Blau's theory of social structure tried to build up society from the simplest relations between individuals. He concedes that most pleasures have their roots in social life: "There is something pathetic about the person who derives his major gratifications from food and drink as such, since it reveals either excessive need or excessive greed, the pauper, . . . the glutton."[6] Anyway, there are no sim-ple processes in the relations between individuals. They can only be postulated arbitrarily, and so Blau's focus upon power is itself an arbitrary and biased restric-tion: "The satisfaction a man derives from exercising power over others requires that they endure the deprivation of being subject to his power; . . . individuals associate with one another because they all profit from the association. But they do not necessarily all profit equally, nor do they share the cost of providing the benefits equally." And so onward to a theory of individualistic social exchange. Blau stands in a low grid/low group position, where the view of a world organized

77

as a competitive, power-seeking game between individuals has *a priori* rightness. His work is a rescue job, salvaging an approach whose reverberations will appeal automatically to other thinkers who also share the same standpoint. But the anthropologist can recognize this approach itself as an example of a cultural bias rooted in a certain kind of social experience. Other cultural biases derive from other social forms. Our ultimate task is to find interpretative procedures that will uncover each bias and discredit its claims to universality. When this is done the eighteenth century can be formally closed, and a new era that has been here a long time can be officially recognized.

The individual human being, stripped of his humanity, is of no use as a conceptual base from which to make a picture of human society. No human exists except steeped in the culture of his time and place. The falsely abstracted individual has been sadly misleading to Western political thought.[7] But now we can start again at a point where major streams of thought converge, at the other end, at the making of culture. Cultural analysis sees the whole tapestry as a whole, the picture and the weaving process, before attending to the individual threads.

At least three intellectual positions being developed today encourage such an approach. One, the philosophical movement styled Phenomenology, started by taking seriously the question of our knowledge of other persons. It sets the individual squarely in a social context, treating knowledge as a joint constructive enterprise. Knowledge is never a matter of the lone individual learning about an external reality. Individuals interacting together impose their constructions upon reality: the world is socially constructed.[8]

Structuralism is a convergent movement whose implicit theory of knowledge transcends the efforts of the individual thinker, and focuses upon social processes in knowledge. In its many forms, modern structural analysis, the offspring of electronic computers, affords possibilities of interpreting culture and of relating cultural to social forms, possibilities that outpace any approaches that doggedly start with the individual.[9]

And finally, closest to the present task, is the Californian movement in sociology called "social accounting" or ethnomethodology. This takes it for granted that reality is socially constructed and also takes it for granted that reality can be analysed as logical structures in use. It focuses upon interpretative procedures – on the methods of verification used by listeners, methods of proving credibility used by speakers, on the whole system of accountability which operates in everyday life.[10] Their approach to the testing and confirming of information starts from the idea that meaning is embedded, that is it is never easily picked from the surface of a communication. Speech is only one channel, and speech itself does not make sense unless it matches the information that is scanned by the hearer from the physical demeanour and surroundings of the speaker – spacing, timing, orientation, clothing, food, and so on. And, of course, this has to include goods. Though for the present it focuses on procedures of interpretation, for its further development this approach will certainly need to turn to cultural analysis. For culture is a possible pattern of meanings inherited from the immediate past, a canopy for the interpretative needs of the present.

Fixed Public Meanings

But what is meaning? It flows and drifts; it is hard to grasp. Meaning tacked to one set of clues transforms itself. One person gets one pattern and another a quite different one from the same events; seen a year later they take a different aspect again. The main problem of social life is to pin down meanings so that they stay still for a little time. Without some conventional ways of selecting and fixing agreed meanings, the minimum consensual basis of society is missing. As for tribal society, so too for us: rituals serve to contain the drift of meanings. Rituals are conventions that set up visible public definitions. Before the initiation there was a boy, after it a man; before the marriage rite there were two free persons, after it two joined as one. Before admission to a hospital, the doctor's certificate of ill health; before the formal declaration of death, the dead is accounted alive; before the body is found, no murder charge sticks; without formal testimony, slander is not slander; without a witnessed signature, the deceased's last will is not valid. To manage without rituals is to manage without clear meanings and possibly without memories. Some are purely verbal rituals, vocalized, unrecorded, but they fade on the air and hardly help to limit the interpretive scope. More effective rituals use material things, and the more costly the ritual trappings, the stronger we can assume the intention to fix the meanings to be. Goods, in this perspective, are ritual adjuncts; consumption is a ritual process whose primary function is to make sense of the inchoate flux of events.

From here it is a short step to the identification of the overall objective that rational beings, by definition, can be supposed to set themselves. Their own rationality must press them to make sense of their environment. The most general objective of the consumer can only be to construct an intelligible universe with the goods he chooses. How does this cognitive construction proceed? To start with, a social universe needs a demarcated temporal dimension. The calendar has to be notched for annual, quarterly, monthly, weekly, daily, and shorter periodicities. The passage of time can then be laden with meaning. The calendar gives a principle for rotation of duties, for establishing precedence, for review and renewal. Another year passed, a new beginning; 25 years, a silver jubilee; 100, 200 years, a centennial or bicentennial celebration; there is a time for living and a time for dying, a time for loving. Consumption goods are used for notching off these intervals: their range in quality arises from the need to differentiate through the calendar year and the life cycle.

This argument does not deny that there is such a thing as private enjoyment. It is developed to assert a straight analytic need to recognize how enjoyment is structured and how much it owes to social standardization. Those who fancy a simple life, with only enough goods for a modest subsistence, should try to imagine a standardized meal, say breakfast, served at all mealtime slots in the weekday, at all meals in the week, at all meals in the year including Christmas Day and Thanksgiving. Food is a medium for discriminating values, and the more numerous the discriminated ranks, the more varieties of food will be needed. The same for space. Harnessed to the cultural process, its divisions are heavy with meaning: housing, size, the side of the street, distance from other centres, special limits, all shore up conceptual categories. The same for clothing, transport and sanitation; they afford sets of markers within the spatial and temporal frame. The choice of goods continuously creates certain patterns of discrimination, overlaying or reinforcing others. Goods, then, are the visible part of culture. They are arranged in vistas and hierarchies that can give play to the full range of discrimination of which the human mind is capable. The vistas are not fixed: nor are they randomly arranged in a kaleidoscope. Ultimately, their structures are anchored to human social purposes.

Hearing this, the economist usually asks: what about the solitary consumer? The man who feeds alone can hardly be said to be sustaining a universe of meanings; the man who reads or listens to music alone, goes for walks alone, what of his consumption of books and shoeleather? The answer comes in three parts. Admittedly, there is a class of solitary feeding, where the person wolfs or bolts his food, probably standing by his refrigerator in his overcoat; this should count as part of a private hygiene, in the same way as his use of soap and toothbrushes. Private hygiene is probably a small item in the sum of consumption goods. But even so, if a person normally chooses his soap and pares his nails for entirely non-social reasons the advertising industry is wildly wrong. The lonely walks may count as private hygiene, too, as long as the walker never shares his experience by speaking or writing about it. But music is another matter. The music lover probably knows a lot about music and is observing the fine discrimination and shifts of practice that are the history of music; he may even be passing judgement (albeit privately) on whether one performance is better than another. He is sharing in an intensely social, cultural process. So, too, is the solitary eater who unthinkingly adopts the sequential rules and categories of the wider society; the man who uses a butter knife when he is alone, even if he doesn't dress for dinner. He would never reverse the conventional sequence, beginning with pudding and ending with soup, or eat mustard with lamb or mint with beef. We may reckon his observance of the rules followed by other consumers as a way of keeping him in practice, or perhaps as a memorial rite. If the gastric juices flow best when the meal is well constructed, well served, and enjoyed in good company, the solitary consumer may be helping his own digestion by adopting the social criteria. But he is certainly helping to uphold the latter. In general, the case of the solitary consumer is a weak counter to the argument that consumption activity is the joint production, with fellow consumers, of a universe of values. Consumption uses goods to make firm and visible a particular set of judgements in the fluid processes of classifying persons and events. We have now defined it as a ritual activity.

But the individual needs compliant fellows if he is to succeed in changing the public categories, reducing their disorder and making the universe more intelligible. His project of creating intelligibility depends heavily on them. He must assure their attending his rituals and inviting him to theirs. By their freely given preferences he obtains a judgement from them of the fitness of the choices he makes of consumer goods for celebrating particular occasions and a judgement on his own relative standing as a judge, as well as a judgement on the fitness of the occasion to be celebrated. Within the available time and space the individual uses consumption to say something about himself, his family, his locality, whether in town or country, on vacation or at home. The kind of statements he makes are about the kind of universe he is in, affirmatory or defiant, perhaps competitive, but not necessarily so. He can proceed, through consumption activities, to get agreement from fellow consumers to redefine some traditional events as major that used to be minor, and to allow others to lapse completely. In England, Guy Fawkes Day comes forward where Halloween used to be. Christmas overshadows New Year in England but not in Scotland, and Mother's Day still hovers on the brink of recognition. The same for the decoration of the home and even the constitution of a meal. Consumption is an active process in which all the social categories are being continually redefined.

For anthropologists the word potlatch sums up this characteristic of feasting, inviting guests, and competing in hospitable honours. There are many variants of the potlatch described in American Northwest Coast ethnography. A Skagit Indian described the potlatch as "shaking hands in a material way". For these Indians of Puget Sound,

the activities of the food cycle and the social season of a single year are posited in socio-religious theory. The cumulative successes and failures of many years were expressed in winter ceremonials. Although a usually prosperous village might have had such a poor summer that its headman could afford few extravagances in the next winter, his success in past winters would nevertheless be commemorated in potlatches, with the attitude that his bad luck was only temporary and that he would recover from his debts in another season. Only repeated misfortune, of several consecutive years, would reduce his standing enough to alter potlatch behaviour toward him. He would postpone potlatching, and hopefully he would avoid loss of status by announcing his obligations on public occasions. Although his demeanour did not convey embarrassment or humility, his words did, expressing an apologetic, almost cringingly guilty attitude about his bad luck. In grandiose language he, or more usually a hired spokes-man, extolled the generosity of the guests and compared it with his own feeble though well-meant efforts to be the same. Because the source of bad luck was invariably bad behaviour, and because good men were honest men, it was necessary that he publicly confess and then promise to reform. But a potlatch leader's confessions and resolutions usually were masked in generalities. He merely alluded to a misdeed that he thought might have become known to his audience. He did not specify who did what or exactly what he as a chief was going to do about it. And his humble words were punctuated by even more elaborate oratory reminding the assemblage of the brilliance of his own past and that of his ancestors. Such a performance was the ultimate expression of upper-class dignity in the face of adversity. A good reputation, mere words of condescension, and a defensive attitude could sustain even a faltering career among the Skagit for quite some years.

While upper-class men lost status gradually as a result of a series of economic setbacks, chiefs in newly formed villages, descendants of commoners, were but grudgingly admitted to one or another potlatch circle as important invited guests. Especially if they had suddenly become rich, they were looked upon as conniving vulgarians without right to such good fortune. Their wealth would be overlooked at give-aways sponsored by hosts of the old guard, who contemptuously identified them, instead, with their former anonymity. And when the *arrivistes* pretentiously potlatched, their betters, the elite who mattered, would not acknowledge invitations. A potlatch of this kind was a fiasco. The etiquette of potlatching made it almost impossible for untested claimants to high station to crash the society of Skagit bluebloods. Unless a new village had steadily grown in numbers and prosperity over a generation or two, during which time its leaders had maintained a mock servility on public occasions, it would never come to be accepted by old, influential villages as a worthy rival. One way by which the Skagit publicly expressed respect for other families and communities was to allow them to compete on the same footing. Trust in people of proven, established lineage, and scorn and fear of Johnnies-come-lately had a sound practical basis, according to Skagit rationalizations about social class behaviour. *Nouveaux riches* potlatchers lacked training for the manipulation of wealth and were liable to provoke, intentionally or unintentionally, embarrassing situations. That is, they might insult the pride of their august guests, which would only have to be avenged to no one's particular social or economic advantage. They were not to be trusted on general principles. Most had reputations for filial impiety, because their leadership was of recent origin and was due to the disloyalty of an ancestor (of several generations ago) and his break with his parental village to found a new one.[11]

Surely we can see here a parallel to the way in which we ourselves proceed to fix or to challenge public meanings.

Notes

1 For other significant anthropological studies of consumption see in particular Sahlins, M. (1976) *Culture and Practical Reason*, Chicago, IL: University of Chicago Press; McCracken, G. (1990) *Culture and Consumption*, Bloomington, IN: Indiana University Press; and more recently Howes, D. (ed.) (1996) *Cross-Cultural Consumption*, London: Routledge.

2   Evans-Pritchard, "The Nuer". In *The Political Institutions of a Nilotic People*, pp. 17–19. Oxford: Clarendon Press, 1940.

3   Durkheim, E. *The Rules of Sociological Method*, edited by E. G. Catlin, Chicago: University of Chicago Press, 1950.

4   Lévi-Strauss, C. *Totemism*, London: Merlin Press, 1962; *The Savage Mind*, London: Weidenfeld & Nicolson, 1966.

5   Douglas, M. *Purity and Danger: An Analysis of Concepts of Pollution and Taboo*, London: Routledge and Kegan Paul, 1966.

6   Blau, Peter, *Exchange and Power in Social Life*, New York: John Wiley, 1964.

7   Dumont, Louis, 'The Modern Concept of the Individual: Notes on Its Genesis and That of Concomitant Institutions.' *Contributions to Indian Sociology*, 8 (13): 61, 1965.

8   Berger, P. and Luckmann, T., *The Social Construction of Reality: A Treatise in the Sociology of Knowledge*, Garden City, NY: Doubleday, 1966.

9   Lévi-Strauss, C., *Anthropologie structurale*, Paris: 1958; English translation *Structural Anthropology*, London: Allen Lane, 1968.

10   Cicourel, A., *Cognitive Sociology*, Harmondsworth: Penguin Books, 1973.

11   Snyder, Sally, "Quest for the Sacred in Northern Puget Sound: An Interpretation of Potlatch." *Ethnology* 14 (2): 154–6.

7

Introduction to *Distinction*

Pierre Bourdieu

In this introduction to his monumental examination of contemporary French culture and class relations, Bourdieu identifies many of the main themes which inform his analysis of class taste formations. He argues that in the reproduction of class relations at the level of culture, the consumption of symbolic goods plays a crucial role. At the moment of consumption, consumers bring to bear upon the objects of consumption their cultural skills, competences, and literacy – their "cultural capital." The more shrewd the manner of investment of this cultural capital, i.e. the more erudite the reading or consumption of the good in question, then the more symbolic capital (recognized prestige) is gained. Here Bourdieu argues that the ultimate axis of determination of what exactly constitutes a more or less erudite reading is the degree to which consumers define and justify their preferences for particular goods via the binary distinction of function vs form.

You said it, my good knight! There ought to be laws to protect the body of acquired knowledge.

Take one of our good pupils, for example: modest and diligent, from his earliest grammar classes he's kept a little notebook full of phrases.

After hanging on the lips of his teacher for twenty years, he's managed to build up an intellectual stock in trade; doesn't it belong to him as if it were a house, or money? (Paul Claudel, *Le Soulier de satin*, Day III, Scene ii)

There is an economy of cultural goods, but it has a specific logic. Sociology endeavours to establish the conditions in which the consumers of cultural goods, and their taste for them, are produced, and at the same time to describe the different ways of appropriating such of these objects as are regarded at a particular moment as works of art, and the social conditions of the constitution of the mode of appropriation that is considered legitimate. But one cannot fully understand cultural practices unless 'culture', in the restricted, normative sense of ordinary usage, is brought

From *Distinction: A Social Critique of the Judgement of Taste*, translated by Richard Nice (London: Routledge and Kegan Paul, 1984), pp. 1–7. Reprinted by permission of the publishers.

back into 'culture' in the anthropological sense, and the elaborated taste for the most refined objects is reconnected with elementary taste for the flavours of food.

Whereas the ideology of charisma regards taste in legitimate culture as a gift of nature, scientific observation shows that cultural needs are the product of up-bringing and education: surveys establish that all cultural practices (museum visits, concert-going, reading, etc.) and preferences in literature, painting or music, are closely linked to educational level (measured by qualifications or length of school-ing) and secondarily to social origin (Bourdieu et al., 1965; Bourdieu and Darbel, 1966). The relative weight of home background and of formal education (the effectiveness and duration of which are closely dependent on social origin) varies according to the extent to which the different cultural practices are recognized and taught by the educational system, and the influence of social origin is strong-est – other things being equal – in 'extra-curricular' and avant-garde culture. To the socially recognized hierarchy of the arts, and within each of them, of the gen-res, schools or periods, corresponds a social hierarchy of the consumers. This pre-disposes tastes to function as markers of 'class'. The manner in which culture has been acquired lives on in the manner of using it: the importance attached to man-ners can be understood once it is seen that it is these imponderables of practice which distinguish the different – and ranked – modes of culture acquisition, early or late, domestic or scholastic, and the classes of individuals which they character-ize (such as 'pedants' and *mondains*). Culture also has its titles of nobility – awarded by the educational system – and its pedigrees, measured by seniority in admission to the nobility.

The definition of cultural nobility is the stake in a struggle which has gone on unceasingly, from the seventeenth century to the present day, between groups differing in their ideas of culture and of the legitimate relation to culture and to works of art, and therefore differing in the conditions of acquisition of which these dispositions are the product.[1] Even in the classroom, the dominant definition of the legitimate way of appropriating culture and works of art favours those who have had early access to legitimate culture, in a cultured household, outside of scholastic disciplines, since even within the educational system it devalues schol-arly knowledge and the interpretation as 'scholastic' or even 'pedantic' in favour of direct experience and simple delight.

The logic of what is sometimes called, in typically 'pedantic' language, the 'read-ing' of a work of art, offers an objective basis for this opposition. Consumption is, in this case, a stage in a process of communication, that is, an act of deciphering, decoding, which presupposes practical or explicit mastery of a cipher or code. In a sense, one can say that the capacity to see (*voir*) is a function of the knowledge (*savoir*), or concepts, that is, the words, that are available to name visible things, and which are, as it were, programmes for perception. A work of art has meaning and interest only for someone who possesses the cultural competence, that is, the code, into which it is encoded. The conscious or unconscious implementation of explicit or implicit schemes of perception and appreciation which constitute picto-rial or musical culture is the hidden condition for recognizing the styles character-istic of a period, a school or an author, and, more generally, the familiarity with the internal logic of works that aesthetic enjoyment presupposes. A beholder who lacks the specific code feels lost in a chaos of sounds and rhythms, colours and lines, without rhyme or reason. Not having learnt to adopt the adequate disposi-tion, he stops short of what Erwin Panofsky calls the 'sensible properties', perceiv-ing a skin as downy or lace-work as delicate, or at the emotional resonances aroused by these properties, referring to 'austere' colours or a 'joyful' melody. He cannot move from the 'primary stratum of the meaning we can grasp on the basis of our ordinary experience' to the 'stratum of secondary meanings', i.e. the 'level of the meaning of what is signified', unless he possesses the concepts which go beyond the sensible properties and which identify the specifically stylistic properties of the work (Panofsky, 1955: 28). Thus the encounter with a work of art is not 'love at first sight' as is generally supposed, and the act of empathy, *Einfühlung*, which is the art-lover's pleasure, presupposes an act of cognition, a decoding operation, which implies the implementation of a cognitive acquirement, a cultural code.[2]

This typically intellectualist theory of artistic perception directly contradicts the experience of the art-lovers closest to the legitimate definition; acquisition of le-gitimate culture by insensible familiarization within the family circle tends to fa-vour an enchanted experience of culture which implies forgetting the acquisition.[3] The 'eye' is a product of history reproduced by education. This is true of the mode of artistic perception now accepted as legitimate, that is, the aesthetic dispo-sition, the capacity to consider in and for themselves, as form rather than function, not only the works designated for such apprehension, i.e. legitimate works of art, but everything in the world, including cultural objects which are not yet conse-crated – such as, at one time, primitive arts, or, nowadays, popular photography or kitsch – and natural objects. The 'pure' gaze is a historical invention linked to the emergence of an autonomous field of artistic production, that is, a field capable of imposing its own norms on both the production and consumption of its prod-ucts.[4] An art which, like all Post-Impressionist painting, is the product of an artis-tic intention which asserts the primacy of the mode of representation over the object of representation, demands categorically an attention to form which previ-ous art only demanded conditionally.

The pure intention of the artist is that of a producer who aims to be autono-mous, that is, entirely the master of his product, who tends to reject, not only the 'programmes' imposed *a priori* by scholars and scribes, but also – following the old hierarchy of doing and saying – the interpretations superimposed *a posteriori* on his work. The production of an 'open work', intrinsically and deliberately polysemic, can thus be understood as the final stage in the conquest of artistic autonomy by poets and, following in their footsteps, by painters, who had long been reliant on writers and their work of 'showing' and 'illustrating'. To assert the autonomy of production is to give primacy to that of which the artist is master, i.e. form, manner, style, rather than the 'subject', the external referent, which involves subordination to functions – even if only the most elementary one, that of representing, signifying, saying something. It also means a refusal to recognize any necessity other than that inscribed in the specific tradition of the artistic discipline in question: the shift from an art which imitates nature to an art which imitates art, deriving from its own history the exclusive source of experiments and even of its breaks with tradition. An art which ever increasingly contains reference to its own history demands to be perceived historically; it asks to be referred not to an external referent, the represented or designated 'reality', but to the universe of past and present works of art. Like artistic production, in that it is generated in a field, aesthetic perception is necessarily historical, inasmuch as it is differential , relational, attentive to deviations (*écarts*) which make styles. Like the so-called naive painter who, operating outside the field and its specific traditions, remains external to the history of the art, the 'naive' spectator cannot attain a specific grasp of works of art which only have meaning – or value – in relation to the specific history of an artistic tradition. The aesthetic disposition demanded by the products of a highly autonomous field of production is inseparable from a specific cultural competence. This historical culture functions as a principle of pertinence which enables one to identify, among the elements offered to the gaze, all the distinctive features and only these, by referring them, consciously or unconsciously, to the universe of possible alternatives. This mastery is, for the most part, acquired simply by contact with works of art – that is, through an implicit learning analogous to that which makes it possible to recognize familiar faces without explicit rules or criteria – and it generally remains at a practical level; it is what makes it possible to identify styles, i.e. modes of expression characteristic of a period, a civilization or a school, without having to distinguish clearly, or state explicitly, the features which constitute their originality. Everything seems to suggest that even amongst professional valuers, the criteria which define the stylistic properties of 'typical works' on which all their judgements are based usually remain implicit.

The pure gaze implies a break with the ordinary attitude towards the world, which, given the conditions in which it is performed, is also a social separation. Ortega y Gasset can be believed when he attributes to modern art a systematic refusal of all that is 'human', i.e. generic, common – as opposed to distinctive, or distinguished – namely, the passions, emotions and feelings which 'ordinary' people invest in their 'ordinary' lives. It is as if the 'popular aesthetic' (the quotation marks are there to indicate that this is an aesthetic 'in itself' not 'for itself') were based on the affirmation of the continuity between art and life, which implies the subordination of form to function. This is seen clearly in the case of the novel and especially the theatre, where the working-class audience refuses any sort of formal experimentation and all the effects which, by introducing a distance from the accepted conventions (as regards scenery, plot, etc.), tend to distance the spectator, preventing him from getting involved and fully identifying with the characters (I am thinking of Brechtian 'alienation' or disruption of plot in the *nouveau roman*). In contrast to the detachment and disinterestedness which aesthetic theory regards as the only way of recognizing the work of art for what it is, i.e. autonomous, *selbständig*, the 'popular aesthetic' ignores or refuses the refusal of 'facile' involvement and 'vulgar' enjoyment, a refusal which is the basis of the taste for formal experiment. And popular judgements of painting and photographs spring from an 'aesthetic' (in fact it is an ethos) which is the exact opposite of the Kantian aesthetic. Whereas, in order to grasp the specificity of the aesthetic judgement, Kant strove to distinguish that which pleases from that which gratifies and, more generally, to distinguish disinterestedness, the sole guarantor of the specifically aesthetic quality of contemplation, from the interests of reason which defines the Good. Working-class people expect every image to explicitly perform a function, if only that of a sign, and their judgements make reference, often explicitly, to the norms of morality or agreeableness. Whether rejecting or praising, their appreciation always has an ethical basis.

Popular taste applies the schemes of the ethos, which pertain in the ordinary circumstances of life, to legitimate works of art, and so performs a systematic reduction of the things of art to the things of life. The very seriousness (or naivety) which this taste invests in fictions and representations demonstrates *a contrario* that pure taste performs a suspension of 'naive' involvement which is one dimension of a 'quasi-ludic' relationship with the necessities of the world. Intellectuals could be said to believe in the representation – literature, theatre, painting – more than in the things represented, whereas the people chiefly expect representations and the conventions which govern them to allow them to believe 'naively' in the things represented. The pure aesthetic is rooted in an aesthetic, or rather, an ethos of elective distance from the necessities of the natural and social world, which may take the form of a moral agnosticism (visible when ethical transgression becomes an artistic *parti pris*) or of an aestheticism which presents the aesthetic disposition as a universally valid principle and takes the bourgeois denial of the social world to its limit. The detachment of the pure gaze cannot be disassociated from a general disposition towards the world which is the paradoxical product of conditioning by negative economic necessities – a life of ease – that tends to induce an active distance from necessity.

Although art obviously offers the greatest scope to the aesthetic disposition, there is no area of practice in which the aim of purifying, refining and sublimating primary needs and impulses cannot assert itself, no area in which the stylization of life, that is, the primacy of forms over function, of manner over matter, does not produce the same effects. And nothing is more distinctive, more distinguished, than the capacity to confer aesthetic status on objects that are banal or even 'common' (because the 'common' people make them their own, especially for aesthetic purposes), or the ability to apply the principles of a 'pure' aesthetic to the most everyday choices of everyday life, e.g. in cooking, clothing or decoration, completely reversing the popular disposition which annexes aesthetics to ethics.

In fact, through the economic and social conditions which they presuppose, the different ways of relating to realities and fictions, of believing in fictions and the realities they simulate, with more or less distance and detachment, are very closely linked to the different possible positions in social space and, consequently, bound up with the systems of dispositions (habitus) characteristic of the different classes and class fractions. Taste classifies, and it classifies the classifier. Social subjects, classified by their classifications, distinguish themselves by the distinctions they make, between the beautiful and the ugly, the distinguished and the vulgar, in which their position in the objective classifications is expressed or betrayed. And statistical analysis does indeed show that oppositions similar in structure to those found in cultural practices also appear in eating habits. The antithesis between quantity and quality, substance and form, corresponds to the opposition – linked to different distances from necessity – between the taste of necessity, which favours the most 'filling' and most economical foods, and the taste of liberty – or luxury – which shifts the emphasis to the manner (of presenting, serving, eating, etc.) and tends to use stylized forms to deny function.

The science of taste and of cultural consumption begins with a transgression that is in no way aesthetic: it has to abolish the sacred frontier which makes legitimate culture a separate universe, in order to discover the intelligible relations which unite apparently incommensurable 'choices', such as preferences in music and food, painting and sport, literature and hairstyle. This barbarous reintegration of aesthetic consumption into the world of ordinary consumption abolishes the opposition, which has been the basis of high aesthetics since Kant, between the 'taste of sense' and the 'taste of reflection', and between facile pleasure, pleasure reduced to a pleasure of the senses, and pure pleasure, pleasure purified of pleasure, which is predisposed to become a symbol of moral excellence and a measure of the capacity for sublimation which defines the truly human man. The culture which results from this magical division is sacred. Cultural consecration does indeed confer on the objects, persons and situations it touches, a sort of ontological promotion akin to a transubstantiation. Proof enough of this is found in the two following quotations, which might almost have been written for the delight of the sociologist:

> What struck me most is this: nothing could be obscene on the stage of our premier theatre, and the ballerinas of the Opera, even as naked dancers, sylphs, sprites or Bacchae, retain an involuable purity.[5]

> There are obscene postures: the simulated intercourse which offends the eye. Clearly, it is impossible to approve, although the interpolation of such gestures in dance routines does give them a symbolic and aesthetic quality which is absent from the intimate scenes the cinema daily flaunts before its spectators' eyes. . . . As for the nude scene, what can one say, except that it is brief and theatrically not very effective? I will not say that it is chaste or innocent, for nothing commercial can be so

described. Let us say it is not shocking, and that the chief objection is that it serves as a box-office gimmick. . . . In *Hair* the nakedness fails to be symbolic.[6]

The denial of lower, course, vulgar, venal, servile – in a word, natural – enjoyment, which constitutes the sacred sphere of culture, implies an affirmation of the superiority of those who can be satisfied with the sublimated, refined, disinterested, gratuitous, distinguished pleasures forever closed to the profane. That is why art and cultural consumption are predisposed, consciously and deliberately or not, to fulfil a social function of legitimating social differences.

Notes

1   The word *disposition* seems particularly suited to express what is covered by the concept of habitus (defined as a system of dispositions) – used later in this chapter. It expresses first the *result of an organizing action*, with a meaning close to that of words such as structure; it also designates a way of being, a habitual state (especially of the body) and, in particular, a *predisposition, tendency propensity* or *inclination* [the semantic cluster of 'disposition' is rather wider in French than in English, but as this note – translated literally – shows, the equivalence is adequate. Translator.] See Bourdieu (1977: 214, n. 1).

2   It will be seen that this internalized code called culture functions as cultural capital owing to the fact that, being unequally distributed, it secures profits of distinction.

3   The sense of familiarity in no way excludes the ethnocentric misunderstanding which results from applying the wrong code. Thus, Michael Baxandall's work in historical ethnology enables us to measure all that separates the perceptual schemes that now tend to be applied to Quattrocento paintings and those which their immediate addresses applied. The 'moral and spiritual eye' of Quattrocento man, that is, the set of cognitive and evaluative dispositions which were the basis of his perception of the world and his perception of pictorial representation of the world, differs radically from the 'pure' gaze (purified, first of all, of reference to economic value) with which the modern cultivated spectator looks at works of art. As the contracts show, the clients of Filippo Lippi, Domenico Ghirlandaio or Piero della Francesca were concerned to get 'value for money'. They approached works of art with the mercantile dispositions of a businessman who can calculate quantities and prices at a glance, and they applied some surprising criteria of appreciation, such as the expense of the colours, which sets gold and ultramarine at the top of the hierarchy. The artists, who shared this world view, were led to include arithmetical and geometrical devices in their compositions so as to flatter this taste for measurement and calculation; and they tended to exhibit the technical virtuosity which, in this context, is the most visible evidence of the quantity or the quality of the labour provided; M. Baxandall (1972).

4   See Bourdieu (1968: 589–612; 1973: 49–126).

5   O. Merlin, 'Mlle. Thibon dans la vision de Marguerite'. *Le Monde*, 9 December 1965.

6   F. Chenique, '*Hair* est-il immoral?' *Le Monde*, 28 January 1970.

References

Baxandall, M. (1972) *Painting and Experience in Fifteenth Century Italy: A Primer in the Social History of Pictorial Style*, Oxford: Oxford University Press.

Bourdieu, P. (1968) 'Outline of a sociological theory of art perception', *International Social Science Journal*, 20, Winter, 589–612.

Bourdieu, P. (1973) 'Le Marché des biens symboliques', *L'Année sociologique*, 22, 49–126.

Bourdieu, P. (1977) *Outline of a Theory of Practice*, Cambridge: Cambridge University Press.

Bourdieu, P. and Darbel, A. (1966) *L'Amour de l'art: les musées et leur public*, Paris: Ed. de Minuit.

Bourdieu, P. et al. (1965) *Un Art moyen: essai sur les usages sociaux de la photographie*, Paris: Ed. de Minuit.

Panofsky, E. (1955) 'Iconography and iconology: an introduction to the study of Renaissance art' in *Meaning in the Visual Arts*, New York: Doubleday.

8

Lifestyle and Consumer Culture

Mike Featherstone

In this essay Mike Featherstone draws heavily on the ideas and evidence presented in Bourdieu's *Distinction* to explore the concept of lifestyle. The term is perhaps most profitably employed, he argues, when applied to the culture and consumption habits and practices of the new petit bourgeoisie - an emerging and increasingly powerful group of "cultural intermediaries" responsible for the production and dissemination of (especially) mass-mediated, and increasingly postmodern, cultural products and symbols.

The term 'lifestyle' is currently in vogue. While the term has a more restricted sociological meaning in reference to the distinctive style of life of specific status groups (Weber, 1968; Sobel, 1982; Rojek, 1985), within contemporary consumer culture it connotes individuality, self-expression and a stylistic self-consciousness. One's body, clothes, speech, leisure pastimes, eating and drinking preferences, home, car, choice of holidays, etc. are to be regarded as indicators of the individuality of taste and sense of style of the owner/consumer. In contrast to the designation of the 1950s as an era of grey conformism, a time of *mass* consumption, changes in production techniques, market segmentation and consumer demand for a wider range of products, are often regarded as making possible greater choice (the management of which itself becomes an art form) not only for youth of the post-1960s generation, but increasingly for the middle-aged and the elderly. Three phrases from Stuart and Elizabeth Ewen's *Channels of Desire* (1982: 249–51) which they see as symptomatic of the recent tendencies within consumer culture, come to mind here: 'Today there is no fashion: there are only *fashions*.' 'No rules, only choices.' 'Everyone can be anyone.' What does it mean to suggest that long-held fashion codes have been violated, that there is a war against uniformity, a surfeit of difference which results in a loss of meaning? The implication is that we are moving towards a society without fixed status groups in which the adoption of styles of life (manifest in choice of clothes, leisure activities, consumer goods, bodily dispositions) which are fixed to specific groups have been surpassed. This apparent

From *Consumer Culture and Postmodernism* (London: Sage, 1991), pp. 83–94. Reprinted by permission of Sage Publications Ltd.

movement towards a postmodern consumer culture based upon a profusion of information and proliferation of images which cannot be ultimately stabilized, or hierarchized into a system which correlates to fixed social divisions, would further suggest the irrelevance of social divisions and ultimately the end of the social as a significant reference point. In effect the end of the deterministic relationship between society and culture heralds the triumph of signifying culture. Are consumer goods used as cultural signs in a free-association manner by individuals to produce an expressive effect within a social field in which the old co-ordinates are rapidly disappearing, or can taste still be adequately 'read', socially recognized and mapped onto the class structure? Does taste still 'classify the classifier'? Does the claim for a movement beyond fashion merely represent a move within, not beyond the game, being instead a new move, a position within the social field of lifestyles and consumption practices which can be correlated to the class structure?

This chapter is an attempt to develop a perspective which goes beyond the view that lifestyle and consumption are totally manipulated products of a mass society, and the opposite position which seeks to preserve the field of lifestyles and consumption, or at least a particular aspect of it (such as sport), as an autonomous playful space beyond determination. An attempt will also be made to argue that the 'no rules only choices' view (celebrated by some as a significant movement towards the break-up of the old hierarchies of fashion, style and taste in favour of an egalitarian and tolerant acceptance of differences, and the acknowledgement of the right of individuals to enjoy whatever popular pleasures they desire without encountering prudery or moral censure) does not signify anything as dramatic as the implosion of the social space but should be regarded merely as a new move within it. A perspective informed by the work of Pierre Bourdieu will be developed to argue that the new conception of lifestyle can best be understood in relation to the habitus of the new petite bourgeoisie, who, as an expanding class fraction centrally concerned with the production and dissemination of consumer culture imagery and information, is concerned to expand and legitimate its own particular dispositions and lifestyle. It does so with a social field in which its views are resisted and contested and within, in Britain, especially, an economic climate and political culture in which the virtues of the traditional petite bourgeoisie have undergone a revival. Nevertheless it would seem to be useful to ask questions about consumer culture not only in terms of the engineering of demand resulting from the efficiencies of mass production or the logic of capitalism, but to discover which particular groups, strata, or class fractions are most closely involved in symbolic production and, in particular, in producing the images and information celebrating styles and lifestyles. What follows is very much a schematic account, written at a high level of generality, and acknowledges that these questions can ultimately only be answered by empirical analyses which take into account the specificity of particular societies.

93

Consumer Culture

To use the term 'consumer culture' is to emphasize that the world of goods and their principles of structuration are central to the understanding of contemporary society. This involves a dual focus: firstly, on the cultural dimension of the economy, the symbolization and use of material goods as 'communicators' not just utilities; and secondly, on the economy of cultural goods, the market principles of supply, demand, capital accumulation, competition, and monopolization which operate *within* the sphere of lifestyles, cultural goods and commodities.

Turning first to consumer culture it is apparent that the emphasis in some popular and academic circles on the materialism of contemporary consumer societies is far from unproblematic. From an anthropological perspective (Sahlins, 1974; 1976; Douglas and Isherwood, 1980 [chapter 6, this volume]; Leiss, 1983) material goods and their production, exchange and consumption are to be understood within a cultural matrix. Elwert (1984) too has referred to the 'embedded economy' to draw attention to the cultural preconditions of economic life. The movement away from regarding goods merely as utilities having a use-value and an exchange-value which can be related to some fixed system of human needs has also occurred within neo-Marxism. Baudrillard (1975; 1981) [chapter 3, this volume] has been particularly important in this context, especially his theorization of the commodity-sign. For Baudrillard the essential feature of the movement towards the mass production of commodities is that the obliteration of the original 'natural' use-value of goods by the dominance of exchange-value under capitalism has resulted in the commodity becoming a sign in the Saussurian sense, with its meaning arbitrarily determined by its position in a self-referential system of signifiers. Consumption, then, must not be understood as the consumption of use-values, a material utility, but primarily as the consumption of signs. It is this refusal of the referent, which is replaced by an unstable field of floating signifiers, which has led Kroker (1985) to describe Baudrillard as 'the last and best of the Marxists'. For Kroker, Baudrillard has pushed the logic of the commodity form as far as it will go until it releases 'the referential illusion' at its heart: the nihilism Nietzsche diagnosed is presented as the completion of the logic of capitalism.

It is this dominance of the commodity as sign which has led some neo-Marxists to emphasize the crucial role of culture in the reproduction of contemporary capitalism. Jameson (1981: 131), for example, writes that culture is 'the very element of consumer society itself; no society has ever been saturated with signs and images like this one'. Advertising and the display of goods in the 'dream-worlds' (Benjamin, 1982; R. H. Williams, 1982) of department stores and city centres plays upon the logic of the commodity-sign to transgress formally sealed-apart meanings and create unusual and novel juxtapositions which effectively rename goods. Mundane and everyday consumer goods become associated with luxury, exotica, beauty and romance with their original or functional 'use' increasingly difficult to decipher. Baudrillard (1983) has drawn attention to the key role of the electronic mass media in late-capitalist society. Television produces a surfeit of images and information which threatens our sense of reality. The triumph of signifying culture leads to a simulational world in which the proliferation of signs and images has effaced the distinction between the real and the imaginary. For Baudrillard (1983: 148) this means that 'we live everywhere already in an "aesthetic" hallucination of reality'. The 'death of the social, the loss of the real, leads to a *nostalgia* for the real: a fascination with and desperate search for real people, real values, real sex' (Kroker, 1985: 80). Consumer culture for Baudrillard is effectively a postmodern culture, a depthless culture in which all values have become transvalued and art has triumphed over reality.

The aestheticization of reality foregrounds the importance of style, which is also encouraged by the modernist market dynamic with its constant search for new fashions, new styles, new sensations and experiences. The formally artistic countercultural notion embodied in modernism that life is/should be a work of art is thus accorded wider currency. William Leiss (1983) has noted in his investigation of advertisements in Canada a shift over the last fifty years (especially marked in television) from advertisements which contain product information to those which incorporated loser, lifestyle imagery.[1]

The concern with lifestyle, with the stylization of life, suggests that the practices of consumption, the planning, purchase and display of consumer goods and experiences in everyday life cannot be understood merely via conceptions of exchange value and instrumental rational calculation. The instrumental and expressive dimensions should not be regarded as exclusive either/or polarities, rather they can be conceived as a balance which consumer culture brings together. It is therefore possible to speak of a calculating hedonism, a calculus of the stylistic effect and an emotional economy on the one hand, an aestheticization of the instrumental or functional rational dimension via the promotion of an aestheticizing distancing on the other. Rather than unreflectively adopting a lifestyle, through tradition or habit, the new heroes of consumer culture make lifestyle a life project and display their individuality and sense of style in the particularity of the assemblage of goods, clothes, practices, experiences, appearance and bodily dispositions they design together into a lifestyle. The modern individual within consumer culture is made conscious that he speaks not only with his clothes, but with his home, furnishings, decoration, car and other activities which are to be read and classified in terms of the presence and absence of taste. The preoccupation with customizing a lifestyle and a stylistic self-consciousness are not just to be found among the young and the affluent; consumer culture publicity suggests that we all have room for self-improvement and self-expression whatever our age or class origins. This is the world of men and women who quest for the new and the latest in relationships and experiences, who have a sense of adventure and take risks to explore life's options to the full, who are conscious they have only one life to live and must work hard to enjoy, experience and express it (Winship, 1983; Featherstone and Hepworth, 1983).

Against the view of a grey conformist mass culture in which individuals' use of goods conforms to the purposes which have been dreamed up by the advertisers, it has often been pointed out that the meaning and use of consumer goods, the decoding process, is complex and problematic. Raymond Williams (1961: 312), for example, argues that cross-class uniformities in housing, dress and leisure are not significant in understanding the class structure. Rather, different classes have different ways of life and views of the nature of social relationships which form a matrix within which consumption takes place. It should also be noted that the uniformities progressively decline with (1) changes in technical capacity which allow greater product variety and differentiation to be built into production runs, and (2) increasing market fragmentation. Effectively, individuals increasingly consume different products. This, coupled with the tendency for more diffuse, ambiguous lifestyle imagery in advertising noted by Leiss, encourages a variety of readings of messages (which increasingly use modernist and even postmodernist formats: a sales-pitch which educates and flatters at the same time). Consequently the consumer culture is apparently able to come nearer to delivering the individuality and differences it has always promised.

The tendency for consumer culture to differentiate, to encourage the play of difference, must be tempered by the observation that differences must be socially recognized and legitimated: total otherness like total individuality is in danger of being unrecognizable. Simmel's (Frisby, 1985) observation that fashion embodies the contradictory tendencies of imitation and differentiation and his assumption that the dynamic of fashion is such that its popularity and expansion lead to its own destruction, suggest that we need to examine more closely the social processes which structure taste in consumer goods and lifestyles, and raise the question of whether the concern for style and individuality itself reflect more the predispositions of a particular class fraction concerned with legitimating its own particular constellation of tastes as the *tastes* of the social, rather than the actual social itself. To do so we must still place the emphasis upon the production of distinctive tastes in lifestyles and consumer goods, but move down from the high level of generality which emphasizes the social and cultural process, the logic of capitalism, which can be regarded as having pushed lifestyle to the fore, to a consideration of the production of lifestyle tastes within a structured social space in which various groups, classes and class fractions struggle and compete to impose their own particular tastes as *the* legitimate tastes, and to thereby, where necessary, name and rename, classify and reclassify, order and reorder the field. This points towards an examination of the economy of cultural goods and lifestyles by adopting an approach which draws on the work of Pierre Bourdieu.

The Economy of Cultural Goods and the Social Space of Lifestyles

In the first place it should be emphasized that when speaking about an economy of cultural goods we do not simply imply a reductionism which reduces the production of goods and lifestyles to *the* economy, rather, to follow Bourdieu's approach is to acknowledge the autonomy of particular practices which need to be understood in terms of the internal dynamic, structuring principles and processes which operate within a particular field, and act in a way which is analogous to an economy. Hence there are processes of market competition, pulls from production and consumption, the tendencies of market segments and groups to monopolize, which operate within all social practices in specific ways - within fields as diffuse as science, sport, art, ageing, linguistic exchanges, photography, education, marriage, religion. In addition each social field is to be regarded as a system in which each particular element (the agents, groups, or practices) receives its distinctive values (in the Saussurian sense) from its relationship to other elements. Bourdieu, however, is no structuralist and is conscious of the need to analyse the history of a field, to examine *process* – the changing trajectories of particular elements within the field over time which alter the relative positions which produce both the structure of the fixed and the meaning of the individual elements within it.

To make the approach more concrete and to introduce the analysis of lifestyles it is useful to examine Bourdieu's *Distinction* (1984) [see chapter 7, this volume]. For Bourdieu taste in cultural goods functions as a marker of class and in *Distinction* Bourdieu seeks to map out the social field of the different tastes in legitimated 'high' cultural practices (museum visits, concert-going, reading) as well as taste in lifestyles and consumption preferences (including food, drink, clothes, cars, novels, newspapers, magazines, holidays, hobbies, sport, leisure pursuits). Both culture in the 'high' sense and culture in the anthropological sense are therefore inscribed on the same social space. The oppositions and relational determination of taste, however, become clearer when the space of lifestyle is superimposed onto a map of the class/occupational structure whose basic structuring principle is the volume and composition (economic or cultural) of capital that groups possess. To give some examples of the resultant correlations (see Bourdieu, 1984: 128–9): those who have a high volume of economic capital (industrialists, commercial employers) have a taste for business meals, foreign cars, auctions, a second home, tennis, water-skiing, right-bank galleries. Those who possess a high volume of cultural capital (higher education teachers, artistic producers, secondary teachers) have a taste for left-bank galleries, avant-garde festivals, *Les Temps modernes*, foreign languages, chess, flea markets, Bach, mountains. Those low in both economic and cultural capital (semi-skilled, skilled and unskilled workers) have a taste for football, potatoes, ordinary red wine, watching sports, public dances.

To pick out examples such as these does an injustice to the complexities of the social space in which the intermediary positions have a definitive role in producing the relational set of taste choices of particular groups (see Featherstone, 1987). It also provides a static account which masks the relational dynamics of the field in which the introduction of new tastes, or inflation, results when lower groups emulate or usurp the tastes of higher groups, causing the latter to respond by adopting new tastes which will re-establish and maintain the original distance (for example, popularity of mass marketing, be it the William Tell Overture or the introduction of a relatively inexpensive champagne in supermarkets and stores such as Marks and Spencer, which will necessarily mean the upper groups move on to more avant-garde pieces of music or purchase a new rarer drink or drink vintage champagne). Dominant groups, therefore, seek to possess or establish what William Leiss (1983) calls 'positional goods', goods which are prestigious because an artificial scarcity of supply is imposed. One of the problems generated by the dynamic of consumer culture is that inflation is constantly introduced as scarce and restricted goods become marketed to the wider population or passed down the market causing a leap-frogging social race to maintain recognizable distinctions. Satisfaction depends upon possession or consumption of the socially sanctioned and legitimate (and therefore scarce or restricted) cultural goods.

It therefore makes sense to talk about the genesis of taste for lifestyles and cultural goods in terms of the possession of volume of cultural as well as economic capital. To attempt to map taste purely in terms of income is to miss the dual principles in operation, for cultural capital has its own structure of value, which amounts to convertibility into social power, independent of income or money. The cultural realm thus has its own logic and currency as well as rate of conversion into economic capital. For the possessors of a high volume of cultural capital, the intellectuals and academics, the prestige, legitimacy, relative scarcity and therefore social value of this cultural capital, is dependent on a denial of the market in cultural goods and a denial of the relevance and necessity to convert cultural capital into economic capital. This misrecognition of the fact that there is an exchange rate, that prestigious cultural goods are redeemable as money, points to the maintenance of a 'higher', 'sacred' cultural sphere in which artists and intellectuals struggle to bring forth the products of their 'natural' talents (the ideology of charisma). It points also to the prestige accorded to symbolic production *vis-à-vis* economic production, and to the way intellectuals have been able to establish a monopoly in defining legitimate taste within the cultural realm, to distinguish, judge and hierarchize between what is tasteful and tasteless, between the pure gaze and the vulgar, between aesthetic distancing and direct sensory enjoyment.

The intellectuals (the dominated fraction of the dominant class), therefore, use the logic of symbolic systems to produce distinctions which contribute to the reproduction of the existing relations between classes and class fractions. In this they share with the bourgeoisie (the dominant fraction of the dominant class) an interest in maintaining the existing state of material class relations in which economic capital enjoys high prestige and a high exchange rate when converted into cultural capital. They will therefore always seek to increase the autonomy of the cultural field and enhance the scarcity of cultural capital by resisting moves towards a democratization of culture.

While the intellectuals as the specialists in symbolic production seek to monopolize access to this field they work within a situation in which inflation and instability increasingly become the norm: the *internal* avant-garde dynamic of artistic modernism creates a new supply of accredited cultural goods, while the *external* dynamic of the consumer market-place itself generates a popular demand for rare artistic goods. It would be useful to examine the latter dynamic in relation to the disseminators of symbolic production, the new petite bourgeoisie, and raise the question of the relationship between this class fraction and the intellectuals which will point us towards some tentative answers to our original speculation about the role of the new petite bourgeoisie in stimulating the demand for the stylization-of-life form of lifestyle.

In one of the most penetrating chapters of *Distinction* (1984: 359) Bourdieu analyses the new petite bourgeoisie, the cultural intermediaries, who provide symbolic goods and services. The important thing to note about the class fraction is its rising trajectory within the social space. In contrast to groups like peasants and farmers who decline numerically through changes taking place in the division of labour and therefore tend towards a pessimistic, nostalgic view of the world, the new petite bourgeoisie is numerically on the increase, and therefore has a progressive view of the world. Bourdieu defines the petit bourgeois as a 'proletarian who makes himself small to become a bourgeois'. Typically they invest in cultural and educational capital. The new petite bourgeoisie stands apart from the old petite bourgeoisie and the working classes in its attraction for the most naive aristocratic qualities (style, distinction, refinement) in the pursuit of expressive and liberated lifestyles.

Here Bourdieu's concept of habitus is useful to outline the set of dispositions which determine tastes and which characterize this stratum. By habitus Bourdieu is referring to the unconscious dispositions, the classificatory schemes, the taken-for-granted preferences which are evident in the individual's sense of the appropriateness and validity of his taste for cultural goods and practices – art, food, holidays, hobbies, etc. It is important to stress that habitus not only operates on the level of everyday knowledgeability, but is inscribed onto the body, being revealed in body size, volume, shape, posture, way of walking, sitting, ways of eating, drinking, amount of social space and time an individual feels entitled to claim, degree of esteem for the body, pitch, tone of voice, accent, complexity of speech patterns, body gestures, facial expression, sense of ease with one's body – these all betray the habitus of one's origins. In short the body is the materialization of class taste: class taste is *embodied*. Each group, class and class fraction has a different habitus, hence the set of differences, the source of the distinctions and the vulgarity of taste, can be mapped onto a social field which should in effect form a third grid to be superimposed onto the space of lifestyles and class/occupational capital discussed earlier.

If we turn to the new petite bourgeoisie habitus it is clear that whereas the bourgeois has a sense of ease and confidence in his body, the petit bourgeois is uneasy with his body, constantly self-consciously checking, watching and correcting himself. Hence the attraction of body maintenance techniques, the new Californian sports and forms of exercise, cosmetics, health food, where the body is treated as a sign for others and not as an instrument. The new petit bourgeois is a pretender, aspiring to more than he is, who adopts an investment orientation to life; he possesses little economic or cultural capital and therefore must acquire it. The new petit bourgeois therefore adopts a learning mode to life; he is consciously educating himself in the field of taste, style and lifestyle.

An approach to life which is characterized by a 'why can't I have my cake and eat it' attitude quests for both security *and* adventure. The new narcissism where individuals seek to maximize and experience the range of sensations available, the search for expression and self-expression, the fascination with identity, presentation and appearance makes the new petit bourgeois a 'natural' consumer. At one point Bourdieu (1984: 370) refers to the new petite bourgeoisie as the 'new' intellectuals

> who are inventing an art of living which provides them with the gratifications and prestige of the intellectual at the least cost: in the name of the fight against 'taboos' and the liquidation of 'complexes' they adopt the most external and easily borrowed aspects of the intellectual life-style, liberated manners, cosmetic or sartorial outrages, emancipated poses and postures and systematically apply the cultivated disposition to not-yet-legitimate culture (cinema, strip cartoons, the underground), to everyday life (street art), the personal sphere (sexuality, cosmetics, child-rearing, leisure) and the existential (the relation to nature, love, death).

They are perfect audience and transmitters, intermediaries for the new intellectual popularization which is not just a popularization of bodies of knowledge, but a popularization of the intellectual *lifestyle* too. An approach which fulfils the functions of distinction since 'it makes available to *almost* everyone the distinctive poses, the distinctive games and other external signs of inner riches previously reserved for intellectuals' (Bourdieu, 1984: 371). In effect the new ethic espoused by the vanguard of the new bourgeoisie and the new petite bourgeoisie may well be in the process of creating the *perfect consumer*.

The new petite bourgeoisie, therefore, identifies with the intellectuals' lifestyle and acts as intermediaries in transmitting the intellectual's ideas to a wider audience. They also act as cultural entrepreneurs in their own right in seeking to legitimate the intellectualization of new areas of expertise such as popular music, fashion, design, holidays, sport, popular culture, etc. which increasingly are subjected to serious analysis. Here it is not a question of the new petite bourgeoisie promoting a particular style, but rather catering for and promoting a general interest in style itself, the nostalgia for past styles, the interest in the latest style, which in an age which itself lacks a distinctive style – what Simmel referred to as the peculiar styleless quality of modern life – have a fascination, and are subjected to constant interpretation and reinterpretation.

While the new petite bourgeoisie has affinities to and similarities with the intellectuals, it also finds a natural ally in the new bourgeoisie. The 'new' in both implies that they are travelling in the same social space, they have abandoned the narrow asceticism of the petite bourgeoisie in favour of promoting more hedonistic and expressive consumption norms. Both groups generate parvenus and an autodidacticism which can be seen in the learning mode they adopt towards culture – to sacred 'high' culture, but also popular culture and also more general consumption style and practices. The generation of a fulfilling, expressive lifestyle mediated through affluent consumption and a stylized presentation of the performing self (Featherstone, 1982), partners and commodities can be seen as central to the worldwide popular TV series about the American sun-belt new rich: *Dallas* and *Dynasty*. Part of their fascination is with the context of a consumer society which asks individuals of all classes, within different targeted markets, to harness their rising expectations to venture along the road to self-improvement and stylization.[2]

Finally, in having pointed to affinities between the intellectuals and new petite bourgeoisie in their role as symbolic producers a number of points can be made about the dynamics of the field of lifestyles and cultural goods which tend to throw the two groups closer together:

1   Time must be introduced into the social space and is one (perhaps the best) dimension for measuring the distance between styles and lifestyles. The introduction of new styles pushes the existing rank order of distinction out of balance. Outmoded styles and lifestyles may generate loyalty from those whose formative years occurred when 'their' style enjoyed endorsement and legitimated popularity. For the avant-garde, of course, the opposite situation pertains. The field, therefore, generates a devaluation of established styles over time. Tastes and styles are subjected to a further market slippage due to the dynamic of popularization within consumer culture. To the avant-garde and cognoscenti popularization is essentially a devaluation. This occurs with a whole range of popular cultural activities and practices, not just in artistic modernism which is the exemplar. Within popular music (itself an unacceptable term to the avant-garde who seek to legitimate their practice by quasi-monopolization and closure practices which impose new hierarchies of expertise and a renaming of the field: 'rock music'), as Bernice Martin (1981) has noted, popularity is double-edged: teenagers abandoned Rod Stewart or the Beatles once they

had been passed down the market to teeny, weeny boppers and kiddypop and up the market to the adults and middle aged.

2   Within strata such as the intellectuals (and here one especially thinks of art and the dynamics of modernism) there is a struggle between the established and the outsiders/newcomers (Bourdieu, 1979; Elias and Scotson, 1965). New-comers adopt subversive strategies, they seek difference, discontinuity and revo-lution or a return to origins to detect the true meaning of a tradition - strategies to create a space for themselves and displace the established. In the postwar era the numbers of individuals entering higher education and intellectual pursuits in the 1960s created a confrontation with the established 'high culture' which can be read in this manner.[3]

3   One of the subversive strategies of outsider intellectuals and the new culture entrepreneurs is to seek to legitimate new fields to stand alongside and under-mine the traditional restricted definitions of taste provided by the established intellectuals and embodied into a high culture. Rock music, fashion, the cin-ema become canonized as the legitimate intellectual areas for critics, interpret-ers and popularizers. The strategy need not be seen as one-way; the imposition of new rules for the game on the part of outsider intellectuals allied with the new petite bourgeoisie cultural intermediaries may also create conditions in which the established intellectuals are forced to enter the new game, to adopt strategies which popularize and interpret texts, styles, practices in the popular media in order to seek to maintain or re-establish some semblance of their former monopoly of cultural authority. Two related points should be noted here: firstly the demand on the part of the cultural intermediaries, with their financial resources and expertise, to present and *realize* their cultural interests (albeit for a mass audience) is flattering to the established intellectuals. It also combats both the accusation of elitism and outmoded taste. Hence 'classical' composers conduct pop operas, conductors of orchestras play jazz, intellectu-als seek to and are drawn into quiz shows, chat shows, etc. via the voracious appetite for 'expertise' and new interpretation of old styles, the discovery of new styles. Secondly, we should note the emergence of the celebrity-intellec-tuals (Vaughan, 1986) who carry out this very process but in doing so under-mine their closed, sacred authority by venturing into popularization. Even without venturing into mass popular programmes (for example, on science and natural history – Magnus Pike and David Bellamy in the UK – where they overplay the stereotype of the mad, arms-flailing scientist) the late-night or minority-channel debates amongst the cultural experts devalue their expertise by putting it on the same level as other programmes. In short their skills as communicators and performers thus have priority over the *sacred* content of their messages.

4   New institutions for recording, preserving, analysing cultural products (for example, an archive or museum of popular culture will appear near to or as an

annexe of 'sacred' art galleries), new journals to popularize television and radio programmes and interpret taste, consumer associations to test products are established. The number of personnel employed in the role of cultural intermediary has also increased. In short, the market in culture is an expanding one which undermines the traditional currency and its authenticators. (See Bourdieu, 1971, on this dynamic in art.)

5 The capacity to circulate information has increased. Styles and works of art are rapidly passed from producers to consumers. Old sacred works of art (such as the *Mona Lisa*) are put on the road to be surveyed by mass audiences in different cultures. Here the globalization process contributes to strengthen the role of the cultural intermediaries who administrate the new global media distribution chains (via satellite, etc.). It also draws in the intellectuals to interpret traditions and styles in a new global circumstance which is one of polyculturalism. This further weakens the (Enlightenment) authority of established Western hierarchies of (high) cultural taste. The intellectuals therefore have to adopt a new role as *interpreters* of the great variety and *wealth* of the different cultural traditions which can be presented to new audiences as meaningful and exotic without venturing into areas of judgement or value-hierarchization (Bauman, 1985).

6 This can be linked to one strategy for outsider intellectuals, which is to appear to attempt to subvert the whole game - postmodernism. With postmodernism, traditional distinctions and hierarchies are collapsed, polyculturalism is acknowledged, which fits in with the global circumstance; kitsch, the popular and difference are celebrated. Their cultural innovation proclaiming a *beyond* is really a *within*, a new move within the intellectual game which takes into account the new circumstances of production of cultural goods, which will itself in turn be greeted as eminently marketable by the cultural intermediaries.

Notes

1 It therefore becomes less important to endorse product quality (although functional information is still required about certain consumer goods) since an experience is associated with and consumed alongside the commodity. While this experience has a psychological dimension in relation to fantasy fulfilment it also has a social dimension which relates to the role goods play as communicators. The more general tendency for not only goods but experiences to become commodified and sold should also be noted – sport spectacles, tourism theme parks, Disney World, etc. – increasingly involve an aesthetically mediated – that is distanced – perception of 'reality'.

2 There is not the space here to provide an analysis of the working class in this respect. Suffice to say that Bourdieu's analysis of the French working class who have to make do with the 'choices of necessity' while ringing true for the lumpen, traditional or unemployed working class does not take into account the privatized, consumer-orientated

fractions, which, of course, have different consumption patterns to the new petite bourgeoise and the bourgeoisie and a very different habitus, but can identify with the latter group via the problematics of autodidacticism: embarrassment and the learning mode.

3   For a discussion of the process of informalization which took place in the 1960s from a perspective which builds upon Elias's theory of the civilizing process, see Cas Wouters (1986)

References

Baudrillard, J. (1975) *The Mirror of Production*, St Louis: Telos Press.

Baudrillard, J. (1981) *For a Critique of the Political Economy of the Sign*, St Louis: Telos Press.

Baudrillard, J. (1983) *Simulations*, New York: Semiotexte.

Bauman, Z. (1985) 'On the Origins of Civilization', *Theory, Culture and Society*, 2 (3).

Benjamin, W. (1982) *Das Passagen-Werk*, 2 vols, edited by R. Tiedermann, Frankfurt: Suhrkamp.

Bourdieu, P. (1971) 'The Intellectual Field and Creative Project', in M. Young (ed.) *Knowledge and Control*, London: Collier-Macmillan.

Bourdieu, P. (1979) 'The Production of Belief: Contribution to an Economy of Symbolic Goods', *Media, Culture and Society*, 2.

Bourdieu, P. (1984) *Distinction: A Social Critique of the Judgement of Taste*, trans. R. Nice, London: Routledge and Kegan Paul.

Douglas, M. and Isherwood, B. (1980) *The World of Goods*, Harmondsworth: Penguin Books.

Elias, N. and Scotson, J. (1965) *The Established and the Outsiders*, London: Cass.

Elwert, G. (1984) 'Markets, Venality and Moral Economy'. Mimeo: Conference on Civilization and Theories of Civilizing Processes: Comparative Perspective, University of Bielfefeld.

Ewen, S. and Ewen, E. (1982) *Channels of Desire*, New York: McGraw-Hill.

Featherstone, M. (1982) 'The Body in Consumer Culture', *Theory, Culture and Society*, 1 (2).

Featherstone, M. (1987) 'Consumer Culture, Symbolic Power and Universalism', in G. Stauth and S. Zaubaida (eds) *Mass Culture, Popular Culture and Lifeworlds in the Middle-East*, Frankfurt: Campus Verlag.

Featherstone, M. and Hepworth, M. (1983) 'The Midlifestyle of George and Lynne', *Theory, Culture and Society*, 1 (3).

Frisby, D. (1985) 'Georg Simmel, First Sociologist of Modernity', *Theory, Culture and Society*, 2 (3).

Jameson, F. (1981) *The Political Unconscious*, Ithaca, NY: Cornell University Press.

Kroker, A. (1985) 'Baudrillard's Marx', *Theory, Culture and Society*, 2 (3).

Leiss, W. (1983) 'The Icons of the Marketplace', *Theory, Culture and Society*, 1 (3).

Martin, B. (1981) *A Sociology of Contemporary Cultural Change*, Oxford: Blackwell Publishers.

Rojek, C. (1985) *Capitalism and Leisure Theory*, London: Tavistock.

Sahlins, M. (1974) *Stone Age Economics*, London: Tavistock.

Sahlins, M. (1976) *Culture and Practical Reason*, Chicago: Chicago University Press.

Sobel, E. (1982) *Lifestyle*, New York: Academic Press.

Vaughan, M. (1986) 'Intellectual Power and the Powerlessness of Intellectuals', *Theory, Culture and Society*, 3 (3).

Weber, M. (1968) *Economy and Society*, 3 vols: Bedminster Press.

Williams, R. (1961) *The Long Revolution*, Harmondsworth: Penguin Books.

Williams, R. H. (1982) *Dream Worlds: Mass Consumption in Late Nineteenth Century France*, Berkeley: California University Press.

Winship, J. (1983) 'Options - For the Way You Want to Live Now, or a Magazine for Superwoman', *Theory, Culture and Society*, 1 (3).

Wouters, C. (1986) 'Formalization and Informalization: Changing Tension Balances in Civilizing Processes', *Theory, Culture and Society*, 3 (2).

9

Object Domains, Ideology and Interests

Daniel Miller

In this chapter Daniel Miller explores the complex ways in which social interests are represented in and through material goods. In a subtle analysis of a variety of different commercial goods, focusing in particular on housing forms, children's sweets, and the conclusions reached by Dick Hebdige on the Italian scooter cycle (see chapter 10), Miller warns against a uniform conception of the representation of interests, arguing instead for a recognition that different material forms embody their own specificities and uniqueness, a fact which plays a significant role in the ways in which those interests are expressed and represented.

Material Ideology

Bourdieu's *Distinction* [see chapter 7, this volume], in common with several other approaches to consumption, such as that of semiotics, is largely based on the mapping of differences between goods on to differences between social groups, which, in the more reductionist instances, are often treated as prior social divisions unaltered by this process of signification. An alternative approach, which will be adopted in this chapter, is to concentrate rather on the possibility of identifying divisions which pertain to particular object domains and which may not be consistent with any cohesive representation of society. In such cases, the significance of the social divisions associated with objects is most evident from the study of the goods themselves.

Within such an approach, objects may not be reducible to the workings of a central hierarchical principle, or be directly related to what are otherwise considered the most important social divisions. In at least one example, the distinction between goods is more closely related to contradictions within one given set of individuals than to differences between social groups. As mass consumption, a particular array of objects may be found to represent and assist in the construction

From *Material Culture and Mass Consumption* (Oxford: Blackwell Publishers, 1987), pp. 158–77. Reprinted by permission of the publishers.

of perspectives relating to control over production or rivalry between consumers, but also to wider issues concerning morality and social ideals. As external forms, however, objects may also be independent of the interpretation of any one particular group, and their consistency as a material presence may belie the actual variety of meanings they invoke.

To set any analysis of the styles of artifacts within the social context of contemporary Britain would appear to require consideration of a wide range of agents and relevant factors. These include forms of production and commerce and the demands of profit, the interests of and constraints on manufacture, design, marketing and advertising, whose role it is to create the images of industrial goods in relation to specified target populations, and the interests of and constraints on the consumer population, who use and in their turn manipulate the meaning of these forms through differential selection, placement, use and association.

As an initial example, one of the most fundamental ranges of objects in contemporary British society will be examined, that is the variety of house styles found in residential developments. Fortunately, major contemporary building styles have been subject to detailed analysis in terms of their social significance. There is the work of Muthesius (1982) on the terraced house, of King (1984) on the bungalow, of Oliver et al. (1981) on the semi-detached house, and of a multitude of authors on the leading architects of the modernist styles, which emerged as the dominant form taken by council properties.

The major distinctions emerge clearly from these accounts. On the one hand (Oliver et al., 1981: 78), there are the attributes held to be exemplified in the half-timbered, suburban, semi-detached, middle-class house: an ambivalent position in relation to town and country, an expression of individualism extended in the modern do-it-yourself tradition, a concern with compromise and a rejection of extremes, all set within statements about tradition and nationalism. Some of these are further extended in the detached bungalow analysed by King (1984), as part of an opposition to elements of modernity and urbanization which constitute the major transformations of the environment over the last two centuries. In stark opposition to the values of suburbia are the images projected by the council estate, which appears on the landscape as a powerful expression of the ideals of communality, of technological supremacy over the slum, and of modernist statements on the possibilities of present and future society, often tied to concepts of socialist planning as formulated by the Bauhaus and promoted by a number of British local councils. Muthesius documents in detail the interests of the professions involved in building streets of terraced properties: the speculators, suppliers of materials, planning controllers and architects. Jackson (1973: 145) shows that these interests were hidden by the demands of style, as in the semi-detached properties which employed a basic frame but added a spurious individuality on the facade in order to make the house more attractive to prospective buyers, or the modernist-style buildings, which proclaimed their scientific nature to the degree that elements of the internal construction which would not normally have been visible were externalized onto the facade to display a commitment to the appropriation of new technologies.

The symbolic function of the different styles present in the built environment which is the context for everyday action suggests that they might fuel an apparently active and sustained debate between suburban individualism and inner-city communalism. The implication, however, that these differences represent actual conflicts in society or the emergence of competing and alternative traditions is quite false. This becomes evident when consideration is given to the processes by which these styles are produced and consumed. The modernist council properties have long been one of the strongest fiefdoms of professionalized architecture, being extremely closely linked to development planning and local political interests, and subject to the intervention of both civic authorities and the state. These links are evident in the modernist style which extends also to the large blocks used for government administration and the offices of major commercial organizations. The development of this style, then, should be credited not only to architects, but to the whole range of bureaucratic and business interests, academics, developers and systems builders, and the various strata of decision makers. When taken together, these amount to a large part of one of the dominant interests of contemporary British society: the professional middle class. As a style, modernism visibly lends itself to this appropriation. It projects an ethos based upon the advances of science, the adaptations to systems technology, and the destruction of tradition, which accords well with those elements of technological dominance discussed by Habermas and his Frankfurt School predecessors in their critiques of modernist rationality and the ideology of technological efficiency.

What is curious is that the members of this same dominant group which may be held responsible for the emergence of modernist architecture, and its appropriation by the state as an authority, do not, by and large, choose family homes of their own built in this style, which is clearly incompatible with their personal desires and images. Instead, their own households are more likely to be typical of the larger examples of the detached, the semi-detached and bungalow, which are extended, in part through emulatory processes, to other sectors of our society with similar aspirations, to such a degree that these styles virtually command modern private development. The consumption of modernist architecture as residential form is almost entirely through state allocation. The consumers of this architecture, the council tenants, have been notoriously restricted in their ability to transform the facade of these dwellings. The suburban dwellers documented by Oliver et al. (1981), who are able to alter the appearance of their homes, tend not to use modernist styles, which, in any case, do not lend themselves to such appropriation.

What this implies is that a group of people who, as consumers, constructed and sustained this image of the individualist tradition also, as producers, constructed the very image of change, community and modernity to which it is opposed. The source of the apparent opposition between these two styles then becomes evident. Clearly, they represent a structural polarity through which the semantic power of the 'semi', as traditional, ambivalent and individualistic, gains its full resonance only by contrast with modernism. To put it the other way around, it is through the state appropriation of the language of change and urbanicity that the construction of an opposite which is perceived as unchanging and suburban becomes sustainable. The representation of the interests of a particular group is greatly clarified if that group is also able to construct an antithetical image (for details of this argument see Miller, 1984). King provides evidence of the power of this structural logic in his example of the attempt by bungalow builders to 'invade' the countryside to such an extent as to threaten the forces which had, until then, controlled the spatial distribution of various styles. The result was legislation curtailing any further extension of this form into 'inappropriate' areas (King, 1984: 184–92).

This suggests that in studies of material representation it should not be assumed that the consumption of a given group will be represented as a coherent and consistent set of forms. The same segment of the population working as producers and consumers here creates quite contrasting images, although analysis reveals them as emanating from a consistent set of interests. This separation allows for further twists in the nature of representation, since the failure of the modernist council estate could be (and was) manipulated by the media to appear as evidence for the failure of the ideals of communality such estates appeared to represent. It was indeed a failure of such imagery, but it must be remembered that the very image of society, and in some cases of socialism, the council estate embodied was that imposed by academics and professionals, and never that of the residents, who have neither a place in the construction of that image, nor the means for its appropriation.

The analysis of the dominant building styles of our society suggests that a set of representations derived from the interests and perspectives of a particular group in society not only denies access to this aspect of culture to alternative perspectives, but at the same time causes these representations to appear to be the image of those who have been excluded. There are comparable cases in other areas of culture studies (e.g. Williams, 1961), where what appears to us as the image of one section of society is actually fabricated by a quite different class. In such cases, the object, in this case building form, may act as a kind of material 'ideology', but the meaning of this term is open to considerable dispute.

The root of the modern use of the term ideology lies with Marx. The theory of value which was the cornerstone of *Capital* [see chapters 1 and 2, this volume] asserts clearly that the very terms and their accepted connotations used in conventional descriptions of the political economy of the time, mystified and suppressed the true nature of, for example, exchange value, as an outcome of the dominance of capitalist interests. Marxism invented itself as the proper understanding of the nature of history seen from the perspective of labour, and should therefore have become the perspective and consciousness of labour. In the later history of Marxism, the re-education of the peasantry and workers, along with the transformation of production processes, has always been a prime instrument in the securing of revolutionary goals (Hinton, 1972). This practice is saved from its apparent idealist overtones by its claimed congruence with inevitable historical transformations whose roots lie elsewhere.

This argument was refined by Lukács's (1971) suggestion that only certain historical transformations could bring the proletariat to realize their true interests and thereby allow them to commence revolutionary action. In view of this, Marxist teaching can be seen as a kind of catalyst. Not surprisingly, this doctrine has become especially important to those who feel as a matter of Marxist science that the proletariat ought by now to have enacted a revolutionary response to the crises which are seen as always present; and their failure to do so is therefore commonly explained as an aspect of false consciousness, which prevented them from recognizing their proper historical duty.

Recent criticisms have been made of several aspects of this approach. Historical analysis suggests that the argument that the perspectives of dominant groups are so pervasive as to permit no alternative or popular forms of representation is untenable (Abercrombie, Hill and Turner, 1980). Marxists influenced by Gramsci's analysis have also asserted the impact of dominant ideas, but, in their view, acquiescence has been always problematic; it has to be worked for through the establishment of hegemony and can never be simply taken for granted. Furthermore, it is commonly met by diverse forms of resistance (e.g. Hall et al., 1976).

One approach to this problem may be derived from the theory of objectification according to which access to culture, as the externalization through which the social group is constructed, is the basis for social development. In so far as society is divided into different interests, of which labour and capital are the prototypical examples, it may well be that some interests have more control than others over the development of representations which accord to their perspective and thus their interests. As Foucault (1981: 92–102) has shown, the power they hold is productive, not merely suppressive, of culture. The concept of perspective implies that understanding is derived from a particular position in the world. If two groups have different perspectives, then, in so far as they are able to create the world, they naturally attempt to do so in accordance with their own perspective, or 'habitus'. Inasmuch, however, as the cultural forms thereby produced become the external environment through which emerge other groups whose interests are not identical, and indeed may be contrary, to their own, we are faced with the situation described in the discussion of building styles above, where the dominated group is forced to attempt to invest itself in the domain of culture represented by the built environment in terms of a set of objects whose initial meanings are antagonistic to its own interests.

What this suggests is that despite valid criticism of their pretensions as theoretical perspectives, the notion of both a dominant ideology and a false consciousness do have at least some place in a theory of ideology. One group may dominate large areas of cultural production, whilst another, through lack of access to cultural form, may be less clear as to the nature of its own interests. The problems arise when these are reified as essential attributes of an entire spectrum of cultural form. The class which is defined in relation to buildings, essentially that of private as against public tenure, is not the same as that defined by another division such as profession. Although dominant as far as building styles and the press are concerned, this same social segment may be less influential in the areas of trade unions and popular culture. Following this expressivist logic, if a group is unable to objectify its interests in certain domains it may attempt to create its own cultural forms in some other field, although some groups without any resources are bereft of both power and prospects in virtually all spheres. One of the results of the quantitative increase in material culture, providing new domains of representation all working in particular ways, is to complicate further the problem of what may be termed material ideology.

The Limits of Objectivism

This complexity is ignored by many of the approaches to ideology which have in common a tendency towards what may be termed 'objectivism', a term which emphasizes a general antipathy towards a subject- or agency-centred perspective. Where the question of ideology is paramount, the concern is with the manner in which control over cultural forms is used to suppress contradictions or conflicts (Larrain, 1982: 15). In recent years, however, analysis based upon a given concept of ideology has been complemented by other projects, some of which also analyse buildings as repressive mechanisms or authoritarian representations (e.g. Foucault, 1977b), but whose overarching concepts such as 'power' or 'discourse' imply a still greater distance between interests and representations, and thereby a greater commitment to objectivism.

Critical objectivist approaches have tended towards a totalizing perspective, by virtue of their style of analysis which tries to rise above culture. When applied to the world of goods, such approaches therefore tend to subsume the whole spectrum of industrial commodities under a variety of notions of cultural dominance. In most cases, this is simply inferred in a phrase about the evils of commodity consumption. There has been, however, a range of attempts to emphasize the place of commodities in exemplifying some general condition of dominance, which goes beyond the more particular implications of ideology. Examples of such studies might include Marcuse's *One Dimensional Man* (1964), the earlier work of Lukács (1971), Barthes' *Mythologies* (1973), Lasch's *The Culture of Narcissism* (1979), and studies by Ewen and Ewen (1982) and Haug (1986) [chapter 20, this volume]. Although these works commonly refer to the bourgeois world as a specific interest group within society, the actual material analysed, such as blue jeans, soap operas or boxing, often represents the cultural forms adopted by the whole spectrum of society.

As an illustration of what appears to be the inevitable result of a strongly objectivist analysis which presupposes its equal relevance for all commodity forms, there follows a brief summary of the trajectory taken by one of the more sustained attempts to focus on the commodity as the central object of research, by the French social theorist Baudrillard. Baudrillard began his studies in the earlier tradition of symbolic analysis, with an attempt to examine the significatory properties of modern mass consumption (e.g. Baudrillard, 1981: 29–87 [chapter 3, this volume]). From the beginning, however, he was concerned to overturn one of the most important of the assumed signifieds, that is utility as defined on the right and use value as defined on the left (Baudrillard, 1975; 1981: 130 –63). His critique of Marx's concept of use value helped to open the way for anthropological studies of the cultural construction of needs (e.g. Sahlins, 1976), and suggested that the ideas of 'true' and 'false' needs sometimes used in critical studies (e.g. Marcuse, 1964) were severely problematic. In time, however, these ideas developed into a much more general critique, in which objects not only did not signify use value but were found not to signify anything outside of themselves. In the modern world, they were held to have become so totally interchangeable that there was no value which could not be reduced to this cycle of exchange. In contrast to Bourdieu, Baudrillard believed that people have become merely the vehicles for expressing the differences between objects. Rather than representing, the sign becomes the front behind which the actual disappearance of the signified goes unnoticed, and we are left merely with the medium itself.

The resulting argument is typical of that current in poststructuralism (e.g. Sturrock, 1979); that is, we think we create objects in history which we use to communicate/signify/represent/constitute, but actually today there is simply a world of objects in terms of which our notions of self and society are created. In short, our identity has become synonymous with patterns of consumption which are determined elsewhere. Taken to its logical conclusion (and the advantage of Baudrillard is that he does just this), this view entails a denial of all signification. Baudrillard's argument becomes highly convoluted, as in his *The Procession of Simulacra* (1983), which postulates the annihilation of all content, but the outcome of this contention is clearly nihilistic, since any opposition to this trend, or any radicalism, would be simply subsumed by this subversion of the sign. Che Guevara, Marx and Baudrillard himself are therefore destined to become merely a set of surfaces to play with as commodities which have lost the possibility of any further depth. In the case of Baudrillard, this appears to have been a self-fulfilling prophecy, and he is mainly quoted today within the avant-garde arts, where he is indeed very much in vogue (Frankovits, 1984).

Baudrillard's biography provides a clear example of the limits of extreme objectivism as an approach to mass commodities (compare Anderson, 1983: 32–55 on poststructuralism in general). In a less sustained form, this is still a much used line of attack. Indeed, some of the ideas developed by Baudrillard in the early 1970s recently resurfaced in a critique of the culture of late capitalism by Jameson (1984; see also Foster ed., 1983). Jameson puts forward the familiar argument that society has lost any possibility of depth or effect, and is reduced to mere pastiche and superficial self-comment. We are left with a play on signs which has no ultimate reference point other than the commodity. The cultural forms of late capitalism have thus become entirely pervasive and able to subsume any attempt at opposition.

The context for this argument is a critique of postmodernism. This term usually refers either specifically to a movement in architecture which emphasizes a return to a popular facade based upon the design of mass commodities (e.g. Jencks, 1977; Venturi, Scott-Brown and Izenours, 1972), or else to the more general movement towards pluralism and primitivism which followed the critique of modernism. In Jameson's critique, it is precisely this populism and celebration of kitsch which is denigrated. This results in a quite misguided emphasis. Jameson seems to object to the fall of modernism and the decline of a critical aesthetic, and fails to learn from the quite genuine failure of modernism itself with regard to its popular acceptability. What he thereby misses is that postmodernism represents simply a new facade or twist to architectural style as ideology discussed earlier. It serves to hide the professional, that is elite, structure through which it continues to operate by assuming the mantle of the popular for itself. It purports to be an appropriation of the public building by the people, when it is actually an appropriation of a particular version of the populist by one dominant group.

Jameson's approach is typical of that conservatism which regards all other periods of history as authentic, but the present as the final inauthentic state. It is a Romantic version of modernism which is viewed as genuinely progressive and critical, rather than merely the means by which capitalism destroyed any tradition which might have opposed its hegemony. A similar point is made by Anderson (1984) with respect to a still more eloquent defence of modernism by Berman (1983). Modernism certainly had its place in the destruction of the *ancien régime*, but it is only one particular form of social change and has recently been most conspicuous in its failures. Furthermore, modernism created a considerable degree of misery and frustration by insisting that only one particular dominant style had the right to be considered the appropriate form for the expression of socialism.

In relation to the object world, all analyses based on strong objectivism tend to produce similar results. They act to reproduce what has been called the mass culture critique (which may come equally from the political right or left; see Hebdige 1981a) [see chapter 10, this volume], in which the objects of mass consumption today are treated as so tainted, superficial and trite that they could not possibly be worth investigating. There may also be the tacit and covert implication that those people who have to live in and through such an object world are equally superficial and deluded, and are unable to comprehend their position. This implies a rejection of any activities undertaken by the mass of the population (always with the exception of direct revolutionary action) as a possible basis for learning about the future development of our society. The argument is that people cannot construct socialism out of kitsch (sometimes with the equally problematic implication that they can out of art). In terms of Bourdieu's *Distinction*, these often esoteric academic critiques tend to align closely with the avant-garde arts as holders of cultural capital.

There are many varied precursors to this modern branch of the mass culture critique, for example, the work of Morris, Adorno and Marcuse (e.g. Horkheimer and Adorno, 1979), as well as several early versions of the notion of false consciousness. A typical contemporary assumption is spelled out by Gortz, who claims that 'working-class demands have turned into consumerist mass demands. An atomized, serialized mass of proletarian demand to be given by society, or more precisely the state, what they are unable to take or produce' (1982: 240). Such a position does not lend itself to anthropological analysis, since one of the objectives of the discipline is to learn something of value from the practices of the people one is studying. The argument that there is a thing called capitalist society which renders its population entirely pathological and dehumanized, with the exception of certain theorists who, although inevitably living their private lives in accordance with the tenets of this delusion, are able in their abstracted social theory to rise above, criticize and provide the only alternative model for society, is somewhat suspicious. The clear lesson of the history of modernism is that the academic left is quite capable of fashioning a central instrument for the reproduction of the interests of the dominant class at precisely the moment when it is making the most strident claims to the contrary.

Recontextualization

It was suggested earlier that the potential for a balance between objectivism and subjectivism in social theory has been demonstrated by a number of recent models (e.g. Bourdieu, 1977; Giddens, 1979). The problem is then how to translate this balance from the more general issues of social theory to the particular context of mass consumption, and certain limitations in the book *Distinction* with regard to just such a translation have been noted. The extreme objectivism which was rejected above is expressed through a variety of images of an overarching class interest or subsuming discourse, usually related either directly to production or to the general term capitalism, which is used to eliminate the possibility of dominated groups as arbiters of cultural form. Clearly, some fields of material culture, such as that of building style, are compatible with such an approach. If other examples can be located which appear to suggest an alternative conclusion, then this raises the more general question as to what appears to determine the suitability of different theoretical emphases to various material forms.

There is a clear tendency for the more anthropological accounts of consumption, such as those of Bourdieu and Douglas [see chapter 6, this volume], to concentrate on consumer interests. Another anthropological study based on an analysis of a particular domain of objects is by James (1979), who analyses the sweets which are purchased by children themselves, as opposed to those bought for them by adults. The suggestion is that these 'kets', as they are called in northeast England, although they are found throughout the country, are generated as an inverse transformation of the acceptable qualities of adult foods. They are, in symbolic terms, systematically 'inedible', for example through the use of strong artificial colours avoided in adult food, the portrayal of 'inedible' animals such as beetles and snakes, 'inedible' objects such as machine tools, bootlaces or flying saucers, and subjects disapproved of by adults, particularly ghoulish representations of corpses, blood, vampires and death. Indeed, since the article was written there has been a considerable increase in the number of skulls and corpses in white chocolate which ooze red when bitten into, and a set of candy bones which form skeletons and are purchased in small plastic coffins for ten pence.

The implications of this example are quite different from those of building forms. Here, a social group which is in a relationship of inferiority to the dominant adult world is able to objectify a perspective which asserts clearly the potential opposition of its interests to that world. This suggests a degree of autonomy in cultural production on behalf of dominated groups. Whilst the sweets are produced by industrial processes for mass consumption, and according to the demands of profit, it would be equally hard to argue that the result is the responsibility of either some evil genius at the production end, or some demonic child at the consumption end. Rather, we have the emergence, over a considerable period of time, of a children's culture. This is not simply the product of a dominant ideology or control over cultural representation, nor a pure act of resistance, but the mutually constituted relationship of two sets of interests and self-images. This example, then, although opposed to the objectivism of the mass culture critique, could not be termed subjectivist in orientation.

Assessed in terms of mass consumption, a balance between subjectivism and objectivism can be seen as a balance between the weight assigned to the two main forces of production and consumption. The relationship between these two forces must be seen as constantly interactive, not largely autonomous as implied by Bourdieu. Despite the enormous efforts made through advertising, design and the media to create markets for given products, well documented by writers such as Galbraith (1969) [see chapter 16, this volume] and Haug (1986), profits are always dependent upon the reciprocal ability of marketing staff to interpret the changes in the way in which goods are used in social relations. Advertising for items such as children's sweets may confirm and help expand the process of objectification of the child's image of the world, but it could hardly be said to have initiated it. If it is the case, as suggested by various studies (Leiss, Kline and Jhally, 1986: 33) [chapter 21, this volume], that advertising, despite all its resources, has little power to affect long-term purchasing trends, then this is an extraordinary finding of contemporary research. Whilst there are other grounds for criticizing the advertising profession, and evidence for a cumulative effect upon social expectations and concepts of lifestyle in general, the failure of any simple correspondence theory should alert us to the complexity of this articulation between production and consumption.

An article by Hebdige (1981b [chapter 10, this volume]; see also 1983) examining the changing meaning of the motor scooter provides an unusually clear picture of the dynamic interaction between the two forces of production and consumption. The development of the object as image is followed through three 'moments': those of design, distribution and consumption. The argument, in very condensed form, is that the motor scooter was developed in Italy as the feminine equivalent of the more macho motorbike. These gender terms stand for a wide range of associated connotations of industrialization and commodification, through which the child-like scooter, with its enclosed machine parts, reproduces in its relationship to the motorbike the basic asymmetry in the status of the sexes. These images are, however, transformed in a manner not intended by the producers (though later picked up and encouraged by them), but which is established rather through articulation with emergent polarities in British youth cultures. The motorbike takes on an association with the rockers which is then contrasted to the motor scooter's place in the construction of the mods' sense of style; the latter representing a more continental 'soft' image against the rocker's 'hard' image. The new grouping is consistent with, but not determined by, the original image created by the industry. Obviously such a brief account omits all the subtlety of the original, which is considerable.

Hebdige's article provides a bridge between those analyses termed 'anthropological', which appear to ignore the direct interests of producers, and those mainly Marxist or commercial, which assume an entirely passive reaction by consumers. It demonstrates both industry's careful reading of the market to try and differentiate material forms on the basis of a prior social division, in this case gender, and also the fact that the transformation of these objects in Britain provided the foundation for the formation of new social groups, to whom consumer style was so integral that they could not be considered prior to those material changes through which they expressed and thereby created themselves (see also Willis, 1978: 11–61). Hebdige's article also permits the reintroduction of elements of intention, and what Giddens (1979: 5) terms 'discursive penetration', to both producer and consumer, whilst retaining a sense of the larger historical forces emanating from social and technological change.

The three examples so far discussed appear to lend themselves to different theoretical perspectives and conclusions, yet they are all drawn from contemporary British consumption patterns. One factor which might be responsible for the differences between them is the properties of the objects themselves as material culture. It is no coincidence that the three sets of objects can be arranged according to a scale of size decreasing from buildings, through motor scooters to sweets. Buildings are enormous artefacts, immovable, extremely expensive, highly visible and highly durable. Their material importance has lead to the extensive involvement of the state in their production and allocation, and their status as major purchases affords opportunities for conspicuous consumption. Such artefacts may tend towards the representation of dominant perspectives, made most explicit in the concept of monuments.

By contrast, there is a vast array of what may be termed 'portable industrial artefacts': the contents of the high streets, supermarkets and shopping catalogues, objects ranging from saucepans, to skirts, to three-piece suites. Compared to buildings, they are cheaper, less durable and therefore more amenable to short-term fashion. They may be less likely to attract the interest of the state or the overall image of industrial production, though many are affected by parallel contrasting images of modernity and tradition. They are, however, the subject of mass marketing and advertising, and the source of much immediate profit. Their very variety suggests that a dynamic interplay between the worlds of business and consumption results in a plethora of relationships and divisions.

Within this area are many objects which are so small, cheap and transient that comparatively little research and investment is likely to be put into the active promotion of new forms determined by production, and the producer may be reduced to a more or less passive respondent to apparent shifts in demand. Obviously, no simple correlation will be found between size of object as a single factor and the nature of the object as representation; but when size is taken as a general gloss for a number of those factors relating to framing, consciousness and triviality . . . it is clear that the nature of material culture itself may be a much underestimated factor in accounting for the patterns and relationships of modern style. The key dimension may not be whether the object is received through the market or some alternative distributive mechanism, but rather its place as a consumption item in constructing social images.

The complexity of the articulation between producer and consumer interests is further illustrated by the case of advertising in women's magazines. In recent years, criticism has been made of the tendency in such magazines to occlude the distinction between text and advert, on the grounds that this is a form of distortion which betrays the trust of the reader in the independent objectivity of editorial content (e.g. Earnshaw, 1984). Clearly, many magazines contain articles merely as a front for the dissemination of the advertisements from which the vast bulk of their income is derived, and in so far as they have editorial comment this reflects those messages (Curren, 1986; Ferguson, 1983). Thus we find advertising features such as articles on holiday resorts and wines in which it is impossible to separate objective opinion from advertising pitch. Does it follow, however, that the readers 'put up' with the bulk of advertising merely because of their interest in the incidental articles?

So evident is the high proportion of adverts in such magazines that the critic who believes that readers are simply fooled by the lack of clear demarcation, must credit them with a remarkably low level of perception. The alternative possibility is that both editors and readers are actually far more interested in the adverts than the rest of the magazine content, and collude in the use of this additional material largely as a legitimation for this practice. The implication that, despite the vast presence of advertising, many people actually want still more of the stuff, is not all that surprising, given the previous argument for the importance of material goods in modern social relations. After all, having possibly spent a great deal of time in unpleasant and unremitting labour, the wage earner may be forgiven for considering the translation of these wages into an act of consumption as being of some importance; obtaining the right object may considerably enhance a reputation or signify membership of a social group, while making the wrong purchase may lead to exclusion and frustration.

This argument is not intended as a defence of the extent of modern advertising, whose interests are clearly derived from company profitability rather than the enhancement of the welfare of the purchaser. It does, however, demonstrate that there is an activity centred on relating goods to larger concerns about the nature of self and society, which may emerge particularly clearly in advertising. Goffman (1979) has demonstrated how central aspects of social inequalities and concepts of self-presentation may be identified through advertisement analysis. The critic who points out that the advertisement appears to have nothing to do with the material and functional nature of the product is merely reproducing the general illusion of vulgar functionalism enshrined in modernism. It is the secondary, often social, but possibly also humorous, moral or sexual connotations which represent the actual value of the 'aestheticized commodity' (Haug, 1986: 72) to the purchaser.

Modern feature writing has started to become more explicit in this collusion. Certain new magazines (and not only free ones) are now distributed explicitly as consumer guides. These magazines have been joined by the colour supplements with long explicit consumer features, and series where potential peers are presented in their own rooms with the full cultural regalia of furnishing, decorations, cars and so forth. Winship's (1983) analysis of *Options*, a recently launched women's magazine, suggests that this close liaison with the modern commodity world plays upon the fantastic in terms of goals which are largely unrealizable in a material sense, but which are clearly lived as fantasy. Fantastic does not, however, mean vicarious, nor does the construction of myth imply mere illusion. The projection of images of possible worlds and cosmologies has always been central to the development of social relations. Neither should this collusion between consumer and producer be seen as always implying an individualistic competitive consumer practice. Adverts may be used as much to help an individual accord with a set of communal values and feelings of social responsibility, as in the explicit advertising of socialism.

The case of advertising complicates another common assumption in critical writing on modern culture, which is that the evaluation of consumption patterns is to be assessed entirely on the basis of hierarchy and the strategies of inclusion or exclusion. Bourdieu is a clear case in point. As a contemporary example, there has been an impressive recent rise of a series of commonly linked 'healthy' practices. These include the wider cultivation and use of wholefoods, organic and pesticide-free crops, homeopathy, acupuncture, biorhythms and other alternative medicines, jogging, aerobics and new sporting activities, all of which appeal to the general desire to prolong individual life. These are linked with a wide diversity of other tastes; for example, many of these consumers tend to be left wing, socially concerned, feminist, well educated, and obviously able to afford these generally expensive alternatives to both the supermarket and the national health service.

If this set of practices is to be condemned as a new form of middle-class oppression through differentiation, then by the same logic many forms of mass culture which have no connection with any 'traditional' working-class regime, but are essentially the results of mechanization and mass production, may become identified with a positive image in the writings of critical sociologists. This tendency emerges in the important body of research entitled popular culture studies (e.g. Bigsby, 1976; Waites et al., 1982), which has developed in Britain as a major instrument of left-wing cultural politics. The perspective taken in most of these studies is closely related to that represented here, in so far as many of them, including the work of Hebdige, are specifically designed to rescue the possibilities of mass materials from the derogatory attitude of the mass culture critique. The subject of such analyses is usually cultural pursuits such as leisure activities and the mass media, rather than material objects *per se*, and mass activities such as shopping have received relatively little critical attention (Mort, 1986 [see chapter 24, this volume]; though see Williamson, 1986a on consumption). Popular culture, however, tends to be ambiguous with respect to mass culture. It often attempts to deal specifically with working-class culture or with sub-cultures which are seen as resistant to the dominant forces in society, so that, as with Bourdieu, though in a somewhat different way, the analysis tends to reduce the material to its place in reproducing or opposing given social positions and conflicts.

The association of the cultural practices of dominated groups with a heroic image is clearly problematic, with writing increasingly assuming that popular means positive (Williamson, 1986b). Modern critical texts often contain contradictory evaluative stances. Should, for example, the hard, macho image of some youth groups be positively evaluated as working class, but negatively evaluated when examined from the perspectives of feminism and racism? Strongly influenced by the pioneering work of Stuart Hall, both the Centre for Contemporary Cultural Studies in Birmingham and, more recently, the Open University have produced an extensive literature on these subjects, in which such contradictions are explicitly addressed.

The problem with reducing the analysis of specific material domains to their place in social differentiation and the reproduction of dominance is not only distributive, in that these may crosscut the given social divisions, but also interpretive, in that this approach may tend to ignore all the other projects in the development of which goods are employed. This is argued by Douglas and Isherwood (1979) [chapter 6, this volume], who stress cognitive demands in the stabilization of categories through their material expression. Objects have always formed an important part of religious and other similar expressive activities. Asceticism, despite its prominence as an ideal, has played a relatively restricted role in most of the world religions, the actual experience of the mass populace having been orientated more towards certain buildings or monuments and the performing of defined, and often elaborate, ritual activities, so that the opposition commonly assumed between materialism and spirituality is based more on an ideal than on a practised dichotomy.

The wider projects encompassed in material appurtenances may be exemplified through an examination of two studies of fashion. Simmel's (1957: 308–15) analysis focuses upon the relationship between individual and social expression not only as posing problems for social theorists, but also as a lived contradiction for the subjects of such theorists. Simmel argues that fashion plays a major part in many people's attempt to live out the contradictory pulls of this perceived duality. Typically, Simmel does not present these as alternatives, a trend towards isolation as opposed to a trend towards integration, but as necessarily contradictory elements of the same actions. Fashion demands an individual conception of a conventional style, thereby allowing the preservation of a private world, a self-conception which is saved from exposure by the expediency of convention. In obeying the dictates of style, it is the social being which takes the responsibility for choice, yet there is simultaneously an arena for personal strategy. Fashion then provides a surface which is partly expressive, but which also in part protects individuals from having to expose their taste in public. This study provides a clear exemplification of the concept of consumption activity as a means of living through necessary contradictions.

In a recent more general study, Wilson (1985: 228–47) argues strongly for the viability of the project of creative recontextualization of these products of mass production against the particular form of the mass culture critique espoused by some feminist perspectives. The approaches discussed above, which tend towards extreme objectivism, are associated by Wilson with a search for authenticity as some natural 'true' female image outside of the context of consumption and patriarchy, leading in practice to a puritanical moralism. Against this, Wilson posits fashion as a mode of modernity providing a more fluid and flexible form of feminist expression which may promote active criticism of the forces it wishes to oppose, but is also creatively self-defining for feminism, employing modes such as fantasy, parody and humour in this project. The reason why Wilson's modernism, unlike either classical architectural modernism or the claimed populism of postmodernism, is acceptable as positive recontextualization, lies in the difference between the practitioners. Within architecture and art, the image of both abstract science and high-street commercial 'pop' is always imposed by professionals, who are in effect interpreting the image of another class. With fashion, on the other hand, there is the possibility of mass participatory modernism, in which images provide groups with a vehicle for appropriating and utilizing cultural forces themselves. Fantasy here may or may not be a mystifying force preventing the housewife from attaining an objective understanding of the forms of her oppression, but like religion before it, it is a world of either idealized morals and possibilities, or else of outrageous alternatives against which everyday life may be both evaluated and understood, and, as such, it has attractions of its own for the consumer.

Conclusion: The Birth of the Consumer

All the examples given above have been used to complicate the problem of analysing the meaning of specific domains. In some cases, the nature of the objects themselves is firmly implicated, as in children's sweets; while in other cases, such as that of motor scooters, the form of the object stays the same and it is their connotations which radically alter. What underlies this complexity is less an appeal for pluralism than a recognition of a pluralism which already confronts us. All the objects discussed are the direct product of commercial concerns and industrial processes. Taken together, they appear to imply that in certain circumstances segments of the population are able to appropriate such industrial objects and utilize them in the creation of their own image. In other cases, people are forced to live in and through objects which are created through the images held of them by a different and dominant section of the population. The possibilities of recontextualization may vary for any given object according to its historical context, or for one particular individual according to his or her changing social environment. Hebdige's work indicates that motor scooters were transformed according to the conceptions of youth groups, but the original distinction promoted in the initial design and marketing of these goods was that of gender. There is nothing in the latter trajectory of the images of these goods which suggests that the ability of the bikes and scooters to reproduce gender asymmetry was in any way deflected by the transformation represented by these later shifts.

Simultaneous with the insistence that recontextualization may be possible has been an avoidance of the other extreme, which is that all such recontextualization is a form of resistance which should be regarded as inevitably positive in its consequence. The term recontextualization implies the concept of text which it-self is open to many readings, and several parallels may be drawn with discussions concerning the death of the author (here perhaps the death of the producer) in the sociology of art (Wolff, 1981: 117–37). Just as modern sociological theory has suggested that the meaning of the text is not simply reducible to the intentions, perspectives or interests of the author, so also the emergence of the object from the world of capitalist or state production does not make it of necessity a direct representation of the interests of capital or the state.

The concept of the death of the author in sociology has, however, rarely led to what might be called the 'birth of the reader'. Most of the writers who have used such ideas (e.g. Barthes, 1977: 142–8; Foucault, 1977a: 113–38) have tended to work within that form of poststructuralism and strong objectivism in which the attack on the author is part of a more general critique of the subject, such that the rejection of the highly individualistic autonomous subject of the liberal tradition develops into a denial of any degree of autonomy or individuality in social rela-tions. The problem with the objectivist foundations for this approach is that the critique of capitalism too often becomes a critique of mass industrial culture *per se*, which has had the effect of stifling any positive advocacy of a potential popular alternative which remains within the context of industrial culture. To that extent, the academic advocates of socialism may be partly responsible for rendering it increasingly unattractive to those sections of society for whom a direct increase in material wealth remains a primary concern.

In contrast to this nihilistic conclusion, the material presented here suggests that the notion of recontextualization permits a more positive reading of the pos-sibilities for the receptor of the commodity. The change from user to consumer is not necessarily the kind of fall from freedom suggested by Raymond Williams (1980), but may lie closer to possibilities which are addressed within other trends within the sociology of art, where interpretation is understood as recreation (Wolff, 1981: 95–116). In the study of mass consumption, this becomes translated from abstract theory into a continual interaction mediated by the specific form of indus-trial commerce through which the material manifestation of this relationship is continually being recreated. Any approach to mass consumption must therefore deal directly with this same mass of objects.

The complexity and contradictions which have been illustrated in contempo-rary material culture may be accounted for in terms of the general characteristics of this media. . . . Objects as diverse concrete forms may be used to create simulta-neous but highly diverse representations whose very materiality acts to prevent them coming into direct conflict at the level of open and conscious dispute. Mate-rial forms therefore lend themselves admirably to the workings of both ideological control and uncontested dissent. This reconfirms the problematic nature of the relationship between culture and society. . . . Rather than postulating some rela-tively consistent phenomenon called 'society' that is distorted or misrepresented by culture, we may dispense with any such assumptions concerning prior subjects, and deal directly with the actual contradictory and complex phenomena of cultural form within which and through which social relations operate. If this argument is not to regress into the objectivist attack on society and the subject, however, it can only be by reaffirming the essentially positive nature of culture as objectification and the possibilities it provides for social development. . . .

References

Abercrombie, N., Hill, S. and Turner, B. (1980) *The Dominant Ideology Thesis*, London: Allen and Unwin.

Anderson, P. (1983) *In the Tracks of Historical Materialism*, London: Verso.

Anderson, P. (1984) 'Modernity and revolution', *New Left Review*, 144, 96–113.

Barthes, R. (1973) *Mythologies*, London: Paladin.

Barthes, R. (1977) 'Death of the author' in *Image-Music-Text*, London: Fontana.

Baudrillard, J. (1975) *The Mirror of Production*, St Louis: Telos Press.

Baudrillard, J. (1981) *For a Critique of the Political Economy of the Sign*, St Louis: Telos Press.

Baudrillard, J. (1983) 'The procession of simulcra', *Art and Text*, 11, 3–46.

Berman, M. (1983) *All That's Solid Melts into Air*, London: Verso.

Bigsby, C. W. E. (ed.) (1976) *Approaches to Popular Culture*, London: Edward Arnold.

Bourdieu, P. (1977) *Outline of a Theory of Practice*, Cambridge: Cambridge University Press.

Curren, J. (1986) 'The impact of advertising on the British mass media' in Collins, R., et al. (eds) *Media, Culture and Society*, London: Sage.

Douglas, M. and Isherwood, B. (1979) *The World of Goods*, Harmondsworth: Penguin Books.

Earnshaw, S. (1984) 'Advertising and the media: the case of women's magazines', *Media, Culture and Society*, 6, 411–21.

Ewen, E. and Ewen, S. (1982) *Channels of Desire*, New York: McGraw-Hill.

Ferguson, M. (1983) *Forever Feminine*, Exeter: Heinemann.

Foster, H. (ed.) (1983) *The Anti-Aesthetic*, Port Townsend: Bay Press.

Foucault, M. (1977a) 'What is an author?' in *Language, Counter-Memory, Practice*, Oxford: Blackwell Publishers.

Foucault, M. (1977b) *Discipline and Punish*, New York: Vintage Books.

Foucault, M. (1981) *The History of Sexuality*, Harmondsworth: Penguin Books.

Frankovits, A. (ed.) (1984) *Seduced and Abandoned: The Baudrillard Scene*, Glebe, Australia: Stonemoss.

Galbraith, J. K. (1969) *The New Industrial State*, Harmondsworth: Penguin Books.

Giddens, A. (1979) *Central Problems in Social Theory*, London: Macmillan.

Goffman, E. (1979) *Gender Advertisements*, London: Macmillan.

Gortz, A. (1982) *Farewell to the Working Class*, London: Pluto Press.

Hall, S., Clarke, J., Jefferson, T. and Roberts, B. (1976) *Resistance Through Rituals*, London: Hutchinson.

Haug, W. F. (1986) *Critique of Commodity Aesthetics*, Cambridge: Polity Press.

Hebdige, D. (1981a) 'Towards a cartography of taste 1935–1962', *Block*, 4, 39–56.

Hebdige, D. (1981b) 'Object as image: the Italian scooter cycle', *Block*, 5, 44–64.

Hebdige, D. (1983) 'Travelling light: one route into material culture' in Miller, D. (ed.) 'Things aint what they used to be', *Royal Anthropological Institute News*, 59, 11–13.

Hinton, W. (1972) *Fanshen*, Harmondsworth: Penguin Books.

Horkheimer, M. and Adorno, T. (1979) *The Dialectic of Enlightenment*, London: Verso.

Jackson, A. (1973) *Semi Detached London*, London: Allen and Unwin.

James, A. (1979) 'Confections, concoctions and conceptions', *Journal of the Anthropological Society of Oxford*, 10, 83–95.

Jameson, F. (1984) 'Postmodernism, the cultural logic of late capitalism', *New Left Review*, 146, 53–92.

Jencks, C. (1977) *The Language of Post-Modern Architecture*, London: Academy.

King, A. (1984) *The Bungalow*, London: Routledge and Kegan Paul.

Larrain, G. (1982) 'On the character of ideology: Marx and the present debate in Britain', *Theory, Culture and Society*, 1.1, 5–22.

Lasch, C. (1979) *The Culture of Narcissism*, New York: Norton.

Leiss, W., Kline, S. and Jhally, S. (1986) *Social Communication in Advertising*, London: Methuen.

Lukács, G. (1971) 'Reification and the consciousness of the proletariat' in *History Class Consciousness*, London: Merlin Press.

Marcuse, H. (1964) *One-Dimensional Man*, London: Routledge and Kegan Paul.

Miller, D. (1984) 'Modernism and suburbia as material ideology' in Miller, D. and Tilley, C. (eds) *Ideology, Power and Prehistory*, Cambridge: Cambridge University Press.

Mort, F. (1986) 'The Texas chain store massacre', *New Socialist*, 35, 15–19.

Muthesius, S. (1982) *The English Terraced House*, New Haven, CN: Yale University Press.

Oliver, P., Davis, I. and Bentley I. (1981) *Dunroamin: The Suburban Semi and Its Enemies*, London: Barrie and Jenkins.

Sahlins, M. (1976) *Culture and Practical Reason*, Chicago: Chicago University Press.

Simmel, G. (1957) 'Fashion', *American Journal of Sociology*, 62, 541–58.

Sturrock, S. (1979) *Structuralism and Since*, Oxford: Oxford University Press.

Venturi, R., Scott-Brown, D. and Izenours, A. (1972) *Learning from Las Vegas*, Cambridge, MA: MIT Press.

Waites, B., Bennett, T. and Martin, G. (eds) (1982) *Popular Culture: Past and Present*, London: Croom Helm.

Williams, R. (1961) *Culture and Society*, Harmondsworth: Penguin Books.

Williams, R. (1980) 'Advertising: the magic system' in *Problems in Materialism and Culture*, London: Verso.

Williamson, J. (1986a) *Consuming Passions*, London: Marion Boyars.

Williamson, J. (1986b) 'The problems of being popular', *New Socialist*, 41, 14–15.

Willis, P. (1978) *Profane Culture*, London: Routledge and Kegan Paul.

Wilson, E. (1985) *Adorned in Dreams*, London: Virago.

Winship, J. (1983) '*Options*. For the way we live now. Or a magazine for superwoman', *Theory, Culture and Society*, 1.3, 44–65.

Wolff, J. (1981) *The Social Production of Art*, London: Macmillan.

10
Object as Image: The Italian Scooter Cycle

Dick Hebdige

Dick Hebdige is at pains to demonstrate that the ways in which commodities move through the various contexts of design, production, distribution, and consumption alter their frame of meaning. Using the example of the shifting meanings and uses of the Italian scooter over the years and in different settings, Hebdige also emphasizes that in order to "read-off" the meanings associated with any consumer commodity we need to pay close attention to the specificities of the place and period in which that commodity is consumed. "Object as Image" is remarkable in many ways, not least because of its meticulous attention to both empirical and anecdotal detail.

One of the difficulties of sociological discourse lies in the fact that, like all discourse, it unfolds in strictly linear fashion whereas, to escape over-simplification and one-sidedness, one needs to be able to recall at every point the whole network of relationships found there. (Pierre Bourdieu, *La Distinction*, 1979)

Nowhere do we encounter 'networks of relationships' more familiar and 'material' yet more elusive and contradictory than those in which material objects themselves are placed and have meaning(s). If linearity is an effect of all discourse then the world of things seems especially resistant to coherent exegesis. And one of the central paradoxes facing those who write about product design must be that the more 'material' the object – the more finite its historical and visual appearance – the more prodigious the things that can be said about it, the more varied the analyses, descriptions and histories that can be brought to bear upon it.

In a sense, each essay in Roland Barthes' *Mythologies* is an equation which depends for its impact on the initial recognition of this perverse formula and Barthes handles the paradox with a relish which alternates between the comic and the macabre ('What I claim is to live to the full the contradiction of my time, which

From *Hiding in the Light* (London: Routledge–Comedia, 1988), pp. 77–115. Reprinted by permission of the author and publishers.

may well make sarcasm the condition of truth.')[1] In 'The New Citroen' Barthes describes how the 'tangible' is made to intersect with the 'ethereal', the 'material' with the 'spiritual', through the convention of the annual motor show where the industry's new product is miraculously 'unveiled' before the public. He refers to the mystique of the object: the dual mystery of its appearance – its magical lines, its 'classical' body and the unanswerable riddle (unanswerable at least for Barthes, the aesthete) of how it came to be made in the first place – to religious myths and archetypes. Here a set of contemporary wonders – the transubstantiation of la-bour power into things, the domestication of the 'miracle' in use – is intimated by Barthes through the manipulation of a single pun: the Citroen DS19 (short for 'Diffusion Special') is pronounced *Déesee* (Goddess) in French.

The essay is, then, a kind of trial by catachresis. It might be argued that this is precisely Barthes' 'method'; that Barthes would have been the first to insist on the validity of constructing an analysis on the strength of a single word – on what it evokes and makes possible for the mythologist. Indeed, for Barthes it is only through 'displacements' of this kind that writing is exalted into Literature:

> For the text is the very outcropping of speech, and it is within speech that speech must be fought, led astray – not by the message of which it is the instrument, but by the play of words of which it is the theatre. . . . The forces of freedom which are in literature depend not on the writer's civil person, nor on his political commitment . . . nor do they even depend on the doctrinal content of his work, but rather on the labour of displacement he brings to bear upon the language.[2]

To be Barthesian, writing is the only practice in which the writer has a 'presence' in which, about which he or she is qualified to speak:

> The paradox is that the raw material, having become in some ways its own end, literature is basically a tautological activity . . . the *écrivain* is one who absorbs the why of the world radically into a how to write.[3]

And for Barthes, that writing which would claim to deal with representation, with myth and the 'doxa' must satisfy certain conditions. It must be self-returning and sensitive to the plurality of verbal signs. It must be capable of 'sarcasm'. A pun is therefore valued in so far as it opens up and undermines the strictures of a 'natural' (i.e. 'bourgeois') speech. So Barthes renders the Citroen back into its 'real' premythical components. He recreates it using purely linguistic materials. Barthes' 'New Citroen' is powered on a figure of speech. None the less the subversive rationale of this replacement is not necessarily visible to everyone who picks up a copy of *Mythologies*. Like the DS revolving slowly on its dais, the argument is simply 'exhibited', turned by a mechanism which remains hidden from the wan-dering eyes of the reader (even, in all likelihood, from the eyes of the reader who appreciates the pun):

> It is obvious that the New Citroen has fallen from the sky inasmuch as it appears at first sight as a superlative object. We must not forget that an object is the best messenger of a world above that of nature: one can easily see in an object a perfection and an absence of origin, a closure and a brilliance – a transformation of life into matter . . . and in a word a silence which belongs to fairy tales.[4]

If writing is regarded as a 'narcissistic activity'[5] as Barthes would have it, then the gross illusion that language is transparent (what has recently been dubbed the 'realist fallacy') is certainly avoided. But the 'new' position has its own attendant fantasies: when language becomes a mirror for the narcissist, other illusions are, of course, possible. We could say that what is 'misrecognized' in (this kind of) language is the depth of perception (the depth of the reflection). To put it another way, what is 'misrecognized' is the illusory 'materiality' of language itself.

For Barthes, the real can only be inserted into language as a 'silence' – 'a silence which belongs to fairy tales'. But instead of the 'silence' of the object, we might like to stress its solidity, its materiality, the simple fact of its 'being there'. And it might be more accurate to say that the problem of representing the material world remains paramount in Barthes and is depicted in that form – i.e. as the relationship of speech to silence – because the problem is itself material: Barthes was, after all, a *litterateur*. Had he been an engineer or a travelling sales rep. who yearned to own a car capable of impressing potential clients ('actualizing (perhaps) . . . the very essence of petit-bourgeois advancement'),[6] then the 'problem' would have been differently conceived and differently presented. And if he had shared the interest in mechanics and 'progress' (mechanics as a metaphor for progress) which no doubt informed the ecstatic response of many of the supplicants who filed past the Citroen stand in 1955 and wanted, themselves, to possess the Goddess, then, no doubt, we too would have been confronted with a different object, a different alienation. For, far from being silent, the number of voices which speak through and for 'dumb things' are legion. The enigma of the object resides for us less in its 'silence', its imagined essence than in the babble which proliferates around it.

Three 'Moments'

> The variability of significance rather than the persistence of qualities should be at the forefront of analysis. (Fran Hannah and Tim Putnam, *Taking Stock in Design History*, *Block 3*)

How then can we hope to provide a comprehensive and unified account of all the multiple values and meanings which accumulate around a single object over time, the different symbolic and instrumental functions it can serve for different groups of users separated by geographical, temporal and cultural location? The problem Bourdieu outlines and Barthes embodies in *Mythologies* has already been acknowledged: there is a tendency amongst those who aspire towards a 'material-ist' conception of design to question the adequacy of the object as the basic unit of analysis and to substitute instead design practice as a more satisfactory point of entry. But this shift in emphasis and the quest for epistemological rigour which motivates it carries its own price. For in the case of design history, there can be no subject without objects. All design practice has as its ultimate ideal and actual destination a tangible result, a real set of objects. Indeed, in design the thing itself is the ideal.

How then is it possible to talk simultaneously about objects and the practices which shape them, determine or delimit their uses, their meanings and their values without losing sight of the larger networks of relationships into which those ob-jects and practices are inserted? The task becomes still more daunting if we ac-knowledge first that there can be no absolute symmetry between the 'moments' of design/production and consumption/use and, further, that advertising stands between these two instances – a separate moment of mediation: marketing, pro-motion, the construction of images and markets, the conditioning of public re-sponse. It is tempting when writing about design either to run these three moments together or to give undue prominence to one of them so that production, media-tion or consumption becomes the 'determining instance' which dictates the meaning of the object in every other context. In either case, the result is more or less the same – a delicately (un)balanced sequence of relationships is reduced to a brutal set of aphorisms, e.g. masses consume what is produced in mass (where produc-tion is regarded as determining); desire is a function of the advertising image (where mediation is regarded as the determining instance); people remain human and 'authentic', untouched by the appeal of either images or objects (where con-sumption or the refusal of consumption is seen as determining). Clearly none of these models is sufficient in itself though each may seem appropriate in particular circumstances when applied to particular objects. It would be preferable to find a way of holding all three instances together so that we can consider the transforma-tions effected on the object as it passes between them. But we are still left with the problem of constructing a language in which that passage can be adequately rep-resented.

If we abandon those solutions to the problem which limit the production of significance to the immanent logic of the object itself – as an internal organization of elements or as a latent essence – if, in other words, we abandon the formalist option and if we also discard the no less abstract language of pure function: 'uses', 'gratifications' and so on, then the criteria for excluding and organizing informa-tion become increasingly uncertain. We are in a field without fences left with an intractable mass: 'cultural significance'.

To construct the 'full significance' of the DS Citroen we would have to do more than merely 'demystify' its reception in the market-place at the point where, as Barthes would have it, the Goddess is 'mediatized' from 'the heaven of Metropolis' and brought within the range of some people's pockets and everybody else's aspirations. If we were to produce a comprehensive analysis we would have to take into account the kinds of significance generated as the object passes through a maze of independent but interlocking frames – drawing back at every point to consider the structures in which each individual frame is housed.

We could trace the passage of the Citroen, then, from its inception/conception through the various preparatory stages: market research, motivational research, design – engineering, styling (division of labour with the design team; relationship of team to management infrastructure), modifications in conception at design stages, constraints of available technological resources on DS design, adaptation of existing Citroen plant to accommodate the new product, production of proto-types and models, production (labour relations, labour processes), exhibitions and launch of new product, press conferences, press releases and handouts, reviews in trade press, advertising campaign (target group), distribution of finished product, retail arrangements, distribution of foreign licences, provision of servicing facili-ties, price, sales figures (consumer profile of target group), formation and compo-sition of the Citroen user groups, etc., etc. Finally, we would have to place the DS alongside other cars available in 1955 in order to assess its difference from equiva-lent products – the extent of its stylistic and technical 'advances' or departures, its potential for 'prestige', etc.

The 'cultural significance' of the Citroen DS19 might be defined as the sum total of all the choices and fixings made at each stage in the passage of the object from conception, production and mediation to mass circulation, sale and use. Nor do the connotations accumulate in an orderly progression from factory to con-sumer. In the production of significance, time is reversible and each stage in the sequence (production–mediation–consumption) can predominate at different times in determining meaning.

For instance, to take a more topical example, the meaning of the Mini Metro is overdetermined by the uncertainty surrounding its production and the reputation for 'bloodymindedness' of the British Leyland workforce – a reputation constructed through press and television coverage of industrial disputes. This in turn enables the Metro to function contradictorily in the news media both as a symbol of 'Brit-ain's hope' and as a symptom of the 'British disease' (where production hold-ups and technical faults are cited as evidence of Britain's decline as an industrial power which, to complete the circle, is 'explained' by reference to the 'problem' of the British workforce). The entire history of British Leyland labour relations is reified in the Mini Metro's public image. The advertising campaign mobilizes that his-tory (the memory of strikes hovers just behind the copy just as in the Hovis televi-sion ads the memory of the Depression looms out of the conjunction of sound and image – the melancholy strains of a northern brass band, the black and white image of 'noble' cloth-capped workers). The Mini Metro advertising campaign overlays two forms of patriotic optimism – that Britain can make it, that British

Leyland can go on making it (and supplying the spares) across the more general-ized faith in the future which purchasing a new car normally implies. The potential purchaser is invited to make all three investments simultaneously – in the future of Britain, in the future of British Leyland, and in his or her own personal future. And newspaper reports make it clear that whenever a dispute threatens production of the Metro, then all three investments are endangered. In this way every reader's stake (as a taxpayer) in the British Leyland Motor Company is realized in the image of the Metro (the car for little people), in the image of the Metro in jeop-ardy and a number of parallel interpellations become possible: 'you' the reader/ taxpayer/consumer/car-owner/Briton/patriot/non-striker. The place of the Mini Metro in the present scheme of things is thus defined by a double address in time – back to British Leyland's past and forward towards a dream of trouble-free con-sumption, a purified economy and a disciplined, docile working class . . .

That, of course, does not exhaust the 'meaning' of the Mini Metro for all time or for all people. It is merely an attempt to isolate some of the themes which already in 1981 have begun to congregate around what we might term the 'offi-cial' fixing of the Mini Metro image – a fixing which brings us back to Barthes and myths and second order signification. And the degree to which that reading of the Metro image proves convincing and even intelligible depends on the reader's prior knowledge of and place within a nexus of political issues and cultural codes which are historically particular and lie quite outside the scope of the list I compiled in relation to the 1955 Citroen. We come back, then, to the original problem: not one object but many objects at different 'moments' (the moments, for instance, of design, assembly and use), at different (real and mythical) times (in different con-junctures in relation to imagined pasts and futures) seen from different perspec-tives and different purposes. How can all these different times, purposes and perspectives be reconciled so that they can be depicted? One solution might be to turn from the object to the text in order to find a more fragmentary mode of representation in which the object can be brought back 'into touch' with that larger, less tangible and less coherent 'network of relationships' which alone can give it order and significance. . . .

The rest of this paper consists of a 'dossier' on one particular genre of com-modities: the Italian motor scooter. The sequence of the narrative corresponds loosely to the progression of the object from design/production through media-tion into use, though there is a good deal of cross-referencing between different 'moments'. Theoretical models have been introduced to frame the material and the narrative has been interrupted at certain points so that sections dealing with larger economic and social developments can be inserted. It is hoped that by pre-senting the 'history of the motor scooter' in this way, some indication of the extent of the variability of its significance can be given as 'echoes' and 'rhymes' build up within the text. The text itself is 'variable' because there is no one 'voice' speaking through it. The same or similar information may be relayed through a different 'voice' in a different section, i.e. its significance may vary according to its placement. In the same way, for the same reason, any 'echoes' which do accumulate cannot be closed off, summed up, reduced to a 'silence' or amplified into a thunderous conclusion.

What follows is premised on the assumption – itself hardly novel – that the facts do not speak for themselves. They are already 'spoken for'. . . .

The scooter as sexed object: early days

The first motor scooters were manufactured in Europe in the years immediately after the First World War (though there are recorded examples of machines called 'scooters' being sold even earlier than this in the United States). From the outset, the word 'scooter' denoted a small, two-wheeled vehicle with a flat, open platform and an engine mounted over the rear wheel. The scooter was further characterized by its low engine capacity: the Autoglider (1921) had a two-and-a-half hp engine. Together these features distinguished the scooter from other categories of two-wheeled transport and marked it off especially from its more powerful, more 'primitive' (i.e. of earlier origin, more 'functional' and 'aggressive') antecedent: the motor cycle. The demarcation between motor cycle and motor scooter coincided with and reproduced the boundary between the masculine and the feminine.

The earliest scooters were designed to meet the imagined needs of the female motor cyclist. For instance, it was possible for women to stand while driving the Scootermotor (1920), thus preserving decorum and the line of their long skirts. (How could the designer have predicted the flattening out of the female silhouette in the women's fashions of the 1920s? How could he have seen the vogue for trousers, breeches and strictly tailored suits which, as Lisa Tickner suggests, were to provide such provocative metaphors for the emancipation of women?)[7] Long before the mass production of Italian Vespas and Lambrettas began to threaten the supremacy of the British motor cycle industry in the 1950s and 1960s, the scooter was interpreted as an alien intrusion – a threat to the masculine culture of the road. It was seen as an absurd omen of a much more general process: the feminization of the public domain (women over thirty were enfranchised in 1918 and one year later the Sex Disqualification Removal Act was passed giving women access to the professions). The machine's lowly status and its vulnerability to ridicule were further reinforced by its visible resemblance to a child's toy scooter. The Zutoped, for instance, was modelled directly on the original toy. Despite modifications in design over the years, the overall conception and placement of the scooter – its projected market, its general shape, its public image – remained fixed in the formula: motor cycles as men; scooters as women and children.

Scooters were permanently wedded to motor cycles in a relation of inferiority and dependence:

The scooter is a device that we refuse to grace with a description of a motor cycle and which, therefore, has no place in this work. (Richard Hough, *A History of the World's Motor Cycles*, Allen and Unwin, 1973)

The gender of machinery

The operative value of the system of naming and classifying commonly called the totemic drives derives from their formal character: they are codes suitable for conveying messages which can be transposed into other codes and for expressing messages received by means of different codes in terms of their own system . . . totemism, or what is referred to as such, corresponds to certain modalities arbitrarily isolated from a formal system, the function of which is to guarantee the controvertibility of ideas between different levels of social reality. (Claude Lévi-Strauss, *The Savage Mind*)

If we start the scooter cycle by following the lead established in 1962 by Lévi-Strauss we do not approach isolated phenomena as the imaginary bearers of substance and meaning but are driven to focus instead on how those phenomena are arranged conceptually and semantically; on what signifying power they possess as elements or functions within codes which are themselves organized into symbolic systems. For the structuralist,

the term totemism covers relations, posed ideologically between two series, one *natural* the other *cultural* . . . [where] the natural series comprises on the one hand *categories*, on the other *particulars*, the cultural series comprises *groups* and *persons*. (Lévi-Strauss, *Totemism*)

In 'primitive' societies, elements from the natural world – flora and fauna – are made to perform these totemic functions. Through the principles of metaphor and metonymy, they guarantee the controvertibility of formal codes into moral, aesthetic and ideological categories. Machines on the other hand, are for Roland Barthes, 'superlative object(s)' invested with a supernatural aura ('We must not forget that an object is the best messenger in a world above that of nature'). They are brought down to earth ('mediatized') by being made to function as differential elements – as markers of identity and difference – organized into meaningful relations through their location within cultural/ideological codes. The first marker of identity is sexual difference. The sexing of the object is the first move in its descent from 'the heaven of *Metropolis*' to its 'proper' place in the existing (i.e. mortal and imperfect) order of things. In advanced industrial societies, the transposition of gender characteristics onto inanimate objects is peculiarly marked. Typically the qualities and status ascribed to the gender of the 'ideal' user are transferred onto the object itself. Paul Willis's study of a Birmingham motor-cycle gang provides an interesting example of this kind of 'anthropomorphization':

The motor cycle boys accepted the motor bike and allowed it to reverberate right through into the world of human concourse. The lack of the helmet allowed long hair to blow freely back into the wind, and this, with the studded and ornamented jackets, and the aggressive style of riding, gave the motorbike boys a fearsome look which amplified the wildness, noise, surprise and intimidation of the motorbike. The motorbikes themselves were modified to accentuate these features. The high cattlehorn handlebars, the chromium-plated mudguards gave the bikes an exaggerated look of fierce power.[8]

This is merely an extreme localized instance of a much more widespread assumption that equates motor cycles with masculinity, machismo, with what Barthes has called the 'bestiary of power'.[9] Once it has been sexed, the machine functions as a material sign of (realizes) imagined gender differences: mechanical sexism.

Advertisements adjudicate in the settling of gender differences. Sometimes the object is split, janus-like, into its two opposed aspects: his and hers. His: functional, scientific, useful. Hers: decorative, aesthetic, gratifying. The distinction corresponds to the separation of design functions: his/engineering; hers/styling. Relations of dominance/subordination inscribed in the sexual division of labour are transposed so that engineering is perceived as superordinate and necessary (masculine/productive), styling as secondary and gratuitous (feminine/non-productive).

These transpositions can colour critical perception of the broadest social and economic developments. For instance, the transition from a production (puritan) economy to a consumer (pagan) one is often condensed in books on economic history into a single image: the image of General Motors' growing ascendency from the mid-1920s onwards over the Ford Motor Company. The success of General Motors is represented as the triumph of sophisticated marketing strategies (obsolescence of desirability – the annual model; massive advertising; 'consumer financing' (the 'trade in', hire purchase); exotic styling) over Ford's more sober approach ('honest' competition in terms of quality and price). Styling is seen as the key to the popularity of General Motors' products: whereas Ford's Model T design remained virtually the same for decades but became relatively cheaper to purchase and produce, GM designers introduced ostentatious styling features to distinguish between markets on status grounds. The development of the modern advertising industry is frequently associated either with the increased spending power of the female consumer or with the growing influence which women are felt to exert over household expenditure. Vance Packard, writing in the late 1950s, quotes the chairman of Allied Stores Corporation to 'illustrate' women's progressive colonization of the consumption sphere:

It is our job to make women unhappy with what they have. We must make them so unhappy that their husbands can find no happiness or peace in their excessive savings.[10]

The 'spread of consumerism' is understood by reference to women's essential gullibility and improvidence. Packard's triple invective against *The Wastemakers* (1960) [see chapter 17, this volume] – the Detroit motor industry; *The Status-Seekers* (1959) – the new breed of consumer; and *The Hidden Persuaders* (1957) – saturation and 'subliminal' advertising – is carried along on a series of analogies between the decline of the 'real' solid/masculine/functional aspects of American industrial design which symbolize the pioneer spirit, and the complementary rise of the 'fantastic'/feminine/decorative elements which symbolize consumer decadence. The fact that terms taken from women's fashion are beginning to infiltrate the language of automobiles is cited as evidence of a more general decline in standards: a car parts dealer from Illinois is quoted as describing a car as a 'woman's fashion item' and Packard claims that in professional design argot, product styling is now referred to as the 'millinery aspect' and designing a new car shell is called 'putting a dress on a model'.[11] The sinister nature of these developments is inferred through the connection between General Motors' success and the investment in styling which is itself indicative of the 'feminization' or 'emasculation' of American society. Throughout the book, indeed throughout much of the critical writing on product design produced in the 1950s, a certain type of car, a certain type of styling, functions totemically to duplicate category distinctions which are collectively predicated on the denial or dismissal of the 'female' and the 'feminine'. Misogynist values are thus relayed mechanically through the medium of objects and attitudes towards objects. The marking out of sexual difference moves along a chain which is constantly slipping: man/woman: work/pleasure: production/consumption: function/form, for example:

> Women have escaped the sphere of production only to be absorbed the more entirely by the sphere of consumption, to be captivated by the immediacy of the commodity world no less than men are transfixed by the immediacy of profit.[12]

This characterization of the 'masculine' and 'feminine' domains and the priorities it encapsulates have been institutionalized in education in the distinction between 'hard' and 'soft' subjects: engineering is installed in universities as a scientific discipline (and seems relatively protected from the cuts?); fashion/fashion history is doubly subordinate – it is only an 'applied art' – and is eminently dispensable.

The patriarchal inflection cuts across the entire field of academic discourse. It is this implicit bias which, at a deep level, orders the Marxian distinction between 'phenomenal forms' and 'real relations'. It is no coincidence that Althusser, in his parody of 'vulgar Marxism', should refer to the economic base as 'His Imperial Majesty':

> When the Time comes, (the superstructures) as his pure phenomena . . . scatter before His Majesty the Economy as he strides along the royal road of the Dialectic.[13]

Hairdrier: motor-cyclists' slang for an Italian scooter.

The 1946 Vespa

Scooter
A machine of less than 250cc engine capacity with body work giving considerable weather protection and having a smart, clean appearance. (J. Simmonds, *Design no. 94*, 1957)

In 1946 and 1947, two new Italian scooters appeared which eclipsed all previous models in terms of sales and served to fix the design concept of the contemporary scooter – the Vespa (Wasp) appeared first and was designed by Corriando D'Ascanio for Piaggio, formerly Piaggio Air, the company which during the war had produced Italy's only heavy bomber, the P108 B. (It was not particularly successful. Mussolini's son, Bruno, was killed piloting an early test flight.)

In 1943, the works at Pontedera were completely destroyed by Allied bombing and a new factory was built with facilities geared towards peace-time production. (Piaggio later diversified into machine tools.) The scooter was originally conceived as a small-scale project which was intended to make maximum usage of available plant, materials and design expertise and to fill a gap in the market, supplying the demand on the part of consumers deprived during the war years of visually attractive, inexpensive luxury goods, for a cheap, stylish form of transport, capable of negotiating Italy's war-damaged roads.

D'Ascanio, who had previously specialized in helicopter design, incorporated aeroplane motifs into the original Vespa. The air-cooled engine and stressed skin framework were commonplace enough in aircraft design but their application to two-wheeled transport was regarded as a major innovation. Equally novel was the idea of mounting the wheels on stub-axles rather than between forks. This made them easier to detach – and thus easier to repair – than motor cycle wheels. D'Ascanio was said to have adapted the idea from the mountings used on aeroplane landing gear though stub-axles were, of course, a standard feature of car design. But the spot-welded, sheet-metal frame represented the most noticeable departure from the conventional idea of the motor cycle. The two-stroke engine was concealed behind removable metal cowlings and the platform frame, which was attached to the central spine, extended upwards almost to the handlebars, providing foot support and protection from the weather. Speed was hardly a consideration: the 98cc engine (subsequently 130cc) had a top speed of only 35 mph but the low fuel consumption (approximately 120mpg) and the ease with which the gear and clutch controls could be mastered, acted as compensatory incentives. (D'Ascanio had substituted handlebar controls for the footpedals favoured by the motor cycle industry.) The two-stroke engine which was mounted over the rear wheel was chosen for its simplicity and, without complicated valve gear or pump lubrication, driving was reduced to a basic set of operations which could be assimilated quickly even by people with no prior motor-cycling experience.

The design, then, made concessions to the rider's comfort, convenience and vanity (the enveloping of machine parts meant that the scooterist was not obliged to wear specialist protective clothing). In addition, the Vespa made a considerable visual impact. It was streamlined and self-consciously 'contemporary'. There was a formal harmony and fluency of line which was completely alien to the rugged functionalism of traditional motor-cycle designs.

The Vespa was launched at the 1946 Turin show and was an immediate commercial success, though reactions in the motor-cycle trade were varied. While the novel styling was on the whole regarded favourably, at least in design circles, attention was drawn to basic engineering faults (the suspension was considered too 'soft' and the sparking was sometimes erratic), and the scooter was criticized on the grounds of general safety (it was unstable at speed, and the eight-inch wheels were considered too small to give adequate road grip, especially in wet or slippery conditions). Piaggio, for their part, argued that these criteria were simply not appropriate: the machine was designed as a small 'gadabout' vehicle suitable for travelling short distances at low speeds. In other words, the Vespa was to be presented to the public not as a poor relation of the motor cycle but as the principal term in a new transport category, as a machine in its own right with its own singular qualities, its own attractions and its own public.

D'Ascanio's Vespa established the pattern for all subsequent scooter designs and its general shape changed little over the years (the headlamp was later moved from the mudguard to the handlebars but this was the only major styling alteration). It combined three innovations – the stub-axles, open frame and enclosed engine – which were reproduced over the next twenty years by manufacturers in France, Germany and Britain so that, by 1966, one journalist could state authoritatively that 'there is hardly a scooter built today which does not incorporate two out of three of these distinctive features'.[14] This fixing of the design concept was made possible through the phenomenal sales (by 1960, 1,000,000 Vespas had been sold, and after a slack period in the late 1960s, the oil crisis led to a market revival and in 1980 Piaggio were reported to be producing 450,000 scooters a year (see *Guardian*, 21 February 1981)). Domination of the market led to domination of the image: the field was secured so effectively that by the mid-1960s the words 'Vespa' and 'scooter' were interchangeable in some European languages. (Traffic signs in Paris still stipulate the times when 'Vespa' can be parked.)

The 1947 Lambretta

In design history the monopoly exerted by the Vespa design over definitions of the scooter has tended to obscure the fact that Piaggio were not the only engineering company in Italy to recognize the emergence of the new 'mood' and market. When the Vespa was entered for the 1946 Milan show it appeared alongside a range of new lightweight motor cycles and mopeds and no fewer than seventeen auxiliary motors for powering pedal-cycles (see Hough, *The History of the World's Motor Cycles*). Moreover, the car industry was just as concerned to make inroads into the revitalized working-class and teenaged markets. By 1953 the Vespa was competing against a peculiarly Continental hybrid: the Isetta three-wheeler, the first of the 'bubble cars'. D'Ascanio was, then, merely the victor in the race to find a metaphor for the *ricostruzione*, to develop a 'popular' commodity capable of translating the more inchoate desire for mobility and change – a desire associated with the re-establishment of parliamentary democracy and given a material boost in the form of Marshall Aid – into a single object, a single image.

In 1947 another scooter appeared which in its basic concept, scale and price bore a close resemblance to the Piaggio prototype – the Lambretta produced by Innocenti of Milan. For almost twenty-five years, until Innocenti's scooter section was bought outright by the Indian government in the early 1970s, the Lambretta range offered the most serious threat to Piaggo's lead in terms of international sales and trade recognition. By 1950 Piaggio and Innocenti had between them opened up a completely new market for cheap motorized transport. Early advertising campaigns were directed at two emergent consumer groups – teenagers and women – neither of which had been considered worthwhile targets for this class of goods before the war. A new machine had been created and inscribed in its design was another new 'invention': the ideal scooterist – young, socially mobile, conscious of his or her appearance. The scooter was defined by one sympathetic journalist as a 'comfortable, nicely designed little vehicle for people who do not care too much about the mechanical side of things'.[15]

As the two companies competed for the same markets, the design of Lambretta and Vespa scooters drew closer together until, by the late 1960s, they were, in styling if not in performance and engineering detail, virtually identical. However, there were marked differences between the Lambretta model A and the D'Ascanio Vespa. Once again, the Lambretta design was a feat of *bricolage*. The material resources – expertise, plant and production processes – of the two component firms (Innocenti SpA which specialized in steel-tube manufacture had amalgamated after the war with the Trussi coach-building concern) were adapted and diverted into scooter production. The model A chassis was based on a double steel-tube structure (similar to the one used on the earlier British Corgi); the front wheel was carried on a fork, the rear wheel on a stub-axle and, as with the Vespa, there was a footboard for the rider. But the Lambretta differed from the Vespa in that it had a larger (125cc) engine and a pillion seat for passengers; on the model A there were footpedal changes for the gears and the clutch, the legshields were shorter and narrower and, most significantly, at least most conspicuously, the engines of the early models were open. Though for safety reasons the gear and clutch controls were subsequently transferred to the handlebars, the Lambretta engine remained fully exposed until 1951 when the C and CL models were introduced. On the C model, the double tube chassis was replaced by a single tube frame and the prospective buyer was confronted with a choice between two different machines: the 'dressed' CL or the 'undressed' C scooter. Demand for the 'dressed' model (which also offered superior weather protection with broader, higher legshields based on the D'Ascanio design) was so great that Innocenti were soon forced to withdraw open Lambrettas from production. Inevitably, the addition of the sleek, protective side panels drew the Lambretta closer to its rival. A pattern of parallel growth emerged: the production of a new model by Innocenti would force a similar design response from Piaggio and vice versa. By 1953 both companies were offering 125 and 150cc models. During the mid- and late 1950s two factors: the demand for sturdier, high performance scooters suitable for long-distance touring and the appearance of powerful German machines – the Heinkel, the Bella, the TWN Contessa – led to adjustments in the engine and wheel sizes of both Vespa and Lambretta models: Piaggio introduced the four-speed GS (*Gran Sport*) and SS (*Super Sport*), Innocenti countered with the Lambretta 175cc TV series.

But throughout, the basic scooter 'silhouette' remained more or less unchanged: the word 'scooter' became synonymous with a streamlined shape and legshields. By the end of the 1950s most of the successful designs for scooters in the popular 125–150cc ranges – the Italian Iso Milano, the French Moby, the German NSU Prima – made clear visual references to the Piaggio original. When British motorcycle manufacturers finally, and with considerable reluctance . . . capitulated to local demand and began producing their own (resolutely unsuccessful) scooters, they tended to turn to Italian models, even, occasionally, to Italian designers (e.g. Vincent Piatti designed a scooter for Cyclemaster in the mid-1950s). The extent to which Continental scooters had penetrated the international motor-cycle market was to lead (for a brief period) to an inversion of the traditional hierarchy. Motor-cycle designers began adopting the 'effeminate' practice of enclosing the machine parts. With the Ariel Leader the engine at last slipped out of sight . . .

The production of consumers

This convergence of form in the design for machines in related categories is not in itself unremarkable. After all, design innovations are meant to set trends. However, the encasement of mechanical parts in metal or plastic 'envelopes' – a development associated historically with the emergence of streamlining – signalled more than just a change in the look of things. It marked a general shift in production processes, in the scale and rate of capital accumulation, in the relationship between commodity production and the market. The drift towards a more systematic 'packaging' of objects, itself linked to the growth of the consultancies, coincided with a much broader development – the rise of giant corporations – the modern conglomerates and multinationals – with the concentration of power and resources into larger and larger units, a movement which in turn had required a fundamental reorganization of social and cultural life: the translation of masses into markets.

The economist Paul Sweezy has outlined some of the changes associated with the development of monopoly capitalism in the postwar period: the automation of the work process; increased specialization and diversification (spreading of risk over a wider product range); expansion of the white-collar sector; control of distribution networks; market sharing between corporations; price fixing (the self-imposed limitation of growth in productive capacity to keep prices pegged at an 'acceptable' level); imperialism (exploitation of Third World resources, domination of Third World market); the displacement of competition from the field of price to the field of sales promotion; increased expenditure on research, design and 'market preparation'. All these developments were motivated by need: 'the profound need of the modern corporation to dominate and control all the conditions and variables which affect its viability'.[16]

It is in this context that the massive expansion of the advertising and marketing industries during the period can be most clearly understood. Given the huge costs involved in producing a new line of goods, if crippling losses were to be avoided, the consumer had to be as carefully primed as the materials used in the manufacturing process. The expedient was, on the face of it, quite simple: the element of risk was to be eliminated through the preparation and control of the market. It was not just the careful monitoring of current market trends that could help to guarantee profits. What was required was a more structured supervision of consumer demands according to the principles of what was later called 'want formation'.[17] In other words, corporate viability was seen to rely increasingly upon the regulation of desire.

It was during this period that design became consolidated as a 'scientific' practice with its own distinctive functions and objectives. From now on, the shape and look of things were to play an important part in aligning two potentially divergent interests: production for profit and consumption for pleasure. The investment on a previously unimagined scale in the visual aspects of design from the 1930s onwards indicated a new set of priorities on the part of manufacturers and marked another stage in a more general (and more gradual) process: the intercession of the image between the consumer and the act of consumption.

These developments were, of course, already well advanced by the time Piaggio's Vespa appeared on the scene. In America there was a thriving, highly organized advertising industry by the mid-1920s and advertising personnel were already formulating policy on the basis of sociological and psychological research (according to Stuart Ewen [see chapter 13, this volume], the work of the early symbolic interactionists which placed the emphasis squarely on the social construction of personal identity was particularly influential).[18] The elaborate cynicism and self-consciously shark-like image of the postwar advertising executive were already fully in evidence by the end of the decade. The following passage appeared in 1930 in *Printer's Ink*, the advertising trade journal:

> Advertising helps to keep the masses dissatisfied with their mode of life, discontented with the ugly things around them. Satisfied customers are not as profitable as discontented ones.[19]

And by 1958 the equivalence between the amounts of money spent on the construction of products and the production of consumers had become so systematized that J. K. Galbraith could present it to his readers as an economic law:

> A broad empirical relationship exists between what is spent on the production of consumer goods and what is spent in synthesizing the desires for that production. The path for an expansion of output must be paved by a suitable expansion in advertising budget.[20]

With the pressure on designers to provide 'product identity' and 'corporate image' a further refinement became possible: a single commodity could be used to promote a range of visually compatible objects produced by different divisions of the same corporation. An Olivetti typewriter or an IBM computer was an advertisement for itself and the company which produced it. The form functioned tautologically: it was a trademark in three dimensions. It 'looked its best' in a 'totally designed environment'.

Developments such as these brought the practical aims of product and graphic design into a close proximity and this tendency to merge design functions became even more pronounced as multidisciplinary approaches – ergonomics and 'management science' – emerged to displace the notion of designer 'intuition' (see *The Practical Idealists*, J. P. A. Blake, Lund Humphries, 1969). By the end of the 1950s the language of contemporary design, peppered with analogies from cybernetics and systems theory, was beginning to reflect the preoccupations with teamwork, integration and total planning which were to provide the dominant themes of the 1960s design boom. The dream of achieving a perfect symmetry between collective desires and corporate designs seemed at last on the point of fruition. An exaggerated formalism took root. The object itself would mediate between the needs of capital and the will of the masses: the consumer would be made over in the image of the object. In an article called 'The Persuasive Image', which appeared in *Design* magazine in 1960, Richard Hamilton wrote:

The media . . . the publicists who not only understand public motivations but who play a large part in directing the public response to imagery . . . should be the designer's closet allies, perhaps more important in the team than researchers or sales managers. Ad man, copy writer and feature editor need to be working together with the designer at the initiation of a programme instead of as a separated group with the task of finding the market for a completed product. The time lag can be used to design a consumer to the product and he can be 'manufactured' during the production span. Then producers should not feel inhibited, need not be disturbed by doubts about the reception their products may have by an audience they do not trust; the consumer can come from the same drawing board.[21]

Mediation

Both Innocenti and Piaggio invested in aggressive advertising campaigns supervised by their own publicity departments. By the early 1950s both companies were publishing their own magazines (in three or four European languages) and had formed their own scooter clubs with massive national, later international, memberships. Through these clubs they organized mass rallies and festivals. They mounted exhibitions, sponsored (sometimes in conjunction with Via Secura, the Italian Road Safety Organization) tours, trials, races, hill climbs, competitions. Against those interests which sought to discredit the scooter's performance, Innocenti and Piaggio set out to display its versatility and range, its resilience, its androgynous qualities ('feminine' and sleek but also able to climb mountains, cross continents . . .).

More than this, by controlling the structures within which the scooter was to be perceived and used, they were attempting to penetrate the realm of the 'popular'. The duty of manufacturers to the market was to extend far beyond the mere maintenance of production standards, the meeting of delivery dates. Now they were to preside over the creation of new forms of social identity, and leisure, a new consumer relation to the 'look of things'. The tests and trials, the spectacles, displays and exhibitions, the social clubs and magazines were part of a more general will – linked, as we have seen, to the expansion of productive forces – to superimpose the image of the factory on the world.

The four sections which follow deal with the public representations of the scooter. Most of the detail is drawn from material put out by Innocenti during the 1950s and 1960s – promotional films, advertisements, copies of *Lambretta Notizario*, etc. This simply reflects the availability of sources – Piaggio's campaigns were no less intensive and incorporated similar themes.

The way in which the material itself has been organized is not entirely arbitrary: the narrative is ordered according to the dictates of an economic principle: the circulation of Image precedes the selling of the Thing. Before looking at what the scooter came to mean in use, it is necessary to consider how it was made to appear before the market. . . .

The dematerialization of the object

The age of the product ended after World War II with industrial design's search to disperse, miniaturize and dematerialize consumer goods. (Ann Ferebee, *A History of Design from the Victorian Era*, 1970)

Innocenti's decision to launch the ('dressed') CL and ('undressed') C Lambrettas simultaneously in 1951 determined once and for all the direction in which consumer preferences were moving in the transport field. It amounted to an unofficial referendum on the issues of styling and taste and the results were unequivocal: the scooter-buying public voted overwhelmingly for convenience, looks, an enclosed engine. The success of the CL merely confirmed the growing trend in product design towards 'sheathing' – defined by one design historian as the encasement of 'complex electronic parts in boxes that are as unobtrusive and easy to operate as possible'.[22]

All these themes were foregrounded in the advertising campaigns and marketing strategies employed by Innocenti and Piaggio. Scooters were presented to the public as clean, 'social appliances'[23] which imposed few constraints on the rider. Design features were cited to reinforce these claims: the panels enclosing scooter engines themselves were easy to remove and the engines were spread out horizontally to facilitate cleaning and the replacement of spares. The stub-axles made it simpler to remove the wheels and by the 1960s most scooters were designed to accommodate a spare. Elegance and comfort were selected as particularly strong selling points: the Lambretta was marketed in Britain as the 'sports car on two wheels' and a variety of accessories – windscreens, panniers, bumpers, clocks, even radios and glove compartments – were available to lend substance to the luxurious image. Innocenti's promotion policies tended to centre directly on the notion of convenience: an international network of service stations manned by trained mechanics was set up to cater for the needs of a new class of scooterists who were presumed to have little interest in even the most routine maintenance (though the stereotype of the 'effeminate', 'impractical' scooterist was resisted by the scooter clubs which encouraged their members to acquire rudimentary mechanical skills, to carry tool boxes, etc.). The concept of 'trouble-free scootering' was taken even further in Spain. At the height of the Continental touring craze in the late 1950s, Innocenti introduced a special mobile rescue unit called the Blue Angels to cope with Lambretta breakdowns and consumer complaints.

All these support structures can be regarded as extensions of the original design project: to produce a new category of machines, a new type of consumer. The provision of a comprehensive after-sales service can be referred back ultimately to the one basic element which distinguished the D'Ascanio Vespa from its competitors – the disappearance of the engine behind a sleek metal cowling. The sheathing of machine parts placed the user in a new relation to the object –

one which was more remote and less physical – a relationship of ease. As such it formed part of what Barthes described in 1957 as the general 'sublimation of the utensil which we also find in the design of contemporary household equipment'[24] – a sublimation effected through the enveloping skin which served to accentuate the boundary between the human and the technical, the aesthetic and the practical, between knowledge and use. The metal skin or clothing added another relay to the circuit linking images to objects. It was another step towards an ideal prospect – the dematerialization of the object; the conversion of consumption into lifestyle.

[An] advertisement[25] . . . incorporates many of the themes explored in the last two sections. A machine, suspended on a circle of glass, is seen through a shop window. The voyeuristic relation is now a familiar one, familiar through the investment made by commerce in the Image, through the reiteration in similar advertisements of the same visual structure. (This is an early example of the genre. It is almost quaint. Almost innocent. The conventions have yet to be refined, obscured.) We look at them looking. We circle round from 'her' to 'him' to 'her', from the 'girl' to the 'boy' to the 'mother' (that, surely, is implied). We have all come by now to recognize the indirect address: desire by proxy. We are all now visionary consumers. Placed through the geometry of looks in a precise relation to the dream machine – a revelation in mechanical parts, we gaze with them from 'outside' at 'her', the object of desire – the scooter/girl poised on their adjacent pedestals. The girl's posture is classical. It is Diana, naked, surprised in the wood: the heel slightly lifted, the mouth slightly open (provocative, ashamed). The model is 'undressed'. But a pane of glass intercedes between 'her' and the boy. Its function is to mediate. This, at least, is made perfectly clear because the cleaning fluid masks it, makes it visible, opaque. The boy's hands, pressed against the glass, mark it as a barrier. Our glance is directed round a circle of glass, through the girl, through the glass, through the boy and his 'mother', through a reflection of a scooter on a circle of glass. All looks are turned at last towards the centre of the image where the engine stands exposed – a still point at the centre of reflection. This is the place where we can all meet – 'her' and 'her' and 'him' and 'her' and you and I – the place where we can come into contact at a distance. A place where we can find contentment (where we can find the 'content' of the 'message'). The transference from 'her' to 'her', from the object–girl to the fetishized object – has taken place. At last – the object that was lost is found. . . .

The mechanism which motivates our gaze is as naked as the machine which motivates the ad. The devices are laid bare: the caption reads: 'A world of dreams is revealed in the shop-window'. A historical transition is arrested in the composition of a single image: the dematerialization of the object, the emergence of what Henri Lefebvre has called the 'Display Myth':

Consuming of displays, displays of consuming, consuming of displays of consuming, consuming of signs, signs of consuming.[26]

Fashion and the feminine

sound: 'The air hostess can become the pilot herself . . . '
image: Air hostess sprints across runway from plane to Lambretta.
sound: '. . . and there's plenty of room on that pillion for a friend!'
image: Man in pilot's uniform leaps on behind her.
(Sequence from *Travel Far, Travel Wide*, promotional film, Innocenti for GB, 1954)

When Innocenti first began exporting Lambrettas to New York in the early 1960s (a time when, according to Vance Packard, the New York *cognoscenti* were turning from Detroit to Europe for their cars seeking that 'Continental, squared-off boxy look')[27] scooters were displayed (and sometimes sold) not in car or motor-cycle showrooms but in exclusive 'ladies' fashion shops. They were thought to be a good thing to dress a window with, regarded less as a means of transport than as chic metal accessories, as jewellery on wheels.

Fashion items appeared regularly in issues of *Lambretta Notizario* (e.g. 'One is all-too-frequently tormented by the sight of badly trousered women on motor scooters [*sic*] . . . Hats? Any hat – provided it is practical and above all else – elegant.') A series of advertisements in the same magazine showed young women seated on scooters in a variety of contexts: the captions ran 'On a Pic-nic', 'Shopping', 'In the Country', 'By the Sea', 'In the Busy City', etc. A reciprocal effect is achieved through the elision scooter/girl: the scooter's versatility is used to advertise the freedom enjoyed by 'modern' young Italian women and vice versa (i.e. look at all the places 'she' can visit, all the things 'she' can do). These two creations – the new Italian woman (an image fixed and disseminated internationally by the postwar Italian film industry through stars like Anna Magnani, Silvano Mangano and Sophia Loren) and the new Italian scooter are run together completely in an article which appeared in the British weekly magazine *Picture Post* entitled 'A New Race of Girls' (5 September 1954). The two inventions – 'untamed, unmanicured, proud, passionate, bitter Italian beauties' – and the 'clean, sporting Vespa scooter' are together alleged to have 'given Italians some sort of "lift" that the creation of the Comet gave the British'. The article is illustrated by a photograph of Gina Lollabrigida on a Vespa.

The scooter is singled out (along with 'beauty competitions and films') as a catalyst in the 'emancipation' of the new Italian woman ('the motor scooter gave her new horizons' . . .) and it is held directly responsible for successive changes in Italian women's fashions since the war:

The pocket handkerchief fashion which swept the women's world in 1949 was devised to keep a pillion girl's hair tidy at speed. The following winter, the headkerchief was developed by the Florentine designer, Emilio Pucci, into a woollen headscarf.

144

Next year, the blown hair problem was solved by the urchin cut. The narrowing of the new look skirt was dictated in order to prevent it getting tangled up with the wheels. The slipper shoe was created for footplate comfort. The turtleneck sweater and the neckerchief were designed against draughts down the neck.[28]

The final sentence reads:

By such means as this was the Italian girl's appearance transformed, and her emancipation consummated.

Tourism and the international context

The entire world becomes a setting for the fulfilment of publicity's promise of the good life. The world smiles at us. It offers itself to us. And because everywhere is imagined as offering itself to us, everywhere is more or less the same. (John Berger, *Ways of Seeing*, 1972)

By 1951 Vespas were being manufactured under licence in Germany, France and Britain. Innocenti had a factory at Serveta in Spain and the motor-cycle company NSU held the licence for Lambrettas in Germany until 1955. As the domestic market reached saturation point (by 1956 there were 600,000 two- and three-wheelers in Italy) Innocenti and Piaggio directed their attention towards Europe and the Third World. (Ironically enough, when Innocenti were forced to sell their scooter operation in 1972 (according to business history sources because of industrial disputes), it was taken over by Scooters India, a state-funded project based in Lucknow which still produces the 'classic' Lambretta models of the 1960s.) By 1977 Vespa were exporting 289,000 scooters a year to 110 countries.

These new horizons were inevitably translated into advertising imagery. During the late1950s Innocenti ran a series of posters entitled 'The Whole World in Lambretta', which showed scooters posed against Buddhist temples or busy London streets. The caption beneath a photograph depicting a Ghanaian scooterist in 'folk costume' invoked the then fashionable notion of youth/style-as-a-universal: 'Wearing a continental suit or a native dress does not change young people's taste for scooters'. It was through strategies such as these that Innocenti and Piaggio could appropriate new markets and convert them into visual capital. One promotion ploy exemplifies the process clearly.

In 1962 Innocenti mounted a 'world wide photographs' competition. Entrants were instructed to submit 'holiday style' snaps of Lambrettas in 'representative' national settings:

For example: a street in Las Vegas with signboards of the famous gambling houses, a picture of a Lambretta amidst the intense traffic of a street of a great metropolis like London, New York, Paris, etc., or against a background of forests, exotic countries, natives in their traditional costumes, wild animals, monuments, and antique vestiges [*sic*] etc. . . . .

Other conditions were stipulated: the Lambrettas should dominate the frame, be 'well centred . . . if possible taken in close-up'. The 'boys and girls' photographed on or directly adjacent to the scooter should be 'young and sports looking' (*sic*). All photographs and negatives were to be retained 'in INNOCENTI files as documentation' and could be used in any future 'advertising exploit considered by INNOCENTI suitable for its purposes'.

The competition rules lay out in a precise, accessible form the criteria which shaped Innocenti advertising policy. The scooter was to be loosely located within a range of connotations – youth, tourism, sport – which were so open-ended that they could be mobilized literally anywhere in the world. In this way it was possible to reconcile the different practical and symbolic functions which the scooter was likely to serve for different national markets. Ultimately, Innocenti ads recognize only one collectivity: the 'international brotherhood' of 'boys and girls': they interpellate the world.

A film produced for Innocenti in 1954 (*Travel Far, Travel Wide*) equates 'freedom' with physical mobility, with the freedom to 'go where you please'. Made against a background of sponsored global marathons and long-distance rallies (one, organized by Innocenti in 1962, went from Trieste to Istanbul), the film was designed to promote the touring potential of the larger 'sporting' scooters. The closing image shows a group of young scooterists approaching a frontier. The voice-over reads:

A frontier. And on the other side a completely different way of life. But whatever country you go to in the world today, you'll find Lambrettas and Lambretta service stations.

This is the paradigm of tourism (everywhere is anywhere, everywhere is different) but here it is especially contradictory. On the one hand, the need for 'national markets' and the impetus to travel demand that national characteristics, 'different ways of life' be accentuated. On the other hand, trouble-free touring (complete with every modern convenience) and the construction of homogenous 'modern' markets require the suppression of national differences and traditional cultures. 'Youth' and 'progress' mediate between these two demands: it is natural for youth to be different, it is the destiny of science to generate change. The scooter serves as the material bridge between different generations, different cultures, different epochs, between contradictory desires. It is a sign of progress. It is for the 'young or young at heart'. It is a passport to the future. Freedom in space becomes freedom in time: 'with a Lambretta you're part of the changing scene'.[29]

The image of the factory

The image of the Innocenti works in Milan appeared as a logo on many of the early Lambretta ads. The image of the factory itself is the final mediation – the moment of production recalled at point of sale. The photograph, taken from an aeroplane, reduces an entire industrial complex to the status of a diagram (the reduction is a display of power in itself). We are left with an abstract 'modern' pattern signifying progress, technology, resources: an echo of the image of the scooter.

The idealization of production and production processes and the related image of the factory-as-microcosm are not of course confined to Innocenti's publicity campaigns. The same motifs can be found in the tradition which led to the development of Italian corporatism under Mussolini and to the 'progressivism' of Giovanni Agnelli, head of Fiat during the period immediately after World War I. They lay behind Adriano Olivetti's attempts to establish 'factory communities' and worker welfare schemes after World War II; they provided the moral and aesthetic basis for Olivetti's concept of 'integrated design'. And the images themselves derived originally from Marinetti, Sant 'Elia and the futurists. . . .

A promotional film called *We Carry On*, made in 1966 soon after Innocenti's death, clearly draws on this native tradition. (The film won first prize in the nonfiction class at Cannes in 1967. The pressure to enter an impressive ('artistic') product must have been intensified after 1961 when Piaggio won the same award.)

. . . The slow aeriel surveillance of the huge Innocenti plant which opens the film suddenly cuts to the production area. The camera work is determinedly 'modern' and avant garde. A scooter is assembled before our eyes. As it moves along the line each stage in its construction is dramatized through the use of expressionist lighting, jump-cuts and skewed camera angles. On the sound-track, harsh *musique concrete* further reinforces the image of inhuman automation and industrial power. The voice-over alternates between the sober recital of statistical facts (. . . 'the production line is one mile long and one-third of a mile wide . . .') and 'poetic' descriptions of technical processes. The style of the latter is 'futurist baroque': 'The factory is a hothouse in which the flowers are pieces of machinery . . . the electro-magnetic test bed is the altar of destruction on which will be sacrificed the body of a Lambretta'. . . . At one point there is a montage sequence which recalls the earlier 'World in Lambretta' series but the rapid juxtaposition of shots – a scooter parked near an oasis, in a city street, on a Mediterranean beach – marks the conjunction of scooter and landscape as 'bizarre'. The contrasts are deliberately violent. (Surrealism in the service of industry: the film seems to have helped determine the stylistic conventions and the 'strangeness' of many present-day (prestige) advertising films. . . .) After an elegiac tribute to Innocenti (the camera circling respectfully round a plinth mounted with a bust of 'our founder') the film ends with another aeriel shot as the camera sweeps across the workers' swimming pool

147

and tennis courts to rest, at last, above the enormous central tower/panopticon. There is a slow final scan along the ranks of completed scooters waiting for dispatch on the factory forecourt . . . 'machines which carry one name and one name only – a name which dominates the whole'. The soundtrack is dominated by the wail of a siren on top of the tower 'calling his [i.e. Innocenti's] people to work. . . . He is gone but we shall carry on. . . .'

The Scooter in Use

The final sections are designed to explore some of the 'cultural meanings' which became attached to the scooter as it was used in Britain.

The reception in Britain

(a) The motorcycle industry

Look, here's a beauty for you. She buys a scooter for a hundred and forty pounds and then she wants to know where the spark comes from. (Motor-cycle dealer, quoted in Jan Stevens, *Scootering*, 1966)

Imports of foreign motorcycles and scooters into Great Britain for the first six months of 1954 – 3,318; for the first six months of 1956 – 21,125. (Figures from J. Symonds, 'Where are the British Scooters', *Design*, no. 94, 1957)

The first Italian scooters appeared in Britain in the early 1950s. Innocenti and Piaggio opted for different distribution strategies. Piaggio granted a manufacturing licence to the Bristol-based Douglas Motorcycle Company in 1951 and, in the same year, P. J. Agg and Son were registered as the Lambretta Concessionaires importing Innocenti's scooters from the Continent. Sales and marketing were also handled differently by the two companies. Innocenti advertising tended to be pitched more directly at the image-conscious youth market and by 1960 the Agg concessionaires had established a nationwide network of over 1,000 service stations and, for the first time in Europe, had secured a market lead for Innocenti over Piaggio.

By the mid-1950s the Italian scooter was beginning to represent a threat to the British motor-cycle industry which until the Second World War had dominated the international market. Demand for the traditionally heavy, high performance machines which British manufacturers produced had been declining steadily since 1945. Within ten years the trend had become pronounced: at the 1955 Earl's Court Motor Cycle Show, three motor-cycles were on display competing against fifty new scooters.

British manufacturers were eventually forced into scooter production, though the transition from heavy, utilitarian vehicles to light, 'visually attractive' ones was never satisfactorily accomplished. (The BSA Dandy, for instance, had narrow legshields and footboard, and there was none of what Stephen Bayley has described as the 'beautiful clothing'[30] of the Vespa or Lambretta.) However, the initial response was one of scorn and dismissal. All the criticisms levelled by the Italian motor-cycle industry in the 1940s were revived. Scooters were defined as 'streamlined' and 'effete'. The original sales line – that this was a form of transport which (even) women could handle – was turned against itself. Scooters were not only physically unsafe, they were morally suspect. They were unmanly. They ran counter to the ethos of hard work, self-sufficiency and amateur mechanics upon which the success of the British motor-cycle industry and the prevailing definitions of masculinity – the 'preferred readings' of manhood – were based.

These objections, formed at least partly in response to commercial pressure, percolated down throughout the motor-cycle producer, retail and user cultures. Motor-cycle shops, many of them owned by former TT veterans, refused to stock the 'gimmicky' new machines, to finance service facilities, or to employ mechanics. The reluctance to legitimate scooters and scooterists lingered on within the motor-cycling fraternity. The scooter remained, for 'committed' motor-cyclists, a sexed (and inferior) object. As recently as 1979 an article appeared in *Motorcycle Sport* which invoked all the old categories and prejudices. The article, entitled 'Is the Scooter making a comeback?' consists of an apparently neutral assessment of scooter performance. The writer endorses only the more powerful machines. The German Maicolette (known in the early 1960s as the 'dustbin' among those British scooterists with Italianate tastes) is praised for 'its beefy two-stroke engine. It could romp along at a confident 70mph holding the road like a motorcycle . . . it went like a rocket.'[31] The author concludes by extracting the 'essence' of 'motor-cycling sport' – its complexity, 'depth', power, its solitary nature – and contrasting these qualities against the 'superficial', 'social' 'fun' of scootering: 'Naturally', the gender of the ideal motor-cyclist is beyond question.

> Motorcycling is a much more complex sport than scootering . . . the enjoyment springs from the pure isolation aboard a fast solo when the rider, for a brief spell, is beyond authority and is in control of his own destiny. Motorcycling is fun of a multi-dimensional variety. Scootering is pleasure of the more superficial sort.[32]

(b) Design

> Somewhere on the lower slopes of clique acceptance was the popular Italian craze which dominated British taste in the later 1950s and which found expression in the vogue for products like motor scooters . . . Olivetti typewriters . . . Espresso coffee machines . . . (Stephen Bayley, *In Good Shape*, 1979)

Those 'superficial' qualities which were interpreted negatively by the motor-cycling industry – the social aspects and the look of the scooter – were regarded as positive assets by those working in the design field, at least by those young enough to appreciate the beauty of a mass-produced but 'well-shaped' machine. The emergent Modern consensus in design which was to become dominant during the 1960s closed more or less unanimously around the Italian scooter and held it up to British industrialists as an example of what a good design should look like. As an everyday artefact invested with some standards of style and utility but which still managed to satisfy all the key criteria – elegance, serviceability, popularity and visual discretion – the scooter fulfilled all the modern ideals.

At least that was the opinion circulated amongst the 'select band of glossy monthly magazines' which, as Banham puts it, decides 'who shall see what' in the design world.[33] Indeed, the first article in the inaugural issue of one of the most influential postwar journals was entirely devoted to the 'Italian look'. Writing in *Design* (January 1949), F. K Henrion compiled a list of tasteful artefacts which 'have together transformed the appearance' of Italian city life. He singled out cars, furniture, ceramics and Gio Ponti coffee machines. But the Vespa scooter – 'a virtual institution' – was especially commended:

> The most important of all new Italian design phenomena is without doubt the Vespa. This miniature motorcycle, streamlined and extremely pleasant to look at, has become an important factor in Italian village and town life.[34]

Henrion drew attention to the scooter's flexibility in use and its capacity for bridging markets:

> You see businessmen with briefcases, commercial travellers with boxes of samples on the vast floorspace. In the evenings, you see young couples ... at the weekends, mother, child and father on picnics. You see these machines parked side by side in front of Ministries and it is surprising how many people afford them at a price equivalent to £80.[35]

Finally, he placed the significance of the Vespa in the context of an overall 'Italian style', as part of the 'second Italian renaissance':

> I seemed to sense a similarity of aesthetic values amongst different products – a similarity which, seen from a distance of many years, might be called the style of the mid 20th century.[36]

Throughout the 1950s and early 1960s Italy tended to epitomize for young, trendsetting British designers everything that was chic and modern and 'acceptable', particularly in automobile and (through magazines like *Domus*) interior design. The cult of the individual designer-as-genius – as a modern Renaissance man blending mathematical skills and artistic flair – seems to have grown up largely round a few Italian names – Ponti, Ghia, Pininfarina, Nizzoli, etc. Sometimes the 'superiority' of the Italian design is 'explained' through its relationship to fine art (e.g. futurism). Ann Ferebee, for instance, compares streamlined Italian products to Boccioni's *Unique Forms of Continuity in Space* and praises 'sheathed' Italian transport for its 'sculptural elegance'.[37] And always the 'refinement . . . and purity . . . of line' – in this case of Pininfarina's 1947 Cisitalia Coupe – is valorized because it sets 'alternative standards against the baroque styles [then] emerging in America'.[38] All these qualities and effects have been attributed at different times to the Italian scooter. It has become installed in the mythology of good Italian taste. It has now become an 'object lesson': it is the only entry for 1946 in Stephen Bayley's *In Good Shape* – it stands in for its time.

A clash, then, between two 'official' versions of the scooter, between two divergent interests. A 'clash of opinion' between, on the one hand, a declining heavy engineering industry with vested interest in preserving the market as it stands, with a fixed conception of both product and market, with material resources geared towards the reproduction of that market, the production of a particular design genre, with a set of established cultural values to mobilize in its defence; on the other, a design industry on the point of boom, with a vested interest in transforming the market, in aestheticizing products, 'educating' consumers, with material resources geared towards the production of a new commodity – Image – with an emergent set of cultural values (a new formation of desire) to articulate and bring to fruition. The Italian origins of the scooter function differently within the two systems. In the first, 'Italianness' defines the scooter as 'foreign competition' and doubles its effeminacy (Italy: the home of 'male narcissism'). In the second, it defines the scooter as 'the look of the future' and doubles its value as a well-designed object (Italy: the home of 'good taste').

The object splits. And is reassembled in use. . . .

The scooter clubs

By the mid-1950s there were British branches of the Lambretta and Vespa user clubs, co-ordinated from separate offices in Central London and sponsored by the Douglas Company and the Agg Concessionaires. Both provided monthly magazines (*Vespa News, Lambretta Leader,* later *Jet Set*). While these organizations were clearly modelled on the lines of the Italian clubs and served a promotional and public relations function, they tended to be less rigidly centralized and local branches, run by amateur enthusiasts, were allowed to organize their own affairs. Moreover, some of the larger branches had their own names – the 'Bromley Innocents', the 'Vagabonds', the 'Mitcham Goons' – their own pennants, badges and colours and, in their informal character, and strong regional affiliations, they bore some resemblance to the prewar cycling clubs. In the 1950s and early 1960s the mass rallies and organized scooter runs were a major attraction for club members. As many as 3,000 scooterists would converge on Brighton and Southend for the national Lambretta Club's annual rally where, at the service marquee, set, according to one enthusiast, amidst 'banners and flags, bunting and a Carnival atmosphere . . . your Lambretta would be repaired and serviced entirely free of charge'.[39] During the evenings there would be barbecues, fancy dress competitions and dances ('this was the day of Rock and Roll . . . Marty Wilde, Tommy Steele, Adam Faith . . .').[40] One of the socially cohesive elements at these events, at least for many of the younger club members, was a shared predilection for Italy and 'Italianate' culture. The clubs organized 'Italy in Britain' weeks to foster the connection. At the Lambretta Concessionaires' headquarters in Wimbledon, an espresso coffee machine dispensed 'free frothy coffee' for club members who brought their machines in to be serviced.[41] One of the records played at the Southend rally dances in the early 1960s was an Italian hit entitled *Lambretta Twist*. . . .

As more scooters came on to the market (by 1963 there were 22 different firms selling scooters in Britain) the emphasis shifted to the competitive events, which tended to be dismissed by the motor-cycling contingent as 'rally-type stuff of an endurance nature'.[42] It seems likely that the British scooter clubs were particularly receptive to the idea of competition because it offered a means of counteracting the stigma (of 'effeminacy' and 'shallowness') which had been attached to the sport in its earlier 'social' phase. Innocenti developed the 200cc Lambretta specifically to meet the demands of the Isle of Man Scooter Rally which, by the late 1950s, had become the most important event of its kind in Europe. Quite apart from the racing and the track events, there were scooter expeditions to the Arctic circle, non-stop runs from London to Milan, ascents of Snowdon on a scooter with a side-car: feats of lone heroism which were intended to display the toughness and stamina of both rider and machine. Some of these gestures had a positively epic quality: one scooterist crossed the English Channel using a Vespa to operate paddles fitted to floats.[43] Club scootering became more muscular, scooter runs longer, trials more arduous. Scooter Tours, an extension of the Lambretta Club of Great Britain, provided couriers to lead 'snakes' of up to forty scooters to Switzerland, Austria and Germany.

As the demand for scooters began to level out (i.e. around 1959) the pressure to win races and break records grew more intense. 'Friendly competition' sometimes gave way to open rivalry and these tensions tended to filter down from the works teams to the ordinary badge-wearing members. The younger, more ardent club supporters began marking out their loyalties in dress. The 'blue boys', for instance, wore sharply cut suits in royal blue – the Lambretta club colour. These rivalries were underscored by the distribution policies of the two firms: dealers were licensed to sell only Vespas or Lambrettas.

None the less, competitiveness never totally dislodged the frame which had been imposed upon the sport at its inception: the 'social aspects' with their attendant connotations of health, open air and cheerful camaraderie. This ideal was reflected in the actual composition of the clubs themselves. Subscriptions were not restricted to a single class or age group (though it seems plausible that there was a bias towards relatively young people (i.e. 16–35) from 'respectable' working-class and lower middle-class backgrounds). Female scooterists figured as prominently as the men, at least on the non-competitive circuit. . . .

Piaggio and Innocenti publicity departments regarded the inclusion of a Vespa or Lambretta in a feature film as a major advertising coup. Film directors were solicited to promote the firms' products. Stars were photographed on set (sometimes in period costume) seated on the latest scooter model.

In the early 1960s two films appeared both of which were, in a sense, made around the Italian scooter (and Cliff Richard): *Wonderful Life* (which featured the Vespa) and *Summer Holiday* (which co-starred the Lambretta). These films articulate precisely the ideal of the 'fun-loving' collective which hovers over the literature, the rallies and the 'socials' of the early scooter clubs, and they recapitulate many of the themes encountered in the scooter ads: 'tourism', 'youth', 'freedom' and 'fashion'. All these categories were brought together in the image of Cliff Richard and a group of 'zany', 'up-to-date' but good-hearted youngsters off on their scooters in search of a Continental coast-line, a holiday romance . . .

The mods

During the mid-1960s Italian scooters became wedded, at least as far as the British press and television were concerned, to the image of the mods (and rockers) – to the image of 'riotous assembly' at the coastal resorts of Southern England. (The marriage has yet to be dissolved: a feature made in 1979 for the television programme *About Anglia* on the Lambretta Preservation Society (a 'respectable' offshoot of the old scooter clubs) began, as a matter of course, with documentary footage of the clashes in 1964 at Margate and Brighton.) The words 'social scootering' had formerly summoned up the image of orderly mass rallies. Now it was suddenly linked to a more sinister collective: an army of youth, ostensibly conformist – barely distinguishable as individuals from each other or the crowd – and yet capable of concerted acts of vandalism. The mods and the scooter clubs, the 'Battle of Brighton', 1964, and the Brighton runs of the 1950s, were connected and yet mutually opposed. They shared the same space like the recto and verso of a piece of paper. After the 'social aspects', the 'anti-social'; after *Summer Holiday*, *My Generation*. . . .

The 'dressed' image

Everyone was trying to look like a photograph, as smooth and flat as a page in a magazine. . . . Everyone wanted to catch the light. (Joan Buck, 'Whatever Happened to the British Model?', *Harpers and Queens*, 1980)

And even here in this Soho, the headquarters of the adult mafia, you could every-where see the signs of the un-silent teenage revolution. The disc shops with those lovely sleeves set in their windows . . . and the kids inside them purchasing guitars or spending fortunes on the songs of the Top Twenty. The shirt-stores and bra-stores with cine-star photos in their windows, selling all the exclusive teenage drag . . . The hair-style salons . . . The cosmetic shops . . . Scooters and bubble-cars driven madly down the roads by kids, who, a few years ago, were pushing toy ones on the pave-ment . . . Life is the best film for sure, if you can see it as a film. (Colin MacInnes, *Absolute Beginners*, 1959)

The first wave of modernist youth emerged in or around London in the late 1950s. Most commentators agree on certain basic themes: that Mod was predominantly working class, male-dominated and centred on an obsessive clothes-consciousness which involved a fascination with American and Continental styles. The endorse-ment of Continental products was particularly marked.

The Dean in Colin MacInnes's *Absolute Beginners* (1959) is a 'typical' (i.e. ideal) early modernist:

College-boy smooth crop hair with burned-in parting, neat white Italian rounded-collar shirt, short Roman jacket very tailored (two little vents, three buttons), no turn-up narrow trousers with seventeen-inch bottoms absolute maximum, pointed toe shoes, and a white mac folded by his side.[44]

His (unnamed) girlfriend is described in similar detail:

Short hem lines, seamless stockings, pointed toe high-heeled stiletto shoes, crepe nylon rattling petticoat, short blazer jacket, hair done up into the elfin style. Face pale-corpse colour with a dash of mauve, plenty of mascara.[45]

But here the absence of precise calibration (no twos or threes or seventeens) pin-points her position within the signifying system of both the novel and the subcul-ture itself. In the same way, though her style is rooted in the Italian connection, derived in all likelihood from the 'new race of [Italian] girls', this isn't stated. The Dean, on the other hand, is defined through a geography of dress. He is English by birth, Italian by choice.

According to sociological and marketing sources, Mod was largely a matter of commodity selection.[46] It was through commodity choices that mods marked them-selves out as mods, using goods as 'weapons of exclusion'[47] to avoid contamina-tion from the other alien worlds of teenaged taste that orbited round their own (the teds, beats and later the rockers).

Mods exploited the expressive potential within commodity choice to its logical conclusion. Their 'furious consumption programme' – clothes, clubs, records, hair styles, petrol and drinamyl pills – has been described as 'a grotesque parody of the aspirations of [their] parents' – the people who lived in the new towns or on the new housing estates, the postwar working and lower middle class . .[48] The mods converted themselves into objects, they 'chose' (in order) to make themselves into mods, attempting to impose systematic control over the narrow domain which was 'theirs', and within which they saw their 'real' selves invested – the domain of leisure and appearance, of dress and posture. The transference of desire ('. . . their parents' . . . aspirations . . .') on to dress is familiar enough. Here the process is auto-erotic: the self, 'its self', becomes the fetish.

When the Italian scooter was first chosen by the mods as an identity-marker (around 1958–9 according to eye-witness accounts),[49] it was lifted into a larger unity of taste – an image made up out of sartorial and musical preferences – which in turn was used to signal to others 'in the know' a refinement, a distance from the rest – a certain way of seeing the world. Value was conferred upon the scooter by the simple act of selection. The transformation in the value of the object had to be publicly marked:

> There was a correct way of riding. You stuck your feet out at an angle of forty-five degrees and the guy on the pillion seat held his hands behind his back and leant back.[50]

Sometimes the object was physically transformed. According to Richard Barnes,[51] Eddie Grimstead, who owned two scooter shops in London during the mid-1960s, specialized in customizing scooters for the mods. The machines were resprayed (Lambretta later adopted some of Grimstead's colour schemes) and fitted with accessories: foxtails, pennants, mascots, chromium, horns, extra lights and mirrors, whip aeriels, fur trim and leopard-skin seats. Such features extended the original design concept organically.

Although the scooter imposed no constraints on the rider's dress (this, after all, was what had originally made the scooter 'suit-able' for the fashion-conscious mods), a style became fixed around the vehicle – a uniform of olive green (parka) anoraks, Levi jeans and Hush Puppies. Sometimes French berets were worn to stress the affiliation with the Continent and to further distinguish the 'scooter boys' from the rockers whose own ensemble of leather jackets, flying boots and cowboy hats signalled an alternative defection to America, an immersion in the myth of the frontier.

The innovative drive within Mod, the compulsion to create ever newer, more distinctive looks was eventually to lead to another customizing trend, one which, once again, seems to contradict the logic of the scooter's appeal. As the banks of lights and lamps began to multiply, a reaction set in amongst the hard core of stylists – scooters were stripped: side-panels, front mudguards, sometimes even the footboards, were removed and the remaining body-work painted in muted colours with a matt finish.[52] These were the last, irreverent transformations. By this time Mod had surfaced as a set of newspaper photographs and Bank Holiday headlines. Fixed in the public gaze, Mod turned, finally, against itself. After baroque, minimalism: the image of the scooter was deconstructed, the object 're-materialized'. . . .

The aestheticization of everyday life

It'll be a great day when cutlery and furniture swing like the Supremes. (Michael Wolff writing in the *SIA Journal* in 1964)

However, Mod's significance (and influence) stretched beyond the confines of the subcultural milieu. It was largely through Mod that the demand for more 'sophisticated' and autonomous forms of teenaged leisure was expressed. And provision expanded accordingly. By 1964 the coffee bars, 'shirt-stores and bra-stores' of McInnes's *Absolute Beginners* had given way to discotheques and boutiques. There was now a Mod television programme, *Ready, Steady, Go* (opening sequence: mod on scooter at traffic lights/voice-over: 'The Weekend Starts Here . . .'). There was a thriving teenaged fashion industry in London based on Carnaby Street and the Kings Road. There were bowling alleys, Wimpey bars and no less than six weekly magazines aimed directly at the Mod market.[53]

At a more general level, Mod highlighted the emergence of a new consumer sensibility, what Raymond Williams might call a 'structure of feeling', a more discriminating 'consumer awareness'. It was, after all, during the late 1950s when the term 'modernist' first came into use, that the Coldstream Council recommended the expansion of Design within Higher Education, that design departments were set up in all the major art schools, that royal patronage was formally extended to industrial design,[54] that the Design Centre itself opened in the Haymarket, that magazines like *Which?*, *Shopper's Guide*, *Home* and *House Beautiful* began publicizing the ideas of 'consumer satisfaction' and 'tasteful home improvement'. And it was in 1964 when 'mod' became a household word, that Terence Conran opened the first of the Habitat shops which, according to the advertising copy, offered 'a pre-selected shopping programme . . . instant good taste . . . for switched on people'.[55]

The mirrors and the chromium of the 'classic' mod scooter reflected not only the group aspirations of the mods but a whole historical Imaginary, the Imaginary of affluence. The perfection of surfaces within Mod was part of the general 'aestheticization' of everyday life achieved through the intervention of the Image, through conflation of the 'public' and the 'personal', consumption and display. In 1966 a Wolverhampton reader of a national newspaper felt concerned enough about a 'decorating problem' to write in for advice:

I have painted walls and woodwork white and covered the floors with Olive Sullivan's 'Bachelor's Button' carpet in burn oak orange chestnut. Upholstery is Donald Bros unbleached linen mullein cloth. Curtains are orange and in a bright Sekers fabric and I am relying upon pictures, books, cushions, and rug for bright contrasting accessories. I have found a winner in London Transport's poster 'Greenwich Observatory' which I think looks marvellous against the white walls.[56]

The separation of a room into its parts (each part labelled, placed), of a suit into its 'features' (each button counted, sited on a map) spring from a common impulse. Together they delineate a new disposition. The reader's room in Wolverhampton, the Dean's suit in Soho – both are 'integrated structures', designed environments. Both are held in high regard. They are subjected to the same anxious and discriminating gaze. This is the other side of affluence: a rapacious specularity: the coming of the greedy I.

Brighton revisited revisited

In 1964, on the stately promenades of the South Coast resorts, a battle was enacted between two groups of adolescents representing different tastes and tendencies. The seaside riots provided a spectacle which was circulated as an 'event' first as news, later, as history (the film *Quadrophrenia* appeared in 1979). The spectacle 'just happened' to be watched (' . . . one local paper carried a photo of a man amongst a crowd of boys swinging deck-chairs holding his child above his head to get a better view . . . ').[57]

According to a survey conducted at Margate, the mods tended to come from London, were from lower-middle- or upper-working-class backgrounds and worked in skilled or semi-skilled trades or in the service industries. (Jimmy, the hero of *Quadrophrenia*, is presented as a typical mod, he works as an office boy in a London advertising agency . . .) The rockers were more likely to do manual jobs and live locally.[58] Most observers agree that mods far out-numbered rockers at the coast. When interviewed the mods used the words 'dirty' and 'ignorant' to typify the rockers. The rockers referred to the mods as 'pansy' and 'soft'.

The clash of opinion between design and motor-cycling interests, between service and productive sectors, 'adaptive' and 'outmoded' elements was translated at Brighton and Margate into images of actual violence. The rocker/mod polarity cannot be so neatly transposed into options on gender (i.e. sexist/counter-sexist). Apparently, girls occupied equally subordinate positions within both subcultures. Male modes sometimes referred to girlfriends as 'pillion fodder'. There were proportionately fewer girls driving scooters within the mod subculture than outside it in the 'respectable' scootering community. . . .

The Mod revival

> The scooter fanatic of eighteen to twenty really doesn't know what it is about. It isn't impossible to be Mod [in 1980], they just go about it in the wrong way – a scooter was a means of transport. You didn't worship it . . . (Original mod quoted in *Observer Magazine*, 1979)

The disappearance of the service stations, the recession, small Japanese motorcycles, compulsory crash helmets, Scooters India, the Red Brigades: the original 'network of relations' transformed over time, and with it the object, and the relationship of the user to the object.

The scooter is 'undressed': all new mods are amateur mechanics. The shortage of spare parts and the collapse of the support structure of garages mean that more scooterists are forced to service and maintain their own machines.

Conclusion

In the *Evening Standard* (24 February 1977), a Mr Derek Taylor, 'one of these new fashionable middle-management people', explained why he sold his car and bought a secondhand Lambretta:

> With road tax at £4 a year, insurance £12 and petrol consumption of nearly 100mpg, I reckon I'm on to a good buy . . . I still enjoy my comfort and want to get to work in a clean and presentable condition.

Fashion remains a significant vector but its significance resides in the fact that it can be turned in on itself: '. . . fashion takes a back-seat, but the practical scooter man has all the accessories on board (monsoon-proof mac . . . RAF long-johns) . . .' (ibid.). The fashion paradigm is punctured by the practical scooter-man. The fuel crisis and the plight of the *Evening Standard*'s 'neglected' middle-management have redefined the object (some traces linger . . . 'comfort . . . clean . . . presentable'). The image falls off into irony.

On the London Underground, a new poster advertising the 'more attractive angular look'[59] of the 'New Line' P range Vespa takes its place alongside the Suzuki and the Mini Metro ads, the images of Adonis briefs, the Elliot twins and the 'This Insults Women' stickers. The Italian scooter cycle kicks off again in slightly higher gear . . .

Notes

Thanks to Mary Rose Young and thanks especially to Mike Karslake, president of the Lambretta Preservation Society for giving me so much of his time and allowing me access to his collection of Innocenti publicity material and memorabilia.

1 Roland Barthes, 'Introduction', *Mythologies*, Paladin, 1972a.
2 Roland Barthes, quoted in J. Bird, *The Politics of Representation, Block 2*, 1980.
3 Roland Barthes, 'Écrivains et écrivaints', in *Critical Eassays*, Evanston, 1972b.
4 Roland Barthes, 'The New Citroen' in Barthes 1972a.
5 Roland Barthes, 1972b.
6 Roland Barthes, 'The New Citroen': 'The bodywork, the lines of union are touched, the upholstery palpated, the seats tried, the doors caressed, the cushions fondled . . . The object here is totally prostituted, appropriated: originating from the heaven of *Metropolis*, the Goddess is in a quarter of an hour mediatized, actualizing through this exorcism the very essence of petit-bourgeois advancement.'
7 Lisa Tickner, 'Women and trousers: unisex clothing and sex-role changes in the 20th century', in *Leisure in the 20th Century*, Design Council, 1977.
8 Paul Willis, 'The Motor Cycle Within the Subcultural Group', in *Working Papers in Cultural Studies* (2), University of Birmingham.
9 Roland Barthes, 1972a.
10 Vance Packard, *The Wastemakers*, Penguin Books, 1963.
11 Ibid.
12 T. Adorno, quoted in Colin McCabe, *Godard: Sound Image: Politics*, BFI Publications, 1981.
13 Louis Althusser, 'Contradiction and Overdetermination', in *For Marx*, Allen Lane, 1969.
14 Jan Stevens, *Scootering*, Penguin Books, 1966.
15 Mike Karslake, *Jet-Set*, Lambretta Club of Great Britain, December 1974.
16 Paul Sweezy, 'On the theory of monopoly capitalism', in *Modern Capitalism and Other Essays*, Monthly Review Press, 1972. Peter Donaldson in *Economis of the Real World*, Penguin Books, 1973, provides some interesting statistics here on the transfer of capital in Britain during the postwar period. He writes: 'Spending on take-overs during the first half of the 1960s was something like ten times that of the 1950s . . . One estimate is that the mergers movement during the 1960s must have involved the transfer of some 20 per cent of the total net assets of manufacturing industry.'
17 See Vance Packard, *The Status-Seekers*, Penguin Books, 1961.
18 Stuart Ewen, 'Advertising as Social Production', in *Communication and Class Struggle*, Vol. I, IG/IMMRC, 1979. Also Stuart Ewen, *Captains of Consciousness: Advertising and the Social Roots of Consumer Culture*, McGraw-Hill, 1977.
19 Quoted ibid.
20 J. K. Galbraith, *The Affluent Society*, Penguin Books, 1970 [see chapter 16, this volume].
21 Richard Hamilton in S. Bayley (ed.), *In Good Shape: Style in Industrial Products 1900–1960*, Design Council, 1979.
22 Ann Ferebee, *A History of Design from the Victorian Era*, Van Nos. Reinhold, 1970.
23 'This exquisite social appliance', a line from *We Carry On*, Innocenti promotional film, 1966.
24 Barthes, 1972a.

25 The advertisiment considered by Hebdige shows a scooter photographed from inside a shop suspended on a circular glass pedestal. Beside it a young, slim and attractive shop assistant, standing on a stool, is cleaning the large, plate-glass display window. Outside the shop, looking in through the window, a boy and a woman, whom we take to be his mother, gaze inwards in awe at the scooter. [Ed.]

26 Henri Lefebvre, *Everyday Life in the Modern World*, Allen Lane, 1971.

27 Vance Packard, 1963.

28 'A New Race of Girls', in *Picture Post*, 5 September 1954.

29 From an advertising jingle used on Australian radio during 1962, sung by the Bee Gees.

30 Bayley, 1979.

31 Jack Woods, 'Is the Scooter Making a Comeback?', in *Motorcycle Sport*, November 1979.

32 Ibid.

33 Reyner Banham, 'Mediated Environments', in C. W. E. Bigsby (ed.) *Superculture: American Popular Culture and Europe*, Paul Elek, 1975.

34 F. K. Henrion, 'Italian Journey', in *Design*, January 1949.

35 Ibid.

36 Ibid.

37 Ann Ferebee, 1970.

38 John Heskett, *Industrial Design*, Thames and Hudson, 1980.

39 Mike Karslake, 1974.

40 Ibid.

41 Personal recollection from Mike Karslake.

42 Woods, 1979.

43 From an article entitled 'The Buzzing Wasp' which appeared in *On Two Wheels*. The series also carried an article on Lambrettas called 'The Alternative Society'.

44 Colin MacInnes, *Absolute Beginners*, re-issued by Allison and Busby, 1980.

45 Ibid.

46 See R. Barnes, *Mods!*, Eel Pie Publishing, 1980, on which I drew heavily for the mod sections in this paper; *Generation X* (eds.) Hamblett and Deverson, Tandem, 1964; Gary Herman, *The Who*, Studio Vista, 1971; S. Cohen, *Folk Devils and Moral Panics*, Paladin, 1972. See also D. Hebdige, 'The Style of the Mods', in S. Hall et al. (eds) *Resistance Through Rituals*, Hutchinson, 1976.

47 Baron Isherwood and Mary Douglas, *The World of Goods: Towards an Anthropology of Consumption*, Penguin Books, 1980 [see chapter 6, this volume]. Isherwood and Douglas define consumption as a 'ritual process whose primary function is to make sense of the inchoate flux of events . . . rituals are conventions that set up visible public definitions'. This idea compares interestingly with Bourdieu's definition of 'taste': 'Tastes (i.e. manifested preferences) are the practical affirmation of an inevitable difference . . . asserted purely negatively by the refusal of other tastes' [see chapter 7, this volume].

48 Barnes, 1980.

49 Ibid.

50 Ibid.

51   Ibid.
52   Ibid.
53   Cohen, 1972.
54   See Fiona McCarthy, *A History of British Design 1830–1970*, Allen & Unwin, 1979. The Design Centre opened in 1956. The Duke of Edinburgh's Prize for Elegant Design was first awarded three years later. Also *The Practical Idealists*, J. and A. Blake, Lund Humphries, 1969.
55   Ibid.
56   Quoted in F. McCarthy, *All Things Bright and Beautiful*, Allen & Unwin, 1972.
57   Cohen, 1972.
58   P. Barker and A. Little, in T. Raison (ed.) *Youth in New Society*, Hart-Davis, 1966. Peter Wilmot gives some interesting figures on patterns of scooter and motor-cycle ownership in a working-class London borough in *Adolescent Boys in East London*, Penguin Books, 1966, during the mod–rocker period. Of his sample of 264 boys, one in ten over sixteen owned scooters (mainly in the sixteen- to seventeen-year range) whilst only one in twenty over sixteen owned a motor bike (they tended to be slightly older, seventeen to eighteen).
59   This comes from a review of the new Vespa P200 in 'The Buzzing Wasp', in *On Two Wheels*.

11

"Making Do": Uses and Tactics

Michel de Certeau

The English translation of Michel de Certeau's *The Practice of Everyday Life* in 1984 coincided with cultural studies' early explorations of alternative conceptualizations of consumption to those rather pessimistic accounts which tended to reduce the practice of consumption to the status of a mere passive assimilation of "dominant ideology." In particular, de Certeau's emphasis on the oppositional and resistive aspects embodied in the practices of everyday life, and especially in consumption, found strong resonances in the work of writers such as Stuart Hall, David Morley, and others who had begun to identify spaces within media texts from which the preferred or dominant readings of those texts could be evaded or even subverted. In this celebrated chapter, de Certeau outlines his subsequently much-used distinction between "strategies," which are adopted by the strong and the powerful, and "tactics," which become the art of the weak and subordinate and are used to undermine and subvert the strictures of an established order.

In spite of the measures taken to repress or conceal it, *la perruque*[1] (or its equivalent) is infiltrating itself everywhere and becoming more and more common. It is only one case amongst all the practices which introduce *artistic* tricks and competitions of *accomplices* into a system that reproduces and partitions through work or leisure. Sly as a fox and twice as quick: there are countless ways of "making do."

From this point of view, the dividing line no longer falls between work and leisure. These two areas of activity flow together. They repeat and reinforce each other. Cultural techniques that camouflage economic reproduction with fictions of surprise ("the event"), of truth ("information"), or communication ("promotion") spread through the workplace. Reciprocally, cultural production offers an area of expansion for rational operations that permit work to be managed by dividing it (analysis), tabulating it (synthesis), and aggregating it (generalization). A distinction is required other than the one that distributes behaviors according to their *place* (of work or leisure) and qualifies them thus by the fact that they are located on one or another square of the social checkerboard – in the office, in the workshop, or at the movies. There are differences of another type.

They refer to the *modalities* of action, to the *formalities* of practices. They traverse the frontiers dividing time, place, and type of action into one part assigned for work and another for leisure. For example, *la perruque* grafts itself onto the system of the industrial assembly line (its counterpoint, in the same place), as a variant of the activity which, outside the factory (in another place), takes the form of *bricolage*.

Although they remain dependent upon the possibilities offered by circumstances, these transverse *tactics* do not obey the law of the place, for they are not defined or identified by it. In this respect, they are not any more localizable than the technocratic (and scriptural) *strategies* that seek to create places in conformity with abstract models. But what distinguishes them at the same time concerns the *types of operations* and the role of spaces: strategies are able to produce, tabulate, and impose these spaces, when those operations take place, whereas tactics can only use, manipulate, and divert these spaces.

We must therefore specify the operational schemas. Just as in literature one differentiates "styles" or ways of writing, one can distinguish "ways of operating" – ways of walking, reading, producing, speaking, etc. These styles of action intervene in a field which regulates them at a first level (for example, at the level of the factory system), but they introduce into it a way of turning it to their advantage that obeys other rules and constitutes something like a second level interwoven into the first (for instance, *la perruque*). These "ways of operating" are similar to "instructions for use," and they create a certain play in the machine through a stratification of different and interfering kinds of functioning. Thus a North African living in Paris or Roubaix (France) insinuates *into* the system imposed on him by the construction of a low-income housing development or of the French language the ways of "dwelling" (in a house or a language) peculiar to his native Kabylia. He superimposes them and, by that combination, creates for himself a space in which he can find *ways of using* the constraining order of the first place or of the language. Without leaving the place where he has no choice but to live and which lays down its law for him, he establishes within it a degree of *plurality* and creativity. By an art of being in between, he draws unexpected results from his situation.

These modes of use – or rather re-use – multiply with the extension of acculturation phenomena, that is, with the displacements that substitute manners or "methods" of transisting towards an identification of a person by the place in which he lives or works. That does not prevent them from corresponding to a very ancient art of "making do." I give them the name of uses, even though the word most often designates stereotyped procedures accepted and reproduced by a group, its "ways and customs." The problem lies in the ambiguity of the word, since it is precisely a matter of recognizing these "uses" "actions" (in the military sense of the word) that have their own formality and inventiveness and that discreetly organize their multiform labor of consumption.

Use, or Consumption

In the wake of the many remarkable works that have analyzed "cultural products," the system of their production,[2] the geography of their distribution, and the situation of consumers in that geography,[3] it seems possible to consider these products no longer merely as data on the basis of which statistical tabulations of their circulation can be drawn up or the economic functioning of their diffusion understood, but also as parts of the repertory with which users carry out operations of their own. Henceforth, these facts are no longer the data of our calculations, but rather the lexicon of users' practices. Thus, once the images broadcast by television and the time spent in front of the TV set have been analyzed, it remains to be asked what the consumer *makes* of these images and during these hours. The thousands of people who buy a health magazine, the customers in a supermarket, the practitioners of urban space, the consumers of newspaper stories and legends – what do they make of what they "absorb," receive, and pay for? What do they do with it?

The enigma of the consumer-sphinx. His products are scattered in the graphs of televised, urbanistic, and commercial production. They are all the less visible because the networks framing them are becoming more and more tightly woven, flexible, and totalitarian. They are thus protean in form, blending in with their surroundings, and liable to disappear into the colonizing organizations whose products leave no room where the consumers can mark their activity. The child still scrawls and daubs on his schoolbooks; even if he is punished for this crime, he has made a space for himself and signs his existence as an author on it. The television viewer can not write anything on the screen of his set. He has been dislodged from the product; he plays no role in its apperition. He loses his author's rights and becomes, or so it seems, a pure receiver, the mirror of a multiform and narcissistic actor. Pushed to the limit, he would be the image of appliances that no longer need him in order to produce themselves, the reproduction of a "celibate machine."[4]

In reality, a rationalized, expansionist, centralized, spectacular, and clamorous production is confronted by an entirely different kind of production, called "consumption" and characterized by its ruses, its fragmentation (the result of circumstances), its poaching, its clandestine nature, its tireless but quiet activity, in short by its quasi-invisibility, since it shows itself not in its own products (where would it place them?) but in an art of using those imposed on it.

The cautious yet fundamental inversions brought about by consumption in other societies have long been studies. Thus the spectacular victory of Spanish colonization over the indigenous Indian cultures was diverted from its intended aims by the use made of it; even when they were subjected, indeed even when they accepted their subjection, the Indians often used the laws, practices, and representations that were imposed on them by force or by fascination to ends other than those of their conquerors; they made something else out of them; they subverted them from within – not by rejecting them or by transforming them (though that occurred as well), but by many different ways of using them in the service of rules, customs, or convictions foreign to the colonization which they could not escape.[5] They metaphorized the dominant order: they made it function in another register. They remained Other within the system which they assimilated and which assimilated them externally. They diverted it without leaving it. Procedures of consumption maintained their difference in the very space that the occupier was organizing.

Is this an extreme example? No, even if the resistance of the Indians was founded on a memory tattooed by oppression, a past inscribed on their body.[6] To a lesser degree, the same process can be found in the use made in "popular" milieux of the cultures diffused by the "elites" that produce language. The imposed knowledge and symbolisms become objects manipulated by practitioners who have not produced them. The language produced by a certain social category has the power to extend its conquests into vast areas surrounding it, "deserts" where nothing equally articulated seems to exist, but in doing so it is caught in the trap of its assimilation by a jungle of procedures rendered invisible to the conqueror by the very victories it seems to have won. However spectacular it may be, his privilege is likely to be only apparent if it merely serves as a framework for the stubborn, guileful, everyday practices that make use of it. What is called "popularization" or "degradation" of a culture is from this point of view a partial and caricatural aspect of the revenge that utilizing tactics take on the power that dominates production. In any case, the consumer cannot be identified or qualified by the newspapers or commercial products he assimilates: between the person (who uses them) and these products (indexes of the "order" which is imposed on him), there is a gap of varying proportions opened by the uses he makes of them.

Use must thus be analyzed in itself. There is no lack of models, especially insofar as language is concerned; language is indeed the privatized terrain on which to discern the formal rules proper to such practices. Gilbert Ryle, borrowing Saussure's distinction between "*langue*" (a system) and "*parole*" (an act), compared the former to a fund of *capital* and the latter to the *operations* it makes possible: on the one hand, a stock of materials, on the other, transactions and uses.[7] In the case of consumption, one could almost say that production furnishes the capital and that users, like renters, acquire the right to operate on and with this fund without owning it. But the comparison is valid only for the relation between the knowledge of a language and "speech acts." From this alone can be derived a series of questions and categories which have permitted us, especially since Bar-Hillel's work, to open up within the study of language (*semiosis* or *semiotics*) a particular area (called *pragmatics*) devoted to use, notably to *indexical expressions*, that is, "words and sentences of which the reference cannot be determined without knowledge of the context of use."[8]

We shall return later to these inquiries which have illuminated a whole region of everyday practices (the use of language); at this point, it suffices to note that these are based on a problematics of enunciation.[9] By situating the act in relation to its circumstances, "contexts of use" draw attention to the traits that specify the act of speaking (or practice of language) and are its effects. Enunciation furnishes a model of these characteristics, but they can also be discovered in the relation that other practices (walking, residing, etc.) entertain with nonlinguistic systems. Enunciation presupposes: (1) a *realization* of the linguistic system through a speech act that actualizes some of its potential (language is real only in the act of speaking); (2) an *appropriation* of language by the speaker who uses it; (3) the postulation of an interlocutor (real or fictive) and thus the constitution of a relational *contract* or allocution (one who speaks to someone); (4) the establishment of a *present* through the act of the "I" who speaks, and conjointly, since "the present is properly the source of time," the organization of a temporality (the present creates a before and after) and the existence of a "now" which is the presence to the world.[10]

These elements (realizing, appropriating, being inscribed in relations, being situated in time) make of enunciation, and secondarily of use, a nexus of circumstances, a nexus adherent to the "context" from which it can be distinguished only by abstraction. Indissociable from the present *instant*, from particular circumstances and from a *faire* (a peculiar way of doing things, of producing language and of modifying the dynamics of a relation), the speech act is at the same time a use *of* language and an operation performed *on* it. We can attempt to apply this model to many nonlinguistic operations by taking as our hypothesis that all these uses concern consumption.

We must, however, clarify the nature of these operations from another angle, not on the basis of the relation they entertain with a system or an order, but insofar as *power relationships* define the networks in which they are inscribed and delimit the circumstances from which they can profit. In order to do so, we must pass from a linguistic frame of reference to a polemological one. We are concerned with battles or games between the strong and the weak, and with the "actions" which remain possible for the latter.

Strategies and Tactics

Unrecognized producers, poets of their own affairs, trailblazers in the jungles of functionalist rationality, consumers produce something resembling the "*lignes d'erre*" described by Deligny.[11] They trace "indeterminate trajectories"[12] that are apparently meaningless, since they do not cohere with the constructed, written, and prefabricated space through which they move. They are sentences that remain unpredictable within the space ordered by the organizing techniques of systems. Although they use their *material*, the *vocabularies* of established languages (those of television, newspapers, the supermarket, or city planning), although they remain within the framework of prescribed *syntaxes* (the temporal modes of schedules, paradigmatic organizations of places, etc.), these "traverses" remain heterogeneous to the systems they infiltrate and which they sketch out their guileful ruses of *different* interests and desires. They circulate, come and go, overflow and drift over an imposed terrain, like the snowy waves of the sea slipping in among the rocks and defiles of an established order.

Statistics can tell us virtually nothing about the currents in this sea theoretically governed by the institutional frameworks that it in fact gradually erodes and displaces. Indeed, it is less a matter of a liquid circulating in the interstices of a solid than of different *movements* making use of the elements of the terrain. Statistical study is satisfied with classifying, calculating, and tabulating these elements – "lexical" units, advertising words, television images, manufactured products, constructed places, etc. – and they do it with categories and taxonomies that conform to those of industrial or administrative production. Hence such study can grasp only the material used by consumer practices – a material which is obviously that imposed on everyone by production – and not the *formality* proper to those practices, their surreptitious and guileful "movement," that is, the very activity of "making do." The strength of these computations lies in their ability to divide, but this analytical ability eliminates the possibility of representing the tactical trajectories which, according to their own criteria, select fragments taken from the vast ensembles of production in order to compose new stories with them.

What is counted is *what* is used, not the *ways* of using. Paradoxically, the latter become invisible in the universe of codification and generalized transparency. Only the effects (the quantity and locus of the consumed products) of these waves that flow in everywhere remain perceptible. They circulate without being seen, discernible only through the objects that they move about and erode. The practices of consumption are the ghosts of the society that carries their name. Like the "spirits" of former times, they constitute the multiform and occult postulate of productive activity.

In order to give an account of these practices, I have resorted to the category of "trajectory."[13] It was intended to suggest a temporal movement through space, that is, the unity of diachronic *succession* of points through which it passes, and not the *figure* that these points form on the space that is supposed to be synchronic or achronic. Indeed, this "representation" is insufficient, precisely because a trajectory is drawn, and time and movement are thus reduced to a line that can be seized as a whole by the eye and read in a single movement, as one projects onto a map the path taken by someone walking through a city. However useful this "flattening out" may be, it transforms the *temporal* articulation of places into a *spatial* sequence of points. A graph takes the place of an operation. A reversible sign (one that can be read in both directions, once it is projected onto a map) is substituted for a practice indissociable from particular moments and "opportunities," and thus irreversible (one cannot go backward in time, or have another chance at missed opportunities). It is thus a mark *in place of* acts, a relic in place of performances: it is only their remainder, the sign of their erasure. Such a projection postulates that it is impossible to take the one (the mark) for the other (operations articulated on occasions). This is a *quid pro quo* typical of the reductions which a functionalist administration of space must make in order to be effective.

A distinction between *strategies* and *tactics* appears to provide a more adequate initial schema. I call a *strategy* the calculation (or manipulation) of power relationships that becomes possible as soon as a subject with will and power (a business, an army, a city, a scientific institution) can be isolated. It postulates a *place* that can be delimited as its *own* and serve as a base from which relation with an *exteriority* composed of targets or threats (customers or competitors, enemies, the country surrounding the city, objectives and objects of research, etc.) can be managed. As in management, every "strategic" rationalization seeks first of all to distinguish its "own" place, that is, the place of its own power and will, from an "environment." A Cartesian attitude, if you wish: it is an effort to delimit one's own place in a world bewitched by the invisible powers of the Other. It is also the typical attitude of modern science, politics, and military strategy.

The establishment of a break between the place appropriated and one's own and its Other is accompanied by important effects, some of which we must immediately note:

1 The "proper" is *a triumph of place over time*. It allows one to capitalize acquired advantages, to prepare future expansions, and thus to give oneself a certain independence with respect to the variability of circumstances. It is a mastery of time through the foundation of an autonomous place.

2 It is also a mastery of places through sight. The division of space makes possible a *panoptic practice* proceeding from a place whence the eye can transform foreign forces into objects that can be observed and measured, and thus control and "include" them within its scope of vision.[14] To be able to see (far into the distance) is also to be able to predict, to run ahead of time by reading a space.

3 It would be legitimate to define the *power of knowledge* by this ability to transform the uncertainties of history into readable spaces. But it would be more correct to recognize in these "strategies" a specific type of knowledge, one sustained and determined by the power to provide oneself with one's own place. Thus military or scientific strategies have always been inaugurated through the constitution of their "own" areas (autonomous cities, "neutral" or "independent" institutions, laboratories pursuing "disinterested" research, etc.). In other words, *a certain power is the precondition of this knowledge* and not merely its effect or attribute. It makes this knowledge possible and at the same time determines its characteristics. It produces itself in and through this knowledge.

By contrast with a strategy (whose successive shapes introduce a certain play into this formal schema and whose link with a particular historical configuration of rationality should also be clarified), a *tactic* is a calculated action determined by the absence of a proper locus. No delimitation of an exteriority, then, provides it with the condition necessary for autonomy. The space of a tactic is the space of the Other. Thus it must play on and with a terrain imposed on it and organized by the law of a foreign power. It does not have the means to *keep to itself*, at a distance, in a position of withdrawal, foresight, and self-collection: it is a maneuver "within the enemy's field of vision," as von Bülow puts it,[15] and within enemy territory. It does not, therefore, have the options of planning general strategy and viewing the adversary as a whole within a distinct, visible, and objectifiable space. It operates within isolated actions, blow by blow. It takes advantage of "opportunities" and depends on them, being without any base where it could stockpile its winnings, build up its own position, and plan raids. What it wins it cannot keep. This nowhere gives a tactic mobility, to be sure, but a mobility that must accept the chance offerings of the moment, and seize on the wing the possibilities that offer themselves at any given moment. It must vigilantly make use of the cracks that particular conjunctions open in the surveillance of the proprietary powers. It poaches them. It creates surprises in them. It can be where it is least expected. It is a guileful ruse.

In short, a tactic is an art of the weak. Clausewitz noted this fact in discussing deception in his treatise *On War*. The more a power grows, the less it can allow itself to mobilize part of its means in the service of deception: it is dangerous to deploy large forces for the sake of appearances; this sort of "demonstration" is generally useless and "the gravity of bitter necessity makes direct action so urgent that it leaves no room for this sort of game." One deploys his forces, one does not take chances with feints. Power is bound by its very visibility. In contrast, trickery is possible for the weak, and often it is his only possibility, as a "last resort": "The weaker the forces at the disposition of the strategist, the more the strategist will be able to use deception."[16] I translate: the more the strategy is transformed into tactics.

Clausewitz also compares trickery to wit: "just as wit involves a certain legerdemain relative to ideas and concepts, trickery is a sort of legerdemain relative to acts."[17] This indicates the mode in which a tactic, which is indeed a form of legerdemain, takes an order by surprise. The art of "pulling tricks" involves a sense of the opportunities afforded by a particular occasion. Through procedures that Freud makes explicit with reference to wit,[18] a tactic bodily juxtaposes diverse elements in order suddenly to produce a flash shedding a different light on the language of a place and to strike the hearer. Cross-cuts, fragments, cracks, and lucky hits in the framework of a system, consumers' ways of operating are the practical equivalents of wit.

Lacking its own place, lacking a view of the whole, limited by the blindness (which may lead to perspicacity) resulting from combat at close quarters, limited by the possibilities of the moment, a tactic is determined by the *absence of power* just as a strategy is organized by the postulation of power. From this point of view, the dialectic of a tactic may be illuminated by the ancient art of sophistic. As the author of a great "strategic" system, Aristotle was already very interested in the procedures of this enemy which perverted, as he saw it, the order of truth. He quotes a formula of this protean, quick, and surprising adversary that, by making explicit the basis of sophistic, can also serve finally to define a tactic as I understand the term here: it is a matter, Corax said, of "making the worst argument seem the better."[19] In its paradoxical concision, this formula delineates the relationship of forces that is the starting point for an intellectual creativity as persistent as it is subtle, tireless, ready for every opportunity, scattered over the terrain of the dominant order and foreign to the rules laid down and imposed by a rationality founded on established rights and property.

In sum, strategies are actions which, thanks to the establishment of a place of power (the property of a proper), elaborate theoretical places (systems and totalizing discourses) capable of articulating an ensemble of physical places in which forces are distributed. They combine these three types of places and seek to master each by means of the others. They thus privilege spatial relationships. At the very least they attempt to reduce temporal relations to spatial ones through the analytical attribution of a proper place to each particular element and through the combinatory organization of the movements specific to units or groups of units. The model was military before it became "scientific." Tactics are procedures that gain validity in relation to the pertinence they lend to time – to the circumstances which the precise instant of an intervention transforms into a favorable situation, to the rapidity of the movements that change the organization of a space, to the relations among successive movements in an action, to the possible intersections of durations and heterogeneous rhythms, etc. In this respect, the difference corresponds to two historical options regarding action and security (options that moreover have more to do with constraints than with possibilities): strategies pin their hopes on the resistances that the *establishment of a place* offers to the erosion of time; tactics on a clever *utilization of time*, of the opportunities it presents and also of the play that it introduces into the foundations of power. Even if the methods practiced by the everyday art of war never present themselves in such a clear form, it nevertheless remains the case that the two ways of acting can be distinguished according to whether they bet on place or on time.

The Rhetorics of Practice, Ancient Ruses

Various theoretical comparisons will allow us better to characterize the tactics or the polemology of the "weak." The "figures" and "turns" analyzed by *rhetoric* are particularly illuminating in this regard. Freud already noticed this fact and used them in his studies on wit and on the forms taken by the return of the repressed within the field of an order: verbal economy and condensation, double meaning and misinterpretations, displacements and alliterations, multiple uses of the same material, etc.[20] There is nothing surprising about these homologies between practical ruses and rhetorical movements. In relation to the legalities of syntax and "proper" sense, that is, in relation to the general definition of a "proper" (as opposed to what is not "proper"), the good and bad tricks of rhetoric are played on the terrain that has been set aside in this way. They are manipulations of language relative to occasions and are intended to seduce, captivate, or invert the linguistic position of the addressee.[21] Whereas grammar watches over the "propriety" of terms, rhetorical alterations (metaphorical drifts, elliptical condensations, metonymic miniaturizations, etc.) point to the use of language by speakers in particular situations in ritual or actual linguistic combat. They are the indexes of consumption and are the interplay of forces. They depend on a problematics of enunciation. In addition, although (or because) they are excluded in principle from scientific discourse, these "ways of speaking" provide the analysis of "ways of operating" with a repertory of models and hypotheses. After all, they are merely variants within a general semiotics of tactics. To be sure, in order to work out that semiotics, it would be necessary to review arts of thinking and acting other than the one that the articulation of a certain rationality has founded on the delimitation of the proper: from the sixty-four hexagrams of the Chinese *I-Ching*,[22] or the Greek *metis*[23] to the Arabic *hila*,[24] other "logics" can be discerned.

I am not concerned directly here with the constitution of such a semiotics, but rather with suggesting some ways of thinking about everyday practices of consumers, supposing from the start that they are of a tactical nature. Dwelling, moving about, speaking, reading, shopping, and cooking are activities that seem to correspond to the characteristics of tactical ruses and surprises: clever tricks of the "weak" within the order established by the "strong," an art of putting one over on the adversary on his own turf, hunter's tricks, maneuverable, polymorphic mobilities, jubilant, poetic, and warlike discoveries.

Perhaps these practices correspond to an ageless art which has not only persisted through the institutions of successive political orders but goes back much farther than our histories and forms strange alliances preceding the frontiers of humanity. These practices present in fact a curious analogy, and a sort of immemorial link, to the simulations, tricks, and disguises that certain fishes or plants execute with extraordinary virtuosity. The procedures of this art can be found in the farthest reaches of the domain of the living, as if they managed to surmount not only the strategic distributions of historical institutions but also the break established by the very institution of consciousness. They maintain formal continuities and the permanence of a memory without language, from the depths of the oceans to the streets of our great cities.

In any event, on the scale of contemporary history, it also seems that the generalization and expansion of technocratic rationality have created, between the links of the system, a fragmentation and explosive growth of these practices which were formally regulated by stable local units. Tactics are more and more frequently going off their tracks. Cut loose from the traditional communities that circumscribed their functioning, they have begun to wander everywhere in a space which is becoming at once more homogenous and more extensive. Consumers are transformed into immigrants. The system in which they move about is too vast to be able to fix them in one place, but too constraining for them ever to be able to escape from it and go into exile elsewhere. There is no longer an elsewhere. Because of this, the "strategic" model is also transformed, as if defeated by its own success: it was by definition based on the definition of a "proper" distinct from everything else; but now that "proper" has become the whole. It could be that, little by little, it will exhaust its capacity to transform itself and constitute only the space (just as totalitarian as the cosmos of ancient times) in which a cybernetic society will arise, the scene of the Brownian movements of invisible and innumerable tactics. One would thus have a proliferation of aleatory and indeterminable manipulations within an immense framework of socioeconomic constraints and securities: myriads of almost invisible movements, playing on the more and more refined texture of a place that is even, continuous, and constitutes a proper place for all people. Is this already the present or the future of the great city?

Leaving aside the multimillenial archeology of ruses as well as the possibility of their anthill-like future, the study of a few current everyday tactics ought not to forget the horizon from which they proceed, nor, at the other extreme, towards which they are likely to go. The evocation of these perspectives on the distant past or future at least allows us to resist the effects of the fundamental but often exclusive and obsessive analysis that seeks to describe institutions and the mechanisms of *repression*. The privilege enjoyed by the problematics of repression in the field of research should not be surprising: scientific institutions belong to the system which they study, they conform to the well-known genre of the family story (an ideological criticism does not change its functioning in any way; the criticism merely creates the appearance of a distance for scientists who are members of the institution); they even add the disturbing charm of devils or bogey-men whose stories are told during long evenings around the family hearth. But this elucidation of the apparatus by itself has the disadvantage of *not seeing* practices which are heterogeneous to it and which it represses or thinks it represses. Nevertheless, they have every chance of surviving this apparatus *too*, and, in any case, they are *also* part of social life, and all the more resistant because they are more flexible and adjusted to perpetual mutation. When one examines this fleeting and permanent reality carefully, one has the impression of exploring the night-side of societies, a night longer than their day, a dark sea from which successive institutions emerge, a maritime immensity on which socioeconomic and political structures appear as ephemeral islands.

The imaginary landscape of an inquiry is not without value, even if it is without rigor. It restores what was earlier called "popular culture," but it does so in order to transform what was represented as a matrix-force of history into a mobile infinity of tactics. It thus keeps before our eyes the structure of a social imagination in which the problem constantly takes different forms and begins anew. It also wards off the effects of an analysis which necessarily grasps these practices only on the margins of a technical apparatus, at the point where they alter or defeat its instruments. It is the study itself which is marginal with respect to the phenomena studied. The landscape that represents these phenomena in an imaginary mode thus has an overall corrective and therapeutic value in resisting their reduction by a lateral examination. It at least assures their presence as ghosts. This return to another scene thus reminds us of the relation between the experience of these practices and what remains of them in an analysis. It is evidence, evidence which can only be fantastic and not scientific, of the disproportion between everyday tactics and a strategic elucidation. Of all the things everyone does, how much gets written down? Between the two, the image, the phantom of the expert but mute body, preserves the difference.

Notes

1   Meaning literally "the wig," de Certeau (*The Practice of Everyday Life*, p. 25) defines *la perruque* as "the worker's own work disguised as work for his employer." It differs from pilfering in that nothing of material value is stolen. It differs from absenteeism in that the worker is officially on the job. *La perruque* may be as simple a matter as a secretary's writing a love letter on "company time" or as complex as a cabinetmaker's "borrowing" a lathe to make a piece of furniture for his living room." [Ed.]
2   See in particular A. Huet et al., *La Marchandise culturelle* (Paris: CNRS, 1977), which is not satisfied merely with analyzing products (photos, records, prints), but also studies a system of commercial repetition and ideological reproduction.
3   See, for example, *Pratiques culturelles des français* (Paris: Secretariat d'État a la Culture – SER, 1974), 2 vols. Alvin Tofler, *The Culture Consumers* (Baltimore: Penguin, 1965), remains fundamental and pioneering, although it is not statistically based and is limited to mass culture.
4   On the premonitory theme of the "celibate machine" in the art (M. Duchamp, et al.) or the literature (from Jules Verne to Raymond Roussel) of the early twentieth century, see J. Clair et al., *Les Machines célibataires* (Venice: Alfieri, 1975).
5   See, for example, on the subject of Aymaras of Peru and Bolivia, J.-E. Monast, *On les croyait Chretiens: les Aymaras* (Paris: Cerf, 1969).
6   See M. de Certeau, "La Longue marche indienne," in *Le Reveil indien en Amerique latine*, ed. Yves Materne and DIAL (Paris: Cerf, 1976), pp. 119–35.
7   G. Ryle, "Use, Usage and Meaning," in *The Theory of Meaning*, ed. G. H. R. Parkinson (Oxford: Oxford University Press, 1968), pp. 109–16. A large part of the volume is devoted to use.
8   Richard Montague, "Pragmatics," in *La Philosophie contemporaine*, ed. Raymond Klibansky (Firenze: La Nuova Italia, 1968), Vol. I, pp. 102–22. Y Bar-Hillel thus adopts a term of C. S. Peirce, of which the equivalents are, in B. Russell, "egocentric particulars"; in H. Reichenbach, "token-reflexive expressions"; in N. Goodman,

"indicator words"; in W. V. Quine, "non-eternal sentences"; etc. A whole tradition is inscribed in this perspective. Wittgenstein belongs to it as well, the Wittgenstein whose slogan was "Don't ask for the meaning, ask for the use" in reference to normal use, regulated by the institution that is language.

9   See "The Proverbial Enunciation," above, p. 18.

10   See Emile Benveniste, *Problemes de linguistique générale* (Paris: Gallimard, 1974), Vol. II, pp. 79–88.

11   Ferdinand Deligny, *Les Vagabonds efficaces* (Paris: Maspero, 1970), uses this word to describe the trajectories of young autistic people with whom he lives, writings that move through forests, wanderings that can no longer make a path through the space of language.

12   See "Indeterminate," below, p. 199.

13   Ibid.

14   According to John von Neumann and Oskar Morgenstern, *Theory of Games and Economic Behavior*, 3rd edn. (New York: John Wiley, 1964), "there is only strategy when the other's strategy is included."

15   "Strategy is the science of military movements outside of the enemy's field of vision; tactics, within it" (von Bülow).

16   Karl von Clausewitz, *Von Kriege*; see *De la Guerre* (Paris: Minuit, 1955), pp. 212–13; *On War*, trans. M. Howard and P. Paret (Princeton: Princeton University Press, 1976). This analysis can be found moreover in many other theoreticians, ever since Machiavelli. See Y. Delahaye, "Simulation et dissimulation," *La Ruse* (*Cause Commune* 1977/1) (Paris: UGE 10/18, 1977), pp. 55–74.

17   Clausewitz, *De la Guerre*, p. 212.

18   Freud, *Jokes and their Relation to the Unconscious*, trans. J. Starchey (London: Hogarth Press and the Institute of Psychoanalysis, 1960).

19   Aristotle, *Rhetoric*, II, 24, 1402a: "by making the worse argument seem the better"; trans. W. Rhys Roberts (New York: Modern Library, 1954). The same "discovery" is attributed to Tisias by Plato (*Phaedrus*, 273b–c). See also W. K. C. Guthrie, *The Sophists* (Cambridge: Cambridge University Press, 1971), pp. 178–9. On Corax's *techne* mentioned by Aristotle in relation to the "loci of apparent enthymemes," see Ch. Perelman and L. Ollbrechts-Tyteca, *Traite de l'argumentation* (Brussels: Université Libre, 1970), pp. 607–9.

20   Freud, *Jokes and their Relation to the Unconscious*, on the techniques of wit.

21   See S. Toulmin, *The Uses of Argument* (Cambridge: Cambridge University Press, 1958); Perelman and Ollbrechts-Tyteca, *Traite de l'argumentation*; J. Dubois et al., *Rhétorique générale* (Paris: Larousse, 1970); etc.

22   See *I-Ching, the Book of Changes*, which represents all the possible situations of beings in the course of the universe's mutations by means of 64 hexagrams formed by 6 interrupted or full lines.

23   M. Detienne and J.-P. Vernant, *Les Ruses de l'intelligence. La Metis des Grecs* (Paris: Flammarion, 1974).

24   See M. Rodinson, *Islam et capitalisme* (Paris: Seuil, 1972); *Islam and Capitalism*, trans. B. Pearce (New York: Pantheon, 1973).

Part II
The Character of the Consumer Society

12

Looking Backwards

Don Slater

Here, Don Slater sets something of the historical context within which Part II is framed. Beginning with the consumer culture we typically associate with the 1980s, Slater traces in reverse order the dominant themes of the various "moments" of consumer society over the last 150 to 200 years. He argues that, perhaps in spite of appearances to the contrary, no one such moment has ever been an entirely unique manifestation of consumer society, but in fact emerges and draws its particular character from precedents set by the previous period.

[The] *longue durée* view of consumer culture contradicts some common-sense views of it. Consumer culture, in fact, inhabits an odd time-frame: on the one hand, modern forms of consumption – like modern forms of the market in much economic theory – are often regarded as effectively universal and eternal; on the other hand, in everyday experience consumer culture lives in a perpetual year zero of newness. Consumer culture is about continuous self-creation through the accessibility of things which are themselves presented as new, modish, faddish or fashionable, always improved and improving. In keeping with the fashionable experience it provides, the very idea of consumer culture is constantly heralded as new: in each generation the Columbuses of capitalism rediscover the promised land of affluent freedom; while critics – both left and right – report our arrival in a frozen land of wealth without value.

In what follows, I want to disrupt this sense of eternal newness by telling the history of consumer culture backwards. This will allow us to trace each 'new age' back to a previous one and at the same time to get a clearer sense of how consumer culture is bound up with 'the whole of modernity'.

The 1980s saw one of the most powerful rediscoveries of consumerism. The consumer was the hero of the hour, not just as the provider of all that buying power which would fuel economic growth (though this was central too, and encouraged through phenomenal credit expansion, deficit financing, and income tax

From *Consumer Culture and Modernity* (Cambridge: Polity Press, 1997), pp. 9–16. Reprinted by permission of the publishers.

reductions) but as the very model of the modern subject and citizen. Exemplified in neo-liberalism – specifically in Reaganomics and Thatcherism – consumer choice became the obligatory pattern for all social relations and the template for civic dynamism and freedom. Collective and social provision gave way to radical individualism (as Thatcher put it, 'There is no such thing as society, only individuals and their families'). And this individual was enterprising – dynamically and unabashedly self-interested – as exemplified in the yuppie and in the character Gekko in the film *Wall Street*. The 1980s also heralded the subordination of production to consumption in the form of marketing: design, retailing, advertising and the product concept were ascendant, reflected in postmodern theory as the triumph of the sign and the aestheticization of everyday life. Much-publicized claims about the reorganization of capitalist production and its relation to the state (post-Fordism, disorganized capitalism, flexible accumulation) all argued that Fordist mass consumption – the pioneer of consumer culture – was giving way or giving birth to a newer and truer consumer culture of target or niche marketing, in which the forging of personal identity would be firmly and pleasurably disentangled from the worlds of both work and politics and would be carried out in a world of plural, malleable, playful consumer identities, a process ruled over by the play of image, style, desire and signs. Consumer culture was now all about 'keeping different from the Joneses'.

Both neo-liberalism and postmodernism proclaimed and seemingly endorsed the murder of critical reason by consumer sovereignty: standards of value other than the preferences expressed by individuals in the market-place were derided as elitist, conservative or simply ungrounded. The ideological consumerism of the 1980s then foregrounds radical individualism and privatism on the one hand, and on another their grounding in a modality of signs and meanings (rather than needs and wants): this consumer culture is profoundly superficial, profoundly about appearances. Materialism is neither good nor bad – it's all there is. And when this situation obtains, as Raymond Williams (1980: 185) puts it, 'we turn out not to be sensibly materialist' at all: unhinged from core social identities and physical want, consumerism becomes a pure play of signs. The ideological miracle carried out by 1980s consumer culture was to tie this image of unhinged superficiality to the most profound, deep structural promises of modernity: personal freedom, economic progress, civic dynamism and political democracy. Through the neo-liberal renaissance and the crumbling of Marxism (in the west and the east), consumer culture was seen in terms of the freedoms of the market and therefore as the guarantor of both economic progress and individual freedom.

Ironically, the 1980s positions on consumer culture, whether neo-liberal, postmodern or critical, largely presented themselves as reactions against the 1950s and 1960s, as commentaries on the bankruptcy of the postwar consensus (both its establishment version and its opponents'). Yet this consensus had presented itself, in its own time, as marking the arrival of the industrial world in the promised land of the consumerist plenty. The great theme of this period is the triumph of economic managerialism, through Keynesian economics and welfare statism, over the crisis tendencies of capitalism exemplified in the Great Depression. The vista of an 'organized capitalism' (Lash and Urry, 1987) with smoothly expanding prosperity placed consumer culture near its centre as simultaneously the engine of prosperity, a pre-eminent tool for managing economic and political stability and the reward for embracing the system. The harmonious marriage of managerial collectivism and consumerist individualism – the mixed economy – is precisely what 1980s neo-liberalism loathed, as exemplified in the idea of regulation and in the split between social provision for welfare and infrastructure on the one hand and private-sector enterprise on the other. At the time, however, 'You never had it so good'. This is the period of the economic miracle that was directly experienced in rising consumption standards. It was so good in fact that – within the ideological climate up to the 1970s – critics of consumer culture had to reach for ever more tenuous accounts of how a world both so systematically stable and individually satisfying could be deemed *unsuccessful* by either intellectuals or their erstwhile revolutionary agents.

In fact the image of the postwar consumer and consumer boom is rather schizoid. On the one hand, consumer culture – especially in the 1950s – appears as a new age of conformity, of 'organization man', of the 'other-directed' narcissist, of the mass cultural dope or couch potato keeping up with the Joneses through the slavish mass consumption of standardized mass production goods, the land of Levittown and American cars (Mills, 1951; Riesman, 1961; Whyte, 1957). The consumer is the 'affluent worker' (Goldthorpe and Lockwood, 1968–9) steadily building up domestic capital within the framework of long-term job security. The stability of the everyday consuming household was itself anchored within the productive harbour of the Keynesian state, which organized itself around a table with chairs set out for organized government, organized business and organized labour. Fordism, it was argued, provided a prosperous yet empty contentment, involving a colonization of everyday life by corporations and consumption norms which rendered it status-driven and conformist, mass and anti-individualist. Prosperity and the good life meant the *ability* to keep up with the Joneses.

On the other hand, the 'affluent society' (Galbraith, 1969) [chapter 16, this volume] could also involve disturbingly explosive and hedonistic consumption patterns among new social groups which were themselves crucially defined by their consumption: the emergence of the teenager, of the Butlins working class, of the suburban family and so on. The affluent society was a consumer society in which economic prosperity brought insatiable and morally dubious wants, a crisis in values over the work ethic, a bifurcation of desire between respectable consumption (consumption within the framework of the family, the spread of bourgeois propriety through the accumulation of domestic capital) and hedonistic, amoral, non-familial consumption (Bell, 1979). On the Marxist side, this period also seemed to confirm a long-worked-out analysis of consumer culture as a form of social and political managerialism, a way to ensure political docility through a mass policy of bread and circuses.

If we date it from the postwar period, consumer culture appears as the culmination of Fordist mass production coupled with Keynesian economic managerialism, both together producing a stable affluence which carries the seeds of its own destruction: moral destruction through conformity or hedonism, socio-economic destruction through the triumph of collectivist regulation, and so on. But postwar consumerism represents the spread of social themes and arrangements which were pioneered in the previous era. The 1920s was probably the first decade to proclaim a generalized ideology of affluence. Above all, it promoted a powerful link between everyday consumption and modernization. From the 1920s, the world was to be modernized partly *through* consumption; consumer culture itself was dominated by the idea that everyday life could and should be *modern*, and that to a great extent it already was. Ewen (1976) [see chapter 13, this volume] and Marchand (1986), for example, demonstrate that the burgeoning advertising and marketing of this era were selling not just consumer goods, but consumerism itself as the shining path to modernity: they incited their publics to modernize themselves, modernize their homes, their means of transport. The exemplary goods of the period are about the mechanization of everyday life, starting with houses themselves, and extending to their electrification; then durables like washing machines, vacuum cleaners, fridges, telephones; then, finally, the automobile for that modern sense of movement into the future and into the jazz age. This is the age of real estate, consumer credit and cars: modern appliances, bought by modern methods, placed in a modern household. The 1920s was probably the first era in which modernity was widely held to be a state that *has already been reached* by the population in general, a state we are in or nearly in, rather than one towards which an avant-garde points: in the consuming activities of the middle class the ultra-modern future was already readable, already beginning to happen.

The 1920s (and, especially in America, the previous two decades as well) exhibit a similar moral split to the postwar era: Sinclair Lewis's (1922) *Babbitt*, on one side, exemplifies consumerism, 'boosterism', the life of selling and goods, as the route to empty mass conformity (especially within the increasingly privatized, suburbanized and nuclearized family); the flapper, the cinema, the automobile and Prohibition represent the other side: the licentious, youth-orientated, pleasure-orientated orgy of the jazz age, Hollywood and Harlem nights. Again, and quite early on, consumerism shows its double face: it is registered on the one hand as a tool of social order and private contentment, on the other side as social licence and cultural disruption.

The 1920s appear as the first consumerist decade, but on closer inspection they seem merely the harvesting of a much longer revolution, commonly periodized as 1880–1930. This era sees the emergence of a mass-production system of manufacture increasingly dedicated to producing consumer goods (rather than the heavy capital goods such as steel, machinery and chemicals which dominated much of the later nineteenth century). If consumer culture is born here it is because we emphasize several interlocked developments: mass manufacture; the geographical and social spreading of the market; the rationalization of the form and organization of production (see, for example, Aglietta, 1979 [see chapter 22, this volume]; Boorstin, 1973; Fraser, 1981; Pope, 1983).

Incontrovertibly, it is in this period that all the features which make up consumer culture take on their mature form, but more importantly it is in this period that a modern *norm* emerges concerning how consumer goods are to be produced, sold and assimilated into everyday life. Only now does the following description become normative if not yet universal: goods are designed with standardized, replaceable components which allow them to be produced in very large volumes at low unit cost through an intensive, rationally controlled and increasingly automated technical division of labour. This is ultimately exemplified in the Fordist model of flow-past assembly lines manned by Taylorized workers. The goods are sold across geographically and socially wider markets – regional, national, global – whose formation is made possible by the interconnection of local markets through new transportation and communications infrastructures (rail, mail, telegraph, telephone); by the concentration of markets into larger cities; by the development of multi-divisional corporations capable of planning and co-ordinating on this scale; by the integration of markets through *marketing*, using such techniques as branding and packaging, national sales forces, advertising, point of sale materials and industrial design – all designed to unify product identity across socially and geographically dispersed markets. This is accompanied by the massive development of retail infrastructures (not just shops but also retail multiples, mail order, vertical integration downwards to the point of sale). This massive volume of cheap standardized goods, rationally sold through ever larger markets, is sold to a population which is increasingly *seen* as consumers: they are not seen as classes or genders who consume, but rather as consumers who happen to be organized into classes and genders.

However, if this period marks the true birth of consumer culture it is only because we define consumer culture in terms of mass production and mass participation in consumption. There is no essential reason to do so. We can equally treat the age of mass consumption as the development of a system whose values and aims were inherited from earlier periods, and as the spreading of a culture that had been already well defined in other classes. Moreover, we can consider the fact that critics did not wait for the emergence of Fordist mass production to engage in full-scale attacks and large-scale theorizations of consumer culture (Miller, 1981; Williams, 1982). Consumer culture existed as a problem for social critics, an ideology for the population and a reality for the bourgeoisie from quite early in the nineteenth century.

Thus we might next look at the prosperous mid-Victorian years from the 1850s to the 1870s. With the industrial and urban pattern of modernization well established as an idea, if not entirely as a reality, and with the economic and political disruptions of the 1840s passed, a new era of confidence is generally held to have been ushered in by the London exhibition at Crystal Palace in 1851. In a stunning anecdote, Rosalind Williams (1982) points out that whereas this first international celebration of progress focused on exhibiting the triumphs of modern science and technology, by the time of the Paris exhibition of 1889 the objects on display were beginning to carry price tags. The transformation of modernity itself into a commodity, of its experiences and thrills into a ticketed spectacle, of its domination of nature into domestic comfort, of its knowledges into exotic costume, and of the commodity into the goal of modernity: all this was brewing well in advance of mass production oriented towards mass consumption (Richards, 1991).

Over this period, consumer culture moves in two contradictory but interrelated directions. On the one hand, consumer culture seems to emerge from the production of public spectacle, from the enervated and over-stimulated world of urban experience so powerfully captured in Baudelaire's image of the *flâneur*: in modernity all the world is consumable experience. And all is display: the development of shopping arcades, department stores, international exhibitions, museums, new forms of entertainment. Cities, department stores and especially international expositions carry powerful collective meanings as symbols of both scientific civilization and national greatness. The world is a cornucopia of consumable experience and goods delivered by modern progress into a modern carnival, and the consumer is the fee-paying audience for the spectacle and experience of modernity (Slater, 1995).

On the other hand, and in opposition to the public culture of commodities, consumerism was made respectable during this period by connecting it to the construction of private, bourgeois domesticity. Consumption is to be turned into respectable culture by wresting it from the hands of both the aristocracy (where it signifies luxury, decadence, terminal superficiality) and the working classes (where it signifies public riotousness, the excesses of the drinking, sporting mob). It is crucial that in this period much debate on consumer culture was carried out in terms not of the consumption of goods but of *time*: a debate about leisure (see, especially Cross, 1993 [see chapter 14, this volume]; Cunningham, 1980) which concerned how to keep this public order outside work hours. How, for example, can (male) working-class leisure consumption be diverted from drinking, gaming and prostitution in public places. Yet once excluded from these public places there are fears about what they get up to in their new privacy – fears about health and morals, about subversion and irreligion. What is Victorian philanthropy and reform but the inculcation of new norms of consumption – of healthy domestic, private consumption in the bosom of the family – calibrated by the scales of bourgeois respectability, medical science and moral discourses on sin and criminality

(Rose, 1992a; 1992b)? In sum, consumer culture of the mid nineteenth century appears to emerge from a series of struggles to organize and tame, yet at the same time to exploit commercially, the social spaces and times in which modernity is acted out.

One more stop before the terminus: bourgeois respectability, as well as its opponents, drew considerably on romanticism . . . [R]omanticism and the concept of culture that it produced were in many respects reactions against industrial, commercial consumer society from Rousseau in the 1750s through revolutionary and nationalist romanticism up to the mid nineteenth century. It has therefore provided probably the most enduring source of critiques of consumer culture, which it sees as part of a materialistic modernity that lacks authentic collective values and truths. Yet paradoxically romanticism also bequeathed to consumer culture many of the themes that we consider most modern or even postmodern. Under the impact of a materialistic and monetarized society, romanticism promoted ideas of personal authenticity, an authenticity that derived from what was 'natural', emotional, irrational, sensual and imaginative in the self. Moreover, it associated these sources of authenticity with aestheticism and creativity: everyday life (at least, in the first instance, the everyday life of the artist or genius) should be a process of making the self. The individual's style of goods, activities and experiences were no longer a matter of pure social performance (as Sennett (1977) argues it was for the eighteenth century) but a matter of personal truth and authenticity. The very idea that acts of consuming are seriously consequential for the authenticity of the self (as opposed to mere physical survival or social climbing) is an unintentional consequence of these early developments, as are many of the 'authentic values' in which modern consumer goods come wrapped: naturalness, emotional gratification, ethnic and national cultural values, images of innocent children, natural women and happy domesticity. It is through romanticism that consumer culture becomes both wildly playful and deadly earnest (Berman, 1970; Campbell, 1989 [see chapter 5, this volume]; Sennett, 1977; Trilling, 1972).

Our reverse narrative has now dropped us off in the early modern period. It is here that consumption comes to be understood in recognizably modern ways and in which recognizably modern ways of consuming begin to appear. It is also the period in which we can see most clearly the ways in which consumer culture and modernity are inextricably interwoven. . . .

None the less, ideas of modern consumption arise firstly in the ideal (or dystopia) of a liberal and commercial society comprising free individuals pursuing their interests through free association in the public sphere. The consumer . . . is one example or one aspect of the private and enterprising individual who stands at the centre of the very notion of modernity. Commercial and civil society required freedom, took liberties and therefore usurped powers. We are familiar with this process in certain areas of historical change: the assertion of reason and science involved a reliance on the individual's resources of knowledge and an independence from received authority, from 'custom and example' (Descartes, quoted in Gellner, 1992), tradition, religious revelation. This is a class struggle in thought, a revolution by and for 'self-made men' (Gellner, 1992). But Enlightenment man – both as an idealized projection and as a real new form of subjectivity – was not just a rational, free-thinking individual in the sphere of science, politics or production: he also learned some of these ways of being by being rational and individual in the experience of going to market and of materially constructing new forms of domesticity, in dressing as a fashionable urbanite and in going to newly commercialized leisure activities.

References

Aglietta, M. (1979) *A Theory of Capitalist Regulation: The US Experience*. London: Verso.

Bell, D. (1979) *The Cultural Contradictions of Capitalism*. London: Heinemann.

Berman, M. (1970) *The Politics of Authenticity*. New York: Atheneum.

Boorstin, D. (1973) *The Americans: The Democratic Experience*. New York: Vintage Books.

Campbell, C. (1989) *The Romantic Ethic and the Spirit of Modern Consumerism*. Oxford: Blackwell Publishers.

Cross, G. (1993) *Time and Money: The Making of Consumer Culture*. London: Routledge.

Cunningham, H. (1980) *Leisure in the Industrial Revolution, c.1780–c.1880*. London: Croom Helm.

Ewen, S. (1976) *Captains of Consciousness*. New York: McGraw-Hill.

Fraser, W. H. (1981) *The Coming of the Mass Market, 1850–1914*. London: Macmillan.

Galbraith, J. K. (1969) *The Affluent Society*. London: Hamish Hamilton.

Goldthorpe, J. and Lockwood, D. (1968–9) *The Affluent Worker*. Cambridge: Cambridge University Press.

Lash, S. and Urry, J. (1987) *The End of Organised Capitalism*. Cambridge: Polity Press.

Lewis, S. (1922) *Babbitt*. New York: Harcourt Brace Jovanovitch.

Marchand, R. (1986) *Advertising the American Dream: Making Way for Modernity – 1920–1940*. Berkeley: University of California Press.

Miller, M. (1981) *The Bon Marché: Bourgeois Culture and the Department Store*. London: Allen and Unwin.

Mills, C. W. (1951) *White Collar*. London: Oxford University Press.

Pope, D. (1983) *The Making of Modern Advertising*. New York: Basic Books.

Richards, T. (1991) *The Commodity Culture of Victorian England: Advertising and Spectacle, 1851–1914*. London: Verso.

Riesman, D. (1961) *The Lonely Crowd: A Study of the Changing American Character*. New Haven, CN: Yale University Press.

Rose, N. (1992a) 'Governing the enterprising self', in Heelas, P and Morris, P. (eds) *The Values of Enterprise Culture: The Moral Debate*. London: Routledge.

Rose, N. (1992b) 'Towards a critical sociology of freedom', inaugural lecture. London: Goldsmiths' College.

Sennett, R. (1977) *The Fall of Public Man*. Cambridge: Cambridge University Press.

Slater, D. R. (1995) 'Photography and modern vision: the spectacle of "natural magic"', in Jenks, C. (ed.) *Visual Culture*. London: Routledge.

Trilling, L. (1972) *Sincerity and Authenticity*. Cambridge, MA: Harvard University Press.

Whyte, W. H. (1957) *The Organization Man*. New York: Doubleday Anchor Books.

Williams, R. (1980) 'Advertising: the magic system', in R. Williams (ed.) *Problems in Materialism and Culture*. London: Verso.

Williams, R. (1982) *Dream Worlds: Mass Consumption in Late C19th France*. Berkeley: University of California Press.

13

Assembling a New World of Facts

Stuart Ewen

In this extract from his influential study of the roots of twentieth-century consumer society, Stuart Ewen presents evidence in support of the claim that the emergence of the particular forms taken by consumer society from the 1920s onwards was not an accidental or piecemeal process. It was, he argues, a very definite and conscious process of ideological engineering. The book as a whole draws very heavily on numerous primary sources taken from the period in question to demonstrate the imperative that was felt to be incumbent on business to establish a consumer culture in favor of the established traditional cultural formations, that were based largely around noncommodified social and cultural practices.

With the wide-scale implementation of mass production in the 1920s, advertising and the ideal of mass consumption were catapulted to the foreground of modern economic planning. In the internal arguments of the business community as well as in their more public expressions, American businessmen celebrated the coming of the new industrial age as one which would accelerate social progress among the masses and at the same time vindicate "the great stream of human selfishness" of which they were an undeniable part (Filene, 1931: 12). And yet the economic and social presence of mass industrial machinery was not something that could arouse popular fidelity by virtue of its productive capacity alone. For as an increasingly large fraction of the material world became the domain of American business enterprise, the organization and manipulation of a responsive social context became clearly imperative. Faced on the one hand with the crisis of overproduction which prompted Bernard Baruch to issue the warning that while "we have learned to create wealth . . . we have not learned to keep that wealth from choking us,"[1] and on the other hand the emergence of tendencies and movements among the working classes which questioned the basis of capitalist wealth *per se*, businessmen sought to utilize their technology for their own political purposes. It became a central function of business to be able to define a social order which would feed and adhere to the demands of the productive process and at the same time absorb,

From *Captains of Consciousness* (New York: McGraw-Hill, 1976), pp. 51–9. Reprinted by permission of The McGraw-Hill Companies.

neutralize, and contain the transitional impulses of a working class emerging from the unrequited drudgery of nineteenth-century industrialization.

More and more, the language of business expressed the imperative of social and ideological hegemony. Such a development was not without its precedents in American history, or that of other nations, however. John Adams had spoken of the political requirements of industry. "Manufacturers cannot live, much less thrive," he cautioned, "without honor, fidelity, punctuality, and private faith, a sacred respect for property, and the moral obligations of promises and contracts" (quoted in Gutman, 1973: 532). So too is much of American industrial development punctuated by attempts to channel thought and behavior into patterns which fitted the prescribed dimensions of industrial life.[2]

In a nineteenth-century society basically devoted to industrialization and regulating patterns of work, the arena of business manipulation was concerned predominantly with the basics of production. As Paul Nystrom, one of America's first consumer economists, wrote retrospectively of that early era: "under such conditions, society itself becomes industrialized. It develops its own ideals of life and puts its high stamp of approval on such virtues as working efficiency, special working ability, industry, thrift and sobriety. Respect and honor are paid to the principles of industrialism, and reverence is offered its founders and leaders. The captains of industry become popular heroes. These are the characteristics of a true industrial society, a society in which ideals of production rather than of consumption rule" (Nystrom, 1929: 5).

With the development of methods of mass production and the expanded notion of markets that this entailed, the ideology of "private faith" to which John Adams had alluded became a matter that extended beyond the strictures of industry and of work. For the "new order" was one which sustained itself not merely around the question of labor fealty to the mechanical process of capitalism, but one which demanded a dedication of *all* social energy to a world being fashioned by industrial technology. It is out of such a modern imperative that Jacques Ellul (1967), critic of technological society, has developed a common conception of *technology* and *technique* as a constellation of devices for the "technical management of physical and social worlds" (Ellul, 1967).

By the 1920s businessmen had reached a considerable awareness of the political and social roles that the process of consumption and the advertising that stimulated it must play. Putting aside the buoyant ad rhetoric of progress and beneficence for a moment, *Printer's Ink* put the need for social control in the frankest terms: "modern machinery . . . made it not only possible but imperative that the masses should live lives of comfort and leisure; that the future of business lay in its ability to *manufacture customers* as well as products."[3] Elsewhere the business community was infused with a political messianism which implied that the mere selling of products was no longer an adequate goal of advertising. Writing in the twenties, Walter Pitkin, professor of marketing at the Columbia School of

Journalism, spoke of goods advertising, even sophisticated "national" market goods advertising, as merely an initial step "in a direction towards which we must go a long way further." Even institutional advertising, a public relations scheme which tried to boost a whole sector of industry, did not meet the political demands of mass industrial society. What was necessary, rather, was a broad-scaled strategy aimed at selling the way of life determined by a profit-seeking mass-productive machinery. Pitkin ordered a campaign for an entire industrial value system, imploring his colleagues "to go beyond institutional advertising to some new kind of philosophy of life advertising" (Pitkin quoted in Rorty, 1934: 392).

Consumerism, the mass participation in the values of the mass-industrial market, thus emerged in the 1920s not as a smooth progression from earlier and less "developed" patterns of consumption, but rather as an aggressive device of corporate survival. Edward Filene, the Boston department store merchant and man who had developed an international reputation as "the mouthpiece of industrial America" (Bernays, 1965: 439), spoke frankly of the role and purpose of consumerizing the broad American population. The attempt to create a national unified culture around the social bond of the consumer market was basically a project of broad "social planning" (Filene, 1931: 271). Industry, Filene argued, could "sell to the masses all that it employs the masses to create," but such a development would require a selective education which limited the concept of social change and betterment to those commodified answers rolling off American conveyor belts. "Mass production demands the education of the masses," Filene axiomized, "the masses must learn to behave like human beings in a mass production world" (Filene, 1931: 272, 144). Such an education, however, was to be one with extremely prescribed horizons. Fearing the implications of the kind of education that might suggest an adversary relationship between the interests of American workers and those of the captains of industry, Filene presented a vision of education into industrial and social democracy within which the element of conflict was eradicated from the world of *knowledge*. Education, for Filene, became a task of building a culture on the basis of "fact-finding." Just looking at the given "facts" about what is being produced rather than questioning the social basis upon which those facts lay was what modern education should be all about. Education should be a process of acclimating and adjusting the population to that world of *facts*, to make it their own. "The schools do their best to teach patriotism – loyalty to the political state . . ." Filene observed, "But what are the schools doing to interpret the machine civilization" to the citizenry? (Filene, 1931: 145–6). "The time has come," he argued, "when all our educational institutions . . . must concentrate on the great social task of teaching the masses not what to think but *how to think*, and thus to find out how to behave like human beings in the machine age" (Filene, 1931: 157; my emphasis).

The concept of "facts" as the essential world to which a worker should address him or herself is something that bore implications beyond the process of consumption. Although Filene's notion of *fact* was largely circumscribed by the wares of the commodity market, the notion of workers feeling comfortable in a world of facts reflects basic transformations in industrial life that characterize machine production and mass production in particular. As long as the apprentice–craftsman system had endured, earning a living was comprised of both productive activity and the social relations of commerce. Goods were made and sold for individuals, and the relationship between craftsmen and individual purchasers essentially affected the definition of work. In a highly mechanized machine production, however, where both commercial interchange and the interchange of long-term training had been eradicated, human intercourse had been largely excised from the work routine of laboring classes. Robert and Helen Lynd, in *Middletown*, their 1924 study of Muncie, Indiana, described how the world of people and the world of things had been cleaved from each other in the industrial process:

> Members of the [working class] . . . address their activities in getting their living primarily to *things*, utilizing material tools in the making of things and the performance of services, while members of [the business class] . . . address their activities predominantly to *people* in the selling or promotion of things, services and ideas. (Lynd and Lynd, 1929: 22)

Presenting "education" as an indoctrination into the world of facts of the marketplace – as opposed to the social relations of production and distribution – was a replication of developments which had shaped patterns of production. Consumption was but a reinforcement of the basic transformation that had increasingly characterized the world of work – a response to *things* rather than *people*, this time extended into daily life and leisure.

Widespread within the socially orientated literature of business in the twenties and thirties is a notion of educating people into an acceptance of the products and aesthetics of a mass-produced culture. Industrial development, then, became far more than a technological process, but also a process of organizing and controlling "long pent-up human impulses" in such a way that these impulses might serve to provide social underpinnings to the industrial system (Filene, 1931:14). Branding all patterns of life which resisted the domination of culture by the industrial machinery as "puritanism in consumption," Leverett S. Lyon's 1920s contribution to the *Encyclopedia of the Social Sciences* called for a training in industrial aesthetics to combat traditional patterns of culture. "What is most needed for American consumption," he wrote, "is training in art and taste in a generous consumption of goods, if such there can be. Advertising," he continued, "is the greatest force at work against the traditional economy of an age-long poverty as well as that of our own pioneer period; it is almost the only force at work against puritanism in consumption. It can infuse art into the things of life; and it will [!] . . ." (Lyon, 1922: 475).

Yet the argument for "education" that became so frequently heard among businessmen in the 1920s, and grew quite frantic as economic crisis appeared at hand,[4] was one which confronted many varieties of historical resistance. First of all, whilst the adoption of a consumerized mentality among working people might affect a political loyalty to the capitalistic premises of the industrial system, there was too little materially – during the 1920s – to secure such loyalties. Despite rhetorical calls among business people for "higher wages" as a tactic of social integration, wages among the vast number of working people remained too low and the desire for expanding profits among business too high to create a high level of material participation by workers in the commodity market.

During the 1920s, notes historian Irving Bernstein, wage earners "did not enjoy as great a rise in income as those in higher brackets" (Bernstein, 1960: 54). Citing figures worked out in Paul Douglas's 1924 study of "Wages and the Family," Bernstein argues that a majority of American working-class families throughout the twenties failed to earn a living which would make them consumers of any great amount of goods beyond subsistence (Bernstein, 1960: 61). If an "American" standard of consumption required at least $2,000 to $2,400 annual income, as Douglas argued, most wage-earning families (16,354,000 families according to Bernstein's calculation) received less than $2,000 per year. While mass consumption rose steadily throughout the twenties, it did not significantly alter the amount of capital in-flow from working-class sectors of the population. Where consumption rose among workers, it rose largely as a result of instalment buying on the one hand (this was also an aspect of middle-class consumption) or the forgoing of one set of goods for another. Regarding the latter, the Lynd's study, *Middletown*, indicates that the widespread consumption of automobiles during the twenties, even among working-class families, was often done at the expense of clothing, food, or the mortgaging of family property, where it existed (Lynd and Lynd, 1929: 254–6).

Beyond this, and perhaps more important to the consciousness of many, were the indigenous networks of social structure that carried premises and values which generated mistrust or open opposition to the corporate monopolization of culture. Traditional family structures, agricultural life styles, immigrant values which accounted for a vast percentage of the attitudes of American working classes, and the traditional realms of aesthetic expression – all of these were historically infused with an agglomeration of self-sufficiency, communitarianism, localized popular culture, thrift, and subjective social bonds and experiences that stood, like Indians, on the frontiers of industrial–cultural development. It was these subjective experiences of traditional culture that stood between advancing industrial machinery and the synthesis of a new order of industrial culture. And it was incumbent on industry, in formalizing the new order, to find a means to sacrifice the old. It was within this historical circumstance that the creation of an industrialized *education* into culture took on its political coloration.

Throughout the 1920s and 1930s the contiguity of industrialization and social control came to the fore in the United States and elsewhere. As Max Horkheimer, a social critic from the Frankfurt School, has noted in discussing monopolizing industrialism: "the rule of economy over all personal relationships, the universal control of commodities over the totality of life" must in the face of historical resistance become "a new and naked form of command and obedience" (Horkheimer, 1941:,379). Much as in the case of totalitarian Nazi Germany which he was addressing himself to, the advance of corporate industrialism required that "the objects of organization [be] . . . disorganized as subjects" (Horkheimer, 1941: 384).

Notes

1   *Forbe's Magazine* (April 1927)
2   In Gutman's (1973) article there is the best extensive discussion of the recurrent tensions between indigenous working-class cultures (largely immigrant) and the problem of industrial organization and ideology. While Gutman's work tends to distil out working-class culture as autonomous and to view capitalism as an obstacle or impediment, rather than as a social system in which workers are involved, this in no way invalidates the value of his work.
3   *Printer's Ink: A Journal for Advertisers, Fifty Years: 1888–1938* (special edition) p. 397.
4   In business writings and pronouncements on the problem of overproduction, the link is often drawn between this and the political/economic function of consumption.

References

Bernays, E. L. (1965) *Biography of an Idea: Memoirs of a Public Relations Counsel,* New York.
Bernstein, I. (1960) *The Lean Years,* Boston.
Ellul, J. (1967) *Technological Society,* New York.
Filene, E. (1931) *Successful Living in the Machine Age,* New York.
Gutman, H. (1973) "Work, culture and society in industrializing America," *American Historical Review,* 78, no 3.
Horkheimer, M. (1941) "The end of reason," *Studies in Philosophy and Social Science,* 9.
Lynd, H. M. and Lynd, R. S. (1929) *Middletown: A Study in Contemporary American Culture,* New York.
Lyon, L. S. (1922) *The Encyclopedia of the Social Sciences,* Vol. 1, New York.
Nystrom, P. H. (1929) *Economic Principles of Consumption,* New York.
Rorty, J. (1934) *Our Master's Voice: Advertising,* New York.

14

Was There Love on the Dole?

Gary Cross

For obvious reasons debates about consumer society have frequently tended to focus upon periods of relative economic affluence. Here, however, Gary Cross looks at the status of consumer culture during the Depression years of the 1930s. He argues that far from representing a period in which the emerging values of consumerism were rejected in favor of the more "traditional" values of self-sufficiency and "making do," the ideological initiative on the part of the business world described in chapter 13 by Ewen had in fact already taken a firm grip on the imaginations of many ordinary people, who, in spite of lack of material access to mass consumption, still saw it as a definite aspirational ideal.

While the Depression undermined the value of free time, it reconfirmed the worth of money. When unemployment became a mark of social difference, the resulting loss of income became a symbol of social exclusion. This was particularly true because the impact of economic hardship was very unevenly distributed. Moreover, daily contact with the affluent on urban streets and nearly universal access to the mass media that nearly continuously displayed luxury only increased the humiliation of poverty.[1]

Those who continued to hold full-time jobs in the US suffered little. In fact, *hourly* wage levels were relatively stable (compared to the massive cuts of earlier depressions). Between 1929 and 1932, hourly wages declined only 13 per cent while the cost of living decreased 20.7 per cent. The problem was with the jobless and those placed on short-time schedules. Average hours were cut 24 per cent and by 1932 the wages in manufacturing were 59 per cent of the 1929 level. The more steadily employed groups of salaried workers, however, saw earnings drop only one quarter.[2] The British pattern was similar. Some regions experienced drastic declines in employment. For example, in 1936, joblessness reached 28 per cent in South Wales but touched only 6.5 per cent in London. Many communities where unemployment was widespread became passive and lowered expectations. But, because prices dropped faster than wages, the steadily employed sectors of the

From *Time and Money: The Making of Consumer Culture* (London: Routledge, 1993), pp. 143–53. Reprinted by permission of the publishers.

British workforce were often better off. Their access to transportation, entertainment, and clothing increased.[3]

Many of the Depression's victims were in daily contact with the more affluent. This probably only intensified the longing for goods among those who experienced real decline in purchasing power. As American sociologist Glen Elder notes (1974):

> Comparisons with past gratifications and standards only served to intensify discontent in deprived families. . . . The higher the climb before the Depression, the greater the investment in the way things were at that time, and the more intense the frustration of downward mobility.[4]

The result was that all associated status and even adulthood with goods.

It is, of course, difficult to find direct evidence to support this thesis. But the fact that 'luxury' consumption did not always drop as fast as did income is a significant indicator. While spending clearly declined during the early Depression years, for expensive items like cars (by 70 per cent between 1929 and 1932 in the US), people kept up spending on gasoline for older cars. Smokers hardly reduced their dependency on cigarettes: American sales dropped merely 6 per cent by 1933 and rose 22 per cent over 1929 levels by 1936. Americans bought new electrical appliances, especially refrigerators. As economic historian Winifred Wandersee notes, 'To many families a radio, the latest movie, a package of cigarettes, or the daily newspaper were as necessary to the family well-being as food, clothing and shelter.'[5]

Contemporaries often stressed the 'escapist' character of working-class leisure consumption in the 1930s when the jobless bought cheap magazines, went to sensational films, gambled to 'forget their troubles'. 'Schoolboy adventure' for men and fashion and gossip magazines for women dominated reading hours. Orwell claimed that 'twenty million people are underfed but literally everyone in England has access to a radio'. John Hilton's *Rich Man, Poor Man* (1944) found that extra income of British workers went to better clothing, housing and food, but it also was spent on 'pools, perms and pints, on cigarettes, cinemas and singles-and-splashes; on turnstiles, totalisators and twiddlems: and on all manner of two pennyworths of this and that'.[6] Sympathetic labour historians, however, often emphasize that indulgence in cheap luxuries, like films and betting, sustained life and that, in any case, austerity was unrealistic. American and British middle-class magazine readers may have been treated to the virtues of thrift (and the benefits of home-canning). But few working people had either the equipment or the will to make much use of this advice. In the early 1930s, one unemployed Briton asked his readers to think of how humiliating it was for the jobless to hear the admonition to 'scrape together a few bones and cabbage leaves . . . [to] make a good dinner'.[7]

Even if the 'escapist' theory is unfair, we cannot entirely discount the psychological effects of poverty.[8] The experience of reduced income on people who

193

expected expanded access to goods 'must have made the pinch of hard times seem intolerable', noted the American sociologist Jesse Steiner in 1937. Steiner and other advocates of the 'new leisure' hoped that old sociability and pleasure might be revived. He was encouraged that surveys showed that Depression-era Americans were spending much more time on cost-free home recreations. But he was ignoring the implication of his own insight about the need for luxury.[9] His counterpart, the Briton C. Northcott Greene, made the same observation: joblessness meant not destitution but a 'lack of a few extra shillings [which] cramps [the jobless] in every way'. Yet too he hoped that this problem could be solved by replacing tea with cheaper cocoa and other forms of domestic economy. But, again, as Orwell made abundantly clear in *Road to Wigan Pier*, poverty increased the need for luxury.[10]

A revealing pattern of 'irrational' consumer behaviour during the Depression was popular gambling in Britain. During the 1930s, gaming gained strength when otherwise unemployed men served bookmakers as runners, gathering bets at pubs. Littlewoods football pools were especially popular, drawing on the 'tanners' of millions; bets were small and the mail-in coupon due the Thursday before the Saturday games became a weekly ritual for perhaps 40 per cent of the adult male population by 1935. Talk on the line at the labour exchange, noted Bakke, was mostly about 'horses and the dogs'.[11] Commercial gambling was, of course, widespread among other urban working-class peoples. For example, in the 1930s, blacks from south Chicago patronized some 500 'policy stations' (almost as many as churches) which provided an illegal, but 'protected', lottery for these poor people. And, in the American West, the gambling towns of Las Vegas and Reno expanded to serve the population centres of southern and northern California.[12]

What attracted people of marginal and insecure income to gamble? As English observer H. L. Smith opined (1935):

> certainly more pleasure is gained in anticipation than is lost in disappointment. The pleasure lasts for some days; but the disappointment is momentary and easily forgotten. Also the fact that many people are excited at the same time about the same event increases the pleasurable excitement of each.

James Hilton's survey of football-pool betters found that few expected more from winnings than the purchase of small gifts for the family or for the financing of home-improvement projects. Historian Ross McKibbin notes that many male British workers despised bingo and the lottery as mindless, preferring their 'learned guesses' based on information gleaned from sporting magazines and 'inside' tips. Winners gained status as skilled practitioners. Betting gave men without public stature one of their few opportunities to make decisions. The competitive tension released in gambling filled a need, denied by the modern division of labour.[13]

But all this is secondary to the essential purpose of gambling – the winning of money that was otherwise unattainable. When, as during the Depression, hard times seemed as arbitrary as did the unearned income of the rich, workers could believe in the possibility of fortuitous gain, no matter how long the odds. The football pools and the Irish sweepstakes seemed 'democratic' opportunities for the people to share in good fortune instead of just hard luck. For many, especially because the cost was nominal, gambling appeared to be a wise investment. 'Why not me?' they asked. As McKibbin notes, 'it was this irregularity of income which generated a rhythm of debt and credit of which gambling was to become an intrinsic part'. British workers gambled rather than saved (except for burial insurance). 'Though the working-class attitude to time was probably fatalistic it was also optimistic.' The future would take care of itself; but it might also bring good luck.[14]

More central still to the social meaning of money was the association of wealth and its display with respectability. This has been a major theme of social historians of the late Victorian worker. English historian Paul Johnson, for example, stresses

the positive desires [of workers] to display the extent of savings and wealth because these were so important in determining the ranking of individuals in the working-class hierarchy. So ornaments were collected and arranged in the parlour for display to visitors, and 'Sunday best' was worn even by the irreligious.[15]

This attitude, of course, survived into the 1930s.

Moreover, spending was psychologically liberating and its lack was devastating. For wage-earners in Jack Common's *Seven Shifts*, Saturday night was not only free from work but it was the time when they could dress up and spend: 'even if the surplus is tiny, people will relax on it, and there's a difference in the way they walk and talk with each other'. Thus the despair of the jobless in Walter Greenwood's novel, *Love on the Dole* (1933), becomes intelligible: he was 'suddenly wakened to the fact that he was a prisoner. The walls of the shops, houses, and places of amusement were his prison walls; lacking money to buy his way into them, the doors were all closed against him.' The jobless or underemployed experienced scarcity in a world of semi-affluence and remembered pleasures. The 'other' was not the employer or powerful but consumers. A young Greenwood character 'felt resentful of everybody who was prosperous'. And, by this, he meant new apprentices, the bookie, and 'cadaverous pawnbroker'.[16]

Resentment was tempered with identification with those who could buy. The jobless dreamed of the respect and freedom that came from the ability to consume. This is why, noted F. Zweig in the 1940s, English workers resisted any effort by government or social elites to control leisure or consumption. For them, 'the spending of money in a spectacular way is marvellous'. Recreation meant freedom and it must constantly change. So-called male 'providers', claimed Zweig, placed great stock in their own spending money; they even reduced the percentage given to their wives for household management when their wages increased. Sons were allowed to withhold much of their apprenticeship pay while parents kept their demands 'more or less on the level of a lodger's pay'.[17] Fathers and teenage boys defined freedom and even manhood in terms of choice in spending. Doubtless many workers shared the explanation of a 'leading citizen' of Middletown of why people judged others by their houses and cars: 'It's perfectly natural. You see, they know money, and they don't know you.'[18] Reduced personal income and the social isolation of joblessness probably reinforced the tendency to make such judgements. This helps explain why the Depression (and postwar austerity) produced neither sustained challenges to capitalism nor support for the cultural alternative of 'democratic leisure'. Instead, these crises heightened the disparity between socially defined consumer expectations and the personal experience of scarcity.

The trauma of austerity centred on frustrating efforts to maintain consumption routines. English workers tried to stick to the 'right sort' of cinema when the family occupied their regular 'pew' on Saturday night. Bakke found that the unemployed of Greenwich, England, still spent 2.6 hours per week at the films and 'the influence of these hours extends far beyond the time spent in the theatre'.[19] Others attempted to carry on the annual habit of summer holidays.[20] Some American families tried to maintain consumption routines through deficit spending. Instalment buying, that had become habitual in the 1920s, continued in the Depression decade. By 1932, about 60 per cent of furniture, autos and household appliances were bought on hire purchase as were up to three quarters of radios and half of other electrical domestic goods. Instalment sales comprised nearly 15 per cent of consumption. Particularly sharp decreases in food prices produced savings that could be used to keep up spending on 'extras' like women's clothing and car maintenance. As the Lynds pointed out, 'car ownership stands to [Middletowners] for a large share of the "American Dream"; they cling to it as they cling to self-respect'.[21]

A major cause of distress was the inability of the jobless to keep up social obligations in spending. For men, this often meant an inability to play the roles of 'mate' and provider. Bakke's jobless men in Greenwich dropped out of the old gang when they could no longer participate in the informal code of reciprocity: 'I like to keep my end up. I can't do it and I know what they think of me even if they don't say it.'[22] This impeded the normal pub life of the jobless who were unable to participate in the ritual of 'standing rounds'. The Briton Max Cohen, in his *I Was One of the Unemployed*, was humiliated by having to borrow from others and frustrated by his inability to join old friends 'somewhere bright and gay, lively and happy'; he had only six shillings per week after rent while on the dole. This same sense of social obligation affected families too. An American couple without work complained:

You can't even have a card game without serving sandwiches and coffee, . . . but all that costs something. We had some people with whom we kept up our contacts, and by common agreement we decided we wouldn't serve refreshments. Somehow it wasn't much fun any longer and we very soon broke up.

But this humiliation particularly obsessed men. Some abandoned old hobbies like photography, embarrassed at having to look at the pictures taken by others.[23] A jobless Greenwood character 'would slink round the by-streets . . . glad to be somewhere out of the way of the public gaze, any place where there were no girls to see him in his threadbare jacket and patched overalls'.[24] Part of the male's identity, developed since apprenticeship years, was the ability to participate in a fraternity of casual consumption with fellow workmates. And this symbol of manhood faded with unemployment.

The frustration of reduced income, of course, extended to the male 'provider' role. English and American fathers were humiliated by their inability to provide children with fashionable clothing for Sunday outings or even 'pennies' for their small offspring.[25] As a jobless English father noted:

It gets on your mind, to see the kids around and you know you're not bringing anything to them. I used to like them have to run to meet me when I came home from work. But now . . . well – I almost wish they wouldn't come. It's hell when a man can't even support his own family.

Note also this comment from a husband: 'It's getting me under to see the wife supporting us, and me who is supposed to be the head of the family doing nothing but look for work.' Manhood was identified with being the provider. An American wife admitted that 'maybe it is not [her husband's] fault that he's unemployed, but it's a man's business to support his family'. Ginzberg found that some women denied sex to their jobless husbands. According to Komarovsky, unemployed American fathers sometimes expected to lose the love of their children while they were jobless, especially if their relationship with their offspring was based on co-erced respect. Income provided breadwinning men both power and 'a margin of toleration' from wives and children for their human frailties. Not only did jobless-ness mean for men a loss of social status and authority in the family, but it seemed to undermine their masculinity and to cause psychosomatic illness.[26] Given this domestic culture, it is hardly surprising that politicians could make points by advo-cating that married men be given priority over women in lay-off decisions in order to preserve male roles as providers.[27]

The provisioning function expressed more than male vanity and the man's do-mestic power. Money greased the wheels of family life. Speaking about American families, Bakke noted:

A large proportion of our problems is solved customarily by the expenditure of money . . . The necessity for undertaking a special campaign for funds every time a necessary

197

expenditure must be made places tremendous strain upon the organizational and planning abilities of the family.

Spending for, and keeping goods within, the family created cohesion.[28] Wandersee observed that 'the man who worked to pay for an automobile, a refrigerator, or a radio was contributing to a family identity, but that identity was maintained through possession rather than production'. The absence of that income reduced not only the status of the provider but threatened the unity of the family. As Margaret Mead would comment some years later, 'when people did not have enough work, no money, and so no symbolic right to play, entertainment was curtailed, movie money was short, dates lacked gaiety, and child bearing was postponed'.[29]

Consumption was part of a complex culture of domestic respectability. Despite the public routine of cinema-going, the Depression led to a turn inward on the home. The English (and American) working-class fixation on keeping 'intact the front room' is well known.[30] The trend towards domestic consumerism was increased by access to cheap radios in the 1930s.[31] The Pilgrim Trust and Mass-Observers were impressed by the efforts of poor families to cling to the dignity and independence symbolized by keeping up life-insurance payments. The traditional obsession with a respectable burial was to avoid the indignity of the 'final dependency'. This, like so many other forms of working-class consumption, expressed a will to privacy and freedom from humiliating reliance on the state or charity.[32]

This quest for familial autonomy doubtless also contributed to the long gradual trend towards married women entering the workforce. The Depression simply exacerbated a complex and still poorly understood movement of mothers into the labour market in the twentieth century. Slowly these women replaced wage-earning children as sources of supplemental family income. Not only reduced domestic production made this possible and necessary, but rising expectations of consumption seemed to have propelled this trend.[33]

But, even when married women held jobs while their husbands did not, role reversals did not necessarily follow. Komarovsky found that only in 13 of the 58 families that she studied did the husband's authority actually decline markedly. Wage-earning married women were far from gaining domestic power, much less independence to pursue outside activities. Many women, as documented in the oral history collection, the 'Voices of American Homemakers Project', filled the gap left by their husband's unemployment with a harried mix of money-making and goods-producing: they sewed, cleaned the homes of the more fortunate, and gardened. They realized the frustration that their granddaughters would later experience – compounded duty in house and wage work.[34] As Wandersee observes, these wage-earning wives 'faced the double task of maintaining [the home] both economically and emotionally. . . . It is thus no wonder that few women exulted in this enforced leadership; it was undertaken at great cost to themselves and their families.' This strain was even more apparent for many women during World War II when the conflict between job and domestic obligations was often unbearable.[35]

It is hardly surprising that this experience, even if short-lived, tended to reinforce the prevailing sexual division of labour, especially among the children of the Depression. Glenn Elder's study of American offspring of families of the 1930s suggests that daughters were denied support for further education and were socialized early to domestic roles, rather than to 'enforced' independence. Responsibility, not fulfilment, was the learned value. Boys were more likely to be freed from parental control, especially if they found jobs at an early age when fathers were laid off. Thus, for males, both the fraternity of spending and the work ethic of the provider were reinforced. The 'feminine mystique' and the ideology of male providing which dominated the 1950s was reinforced by the experience of the 1930s. This gender system was founded on consumption and 'full-time employment'.[36] For many, the Depression solidified the gender order by revealing its stress points: the wife's domestic domain and the male's role of provider. The slump showed that neither women nor men wished to abandon these roles. This gendered system created the ideal 'balance' of wage-work and consumption time that emerged after World War II around the 40-hour workweek.

It never made sense for populist intellectuals to project on to working people their nostalgia for an ascetic community of neighbours around leisure. But neither was it accurate for more conservative observers to presume that wage-earners with free time would do nothing but become victims of the con men of consumerism or, in the frustration of unstructured time, escape freedom in overtime and moonlighting. That intellectuals vacillated between these extremes is proof of the persistence of the chasm that separates intellectuals from working people. In reality, wage-earners seemed to respond to the opportunities of time and money in the ever-changing context of their concrete lives. Openings for the quest for free time have been very brief, coinciding with unusual periods of organizational power and consciousness. In their absence, the disciplinary power of the market reduced the range of choice to a defence of present living standards within the prevailing gender system.

A nascent mass consumerism in the 1920s, in the US especially, may well have begun to lash wage-earners to the wheel of work. But the traumas of the Depression decade which followed also had an impact. In that situation, where poverty was not general but restricted to 'deindustrializing' regions, economic scarcity meant loss of self-respect. Workers defined themselves less as jobholders and more as consumers. Instead of creating a militant class against capitalism, unemployment humiliated working families with unfunded leisure. This was inevitable in a society where, especially for men, free time was a compensation for work and leisure was inherently dependent upon income beyond subsistence. Not only was the value of free time diminished and money endowed with special social power, but commitment to work was reinforced. Few jobless families found that 'all of our friends are in the same boat'. Many believed that others in their status group were better off. This made deprived families unwilling either to accept relief or to identify with the jobless even if they themselves were among the unemployed.[37] Despite the emergence of new social solidarities of trade unionism, these movements only temporarily reversed the logic of individualism: free time became, if anything, more privatized; and money increasingly became the mark of personal family status. Even if some recognized the value of non-waged domestic labour in the 1930s and the economic disruptions to the sexual division of labour made possible a domestic power shift, the Depression tended more to reinforce the existing status quo in gender relations. The identity of men as providers and women as keepers of a private domestic order was reconfirmed.

Finally, the interwar experience advanced the notion of personal fulfilment through consumption. Advertising, the media, and instalment buying created a precocious consumerism in America from the 1920s. As historian Richard Fox summarizes, by the 1950s: 'All seemed united by their commitment to acquiring the mass marketed tokens of "the American standard of living"'.[38] Britain and later France were not far behind. The identification of leisure with consumption won many to hard and steady work in disagreeable jobs.

But the relative deprivation experienced by the unfortunate in the Depression surely intensified this association of free time and money. In reaction, after World War II, millions of working-class Americans and even Europeans sought to join the middle class in sampling the satisfactions that advertisers and their more fortunate neighbours had continuously displayed during the lean years.

Nevertheless, the social bias towards goods was not merely a product of the traumas of market discipline or even the distortions of the Depression. Rather that prejudice reflected the social power of consumerism that extended far beyond social emulation. This neither the intellectual nor activist of democratic leisure recognized. Commodities did not simply subvert 'traditional' ways of life; rather consumerism met accustomed social needs while undermining social contacts. Through mundane domestic consumption and exceptional purchases for vacations, spending both comforted and fulfilled dreams. And, the tensions between free time and consumption that intellectuals insisted on maintaining were attenuated. . . .

Notes

1   Recent British studies on the 1930s are Aldcroft, *Interwar Economy*; John Stevenson and Chris Cook, *The Slump, Society and the Politics of Depression*, (London, 1977); and Steven Constantine, *Unemployment in Britain Between the Wars* (London, 1988). A very good survey of scholarly opinion is Sean Glynn and Alan Booth, eds., *The Road to Full Employment* (London, 1987).

2   Lescohier, *History of Labor*, pp. 92–3. Of course per capita disposable income of Americans dropped from $682 to $363 between 1929 and 1933, rising only to $576 by 1940. US Bureau of the Census, *Historical Statistics*, p. 139.

3   Glynn and Oxborrow, *Interwar Britain*, p. 43 and n. 70.

4   Elder, *Children of Depression*, pp. 26, 53 and 61.

5   Roland Vaile, *Research Memorandum on Consumption in the Depression* (Washington, 1937), pp. 19 and 38. See also Frederic Mishkin, 'The Household Balance Sheet and the Great Depression', *Journal of Economic History* 38 (December 1978), pp. 918–36; Jesse Steiner, 'Recreation and Leisure Time Activities', in Committee on Social Trends, *Recent Social Trends*, vol. 2, p. 896; Wandersee, *Women's Work*, p. 43.

6   Orwell, *Road to Wigan Pier*, p. 80; Pilgrim Trust, *Without Work*, pp. 244–5. Hilton cited in John Stevenson, *British Society 1914–45* (London, 1984), p. 127.

7   Stephen Jones, *Workers at Play: A Social and Economic History of Leisure, 1918–1939* (London, 1986), p. 118; Charles Mowat, *Britain Between the Wars, 1918–1940* (London, 1955), p. 485; Wandersee, *Women's Work*, pp. 46–54; 'How We Live on $2,500 a Year', *Ladies Home Journal* 47 (October 1930), p. 104; Deidre Beddoe, *Back to Home and Duty: Women Between the Wars, 1918–1939* (London, 1989), pp. 102–3; and Greene, *Time to Spare*, p. 89.

8   As J. S. Dusenberry pointed out, atomistic models of spending behaviour, mathematically correlated to income, are inadequate for they ignore the social pressures to consume. J. S. Dusenberry, *Income, Saving and the Theory of Consumer Behavior* (Cambridge, MA, 1949).

9   Jesse Steiner, *Research Memorandum on Recreation in the Depression* (New York, 1937), pp. 16, 40, 43 and 45–6; National Recreation Association, *The Leisure Hours of 5,000 People* (New York, 1934), p. 15. See also Marion Flad, 'Leisure Time Activities of Four Hundred Persons', *Sociology and Social Research* 18 (January 1934), pp. 265–74.

10 C. Northcott Greene, 'Filling In the Workless Day', in Greene, *Time to Spare*, pp. 119–21 and Orwell, *Road to Wigan Pier*, pp. 88–104.

11 Although often associated with professional sporting matches, most of it was off-site and many betters had no real interest in the game itself. While an 1899 law prohibited street betting in Britain, bookies freely practised their trade in and around pubs, drawing bets of sixpence to two shillings on the horses. In one English survey, 90 per cent of male betters on the greyhounds never visited the tracks despite the availability of dog tracks (23 greyhound tracks as compared to nine horse racetracks in the London area in 1929). Perhaps 80 per cent of the working-class families of London engaged in some form of gambling in the interwar years. Mass-Observation, *The Pub and the People* (London, 1943), pp. 262–6; Burns, *Leisure in the Modern World*, p. 102; Durant, *Problem of Leisure*, pp. 158, 169, 185; Rowntree, *Progress and Poverty*, pp. 399–406; B. S. Rowntree, *English Life and Leisure* (London, 1951), ch. 2; John Hilton, *Why I Go In For the Pools* (London, 1935); and Bakke, *Unemployed Man*, p. 188. Note especially Jones, *Workers at Play*, pp. 38–40; and Ross Mckibbin's essay, 'Working-class Gambling in Britain, 1880–1939', reprinted in McKibbin's *The Ideologies of Class: Social Relations in Britain, 1880–1950* (Oxford, 1990), pp. 101–39.

12 Note the classic St Clair Drake and Horace Cayton, *Black Metropolis* (1945; repr. New

York, 1962), vol. 2, pp. 470–94; and John Findlay, *A People of Chance* (New York, 1986), chs 4 and 5.

13 Smith, *London Life and Labour*, 9, p. 271; Rowntree, *Life and Leisure*, pp. 133–4; Hilton, *Why I Go In For the Pools*; McKibbin, 'Working-class Gambling', pp. 116–23; and Ross McKibbin, 'Work and Hobbies in Britain, 1880–1950', in Jay Winter, ed., *The Working-class in Modern British History* (Cambridge, 1983), p. 144.

14 McKibbin, 'Working-class Gambling', pp. 114–15.

15 Paul Johnson, 'Credit and Thrift in the British Working Class, 1870–1939', in Winter, *Working Class in British History*, pp. 169–70.

16 Jack Common, *Seven Shifts* (London, 1937), p. 165; and Walter Greenwood, *Love on the Dole* (1933; repr. Harmondsworth, 1987), pp. 171 and 77.

17 Ferdynand Zweig, *Labour Life and Poverty*, (London, 1948), pp. 75–6, 44–7. A 'good marriage' depended upon fulfilling roles – men providing money and women managing it. But, because of the male's economic and sometimes physical dominance, the failure of wives to manage, even without decreasing household income, forced many women into a shadow economy of taking in laundry and sewing, petty trade, and even borrowing to avoid domestic violence. See Jane Lewis, 'Marriage Relations: Money and Domestic Violence in Working-class Liverpool, 1919–39', in Jane Lewis, ed., *Labour and Love: Women's Experience of Home and Family, 1850–1940* (London, 1986), pp. 195–219.

18 R. and H. Lynd, *Middletown*, p. 81.

19 Bakke, *Unemployed Man*, ch. 6.

20 Cross, *Blackpool*, chs 3 and 4.

21 Instalment buying shifted spending towards consumer-durable goods rather than an increase in total consumption. Comparisons of the distribution of American wage-earners' income between 1929 and 1932 show decreases in food and clothing spending but an increased share in miscellaneous consumption by 4.5 per cent. Vaile, *Research Memorandum on Consumption*, pp. 19, 28; Lynd, 'People as Consumers', pp. 862–3, 892, and 896; and R. and H. Lynd, *Middletown in Transition*, pp. 11 and 26.

22 Bakke, *Unemployed Man*, p. 197.

23 Mass-Observation, *The Pub*, pp. 178–82; Max Cohen, *I was One of the Unemployed* (London, 1945), especially p. 103; Beales and Lambert, *Memoirs*, p. 245; Bakke, *Citizens Without Work*, pp. 11 and 192; and Komarovsky, *Unemployed Man*, pp. 122–8, quotation from pp. 122–3.

24 Greenwood, *Love on the Dole*, p. 70.

25 See, for example, Greene, *Time to Spare*, p. 122; Bakke, *Citizens Without Work*, p. 197; and Brierley, *Means Test Man*, pp. 141 and 226.

26 Ginzberg, *Unemployed*, p. 74; and Komarovsky, *Unemployed Man*, p. 37.

27 Bakke, *Unemployed Man*, pp. 69–70; and Komarovsky, *Unemployed Man*, p. 77. See Gabriel Wells, *The Inwardness of Unemployment* (London, 1925), p. 12, where he advocates differential lay-off for men and women because 'civilization is a process of progressive polarization, distinct sphere and mission, usually supplemental'. Of course, this ideal had little practical impact given the sexual division of the labour market.

28 Bakke, *Citizens Without Work*, p. 190.

29 Wandersee, *Women's Work*, p. 26; and Margaret Mead, 'The Pattern of Leisure in

Contemporary American Culture', *Annals of American Academy of Political and Social Science* (September, 1957), pp. 11–15.

30 Pilgrim Trust, *Without Work*, p. 189; and Bakke, *Unemployed Man*, pp. 158–9.

31 See, for example, Rowntree, *Progress and Poverty*, pp. 408 and 429–45; and Richard Hoggart, *Uses of Literacy* (London, 1957), p. 24.

32 Pilgrim Trust, *Without Work*, p. 184; and Cross, *Blackpool*, p. 40.

33 This theme can be easily exaggerated: for example, the percentage of married women in an American workforce rose only from 11.7 per cent in 1930 to 15.6 per cent in 1940 and never more than 12 per cent of British married women held paid jobs in the 1930s. Of course, these figures doubtless ignore much work done in the 'informal' economy. US Bureau of the Census, *Historical Statistics of the United States*, part 1, p. 133; and UK Department of Employment, *Historical Abstract of Statistics (1921–63)* (London, 1962), p. xxx. See also, for Britain, Jane Lewis, ed., *Labour and Love: Women's Experience in Home and Family* (London, 1986); and Deidre Beddoe, *Back to Home and Duty: Women Between the Wars, 1918–1939* (London, 1989). For the US, the standard work is Ruth S. Cowan, *More Work for Mother: The Ironies of Household Technology* (New York, 1983), in addition to Wandersee, *Women's Work*.

34 National Extension Homemakers Council, 'Voices of American Homemakers Project', a four-volume typescript of interviews with American homemakers, mostly from small towns and farms, who lived during the Depression. See, for example, the comments of Essie Summers, 'Arkansas', pp. 12–13, Masa Scheer, 'Indiana', pp. 28–33, and Mrs Meyers, 'Michigan', pp. 27–8.

35 Komarovsky, *Unemployed Man*, p. 42; and Wandersee, *Women's Work*, chs 3–6, quotation on pp. 112–13. On British women's wartime experience, see Gail Braybon and Penny Summerfield, *Out of the Cage: Women's Experience in Two World Wars* (London, 1988), chs 4,5 and 14.

36 Wandersee, *Women's Work*, pp. 115–16; and Elder, *Children of the Depression*, pp. 279–82 and 290–1.

37 Komarovsky, *Unemployed Man*, p. 128.

38 R. and H. Lynd, *Middletown*, pp. 81–3; and Richard W. Fox, 'Epitaph for Middletown', in Richard Wightman Fox and T. J. Jackson Lears, eds, *Culture of Consumption* (New York, 1983), p. 103.

15

A Child's Cartography

Sharon Zukin

One aspect of the transition from pre-Fordist forms of consumption to those we typically associate with mass consumption has been the changing conception of the local neighborhood and, with it, notions of "the local community." At the heart of this neighborhood and community has usually been situated the neighborhood shopping street which, as Sharon Zukin so eloquently describes here, became a primary focus for the reproduction of social relationships and established cultural patterns. Zukin also places the decline of the local shopping street during the 1950s and beyond within the broader context of the various ethnic and racial migrations and the contemporary US city.

Sometimes at night I dream about the shopping street in the neighborhood in North Philadelphia where I grew up in the 1950s. It was an older middle-class and lower-middle-class neighborhood, all white, with both synagogues and churches. Tall sycamore trees lined both sides of the street. The houses were undoubtedly smaller than I remembered them. Many were six-room rowhouses, but all had lawns and porches in front and fenced gardens in back. Our house was built in the 1920s; my parents were the second owners. As in even older neighborhoods that stretched northwards from city center, our garden faced an alley.

Every morning the city sanitation workers wheeled their carts through the alley, clanging the metal lids of garbage cans as they picked up the garbage. From time to time, a knife grinder called his way up the alley. I remember the dairy delivering milk to our front door in glass bottles, and a fruit and vegetable peddler and a large, regional bakery sold food from trucks that parked on our street once or twice a week. The shopping street my mother favored was two blocks away. I realize now it was an outpost of urban Jewish culture – not that we thought of it as either urban or Jewish in the 1950s, or that the children were even conscious of being "European" Americans and white. To us, it was just Eleventh Street: a compact assortment of two-story brick houses, with store fronts at street level and apartments on top.

From 'While the city shops' in *The Culture of Cities* (Oxford: Blackwell Publishers, 1995), pp.192–207. Reprinted by permission of the publishers.

Among the stores were three "Jewish" delicatessens that sliced red salty lox from big sides of salmon and sold silver herrings and sour pickles from deep barrels of brine. There were three bakeries that sold their own bagels, challah, rye bread with caraway seeds, onion rolls and salt sticks, as well as coffee crumb cakes and the spirals of butter pastry I called pigs' ears until I went to France and learned to call them *papillions.* The baker's daughter was my classmate in elementary school. Her mother worked behind the counter. Mrs Fox sold butter, cheese, and eggs next door. She spoke with an East European accent that I could not identify even now and wore a white apron and brown cardigan over her housedress. She always gave me a taste of Emmenthaler, which we called *schweitzer* cheese, or the sweeter domestic Munster.

Mrs Fox and the baker's family and the extended family of the delicatessen owner all lived above their shops. There were also both kosher and nonkosher butcher shops and a fish store where live carp swam in a tank. My T-shirt and jeans came from a dry goods store on one block of the cross street and my saddle shoes from a children's shoe store on another. While there must have been several green-grocers, my mother shopped at only one. She might feud with Ben for selling her a bad tomato, but we always returned to his store. The same with Meyer the butcher, who kept a cigar stub clenched between his teeth as he split a chicken, his wife Ethel who sat at the cash register, and their son Harvey, who worked in the shop and reminded me of Elvis.

As intimate as we were with our local shopping street, we knew it was at the bottom of a cultural and geographical hierarchy. Movie theaters, banks, and super-markets – outposts of the dominant commercial culture – were farther away but still within walking distance. Near them was the local public library. While there were not yet fast food franchises on Broad Street, we could eat at the counter of a small Horn and Hardart's restaurant and shop at a branch of the Pep Boys auto supplies chain. For serious clothes shopping in department stores and for the treat of lunch and a first-run movie, we took the bus downtown.

Eleventh Street, and many other local shopping streets like it, reflect both the identity and the assimilation of an urban, secular, ethnic culture. The social repro-duction of this culture is carried out with a certain degree of separation from other groups: to some extent, in our case, from non-Jews, but mainly from non-Europe-ans and especially African Americans (see Massey and Denton, 1993). Yet the intimacy in a public space represented by a neighborhood shopping street reflects more than the insularity of an ethnic community. It also represents the relatively small scale of social life that we associate with neighborhood geography and the coherent social space of gender and social class. Neighborhood shopping streets challenge critical urban social theory because they produce both difference and continuity. Shopping streets make it necessary to understand ethnicity as a negoti-ated identity made up of a thousand different social interactions in public space, from face-to-face relations to more abstract transactions of commercial exchange (see Harvey, 1985; Sennett, 1990, 163–8).[1]

On these streets, ethnicity is in some way a substitute for intimacy. While we usually did not meet our immediate neighbors on Eleventh Street, we did know a lot about the shopkeepers. And by virtue of the talkative shopping practices of mothers and children, they knew a lot about us. Eleventh Street speaks to the old connection between proximity and survival, when locality excluded strangers (see Shields, 1992), and neighborhood shopping streets rather than regional malls, franchise stores, and home shopping networks satisfied a need for both social community and material goods.

Yet if the neighborhood shopping street of my childhood is quite distant from today's standardized, regional mall, it was also distant from the downtown commercial center of its time. Except for storekeepers, the neighborhood was not a place to work – and has not been, for most Americans, since the middle of the late nineteenth century. On weekdays, especially, the shopping street was a woman's world. Most of the women in my neighborhood when I was growing up were nonworking mothers who prepared lunch each day when their children (the post-war "babyboom") walked home from the local public school. While there were no sidewalk vendors or discount stores, customers could negotiate some prices, within limits, with storeowners, whom they knew by name. Customers also had favorite employees whom they wanted to wait on them. Because stores were small, display space was minimal. Mrs Fox kept eggs in a back room; her small refrigerated glass case held only a few cheeses and two large mounds of butter, salted and sweet. In the delicatessen, cans were wedged so tightly onto shelves only the owner's grandson could pry them loose. The plate glass windows were large but irrelevant to the display of goods. Except for seasonal fruits and vegetables, the goods never changed. The windows were useful for looking into the stores, reflecting and moving the street indoors.

By contrast, downtown was a fairyland of diversity and display. The long century of department stores (1860–1970) had so balanced rationalization and desire that shoppers, especially women, felt their inner needs were met by an intimacy with the goods (Leach, 1993). Display windows reached their apotheosis at holiday times, especially Christmas, when mechanical dolls, blinking lights, and falling "snow" attracted crowds. There seemed no end to the abundance of goods displayed on countertops and in glass showcases, and there were even goods stored away out of sight, which we glimpsed when saleswomen searched through deep drawers for a particular size or color.

One cluster of department stores at Eighth and Market Street carried a wide variety of clothes and furniture, housewares and toys, at low to moderate prices. Each had a slightly different social status: Lit Brothers' was probably lowest, Gimbel's was higher because the store stretched through the block to the more prestigious Chestnut Street and included a small branch of Saks Fifth Avenue, Stawbridge and Clothier's was higher still because it was associated by ownership and probably clientele with the WASP elite. The larger and grander John Wanamaker store was a few blocks away. Dominating both Market and Chestnut Streets, it competed with City Hall as the true center of the city. A few women's and girls' speciality clothing stores, shoe stores, restaurants, and movie theaters completed our map of the downtown, with my pediatrician's and ophthalmologist's offices, and a theater where I saw my first live stage show, on the western edge of the main shopping district. There were also stores for window shopping only; they were off limits because they were either too expensive or too tawdry.

We shopped mainly in the department stores. I knew the children's floors – toys and clothing – as well as I knew my bedroom, and I savored the separate floors in each store where sheets, lingerie, sofas, and shoes were sold. The escalators were always miraculous to me: little did I think that old John Wanamaker had to have them for his store when he realized their usefulness in moving shoppers to all the different buying areas (Leach, 1993, 73–4). In fact, the vertical stratification of the department stores, from bargain basement to luxury furs and millinery and up to linens, struck me as a natural order. It matched the horizontal stratification of the city from Eleventh Street to Broad Street and downtown, and from our neighborhood to city center through a band of inner-city ghettos, of which I gradually became more aware.

Writing about my early life as a shopper confronts both the limitations of child-hood memory and the gap between experience (*espaces vécus*) and epistemology (*espaces conçus*). What, after all, despite lives devoted to shopping, do any of us know about the public life of these streets? It seems to me that urban memoirs establish three big historical, methodological, and theoretical points about neighborhood shopping streets that could well be nursed by social critics: their importance to the social reproduction of different social groups, the distance be-tween them and the hegemonic sociospatial forms of shopping such as "down-town" and malls, and the connections they make between global and local sources of identity, and between ethnic change and commercial decline.

Memoirs suggest, at the very least, that girls develop a rather "domestic" con-ception of neighborhood shopping streets, while boys experience them as part of a more aggressive public life, a public culture of territories and display, and even gangs. Social class also shapes conceptions of the streets: wealth and cultural capi-tal affect whether knowledge of the street is mediated by hired caregivers and parents, whether a child is – like Walter Benjamin – a *flâneur* or, like Alfred Kazin, "a walker in the city." Another issue concerns the nature of the public in these public spaces. Are shopping streets best understood, as I have suggested, as the moral basis of an insular community? Are they sites of conflict between customers of one ethnic group and shopkeepers of another, often blacks and Jews, or are they sites of integration? After all, the postwar Jewish immigrants who bought stores on Eleventh Street were integrated with their American-born Jewish customers. African street vendors today sell their goods outside shops owned by African Ameri-cans.

The easy slippage between "neighborhood" and "ethnic" shopping streets raises questions about time and space, as well as about social identity. Does neighborhood refer only to the scale, while ethnicity refers to the character, of public life? To what degree does the social reproduction of difference depend on the negotiation of sameness? Does identity depend on defining oneself with or defining oneself against the city?

Let us take the urban memoirs of three members of my ethnic group: the European cultural theorist Walter Benjamin, the American travel writer Kate Simon, and the American literary critic Alfred Kazin (the only one of the three who is still alive). Despite the differences in space and time – their childhoods were spent in Berlin, Brooklyn, and the Bronx either before or after World War I – I am always astonished by the likeness between their experience of the modern city and mine. Yet the difference in social class between Benjamin and Kazin, and the difference in gender between Kazin and Simon, shape differences in their child's cartography of the city. Benjamin and Kazin are "white European males." Benjamin was raised in a bourgeois Jewish family in Berlin and so "represents" a burden of modern European history that includes ethnic assimilation, political and artistic leftism, a cosmopolitan palette of urban crowds, cafés, and patrician architecture. Kazin is, like Benjamin, a Jew. But he was born in Europe and raised in a working-class Jewish neighborhood in Brooklyn. His family spoke Yiddish at home and practiced the socialism of Jewish labor unions and immigrant politics. Kazin grew up to "represent" modern American literature, a representation of eternal conflicts between nature and cities, art and politics.

Almost the first words of their early memoirs – of Berlin and Brownsville, respectively – introduce the city seen through the filter of social class. "Now let me call back those who introduced me to the city," Benjamin so evocatively begins "A Berlin Chronicle" (1979: 293). "For although the child, in his solitary games, grows up at closest quarters to the city, he needs and seeks guides to its wider expanses, and the first of these – for a son of wealthy middle-class parents like me – are sure to have been nursemaids." From there he plunges directly into the central pleasure spaces of the city, spaces that he, by his social class and class culture, inherits: "With them I went to the Zoo . . . – or, if not to the Zoo, to the Tiergarten." Kazin, by contrast, begins his early memoirs in Brownsville, a neighborhood so distant from the central spaces of Manhattan that its residents identify going to Manhattan with going to "the city." And his memories are acrid ones: "From the moment I step off the [subway] train at Rockaway Avenue and smell the leak out of the men's room, then the pickles from the stand just below the subway steps, an instant rage comes over me, mixed with dread and some unexpected tenderness" (Kazin, 1951: 5). Kazin's rage, so immediately identified with the neighborhood shopping street, springs from his neighborhood and ethnicity, which stands in turn for the status of being an immigrant of the lower social class. Benjamin (1979: 294), quite differently, directs his rage against his mother, whom he so unwillingly accompanied on her mercilessly efficient shopping expeditions downtown that he could not for years (so he says) distinguish between his right foot and his left.

Benjamin does not write about neighborhood shopping streets. In addition to cafés and apartments, his memories of Berlin are all "downtown." From childhood, he is the true *flâneur*, disdainful yet appreciative of novelty, money, and designer labels:

> In those early years I got to know "the town" only as the theater of purchases, on which occasions it first became apparent how my father's money could cut a path for us between the shop counters and assistants and mirrors, and the appraising eyes of our mother, whose muff lay on the counter. In the ignominy of a "new suit" we stood there, our hands peeping from the sleeves like dirty price tags, and it was only in the confectioner's that our spirits rose with the feeling of having escaped the false worship that humiliated our mother before idols bearing the names of Mannheimer, Herzog and Israel, Gerson, Adam, Esders and Madler, Emma Bette, Bud and Lachmann. An impenetrable chain of mountains, no, caverns of commodities – this was "the town". (1979: 327)

Kazin's shopping street in Brownsville is made up of scant displays of bare commodities and their representations of repetition and defeat. Memory of the street is joined with memory of the fear of not being able to escape living close, in all senses, to the margins:

> The early hopelessness burns at my face like fog the minute I get off the subway. I can smell it in the air . . . It hangs over the Negro tenements in the shadows of the El-darkened street, the torn and flapping canvas sign still listing the boys who went to war, the stagnant wells of candy stores and pool parlors, the torches flaring at dusk over the vegetable stands and pushcarts, the neon-blazing fronts of liquor stores, the piles of Halvah and chocolate kisses in the windows of the candy stores next to the News and Mirror, the dusty old drugstores where urns of rows and pink and blue colored water still swing from chains, and where next door Mr A's sign still tells anyone walking down Rockaway Avenue that he has pants to fit any color suit. (1951: 6)

We see already the intimations of postwar racial change. The hopelessness, the degradation of his class Kazin also projects onto the first blacks who moved into the most dilapidated tenements. But even in the ordinary wares of the stores and their immigrant Jewish owners, Kazin finds little to attract and less to fascinate him.

Yet Kate Simon, who immigrated to a working-class neighborhood in the Bronx with her Polish Jewish parents around the same time, after World War I, still remembers the shopping streets with the pleasure – dare I say? – of domestic attraction, of identification with a woman's domestic role.

Bathgate, moving southward from Tremont towards Claremont Parkway, was the market street where mothers bought yard goods early in the week, as well as dried mushrooms and shoelaces. On Wednesdays they bought chickens and live fish to swim in the bathtub until Friday when they became Gefilte fish. Most women plucked their own chickens. . . . On the next block, Washington, was the public library, and a block north of it, on the corner with Tremont, the barber shop where I went for my Buster Brown haircut. Tremont west of Third also held the delectable five-and-ten, crisscrosses of rainbows and pots of gold. (1982: 3)

Removed in time and space from us, Benjamin's, Kazin's, and Simon's memoirs teach us much about the actual production of difference in urban streets. Benjamin inherited entry into a central, affluent space of the city; Simon and Kazin earned their way into the city by getting a university education and chosing an intellectual career. They all escaped their childhood homes: Benjamin, moving easily through the streets of Paris; Simon and Kazin, moving to Manhattan. All came to different ends. Simon died, Kazin has written his memoirs, and Benjamin, unwilling or unable to escape from the Nazis, killed himself in Europe during World War II. Yet their memoirs still speak to me. There were no kosher chicken pluckers on Eleventh Street, but the ethnic identity of Simon's and Kazin's neighborhoods resonates with the sameness-in-difference, or the difference-in-sameness, of my own, more secular shopping street. Downtown Philadelphia also has the patrician architecture and bourgeois interiors that Benjamin wrote about. While our experiences differ, our subjective maps of the city are more or less the same. Benjamin's memories of downtown evoke the social ambitions I remember of shopping on Chestnut Street and strolling through Rittenhouse Square.

African-American urban memoirs, roughly contemporaneous with those of Kazin and Simon, emphasize many of the same neighborhood sights: home, school, church (rather than synagogue), public library, and sometimes early jobs. Yet there are crucial differences, differences born of exclusion rather than insularity. Black authors remember being excluded from racially segregated schools in midwestern and northern cities or being the only African American in their classes. They remember the paradox of neighborhood shopping streets where stores were owned and staffed by whites, a situation that practically prohibits the easy intimacy I found on Eleventh Street. Their experience of downtown was shaped not only by differences of social class and wealth, but also by racial segregation. African Americans had limited opportunities to get summer jobs – compared to whites – and few opportunities to enter stores as customers. As far back as the 1820s, some streets in black neighborhoods were marked by danger, crime, the "lowlife" that other groups had created and patronized.

The novelist Chester Himes, although born into the middle class, lived for years in his young manhood as a hustler, thief, and pimp. He was introduced to city life as Walter Benjamin was, by the commercial exchanges and romantic alliances of prostitution. He chose the life of the streets. Unlike Benjamin, however, Himes is unable just to be a *flâneur*. Himes constructs his identity by emphasizing an inability to escape the streets in a way Benjamin cannot experience or perhaps even conceive of. Neither does his rage permit him Kazin's rejection of neighborhood streets: he is compelled to identify with other African Americans and with the streets. In 1926, he remembers (1990: 18), when he was a teenager in Cleveland,

> Scovil Avenue ran from 55th Street to 14th Street on the edge of the block ghetto and was the most degraded slum street I had ever seen. The police once estimated that there were 1500 black prostitutes cruising the 40 blocks of Scovil Avenue at one time. The black whores on Scovil for the most part were past their thirties, vulgar, scarred, dimwitted, in many instances without teeth, diseased, and poverty-stricken. Most of the black men in the neighborhood lived on the earnings of the whores and robbed the "hunkies." They gambled for small change, fought, drank poisonous "white mule," cut each other up, and died in the gutter.

Several years later, Himes did research on the history of Cleveland and discovered the complicity of whites in creating this neighborhood street. Unskilled East European immigrants, called *hunkies,* or Hungarians, were recruited by white employers to work in the steel mills. They came to the United States without their wives and children, often patronizing African-American prostitutes, creating a base of local employment for black women when black men were hired only as strikebreakers. While knowing this history helps Himes put Scovil Street in perspective, it does not remove the hurt of experiencing Scovil as your neighborhood shopping street.

No matter how mean the streets, or how extensive the cultural capital of some individuals, it is the black ghetto where all blacks "belong," or are relegated, by their exclusion from other social sites. When Himes was a college student at Ohio State University in Columbus, also in 1926, he saw "all the black musicals on Warren Street, which was the next street over from Long and ran through the worst of the black slums. So many soul brothers killed each other for one reason of another on Warren Street, that it was known as the Burma Road" (1990: 26). So why did a college student withdraw to the ghetto? "All the movie theaters in downtown Columbus and the white neighborhoods either segregated blacks in the upper balconies or did not receive them at all. And no white restaurants served blacks anywhere in the city, not even those near Ohio State University. I always tightened up inside whenever I passed one of them" (1990: 26).

These exclusions complicate neighborhood shopping streets in black ghettos, making them both "lower class" because they sell low-price goods and "ethnic" because they cater to a specific cultural group. For the same reasons, these streets are both "regional" commercial centers for blacks from all over the city and the metropolitan region and "local" shopping streets. Seventh Avenue or 125th Street in Harlem, South State Street in Chicago, and Pennsylvania Avenue in Baltimore are African-American downtowns. They become places to see the latest and best in "black" entertainment and well as centers of political information and organization. They attract tourists from white areas of the city and overseas. The diversity of uses explodes boundaries between upper and lower social classes among blacks, between entertainment and danger, between day and night. "South State Street was in its glory then," Langston Hughes writes in his autobiography about this area near the loop in 1916 (Hughes, 1940: 33),

> a teeming negro street with crowded theaters, restaurants, and cabarets. And excitement from noon to noon. Midnight was like day. The street was full of workers and gamblers, prostitutes and pimps, church folks and sinners. The tenements on either side were very congested. For neither love nor money could you find a decent place to live. Profiteers, thugs, and gangsters were coming into their own.

Even a more mundane, local shopping street – 145th Street on the west side of Harlem – was much more heterogeneous than similar streets in Jewish memoirs – even Brownsville's Pitkin Avenue. The Caribbean American poet Audre Lorde remembers (Lorde, 1982: 50) walking on 145th Street with her two sisters, "three plump little Black girls, dimpled knees scrubbed and oiled to a shine, hair tightly braided and tied with threads," in the late 1930s:

> We trudged up the hill past the Stardust Lounge, Mickey's Hair-Styling – Hot and Cold Press, the Harlem Bop Lounge, The Dream Café, the Freedom Barber Shop, and the Optimo Cigar Store . . . There was the Aunt May Eat Shoppe, and Sadie's Ladies' and Children's Wear. There was Lum's Chop Suey Bar, and the Shiloh Mission Baptist church painted white with colored storefront windows, the Record Store with its big radio chained outside setting a beat to the warming morning sidewalk. And on the corner of Seventh Avenue as we waited for the green light arm in arm, the yeasty and suggestively mysterious smell issuing from the cool dark beyond the swinging half-doors of the Noon Saloon.

The mix of store names speaks to corporate identity (the Optimo cigar) and individual ownership (Aunt May, Sadie), to African-American history (the Freedom Barber Shop), to the links between ethnicity and exclusion (the beauty shop and Baptist church), and to the neighborhood Chinese restaurant more typical of Manhattan in the past than of most other American cities. But the diversity also suggests a different pattern of "going out" from that of old Jewish neighborhoods. This is less exclusively a "shopping" street for daily goods, and it speaks of a strong male presence: of men who are unemployed during the day because of night jobs or no job, of men who go to church, listen to popular music, and drink in bars.

There is less of a male presence in Jewish shopping streets, at least, outside the neighborhoods of Hasidic Jews. In my neighborhood, during the postwar years, most mothers did not work outside the home. In Kazin's and Simon's time, many Jewish women worked at home on the "putting out" system of garment factories.

Black women, by contrast, worked in other people's homes as domestic workers, in stores and restaurants, and eventually in offices. They could not shop on the streets during most weekday hours. Yet black women are also important customers of neighborhood shops. Audre Lorde is impressed by her mother's aura of authority, an identity partly established by her bearing and partly by her acting out a domestic role as food gatherer in the local context of a neighborhood shopping street.

> Total strangers would turn to her in the meat market and ask what she thought about a cut of meat as to its freshness and appeal and suitability for such and such, and the butcher, impatient, would nonetheless wait for her to deliver her opinion, obviously quite a little put out but still deferential. Strangers counted upon my mother and I never knew why, but as a child it made me think she had a great deal more power than in fact she really had. (1982: 17)

Perhaps this was an exchange made on neighborhood shopping streets: as women assumed their domestic roles, and girls identified with their mothers, so they established an authority outside the home, in public space, in shopping (see also Ewen, 1985). Perhaps this memory brings Audre Lorde closer to Kate Simon and, in a way, to Walter Benjamin's mother and to mine.

Yet Lorde also experiences neighborhood shopping streets through a dual exploitation: as a girl and a black.

> In 1936–1938, 125th Street between Lenox and Eighth Avenues, later to become the shopping mecca of Black Harlem, was still a racially mixed area, with control and patronage largely in the hands of white shopkeepers. There were stores into which Black people were not welcomed, and no Black salesperson worked in the shops at all. Where our money was taken, it was taken with reluctance; and often too much was asked. (It was these conditions which young Adam Clayton Powell, Jr., addressed in his boycott and picketing of Blumstein's and Weissbecker's market in 1939 in an attempt, successful, to bring Black employment to 125th Street.) Tensions on the street were high, as they always are in racially mixed zones of transition. As a very little girl I remember shrinking from a particular sound, a hoarsely sharp, gutteral rasp, because it often meant a nasty glob of grey spittle upon my coat or shoe an instant later. My mother wiped it off with the little pieces of newspaper she always carried in her purse. (1982: 17)

As in Kazin's memoir of Brownsville, there are strong sensual memories of revulsion in Lorde's memoir and also intimations of racial change. Yet both the degradation and the change are different for a black woman than for a white man. While for Kazin the transition from Jews to blacks suggests sinking into deeper defeat, for Lorde it is a means of liberation.

Lorde also describes repeated sexual molestation by a white storeowner in Washington Heights, not far from her home in Harlem, which sets new parameters to the dangers of neighborhood shopping streets – when the customer is young, female, and black. The storeowner was "a fat white man with watery eyes and a stomach that hung over his belt like badly made jello" (1982: 49). He sold secondhand comic books, both fascinating the author by his stock and repulsing her by his body and his cigar, offering her the usual sexual trade:

> "Lemme help you up, sweetheart, you can see better." And I felt his slabby fingers like sausages grab my ribs and hoist me through a sickening arc of cigar fumes to the edge of the bins full of Bugs Bunny and Porky Pig comics . . . By the time he loosened his grip and allowed me to slide down to the blessed floor, I felt dirtied and afraid, as if I had just taken part in some filthy rite.

In return, she got an extra comic for free, no small treat for a child whose parents counted the pennies.

Even for my near contemporary, the novelist John Edgar Wideman, who grew up, as did his mother, in Homewood, an historic black ghetto in Pittsburgh, the specific configuration of neighborhood shopping streets in black areas is a source of cultural identity in an otherwise alien environment. When Wideman came to Philadelphia in 1959 as a freshman at the University of Pennsylvania, he and one of his few black classmates "would ride buses across Philly searching for places like home. Like the corner of Frankstown and Bruston in Homewood. A poolroom, barbershop, ribjoint, record store strip with bloods in Peacock colors strolling up and down and hanging out on the corner" (1984: 32). Finally, they "found South Street. Just over the bridge, walking distance if you weren't in a hurry, but as far from school, as close to home, as we could get. Another country." Thirty and forty years after Chester Himes and Langston Hughes, Wideman renegotiates their experience, and to some degree also that of their contemporaries among Jewish immigrants. Finding himself in the city is based on finding "home"; an identity of difference is reproduced by both exclusion, or the feeling of being excluded, and the reproduction of sameness on an ethnic shopping street.

Around the same time I moved away from Philadelphia, away from Eleventh Street, Wideman's mother became aware of the "decline" of Homewood. Decline there did not reflect racial transition so much as the denigration of the once stable, working-class black community. While the small shops of neighborhood shopping streets must have shown clear but gradual signs of the net closing in, as Wideman says, he chooses the example of a supermarket, part of a national chain, supposed to be one of those hegemonic forms of shopping – standardized, centralized, clean. "Some signs were subtle, gradual. The A&P started to die. Nobody mopped filth from the floors. Nobody bothered to restock empty shelves. Fewer and fewer white faces among the shoppers. A plate-glass display window gets broken and stays broken. When they finally close the store, they paste the going-out-of-business notice over the jagged, taped crack" (1984: 75).

This memory, too, voices regret at a "world we have lost." No matter what kinds of goods were sold on ethnic shopping streets, or how deep the ethnic groups' exclusion from other shopping sites, since the 1960s, shopping experiences in the ghetto have been degraded. "This used to be the downtown of Southeast Side," says Curtis Strong, a professional boxer, Illinois state champion, and subject of a video made by the sociologist Loïc Wacquant, talking about 63rd Street in Chicago. "This used to be a hot spot in the 60s. You could get anything here . . . [There was] an A&P, Buster Browns [a national brand of children's shoes], McDonald's burgers."

These memories bring us to our recent history. In the 1960s, we enter a different period, the period of the postmodern city – or what from a different view appears to be the abandonment, the reshaping, and the selective revitalization of the modern city. This happened in a context of long-term suburbanization and a shift of capital investment., white-collar employment, and cutting-edge industries away from older cities. But the central change that occurred in public discourse about American cities at this time was a connection between race and economic decline, an equation of "the urban problem" with "the Negro problem" (Beauregard, 1993: ch. 7). This change was embedded not only in demographic movements and housing markets, but also in the transformation of neighborhoods and downtown shopping streets. Following the urban riots of the middle to late 1960s, white storeowners and shoppers fled many of the neighborhoods that a generation or two of immigrants and their children had called their own. Whether they feared arson, reprisals, or theft, loss of social status or simply physical contact, people left. Many shopping streets abruptly changed their ethnicity. The "ghetto" spread to my neighborhood of North Philadelphia. Eleventh Street receded – like Marshall Street, where my parents had shopped in their youth – to a childhood memory.

Note

1 Sociologists will recall the work of the University of Chicago professor Gerald Suttles (1968), whose concept of "ordered segmentation" suggests the importance ethnic groups assign to local territory in their efforts to develop moral communities. My work differs from his because I am concerned less with ethnic differentiation than with public space, I am especially interested in commercial spaces, and I am not limiting the analysis to "slum" communities. I also see both ethnicity and urban space as responding to larger political economic factors.

References

Beauregard, R. A. (1993) *Voices of Decline: The Postwar Fate of US Cities*, Oxford: Blackwell Publishers.

Benjamin, W. (1979) "A Berlin Chronicle," in *One-Way Street and other Writings*, trans. E. Jephcott and K. Shorter, London: NLB.

Ewen, E. (1985) *Immigrant Women in the Land of Dollars*, New York: Monthly Review Press.

Harvey, D. (1985) "Money, Time, Space and the City," in *Consciousness and the Urban Experience: Studies in the History and the Theory of Capitalist Urbanization*, Baltimore: Johns Hopkins University Press.

Himes, C. (1990) *The Quality of Hurt: The Early Years*, New York: Paragon House.

Hughes, L. (1940) *The Big Sea*, New York: Hill and Wang.

Kazin, A. (1951) *A Walker in the City*, New York: Harcourt Brace and World.

Leach, W. R. (1993) *Lands of Desire: Merchants, Power and the Rise of a New American Culture*, New York: Pantheon.

Lorde, A. (1982) *Zami: A New Spelling of My Name*, Freedom, CA: Crossing Press.

Massey, D. S. and Denton, N. A. (1993) *American Apartheid: Segregation and the Making of the Underclass*, Cambridge, MA: Harvard University Press.

Sennett, R. (1990) *The Conscience of the Eye*, New York: Norton.

Shields, R. (1992) "A Truant Proximity: Presence and Absence in the Space of Modernity," *Environment and Planning D: Society and Space*, 10: 181–98.

Suttles, G. D. (1968) *The Social Order of the Slum*, Chicago: University of Chicago Press.

Wideman, J. E. (1984) *Brothers and Keepers*, New York: Holt, Rinehart and Winston.

16

The Dependence Effect

John Kenneth Galbraith

In this extract from his celebrated *Affluent Society*, originally published in 1958, John Kenneth Galbraith, long-standing hero of American liberalism, presents his most cogent critique of the traditional defence of Fordist mass production. Galbraith argues that the established orthodoxy – that the production of more and more goods simply enables the satisfaction of more and more human needs and wants – is rendered fallacious in the face of the actual evidence that it is production itself, aided by the powerful institutions of "advertising and salesmanship," that has created these needs and wants in the first place.[1]

The notion that wants do not become less urgent the more amply the individual is supplied is broadly repugnant to common sense. It is something to be believed only by those who wish to believe. Yet the conventional wisdom must be tackled on its own terrain. Intertemporal comparisons of an individual's state of mind do rest on technically vulnerable ground. Who can say for sure that the deprivation which afflicts him with hunger is more painful than the deprivation which affects him with envy of his neighbor's new car? In the time that has passed since he was poor, his soul may become subject to a new and deeper searing. And where a society is concerned, comparisons between marginal satisfactions when it is poor and those when it is affluent will involve not only the same individual at different times but different individuals at different times. The scholar who wishes to believe that with increasing affluence there is no reduction in the urgency of desires and goods is not without points for debate. However plausible the case against him, it cannot be proven. In the defense of the conventional wisdom, this amounts almost to invulnerability.

However, there is a flaw in the case. If the individual's wants are to be urgent, they must be original with himself. They cannot be urgent if they must be contrived for him. And above all, they must not be contrived by the process of production by which they are satisfied. For this means that the whole case for the urgency of production, based on the urgency of wants, falls to the ground. One

From *The Affluent Society* (Harmondsworth: Penguin Books, 1987), pp. 126–33.

cannot defend production as satisfying wants if that production creates the wants.

Were it so that a man on arising each morning was assailed by demons which instilled in him a passion sometimes for silk shirts, sometimes for kitchenware, sometimes for chamber pots, and sometimes for orange squash, there would be every reason to applaud the effort to find the goods, however odd, that quenched this flame. But should it be that his passion was the result of his first having cultivated the demons, and should it also be that his effort to allay it stirred the demons to greater and greater effort, there would be question as to how rational was his solution. Unless restrained by conventional attitudes, he might wonder if the solution lay with more goods or fewer demons.

So it is that if production creates the wants it seeks to satisfy, or if the wants emerge *pari passu* with the production, then the urgency of the wants can no longer be used to defend the urgency of the production. Production only fills a void that it has itself created.

II

The point is so central that it must be pressed. Consumer wants can have bizarre, frivolous, or even immoral origins, and an admirable case can still be made for a society that seeks to satisfy them. But the case cannot stand if it is the process of satisfying wants that creates the wants. For then the individual who urges the importance of production to satisfy these wants is precisely in the position of the onlooker who applauds the efforts of the squirrel to keep abreast of the wheel that is propelled by his own efforts.

That wants are, in fact, the fruit of production will now be denied by few serious scholars. And a considerable number of economists, though not always in full knowledge of the implications, have conceded the point. In the observation cited at the end of the preceding chapter, Keynes noted that needs of the "second class," i.e. those that are the result of efforts to keep abreast or ahead of one's fellow being, "may indeed be insatiable; for the higher the general level, the higher still are they" (Keynes, 1931: 365). And emulation has always played a considerable role in the views of other economists of want creation. One man's consumption becomes his neighbor's wish. This already means that the process by which wants are satisfied is also the process by which wants are created. The more wants that are satisfied, the more new ones are born.

However, the argument has been carried farther. A leading modern theorist of consumer behavior, Professor Dusenberry, has stated explicitly that "ours is a society in which one of the principal social goals is a higher standard of living ... [This] has great significance for the theory of consumption ... the desire to get superior goods takes on a life of its own. It provides a drive to higher expenditure which may even be stronger than that arising out of the needs which are supposed to be satisfied by that expenditure" (Dusenberry, 1949: 28). The implications of this view are impressive. The notion of independently established need now sinks into the background. Because the society sets great store by the ability to produce a high standard of living, it evaluates people by the products they possess. The urge to consume is fathered by the value system which emphasizes the ability of society to produce. The more that is produced, the more that must be owned in order to maintain the appropriate prestige. The latter is an important point, for, without going as far as Dusenberry in reducing goods to the role of symbols of prestige in the affluent society, it is plain that his argument fully implied that the production of goods creates the wants that the goods are presumed to satisfy.[2]

III

The even more direct link between production and wants is provided by the institutions of modern advertising and salesmanship. These cannot be reconciled with the notion of independently determined desires, for their central function is to create desires – to bring into being wants which previously did not exist.[3] This is accomplished by the producer of the goods or at his behest. A broad empirical relationship exists between what is spent on production of consumer goods and what is spent on synthesizing the desires for that production. A new consumer product must be introduced with a suitable advertising campaign to arouse an interest in it. The path for an expansion of output must be paved by a suitable expansion in the advertising budget. Outlays for the manufacture of a product are not more important in the strategy of modern business enterprise than outlays for the manufacturing of demand for the product. None of this is novel. All would be regarded as elementary by the most retarded student in the nation's most primitive school of business administration. The cost of this want formation is formidable. In 1974, total advertising expenditure – though, as noted, not all of it may be assigned to the synthesis of wants – amounted to approximately twenty-five billion dollars. The increase in previous years was by about a billion dollars a year. Obviously, such outlays must be integrated with the theory of consumer demand. They are too big to be ignored.

But such integration means recognizing that wants are dependent on production. It accords to the producer the function both of making the goods and of making the desires for them. It recognizes that production, not only passively through emulation, but actively through advertising and related activities, creates the wants it seeks to satisfy.

The business man and the lay reader will be puzzled over the emphasis which I give to a seemingly obvious point. The point is indeed obvious. But it is one which, to a singular degree, economist have resisted. They have sensed, as the layman does not, the damage to established ideas which lurks in these relationships.

As a result, incredibly, they have closed their eyes (and ears) to the most obtrusive of all economic phenomena, namely, modern want creation.

This is not to say that the evidence affirming the dependence of wants on advertising has been entirely ignored. It is one reason why advertising has so long been regarded with such uneasiness by economists. Here is something which cannot be accommodated easily to existing theory. More previous scholars have speculated on the urgency of desires which are so obviously the fruit of such expensively contrived campaigns for popular attention. Is a new breakfast cereal or detergent so much wanted if so much must be spent to compel in the consumer the sense of want? But there has been little tendency to go on to examine the implications of this for the theory of consumer demand and even less for the importance of production and productive efficiency. These have remained sacrosanct. More often, the uneasiness has been manifested in a general disapproval of advertising and advertising men, leading to the occasional suggestion that they shouldn't exist. Such suggestions have usually been ill received in the advertising business.

And so the notion of independently determined wants still survives. In the face of all the forces of modern salesmanship, it still rules, almost undefiled, in the textbooks. And it still remains the economist's mission – and on few matters is the pedagogy so firm – to seek unquestioningly the means for filling these wants. This being so, production remains of prime urgency. We have here, perhaps, the ultimate triumph of the conventional wisdom in its resistance to the evidence of the eyes. To equal it, one must imagine a humanitarian who was long ago persuaded of the grievous shortage of hospital facilities in the town. He continues to importune the passerby for money for more beds and refuses to notice that the town doctor is deftly knocking over pedestrians with his car to keep up the occupancy.

And in unravelling the complex, we should always be careful not to overlook the obvious. The fact that wants can be synthesized by advertising, catalyzed by salesmanship, and shaped by the discreet manipulations of the persuaders shows that they are not very urgent. A man who is hungry need never be told of his need for food. If he is inspired by his appetite, he is immune to the influences of Messrs. Batten, Barton, Durstine & Osborn. The latter are effective only with those who are so far removed from physical want that they do not already know what they want. In this state alone, men are open to persuasion.

IV

The general conclusion of these pages is of such importance for this essay that it had perhaps best be put with some formality. As a society becomes increasingly affluent, wants are increasingly created by the process by which they are satisfied. This may operate passively. Increases in consumption, the counterpart of increases in production, act by suggestion or emulation to create wants. Expectation rises with attainment. Or producers may proceed actively to create wants through advertising and salesmanship. Wants thus come to depend on output. In technical terms, it can no longer be assumed that welfare is greater at an all-round higher level of production than at a lower one. It may be the same. The higher level of production has, merely, a higher level of want creation necessitating a higher level of want satisfaction. There will be frequent occasion to refer to the way wants depend on the process by which they are satisfied. It will be convenient to call it the Dependence Effect.

We may now contemplate briefly the conclusions to which this analysis has brought us.

Plainly, the theory of consumer demand is a peculiarly treacherous friend of the present goals of economics. At first glance, it seems to defend the continuing urgency of production and our preoccupation with it as a goal. The economist does not enter into the dubious moral arguments about the importance or virtue of the wants to be satisfied. He doesn't pretend to compare mental states of the same or different people at different times and to suggest that one is less urgent than the other. The desire is there. That for him is sufficient. He sets about in a workmanlike way to satisfy desire, and accordingly, he sets the proper store by the production that does. Like woman's, his work is never done.

But this rationalization, handsomely though it seems to serve, turns destructively on those who advance it once it is conceded that wants are themselves both passively and deliberately the fruits of the process by which they are satisfied. Then the production of goods satisfies the wants that the consumption of these goods creates or that the producers of goods synthesize. Production induces more wants and the need for more production. So far, in a major *tour de force*, the implications have been ignored. But this obviously is a perilous solution. It cannot long survive discussion.

Among the many models of the good society, no one has urged the squirrel wheel. Moreover . . . the wheel is not one that revolves with perfect smoothness. Aside from its dubious cultural charm, there are serious structural weaknesses which one day may embarrass us. For the moment, however, it is sufficient to reflect on the difficult terrain which we are traversing. In Chapter VIII, we saw how deeply we were committed to production for reasons of economic security. Not the goods but the employment provided by their production was the thing by which we set ultimate store. Now we find our concern for goods further undermined. It does not arise in spontaneous consumer need. Rather the dependence effect means that it grows out of the process of production itself. If production is to increase, the wants must be effectively contrived. In the absence of the contrivance, the increase would not occur. This is not true of all goods, but that it is true of a substantial part is sufficient. It means that since the demand for this part would not exist, were it not contrived, its utility or urgency, *ex* contrivance, is zero. If we regard this production as marginal, we may say that the marginal utility of present aggregate output, *ex* advertising and salesmanship, is zero. Clearly the attitudes and values which make production the central achievement of our society have some exceptionally twisted roots.

Perhaps the thing most evident of all is how new and varied become the problems we must ponder when we break the nexus with the work of Ricardo and face the economics of affluence of the world in which we live. It is easy to see why the conventional wisdom resists so stoutly such change. It is far, far better and much safer to have a firm anchor in nonsense than to put out on the troubled seas of thought.

Notes

1 See also J. K. Galbraith, *The New Industrial State*, Harmondsworth: Penguin Books, 1974.
2 A more recent and definitive study of consumer demand has added even more support. Professors Houthakker and Taylor (1970), in a statistical study of the determinants of demand, found that for most products price and income, the accepted determinants, were less important than past consumption of the product. This "psychological stock," as they called it, concedes the weakness of traditional theory; current demand cannot be explained without recourse to past consumption. Such demand nurtures the need for its own increase.
3 Advertising is not a simple phenomenon. It is also important in competitive strategy and want creation is, ordinarily, a complementary result of efforts to shift the demand curve of the individual firm at the expense of others or (less importantly, I think) to change its shape by increasing the degree of product differentiation. Some of the failure of economists to identify advertising with want creation may be attributed to the undue attention that its use in purely competitive strategy has attracted. It should be noted, however, that the competitive manipulation of consumer desire is only possible, at least on any appreciable scale, when such need is not strongly felt.

References

Dusenberry, J. S. (1949) *Income, Saving and the Theory of Consumer Behavior*, Cambridge, MA: Harvard University Press.
Houthakker, H. S. and Taylor, L. D. (1970) *Consumer Demand in the United States*, 2nd edn, Cambridge, MA: Harvard University Press.
Keynes, J. M. (1931) "Economic possibilities for our grandchildren", in *Essays in Persuasion*, London: Macmillan.

17

"Growthmanship"

Vance Packard

Along with Galbraith, Vance Packard is perhaps the most widely read among a populist readership of those liberal critics of the postwar US consumer society. Primarily through three books (*The Hidden Persuaders* (1957), *The Status Seekers* (1959), and, here, *The Wastemakers*) Packard launched a fierce assault on the perceived imperatives that are held to be coterminous with mass production and consumption. In this extract he attacks the economists' and governments' mantra-like incantations that more and more growth is not only good but is indeed virtually an essential aspect of the modern US economy.

Men's appetite for goods must be quickened and increased. (Paul Mazur)

Out of all the anxieties created by the desire to escape the developing dilemma and to make the economy hum at ever-higher levels has come a clamour for 'growth.' Economic thinkers of many stripes have joined in the call. Certainly this is the first time in history that the felt need for growth has been so self-consciously vocalized. Marketers talk of the need to increase sales of consumer goods and services by a hundred and fifty to two billion dollars within the decade. Labour spokesmen have called for 'rapid expansion'. Political candidates for the presidency in both parties have called for more growth. Conservatives who became uneasy about some of the novel ideas their rivals were offering to promote growth sneered that the rivals were making a high-level game of 'growthmanship'. In 1960, both party platforms called for more growth and differed only on how it should be achieved.

Some people have pointed to the Russian claims of rapid growth as a justification for the United States to embark on a crusade to increase its total output. With many of these, any output is considered to add to the military potential of the nation whether it involves more deodorants, more hula hoops, more electric rotisseries, or pinball machines. The fact that the United States is already out-producing Russia in consumer durables by at least twenty to one is generally ignored. Also ignored is the

From *The Wastemakers* (London: Longman, 1960), pp. 20–5.

fact that Russia has managed to startle the world by sending a giant satellite around the moon with a total national output that has been less than half of that of the United States. Russia simply has a different set of national priorities.

Furthermore, the Soviet example being held up as a challenge to the United States becomes less impressive on close inspection. Its rate of economic growth, for example, is less remarkable than that of Mexico, Japan or West Germany. Compared with that of the United States, its percentage of annual growth of output seems impressive simply because it is starting from a lower base and because it is an underdeveloped country trying to catch up with an overdeveloped one. Economist W. Allen Wallis, special assistant to the President, observed in 1960: 'Even if Russian growth rates continue higher than ours, the absolute gap between us will continue to increase for some time to come. . . . There is no possibility that the Russian economy will overtake ours at any time in the visible future – certainly not in this century.'

Still, the Russian growth rate is widely held up as a minimum challenge for Americans if they are to hold up their heads in the world. Whether the growth is particularly needed to promote the well-being of the American people is rarely even considered. No one has considered that you can make a country overgrow just as the Pentagon has concluded that you can 'over-kill' any possible enemy if you keep on producing hydrogen bombs beyond any rational need. And few have considered that some selective kinds of growth may well be needed in the United States, other kinds are undesirable or would produce only surfeit. It is just assumed that any growth is good. Growth is fast becoming a hallowed word alongside Democracy and Motherhood.

Some – but not all – planners in the federal government have also been preoccupied with the idea that any growth is good for the country. As novelist John Keats pointed out, 'Washington's planners exult whenever a contractor vomits up five thousand new houses on a rural tract that might better have remained in hay' (Keats, 1958: 230). In mid 1960, reports from Washington revealed that there was a strong feeling within the administration that more liberal allowances should be made for the obsolescence of business equipment in order to 'foster economic growth', by permitting faster tax write-offs of existing equipment.

How will all the sought-after growth be achieved? That has been the chief point of contention. Businessmen have been wary of some of the ideas tossed around by politicians and liberals as smacking of boondoggling. They are passionately convinced that the great challenge facing the nation is to make sure the citizenry will be induced to enjoy more and more of the good things in life – which they, of course, will be more than happy to produce.

To a pre-1950 economic thinker this would seem like no challenge at all. Historically, economists have assumed that people will automatically consume eagerly everything that their nation's economy can turn out for them. This concept is often referred to as Say's Law. A French economist of the past century, Jean-

Baptiste Say, concluded that production is bound to equal distribution. Say's law was conceived in an era of scarcity. There was so much poverty of even the necessities of life that a ready and eager market was assumed.

In the mid-twentieth century's era of abundance, however, his law became less and less relevant. Desire did not necessarily keep pace with productive capacity. More pertinent for the new era were the concepts of Paul Mazur, partner of a Wall Street investment house, who has become widely accepted as a leading apostle of 'consumerism'. Early in the fifties, he pointed out that every recent United States recession had been caused by the failure of business to gear its production down to what could clearly be consumed, or a failure to see that consumption kept pace with production. The result was jammed warehouses and a depressed market. In his *The Standards We Raise*, widely admired at least by the marketers of industry, he asserted:

> The giant of mass production can be maintained at the peak of its strength only when its voracious appetite can be fully and continuously satisfied. . . . It is absolutely necessary that the products that roll from the assembly lines of mass production be consumed at an equally rapid rate and not be accumulated in inventories.

Thus the challenge was to develop a public that would always have an appetite as voracious as its machines. The chief economists of the world's largest advertising agency, J. Walter Thompson, asserted in 1960 that Americans would need to learn to expand their personal consumption by sixteen billion dollars per year if they were to keep pace with this production ability. All this backlog of what he called consumer need was awaiting 'activation by advertising'. This, he said, represented the 'real opportunity' of the day.

The central problem was to stimulate greater desire and to create new wants. And this was becoming a little more difficult each year. In the late fifties, *Advertising Age* carried this headline: 'Creating Desire for Goods Gets Harder'. It quoted the chief of research of a Los Angeles newspaper who stated: 'Productive capacity has outstripped our efficiency in creating desire for goods'. He added that it was becoming increasingly hard to create a burning desire for things.

People should be persuaded to expand their wants and needs, and quickly. The head of J. Walter Thompson made that point and explained: 'We must cut down the time lag in expanding consumption to absorb this production'. This agency's various pronouncements on the state of the nation indicated that it had become infatuated with the phrase 'time lag'. Everything could be blamed on the time lag. This implied that Americans had great unrecognized wants which they would inevitably discover eventually. They just had to be educated and activated. The agency's research director, however, warned that 'the velocity of change in living standards needed to match the most conservative estimates of future productive ability nearly staggers the imagination.'

The emerging philosophy was most fervently and bluntly stated perhaps in two long articles in *The Journal of Retailing* during the mid-fifties. The author was Marketing Consultant Victor Lebow. He made a forthright plea for 'forced consumption' (Lebow, 1955: 166).

> Our enormously productive economy . . . demands that we make consumption our way of life, that we convert the buying and use of goods into rituals, that we seek our spiritual satisfactions, our ego satisfactions, in consumption. . . . We need things consumed, burned up, worn out, replaced, and discarded at an ever increasing rate.

At other points he spoke of the 'consumption requirements of our productive capacity' and of the 'obligation' of retailers 'to push more goods across their counters'.

As businessmen caught a glimpse of the potentialities inherent in endlessly expanding the wants of people under consumerism, forced draft or otherwise, many began to see blue skies. In fact, *Sales Management* featured a blue sky on the cover of one of its issues as the sixties approached with this exhortation from management to marketers: 'Go Get Us a Trillion Dollar Economy'.

At the time this order was given, the United States' economy was still approaching the *half* trillion mark.

Such heady resolutions could be implemented if the public could somehow be induced to feel the need to buy more and more products and services. Men's appetite for goods needed indeed to be quickened and increased.

Old-fashioned selling methods based on offering goods to fill an obvious need in a straightforward manner were no longer enough. Even the use of status appeals and sly appeals to the subconscious needs and anxieties of the public – which I have examined in earlier works (see Packard, 1957; 1959) – would not move goods in the mountainous dimensions desired.

What was needed was strategies that would make Americans in large numbers into voracious, wasteful, compulsive consumers – and strategies that would provide products assuring such wastefulness. Even where wastefulness was not involved, additional strategies were needed that would induce the public to consume at ever-higher levels.

Happily for the marketers, such strategies were emerging or were at hand. They had been forged in the fires of the fifties and were being perfected for use in the sixties.

It is nine such strategies and their implementation that we shall explore in detail in the next thirteen chapters. They need to be understood because, for better or worse, they are influencing profoundly the climate in which the people of the United States – and, to a growing extent, the people of the rest of the Western world – live.

References

Keats, J. (1958) *The Insolent Chariots*, Philadelphia: J. B. Lippincott.

Lebow, V. (1955) *The Journal of Retailing*, winter.

Packard, V. (1957) *The Hidden Persuaders*, London: Longmans.

Packard, V. (1959) *The Status-Seekers*, New York: David McKay.

18

Textiles: The Fabric of Life

Ernest Dichter

One of the leading figures of "motivation research," a practice that was important in informing the thinking of the advertising and marketing industries of the 1950s and 1960s, Ernest Dichter is perhaps better remembered among academics for being one of the chief targets of Jean Baudrillard's early writings. In this extract from *The Strategy of Desire*, a sort of pauper's anthropology-cum-semiotics of everyday objects and beliefs, Dichter discusses the associational qualities of a variety of textiles.

Every undergraduate student of economics is taught that such industries as steel and power are 'basic' while such other industries as textiles are not. There is no better indication of the great gap which so often appears between social truth and psychological truth. For, although steel is indeed basic to the functioning of our society, it is not basic to the functioning of human life itself.

Textiles, on the other hand, are as psychologically basic to human life as food. Biologically, man is a basic creature – 'naked' in the full sense of 'standing unprotected and exposed to the world'. All creatures need a barrier which enables them to resist the changes in the environment to which they cannot adjust. But, alone among the animals, the human species has no such adequate natural barrier between itself and the world. Only in the context of this basic situation of humankind can the psychology of textiles be understood.

'Cloth' – a synonym for textile – has the same meaning as 'clothe' – to cover. Naked things, like naked people, demand to be covered. In covering nakedness, whether of people or of things, we accomplish these five basic purposes: we protect and insulate; we facilitate contact with the world; we hide defects and weaknesses; we give the appearance we wish to give; and we decorate.

Man's basic need for a barrier between his nakedness and the world is met by his use of textiles. In all the thousands of years since the first appearance of the arts of spinning and weaving to produce cloth, no better solution to this basic human problem has been found.

From *The Strategy of Desire* (London: Boardman, 1960), pp. 104–10.

How do textiles protect? To some degree, textiles 'ward off' physical dangers to both people and objects. But their main purpose as protectors is *to insulate – to prevent contamination* of one thing by another. Clothing, for example, doesn't give warmth of itself. It wards off cold and holds in the warmth we ourselves generate. Bandages have no healing power of their own. They keep out 'bad' bacteria and allow the body's own curative powers to work. Similarly, sheets on a bed, undergarments, table linen, all serve the same basic function of acting as a barrier to contamination.

This function is psychological as well as physical. Proper clothing, people tell us, permits them to keep their psychological balance as well as their temperature balance. White lace curtains at the window are a symbolic barrier keeping the home atmosphere uncontaminated. Appeals based on these factors will be powerful motivators for they touch upon fundamental relationships in the web of human life.

Because textiles insulate – prevent contamination of one thing by another without hampering freedom of action – they also facilitate contact between people and people as well as between people and things. Fresh sheets allow us to sleep in a bed that others have occupied. Fresh tablecloths renew the dirtied table. Clothing, similarly, not only insulates us but promotes social contact at the same time.

We find that the protecting barrier of textiles softens as well as insulates. The hardness of the chair is softened by its covering. Similarly, our respondents speak of the inner hardness of a person as softened by his clothing or the hardness of the bare window as softened by draperies.

The ancient Bible story tells us that when Adam and Eve ate the fruit of the tree of knowledge, they looked at their nakedness and were ashamed. Ashamed of what? Not, we may be sure, of the exposure of their sex organs. We now know that this kind of shame depends solely upon social conditions. And in any event, such biblical allusions always refer to far deeper human forces than mere embarrassment.

Man's shame at his own nakedness to which the Bible refers is a shame arising from the awareness of being exposed in the fullest sense: exposed to the world as a creature of weakness. No force in man is more basic than his need to maintain his inner privacy – to prevent the exposure of his naked thought and his inner weaknesses.

But the great *strength* of human beings lies in the fact that they can become aware of their weaknesses – and do something about them. (The essential meaning of the Bible story then can be schematized like this: Discovery of knowledge – awareness of weakness – shame – action to overcome weakness.)

Against this background of basic functions we can now analyse a few of the basic textile materials and understand their particular appeals and lack of appeals.

Cottons, women tell us, seem 'chaste' and 'innocent' – 'fresh, clean, cool'. They give an appearance of 'inner calm' and 'unostentatious confidence'. On the other hand, they speak of cottons as 'very feminine,' 'attractive,' 'sexy in a quiet way'. The 'purity' appeal of cottons is enormously enhanced by the fact that women see them as wonderfully easy to launder, to starch and iron, to keep clean.

Cottons are 'soft and friendly', our female respondents say, yet even for the most intimate clothing are 'kind of impersonal'.

Curiously enough, men don't share this enthusiasm for cotton, but on the contrary have a strong prejudice against the idea of cotton fabrics. Even though in practice they find cotton shirts, skirts, blouses, etc., quite pleasant, in principle cotton connotes to men 'cheapness', 'shoddiness', 'lack of durability'. Partly, we find, this stems from a lack of awareness of the advances made by the textile industry in improving styles of cotton, and of the durability of this material. Partly, the prejudice comes from the fact that where women think of cottons as soft and yielding, men think of them as a neutral material – neither soft enough for the intimate, nor 'hard' enough for the impersonal functions of everyday work life. A major task of advertising for cottons in the immediate future will be to overcome this strong male prejudice.

Wool, in contrast to neutral cotton, is seen as strongly male by men and women alike. To be 'male' in our society means, among other things, to be 'without inner weakness' – and wool almost perfectly conveys this impression. As a result, wool, above all the materials which we tested, fulfils best the function of hiding inner weakness, is best for presenting the impression of unquestioned ability to withstand and deal with the rigours of the world.

Wool, our respondents say, is 'out-doors', 'belongs in the woods'; 'pipe, fire, lodge, rich pine smell, man in a red check wool shirt'. Thoughts of a rigorous environment make respondents think of wool and vice versa. The two belong together, as 'Children playing in the snow, clad in wool snow suits'.

While wool itself is not personal nor intimate, it is a shield to the personal and intimate – a protector that permits personal and intimate things to happen. One of our respondents from Maine said, 'I never seen it to fail. Get a man and woman together in a sleigh wrapped around with the same wool blanket and you can't keep 'em from getting all over from one another'. Several of our respondents had a train of thought like this – 'cold night, warm wool blanket, warm and cosy inside and umm . . .'.

Yet wool itself is sedate, conservative, refined despite its rough ruggedness. Nearly every respondent thought of English tweeds in a setting of old ivy-covered buildings – the English country squire, or the American college professor.

Because of the impersonal quality of wool, it serves perfectly to symbolize the group membership of its wearer – tweeds for university people, grey flannel for Madison Avenue, olive drab for the military.

Men relate to wool with strong emotions – it expresses exactly the qualities they wish to possess. Women, too, respond to wool warmly.

Silk is at the opposite pole from wool. It is as feminine as wool is masculine. It is as intimate as wool is impersonal. Wool connotes rugged gentility; silk is refined, delicate, and tenderly gentle. Wool belongs in the rigorous outdoors; silk belongs in the 'inner chamber'. Wool conceals; silk reveals.

Silk is sexually exciting; for many men, far more exciting than the woman in the flesh. Again, the Bible story comes to mind – man's shame at the appearance of his nakedness. Silk, however, enhances all the personal, warm, tender qualities of the wearer, while at the same time causing the 'animal' side of nakedness to disappear.

Clinical psychologists have long known the role of silk for those whose fear of the 'animal' side of their nature inhibits their sexual responses. Silk can become a fetish for such people – silk 'worship' is, in fact, a surprisingly frequent 'secret vice' in our society and is found in a great many otherwise well-adjusted people. Many, many children are ardent silk fetishists and cannot go to sleep without a 'piece of silk' to hold and rub between their fingers. (This behaviour does not, of itself, indicate any serious psychological disturbance. Usually it is merely compensation for some slight lack of mothering or indicates some degree of lack of assurance about the real depth of mother's love.)

Where the fear of the intimate, the personal, the 'naked' becomes really strong, however, it extends to silk itself and there are many men and women who for this reason violently dislike silk.

In spite of the passionate references to silk, silk itself is 'cool – like soft skin'. It is 'elegant', 'luxurious'. Everyday speech acknowledges it as a standard of excellence – 'as fine as silk'. A special value is attached to hair which is 'silken'. In other words silk is seen as the ultimate in refinement. Silk evokes images of palaces, of kings and queens and princesses, images of 'graceful oriental luxury'.

A fascinating series of studies on the nature of love was reported for the sixteenth annual convention of the American Psychological Association, August 31, 1958. In an address by Professor Harry F. Harlow, University of Wisconsin, he stated neonatal and infant macaque monkeys were used as the subject for the analysis of basic affectional attitudes. Real monkey mothers were replaced by wire and cloth mother-surrogates. The almost frightening conclusions of these studies were that the baby monkeys developed strong affection and love for the artificial cloth mothers. Further detailed experiments showed that while these cloth mothers could be made to provide milk to the infant monkeys, it was not the lactation, but almost exclusively the softness of the cloth that appealed to the infants. The experimenters talked therefore about the 'contact need', which apparently operates as well in these mother-surrogates as it does in the attitudes of people towards their pillows, blankets, and soft, cuddly stuffed toys. As Professor Harlow says: 'We were not surprised to discover that contact comfort was an important basic affectional love variable, but we did not expect it to overshadow so completely the variable of nursing; indeed, the disparity is so great as to suggest that the primary function of nursing as an affectional variable is that of insuring frequent and intimate body contact of the infant with the mother'.

231

In one of the delightful poems accompanying this article, the following struck me as particularly revealing: 'The rhino skin is thick and rough / And yet the skin is soft enough / That baby rhinos always sense / A love enormous and intense'.

The point of this chapter then is that to separate materialism from idealism, one with a negative, the other with a positive and more desirable connotation, is naive, to say the least. What we do day after day has to be the staying point for any strategy for change. We have to accept the realistic behaviour of people and eliminate morality judgements in a scientific approach.

Our problem is always how we can get people to behave the way we think they should. The discussion of the desirability of material goods and the need to turn our interests more in the direction of ideals can only be solved if we drop this superficial distinction. There are ideals that are good and those that are bad, just as much as there are good and bad possessions. What makes either one of them good or bad? To answer this we have to go back to the problems of human goals and purpose . . . [T]hese goals are growth and self-realization. A product whose possession does contribute to growth, new experiences, and dynamic forms of happiness, one which opens up new horizons, I would consider good. The word 'good' has to be used in the human, clinical sense; that is, good for human beings, their final goals in life, contributing to a richer rather than poorer life in the psychological sense.

If you keep on buying new cars, new clothes, in order to impress your friends or to follow the crowd, it is the object that possesses you. You are not getting psychologically richer. If, however, you only choose those tangible things that permit you to express yourself in a wider way, providing you with self-realization, then the object is being mastered by you.

The real role of motivational research and strategy of desire, then, in the ideal sense should be one where only those goals and objects are being praised that permit new discoveries, new experiences, self-realization. Of course, we are far from such an ideal stage. But the motivational researcher in advising the communicator, the educator, and the advertiser to stress the new horizons opened by his ideals or products would at the same time help the advertiser not only to sell his product but also reorient, re-evaluate the system of values prevalent in our society. Even buying of tangible goods, instead of arousing guilt feelings, could very well then be interpreted as one form of translating aspects of your personality into tangible form.

19
A New Language?

Jean Baudrillard

This extract comes from one of Baudrillard's earliest assaults on the consumer society in general and the advertising industry in particular. Baudrillard explores the proposition that the "system of objects," i.e. the system of consumer goods, is structured semiotically to constitute a new language. This new language materializes itself in its essential character through the brand name. However, while the system of objects is indeed a system of signification, it is also a profoundly regressive and impoverished one in which everything and everyone is reduced to a basic equivalence in consumer objects.

. . . Does the object/advertising system form a language? The idealist–consumerist philosophy is based on the substitution of lived and conflictual human relations with "personalized" relations to objects. According to Pierre Martineau, "Any buying process is an interaction between the personality of the individual and the so-called 'personality' of the product itself."[1] We make believe that products are so differentiated and multiplied that they have become complex beings, and consequently purchasing and consumption must have the same value as any *human* relation.[2] But precisely: is there an active syntax? Do objects instruct needs and structure them in a new way? Conversely, do needs instruct new social structures through the mediation of objects and their production? If this is the case, we can speak of a language. Otherwise, this is nothing more than a manager's cunning idealism.

Structure and Demarcation: The Brand

The act of buying is neither a lived nor a free form of exchange. It is a preconditioned activity where two irreducible systems confront each other. At the level of the individual, with his or her needs, conflicts, and negativity, the system is fluid

From "The system of objects" in *Selected Writings*, edited by Mark Poster (Oxford: Polity Press, 1988), pp. 14–21. Published originally as *Le Systèm des objets* (Paris: Gallimard, 1968).

and disconnected. At the level of products, in all of their positivity, the system is codified, classified, discontinuous, and relatively integrated. This is not interaction but rather the forced integration of the system of needs within the system of products. Of course, together they constitute a system of signification, and not merely one of satisfaction. But a syntax is necessary for there to be "language": the objects of mass consumption merely form a repertoire. Let me explain.

At the stage of artisanal production objects reflect the contingent and singular character of needs. While the two systems are adapted to one another they are no better integrated since they depend on the relative coherence of needs, which are fluid and contingent: there is no objective technological (*technique*) progress. Since the beginning of the industrial era, manufactured goods have acquired coherence from technological organization (*l'ordre technique*) and from the economic structure. The system of needs has become less integrated than the system of objects; the latter imposes its own coherence and thus acquires the capacity to fashion an entire society.[3] We could add that "the machine has replaced the unlimited series of variables (objects 'made to measure' in accordance with needs) with a limited number of constants."[4] Certainly we can identify the premises of a language in this transformation: internal structuration, simplification, transition to the limited and discontinuous, constitution of *technemes* and the increasing convergence of these technemes. If the artisinal object is at the level of speech (*parole*), industrial technology institutes a set of expressions (*langue*). But a set of expressions (*langue*) is not language (*langage*):[5] it is not the concrete structure of the automobile engine that is expressed but rather the form, color, shape, the accessories, and the "social standing" of the object. Here we have the tower of Babel: each item speaks its own idiom. Yet at the same time, through calculated differences and combinatorial variations, serial production demarcates significations, establishes a repertoire and creates a lexicon of forms and colors in which recurrent modalities of "speech" can be expressed: nevertheless, is this language? This immense paradigm lacks true syntax. It neither has the rigorous syntax of the technological level, nor the loose syntax of needs: floating from one to the other like an extensive repertoire, reduced, at the level of the quotidian, to an immense combinatorial matrix of types and models, where incoherent needs are distributed (*ventiler*) without any reciprocal structuration occurring. Needs disappear into products which have a greater degree of coherence. Parceled out and discontinuous, needs are inserted arbitrarily and with difficulty into a matrix of objects. Actually, the world of objects is overwhelmed by the absolute contingency of the system of individual needs. But this contingency is in some way indexed, classified, and demarcated by objects: it can therefore be directed (and this is the system's real objective on the socioeconomic level).

If the industrial technological order is capable of shaping our society it is, in a way that is contradictory, a function of society's coherence and incoherence: through its structural (technological) coherence "at the top"; and through the astructural (yet directed) incoherence of the process of product commercialization and the satisfaction of needs "at the base." We can see that language, because it is actually neither consumed nor possessed by those who speak it, still maintains the possibility of the "essential" and of a syntax of exchange (the structuration of communication). The object/advertising system, however, is overwhelmed by the "inessential" and by a destructured world of needs; it is content to satisfy those needs in their detail, without ever establishing any new structures of collective exchange.

Martineau adds: "There is no simple relationship between kinds of buyers and kinds of cars, however. Any human is a complex of many motives . . . which may vary in countless combinations. Nevertheless the different makes and models are seen as helping people give expression to their own personality dimensions."[6] He goes on to illustrate this "personalization" with a few examples.

> The conservative, in choosing and using a car, wishes to convey such ideas as dignity, reserve, maturity, seriousness. . . . Another definite series of automotive personalities is selected by the people wanting to make known their middle-of-the-road moderation, their being fashionable. . . . Further along the range of personalities are the innovators and ultramoderns.[7]

No doubt Martineau is right: it is in this way that people define themselves in relation to objects. But this also shows that it is not a language, but rather a gamut of distinguishing criteria more or less arbitrarily indexed on a gamut of stereotyped personalities. It is as if the differential system of consumption significantly helped to distinguish:

1 within the consumer, categories of needs which now have but a distant relation with the person as a lived being;
2 within society, categories or "status groups," recognizable in a specific collection of objects. The hierarchized gamuts of objects and products play exactly the same role as the set of distinguishing values played in previous times: the foundation of group morality.

On both levels, there is a solicitation, coerced grouping, and categorization of the social and personal world based on objects, developing into a hierarchical repertoire without syntax; that is, into *a system of classification, and not a language*. It is as if, through the demarcation of the social, and not by a dialectic, an imposed order was created, and through this order, for each group, a kind of objective future (materialized in objects): in short, a grid in which relations become rather impoverished. The euphoric and wily "motivation" philosophers would like to persuade themselves and others that the reign of the object is still the shortest path to freedom. They offer as proof the spectacular melange of needs and satisfactions, the abundance of choice, and the festival of supply and demand whose effervescence can provide the illusion of culture. But let us not be fooled: objects are *categories of objects* which quite tyrannically induce *categories of persons*. They undertake the policing of social meanings, and the significations they engender are controlled. Their proliferation, simultaneously arbitrary and coherent, is the best vehicle for a social order, equally arbitrary and coherent, to materialize itself effectively under the sign of affluence.

The concept of "brand," the principal concept of advertising, summarizes well the possibilities of a "language" of consumption. All products (except perishable foods) are offered today as a specific acronym: each product "worthy of the name" has a brand name (which at times is substituted for the thing itself: Frigidaire or Xerox). The function of the brand name is to signal the product; its secondary function is to mobilize connotations of affect:

> Actually, in our highly competitive system, few products are able to maintain any technical superiority for long. They must be invested with overtones to individualize them; they must be endowed with richness of associations and imagery; they must have many levels of meaning, if we expect them to be top sellers, if we hope that they will achieve the emotional attachment which shows up as brand loyalty.[8]

The psychological restructuration of the consumer is performed through a single word – Philips, Olida, General Motors – a word capable of summing up both the diversity of objects and a host of diffuse meanings. Words of synthesis summarizing a synthesis of affects: that is the miracle of the "psychological label." In effect this is the only language in which the object speaks to us, the only one it has invented. Yet, this basic lexicon, which covers walls and haunts consciences, is strictly asyntactic: diverse brands follow one another, are juxtaposed and substituted for one another without an articulation or transition. It is an erratic lexicon where one brand devours the other, each living for its own endless repetition. This is undoubtedly the most impoverished of languages: full of signification and empty meaning. It is a language of signals. And the "loyalty" to a brand name is nothing more than the conditioned reflex of a controlled affect.

But is it not a beneficial thing, our philosophers object, to tap into deep motives (*forces profondes*) (in order to reintegrate them within the impoverished system of labels)? Liberate yourself from censorship! Overcome your superego! Take courage in your desires! Yet, are we actually tapping into these deep motives in order to articulate them in language? Does this system of signification give meaning to presently hidden aspects of the individual, and if so, to which meanings? Let us listen once again to Martineau:

> Naturally it is better to use acceptable, stereotyped terms. . . . This is the very essence of metaphor. . . . If I ask you for a "mild" cigarette or a "beautiful" car, while I can't define these attributes literally, I still know that they indicate something desirable. . . . The average motorist isn't sure at all what the "octane" in gasoline actually is. . . .

But he does know vaguely that it is something good. So he orders "high-octane" gasoline, because he desires this essential quality behind the meaningless surface jargon.[9]

In other words, the discourse of advertising only arouses desire in order to generalize it in the most vague terms. "Deep motives," rephrased in their simplest expression, are indexed on an institutionalized code of connotations. And in fact, "choice" only confirms the collusion between this *moral* order and my most profound whims (*velleites*): this is the alchemy of the "psychological label."

The stereotyped evocation of "deep motives" is simply equivalent to *censorship*. The ideology of personal fulfilment, the triumphant illogicality of drives cleansed of guilt (*deculpabilisées*), is nothing more than a tremendous endeavor to materialize the superego. *It is a censor, first of all, that is "personalized" in the object.* The philosophers of consumption may well speak of "deep motives" as the immediate possibilities of happiness which need only be liberated. But the unconscious is conflictual and, insofar as advertising mobilizes it, it is mobilized as conflict. Advertising does not liberate drives. Primarily, it mobilizes phantasms which block these drives. Hence, the ambiguity of the object, in which individuals never have the opportunity to surpass themselves, but can only re-collect themselves in contradiction, in their desires and in the forces that censor their desires. We have here a general schema of gratification/frustration:[10] under the formal resolution of tensions and an incomplete regression, the object serves as a vehicle for the perpetual rechanneling of conflicts. This could possibly be a definition of the specific form of contemporary alienation: in the process of consumption internal conflicts or "deep drives" are mobilized and alienated in the same way as labor power is in the process of production.

Nothing has changed, or rather it has: restrictions in personal fulfilment no longer manifest themselves through repressive laws, or norms of obedience. Censorship operates through "unconstrained" behaviors (purchasing, choice, consumption), and through spontaneous investment. In a way, it is internalized in pleasure (*jouissance*).

A Universal Code: Social Standing

The object/advertising system constitutes a system of signification but not language, for it lacks an active syntax: it has the simplicity and effectiveness of a code. It does not structure the personality; it designates and classifies it. It does not structure social relations: it demarcates them in a hierarchical repertoire. It is formalized in a universal system of recognition of social statuses: a code of "social standing."

Within "consumer society," the notion of status, as the criterion which defines social being, tends increasingly to simplify and to coincide with the notion of "social standing." Yet "social standing" is also measured in relation to power, authority, and responsibility. But in fact: There is no real responsibility without a Rolex watch! Advertising refers explicitly to the object as a necessary criterion: You will be judged on. . . . An elegant woman is recognized by . . . etc. Undoubtedly, objects have always constituted a system of recognition (*repérage*), but in conj[unction] . . . [sy]stems of recognition (gestural, ritual, cere[monial]. . . noral values, etc.) What is specific to our s[ociety]. . . on (*reconnaissance*) are progressively withdr[awn]. . . he code of "social standing." Obviously t[he code]. . . given the social and economic level; nevert[heless]. . . sing is to convert us all to the code. Since . . . is moral, and in every infraction is more . . . totalitarian; no one escapes it: our indiv[idual]. . . each day we participate in its collective . . . equires at least that we believe that oth[ers]. . . enter the game, even if only ironically. . . ried out in relation to a society that confo[rms]. . . , however:

[handwritten marginal annotations: "Newspeak", "Total libertarianism (doublethink)", "(3)"]

1 It . . . de: the manifestation of value, even fo[r]. . . de in, the neighborhood we live in, an[d]. . . d us and distinguish us from others. But that's not all. Have not all codes of value always been partial and arbitrary (moral codes to begin with)?

2 The code is a form of socialization, the total secularization of signs of recognition: it is therefore involved in the – at least formal – emancipation of social relations. Objects do not only facilitate material existence through their proliferation as commodities, but, generalized into signs of recognition, they facilitate the reciprocation of status among people. The system of social standing, at least, has the advantage of rendering obsolete the rituals of caste or of class and, generally, all preceding (and internal) criteria of social discrimination.

3 The code establishes, for the first time in history, a *universal* system of signs and interpretation (*lecture*). One may regret that it supplants all others. But conversely, it could be noted that the progressive decline of all other systems (of birth, of class, of positions) – the extension of competition, the largest social migration in history, the ever-increasing differentiation of social groups, and the instability of languages and their proliferation – necessitated the institution of a clear, unambiguous, and universal code of recognition. In a world where millions of strangers cross each other daily in the streets the code of "social standing" fulfils an essential social function, while it satisfies the vital need of people to be always informed about one another.

Nevertheless:

1 This universalization, this efficiency is obtained at the price of a radical simpli-fication, of an impoverishment, and of an almost irrevocable regression in the "language" of value: "All individuals are described in terms of their objects." Coherence is obtained through the formation of a combinatorial matrix or repertoire: hence a functional language is established, but one that is symboli-cally and structurally impoverished.

2 The fact that a system of interpretation (*lecture*) and recognition is today ap-plied by everyone, or that value signs are completely socialized and objectified, does not necessarily lead to true "democratization." On the contrary, it ap-pears that the *constraint of a single referent only acts to exacerbate the desire for discrimination*. Within the very framework of this homogenous system, we can observe the unfolding of an always renewed obsession with hierarchy and distinction. While the barriers of morality, of stereotypes, and of language col-lapse, new barriers and new exclusions are erected in the field of objects: a new morality of class, or caste, can now invest itself in the most material and most undeniable of things.

Society is not becoming any more transparent, even if today the code of "social standing" is in the process of constituting an immediately legible, universal struc-ture of signification, one that enables the fluid circulation of social representations within the group hierarchy. The code provides the image of a false transparency, of a false legibility of social relations, behind which the real structures of production and social relations remain illegible. A society would be transparent only if knowl-edge of the order of signification was also knowledge of the organization (*ordre*) of its structures and of social facts. This is not the case with the object/advertising system, which only offers a code of significations that is always complicit and opaque. In addition, if the code's coherence provides a formal sense of security, that is also the best means for it to extend its immanent and permanent jurisdiction over all individuals in society.

Notes

1 Martineau, P. (1957) *Motivation in Advertising: Motives that Make People Buy*, New York: McGraw Hill.

2 Other more archaic methods exist which personalize the purchase: bartering, buying second-hand [shopping] (patience and play), etc. These are archaic for they assume a passive product and an active consumer. In our day the whole initiative of personaliza-tion is transferred to advertising.

3 Gilbert Simondon, *Du Mode d'existence des objects techniques* (Paris: Aubier, 1958), p. 24.

4   L. Mumford, *Technique et civilisation* (Paris: Seuil, 1959), p. 246. English edition: Lewis Mumford, *Technics and Civilisation* (New York: Harcourt, Brace, 1934).

5   The trilogy *parole/langue/langage* finds no unmediated (immediate) articulation in English: *Parole* as speech/word; *langue* as specific language (e.g. Serbo-Croatian); and *langage* as language (e.g. the structure of language). I have translated lange in this sentence ("*Mais langue n'est pas langage*") as "set of expressions" to keep in line with Baudrillard's argumentation. [Trans.]

6   *Motivation in Advertising,*. p. 75.

7   Ibid.

8   Ibid., p. 50.

9   Ibid., p. 100.

10 In fact, we are giving too much credit to advertising by comparing it with *magic*: the nominalist lexicon of alchemy has already in itself something of an actual language, structured by a research and interpretive (*déchiffrement*) praxis. The nominalization of the "brand name," however, is purely immanent and fixated (*figé*) by an economic imperative.

20

Aesthetic Abstraction of the Commodity: Surface – Package – Advertising Image

Wolfgang Fritz Haug

The work of the German Marxist critic Wolfgang Fritz Haug follows on directly from the intellectual and theoretical precedents set by writers such as Theodor Adorno, Max Horkheimer, Herbert Marcuse, and others associated with the Frankfurt School. In common with that tradition of criticism, Haug employs both Marxist and Freudian ideas in his critique of the contemporary commodity form. In this brief extract Haug examines the role of packaging in the fetishization process.

The contradiction of interests between buyer and seller, use-value and exchange-value (or valorization), which ultimately dominates the unleashed commodity–cash nexus, exposes the object of use, which was made and acts as a carrier of value, to a field of antagonistic forces: in this dissection, to which the commodity is subjected under the calculated control of the valorization standpoint, the commodity's surface appearance and its meaning detach themselves and form a hybrid which performs a highly specific function. This hybrid is the expression, and carries out the function, of a social relationship as it appears in the relationship of the character-masks worn by buyer and seller. This antagonistic relationship constitutes the function: the economic function in turn leads to the emergence of the techniques and phenomena which become their carrier. In concrete terms this process can be imagined as a situation where everything functional contributes to phenomenal economic successes, which, once established and consciously repeated, go on to cripple economically anything which does not further this development. The function leading to the aesthetic abstraction of the commodity is realization, which, through the aesthetic promise of use-value, creates the means that trigger the sale.

   The aesthetic abstraction of the commodity detaches both sensuality and meaning

From *Critique of Commodity Aesthetics* (Cambridge: Polity Press, 1986), pp. 49–50. Reprinted by permission of the author.

from the object acting as a carrier of exchange-value and makes the two separately available.[1] At first the functional already separate form and surface, which already have their own manufacturing processes, remain with the commodity to develop as naturally as skin covers a body. Yet functional differentiation is preparing the actual process of replacement, and the beautifully designed surface of the commodity becomes its package: not the simple wrapping for protection during transportation, but its real countenance, which the potential buyer is shown first instead of the body of the commodity and through which the commodity develops and changes its countenance, like the fairytale princess who is transformed through her feathered costume in which she seeks her fortune in the marketplace.[2] As an example of this, a US bank, in order to facilitate the exchange of money, recently changed even the design of its cheques to make use of new psychedelic colours.

But to return to the commodity: now that its surface has been detached and become its second skin, which as a rule is incomparably more perfect than the first, it becomes completely disembodied and drifts unencumbered like a multicoloured spirit of the commodity into every household, preparing the way for the real distribution of the commodity. No one is safe any longer from its amorous glances, which the realization motive casts at the consumers with the detached yet technically perfect appearance of a highly promising use-value.[3] For the time being at least, the customers' wallets still hold the equivalent of this disguised exchange-value.

Notes

1 The fact that an object's mere appearance can be detached and used for purposes of deception is so acceptable to bourgeois jurisdiction that it refuses to prosecute photocopying offences even in the area of forgery. According to a ruling in the first Federal Criminal Court, in Germany a photocopy cannot have the basic characteristics of a document and thus its forgery cannot constitute a documentary forgery. The proof given was that a document is 'the embodiment of a declaration', a piece of evidence in itself which reveals its author, while a photocopy produces only a 'more or less faithful duplicate' which, like a written copy, is a mere reproduction presented as the embodiment of a declaration, but which unlike a written copy, is pictorial (cf. 'Fotokopien gelten nicht als Urkunden', *Tagesspiegel*, 13 October 1971). In the right of ownership, bourgeois law defends through the claims of the embodied appearance its own claims to private property, which conversely generates the systematic disembodiment of the appearance of things in commodity production.

2 Even polished, shiny or transparent surfaces are sold as calculated methods of creating an illusion in the packaging market, which is also an advertising market. 'Almost any object', the tin-foil manufacturer, Forchheim GmbH advertised in 1964, 'becomes a winner when wrapped in tin-foil: such an attractive face cannot fail to promote sales.' A

special issue of foil 'is especially suited to wrap chocolates, biscuit and cigarette boxes and is excellent too for wrapping up different articles as special offers . . . its shiny surface is a sure-fire sales success'. (Advertisement in *Der Spiegel*, 6 May 1964, p. 77 and in the edition of 1 April 1964).

3   One of the forms in which the colourful appearance of commodities is circulated belongs to the distribution method of the mail-order company, namely the mail-order catalogue. The firm 'Quelle' alone calculates around DM130 in catalogue costs (cf. 'Der Katalog enthalt 40,000 Artikel', *Tagesspiegel*, 19 September 1971, p. 12). These costs cover a huge outlay in technical equipment and personnel.

> For around seven months two hundred graphic experts, copywriters, photographers, designers and managerial staff have been busy preparing the catalogue with more than seven hundred pages. Seventy-six photographic models posed for the catalogue in Majorca, on the Zugspitze, in Frankfurt and in Scotland. But of a correspondingly huge number of shots, exactly 10,001 photos had to be selected, and twelve major printers used 8,500 tonnes of paper and 560 tonnes of ink in the four or five weeks it took to print them. (*FAZ*, 10 August 1971)

No actual commodity-body can actually keep up with the overwhelming technical perfection that stage-manages and reproduces its appearance in this way.

21
The Bonding of Media and Advertising

William Leiss, Stephen Kline, and Sut Jhally

In their book *Social Communication in Advertising* William Leiss, Stephen Kline, and Sut Jhally explore, through an empirical study of twentieth-century Canadian advertisements, the manner in which the advertising industry has changed its mode of symbolic representation. They argue that advertising has passed through quite distinct phases, moving from forms of representation based around informational formats to those which currently predominate and which are based on "lifestyle" imagery. In this extract they examine some of the ways in which this shift in advertising language is bound-up with the industry's changing relationship with the media.

We hold the view that an adequate appreciation of advertising's place in modern society arises out of a detailed examination of its historical evolution. This conviction is shared by others. Daniel Pope's (1983) *The Making of Modern Advertising* divides the history of advertising into three periods: the Gilded Age (about 1870–90), the Progressive Era (1890–1920) and the Modern Era (1920–present).

The Gilded Age is the period of regional production and distribution when early industrial expansion led to increased advertising, largely in old-fashioned formats. The agencies acted as space brokers only, promoting the interest in advertising mainly on behalf of the print media. Growth in advertising was due to new products, proprietary medicines, department stores and a very few national advertisers of branded goods; advertising played a very minor part in industrial production, and agency practice was in a rudimentary state of development.

The Progressive Era is the period of expanding mass production and the rise of national branded products. The broad institutional structure of advertising was established, with the service agencies moving to the centre of national campaigns. The business practices, ethics and institutional structures of advertising

From *Social Communication in Advertising* (London: Routledge, 1990), pp. 148–59.

were all put in place and regularized at this time, making it the formative period for the industry. Mass-media advertising expanded dramatically and came to be regarded as a legitimate feature in the market-place. Yet many remained unconvinced of either the necessity or desirability of product advertising on a large scale.

Pope's third phase, the Modern Era or 'the era of market segmentation', stretches from the 1920s to the present. In this period the market-place begins to move from production for mass consumption – that is, for an undifferentiated group of consumers – to one of production for consumption in a stratified market-place increasingly defined by consumers organized into relatively well-defined subgroups. Pope suggests that by the end of the 1920s most of the important features of the modern advertising industry had already been established: the agencies' role in advertising, their strong links with various media, and their business practices (methods of payment and so forth). Thus there remained only the need for advertisers to define market segments with increasing precision and for agencies to learn how to address them. In this sense the addition of new media and the changes in advertising approaches were of minimal consequence for the role of advertising or its eventual function in the contemporary market-place.

Pope places comparatively little emphasis on the impact that agency practice, relations with the media and marketing theory had on the evolution of the industry, however; he views its development as largely conditioned by the apparently irresistible wave of national product advertising itself. Once the agencies had responded to this wave by laying the foundations for their full-service capabilities, as they did in the 1920s, the institutional arrangements supporting modern advertising – according to this view – were in place. What happened thereafter was essentially the story of their reaction to, and absorption of, the special features of later media revolutions.

However, there is more to the story of modern advertising than its institutional link to national manufacturing and the markets it developed. For us, no less important is the role that the agencies played in constructing the bridge between selling and communicating in contemporary society. Some other observers have also focused on a wider network of changes in seeking to address advertising's social impact, among them Michael Schudson (1984). His interpretation isolates four important and interrelated dimensions: market forces, notably changes in the system of distribution; changes in methods of industrial production, especially the volume and types of goods; media forces and the way they adjust to advertising; the agencies and how they organize, promote and redefine advertising practice.

Other authors – for example, Stephen Fox in *The Mirror Makers* (1984) – also identify innovations in advertising practice itself as the key factor in the industry's development. Fox argues that the influence of strong individuals within the business has taken advertising through periodic reconceptualizations of what constitutes good practice. He depicts its history as governed by alternating cycles of emphasis, shifting back and forth between 'hard-sell' persuasive formats (reason why, unique selling point) and 'soft-sell' suggestive ones (emotive or 'creative', emphasizing design, lifestyles and personal images). Although his biographical approach identifies the major advocates of these alternative positions and their arguments, it is less helpful in filtering out the essential differences between the creative approaches of the 1960s and those of the 1920s. Clearly both styles, the persuasive and the creative, have been a part of the repertoire of advertising for the past one hundred years and they seem to come in and out of favour with different agencies at different times, for different classes of product, or with different types of audiences. But such cycles in themselves do not reveal the broader dimensions of change that make the two approaches so very compatible within the world of advertising. As one of our interviewees put the point:

> There has always been the distinction between the two appeals: the rational and the emotional. They were separate. Either you had a rational product like a car or else you had an emotional one like cosmetics. We used to say, don't mix the two appeals. In the eighties you have to mix them.

The type of appeal used depended on circumstances. Fashion rules the industry, and approaches come in and out of fashion, with different agencies profiting, depending on their orientation. But during the 1950s, for example, both heavily research-orientated agencies and those that stressed intuition and creativity thrived.

The idea that the industry just swings back and forth between two well-established poles leads to the belief that advertising has grown in sophistication over the years without really changing: for almost every type of ad today, there is some historical precedent. The alternation between persuasion and suggestion, so the story goes, is a struggle between the view of human beings as rational creatures and the view of them as emotional and creative.

Merle Curti found a smoother evolutionary development in the views of human nature held by advertisers, basing his study of changes in marketing outlook held by advertising practitioners on the contents of *Printer's Ink* for the period between 1890 and 1954. Curti sought to pinpoint the evolution of the dominant attitude in advertising thought. He divided the period into three phases.

During the first phase, the Rationalistic Image of Human Nature, advertisers tended to think of consumers essentially as rational and not easily persuaded by gimmicks. 'Most experts who held to the informative purpose of advertising emphasized the basically rational, logical and sensible qualities of man without indicating further what these views were' (Curti, 1967: 338). They assumed that a person wanted to know first price, then function, craftsmanship, durability, and benefits, that is, all the reasons why one should buy, in order to make some estimation of the product's worth in terms of one's own priorities. The rational view is reflected both by practitioners of reason-why advertising and by rationalistic academic psychology around the turn of the century.

In the second phase, the Irrational Conception of Human Nature, which lasted from about 1910 to 1930, 'the dominant idea came to be that man is actuality more irrational than rational. Merchandising techniques, techniques to appeal to various nonrational impulses, now received emphasis' (Curti, 1967: 347). Human nature was viewed as malleable, not fixed. Advertising operated by suggestion, pictures, attention-gathering stimuli, and playing on human sympathy to persuade the consumer to desire the product. Campaigns were based on 'appeals' and imputed motives, and sales would depend on how well the advertiser could take advantage of people's competitiveness, shame, desire for approval or need for reward for achievement. Appeals to personal appearance, prestige, family and home were also featured.

In the third phase, which emphasized the behavioural sciences and originated during the Great Depression and extended through the postwar years, the rational and irrational views of human nature were merged and modified. Advertisers began to talk more of satisfying consumer wants as opposed to creating them, and social science became a major influence introducing new research methods and techniques to the industry. Psychological conceptions of human nature were very influential in this period; the tension between rationalist and irrationalist notions was dealt with by accepting both. Advertisers learned from psychologists 'that whatever decision we make, however purely rational it may seem, is deeply influenced by emotional forces, conscious, subconscious or unconscious. Of special importance was the increasing recognition of symbols in invoking emotional responses' (Curti, 1967: 354). Personality traits such as self-esteem, impulses for creative expression, and concerns for social relations that had been highlighted in the behavioural sciences, were explored minutely by marketers as bases for selling.

Curti linked variations in thinking about advertising to social and institutional ones. His analysis does not cover the contemporary period, but this has been addressed by Monte Sommers (1983), who traces the transition from psychological approaches to a broader marketing management approach which trickled down into advertising practice from marketing theory. This strategy integrated advertising into a 'global' marketing framework, brought new statistical methods to bear on decision-making tasks (including the concepts of product and consumer life cycles and the hierarchy of needs), and generally defined new goals and purposes for advertising around the concept of market segmentation. In this strategy the main concern shifts from the consumer to the market, specifically the description of, and access to, segments or groups of buyers.

Thus the understanding of the advertising industry is based in changes in its structure and relationships in the larger business sphere, and on changes in advertising thought and practice within the industry itself. The advertising industry is depicted as responding to shifts in the market or to broader conceptions of man and society. For the most part it is not regarded as a 'transformative institution' in its own right, or a factor of significant proportions in modern society.

A comment by one of our interviewees illustrates this outlook: 'After factoring out TV and media change, I honestly believe that North American commercial society has used advertising in 1910 the same as in 1980, except that advertising has adjusted as society has matured and the market has increased.' However, we simply cannot factor out variations in media when we are attempting to understand the changing qualities of advertising. For if we view it as primarily an extension of the industrial process of manufacture and distribution, and downplay its own interpretation of and contribution to mediated communication and its impact on modern popular culture, we run the risk of ignoring much of what happened in the twentieth century – the novel use of visuals, dialogue, story-telling, film demonstration, characters, persuasive design and marketing strategy.

Our own portrait places much greater emphasis than others on the close interconnections among advertising, the goods-producing sector, and media, and especially advertising's connective or bridging function in relation to production and media. The advertising industry, led by its agencies, transferred knowledge about the media to producers, knowledge about audiences to media, and knowledge about consumers and how to reach them more effectively with marketing campaigns back and forth between producers and the media.

Advertising, especially the agencies, never responded just passively to changes in media, but in many cases became an active force in their development. Advertisers have been active lobbyists in the commercialization of the media and in reorganizing them to suit their own particular needs and orientations. It is impossible to write a history of the media in the modern world without giving significant attention to the role of advertising in shaping them, and at the heart of this story is the relationship between media and advertisers established by the agencies and the impact of this relationship on the concepts and practice of marketing thought. Advertising can never be thought of as simply an extension of what is happening in marketing or mass production or mass consumption: the key to its growing impact in society is what is happening in communications media.

Successive waves of innovation in magazine production, radio and television are reflected in changes in advertising practices, from which resulted equally profound transformations in the way that advertisers thought about and approached consumers through the design of campaigns and marketing strategies. In order to map out these interconnections we have constructed a historically based account that includes changes over time in the cultural determinants of consumption behaviour, the system of industrial production and distribution, the organization of the advertising business, the communicative models brought into the practice of advertising, and media technologies. Our account draws on the earlier work of Pope and Curti, but emphasizes a broader set of factors.

The bonding of media and advertising, which is the principal force in these varied dimensions, develops in four stages during the twentieth century. Of course reality is not so neatly demarcated as the dating of the stages presents it, and the latter phases of each, representing times of realignment and transformation, shade into their successors. Most importantly, the characteristics of each period do not disappear, but rather become subordinate components in a newer and more complex environment. For example, rationalistic–informative approaches dominant in the early stages are not so much subverted by the development during the 1920s of new ideas about the consumer and new media as channelled into specific media and product categories; classified ads do not disappear but are gradually restricted to personal and small retail selling in the major newspapers. The development of advertising is a process of 'layering' techniques and strategies, culminating in a versatile, multi-dimensional armory. Few ingredients have ever been simply discarded or forgotten; almost everything in the storeroom is subsequently dusted off, refitted and returned to service in a more specialized niche.

Stage One: The Product-orientated Approach (1890–1925)

The development of commercialized print media is closely related to our first stage, when advertising was orientated toward the product. The service agencies, reaching beyond their earlier functions as space sellers, concentrate on copywriting and advertising design to sell the new national branded products. The agencies established communication as the unifying element in the services they offer. They systematize and develop new styles of appeal, leaving behind the 'announcements' of earlier periods in favour of a persuasive informational approach arguing the merits of the product. The appeals are predominantly rationalistic in the sense that 'reason-why' demands an explanation of the motivation for using a product. The written text is the core of this explanation, although new technologies first in magazines and then in newspapers allow the increasing use of illustration and visual layout elements in the development of arguments about the qualities of the product. The agencies focus mainly on national campaigns and become particularly important to the consumer magazine industry. They extend their explorations of the stylistic elements of campaign design, merging visual and rhetorical devices and codifying these in agency practice.

Stage Two: Product Symbols (1925–45)

The professionalization of the agencies now makes advertising capable of influencing public policy on the development of radio, and responding positively and opportunistically to the national advertising possibilities of this new medium. Research into audiences for media broadens the marketing services offered by the agencies. The agencies move closer to the marketing concept, in which consumer disposition is a crucial element in advertising even though knowledge about the consumer at this time is limited to very broad demographic or polling-based evidence. In this context marketing thought begins to shift towards the non-rational or symbolic grounding of consumption based on the notion of appeals or motives, putting less emphasis on the product and its uses. More precisely, product-orientated advertising gradually is confined to particular media and types of goods.

The experience with new media changes the practice of advertising. In magazines photography and art allow for innovations in the associational dimension of argumentation. Products are presented less and less on the basis of a performance promise, and more on making them 'resonate' with qualities desired by consumers – status, glamour, reduction of anxiety, happy families – as the social motivations for consumption. In radio, institutional association is the early basis for sponsorship of programming, but during the 1930s experience with the role of dialogue, stars and the development of characters allows the advertiser to assimilate much more about the social context of consumption as the basis of advertising strategy. 'Tie-ins' between product and programme, attention-getting devices, consistent and strong brand images, and testimonials knit together goods with the social, rather than the functional, basis of consumption.

Stage Three: Personalization (1945–65)

The agencies transfer their knowledge of and contacts with the entertainment world made through radio and magazines to the new medium of television. Television quickly becomes the major medium for national branded product campaigns and in many cases the major source of income for the agencies. The new medium could combine design and cultural symbolism with characterization, story line and dialogue. The communicative potential of television offers many new avenues as the personnel, stylistics of imagery, patterns of attention and programming format are bent to advertising purposes. The agencies are also major players in the realignment of context orientations in older media, as both radio and magazines adjust to the loss of certain types of major national accounts by tailoring their subject matter and editorial slants to new target audiences.

Both creative- and research-orientated professionals believe that knowing more about the consumer is central to effective advertising. Agencies once more expand advertising practice so as to include new types of research, most notably the application of psychological concepts and techniques to studying consumers and what makes them buy. The advertisers seeks to gain access to the psychological makeup of consumers through personnel who are 'in tune with the times' and who understand the ordinary consumer. Marketing strategy and advertising styles revolve around the idea of a prototypical mass consumer accessible through television, the quintessential mass medium, and characterized by a limited set of traits (interest in convenience, fascination with technology and science, desire for glamour).

Stage Four: Market Segmentation (1965–85)

After about 1965 advertising practice adapts to the multimedia conditions of the present market-place. Television itself is forced to target specific types of audiences desired by advertisers in order to compete with other media offering better access to local and specialized markets. Advertising is now seen as part of the marketing mix rather than as the main route to promoting consumption, and the agencies modify their routines accordingly, embrace marketing management, a philosophy that incorporates a whole new set of statistical and marketing research procedures into the preparation of advertising campaigns. These statistical packages concentrate not on personality but on activities of different subgroups of consumers, providing some analysis of their use of media, their consumption preferences and their lifestyle attitudes. The breakouts of marketing research become the basis for decisions on design and media buying, allowing the agency to formulate marketing campaigns precisely targeted at particular groups of buyers. There is no point in broadcasting expensive messages to those who a bit of judicious investigation reveals are bound and determined to remain indifferent to them.

As we mentioned, no phase supplants the foregoing ones, but rather each complements the others, adding variations and new operations to the existing repertoire. Posters, signs and flyers – the classic means of publicity in early times – still flourish. Classified and local advertising still provide up to one-third of newspaper revenue. 'Rationalist', test-orientated ads still frequently appear in the pages of newspapers and magazines, especially for certain types of consumer goods (stereo equipment, personal computers, more expensive automobile lines). The status-envy appeal formats of the 1930s, the testimonial pitches and the celebrity appearance all persist for specific uses.

This is an 'articulated' communication system, a collection of distinct yet interconnected parts, composed of products, persuasive strategies, and media channels whose unity is forged by the accumulated experience of the advertising agencies.

References

Curti, M. (1967) 'The changing concept of human nature in the literature of American advertising', *Business History Review*, 41.

Fox, S. (1984) *The Mirror Makers*, New York: William Morrow.

Pope, D. (1983) *The Making of Modern Advertising*, New York: Basic Books.

Schudson, M. (1984) *Advertising, The Uneasy Persuasion*, New York: Basic Books.

Sommers, M. (1983) 'The evolution of marketing thought and its implications for the study of advertising'. Paper presented at a meeting of the Canadian Communication Association, Vancouver, BA

22

The Characteristic Mode of Consumption of Fordism

Michel Aglietta

Michel Aglietta is a leading figure of the French "Regulation School." In his seminal work *A Theory of Capitalist Regulation* he draws exclusively on Marxist political economy to explore the historically contingent character of twentieth-century capitalism and in particular that of Fordism. In this extract Aglietta emphasizes the central role of the commodity-form in constituting a direct and indeed material relationship between production and consumption. The primary commodities of Fordism, especially those of standardized housing and the automobile, Aglietta argues, reflect for very practical and technical reasons the nature of Fordist production itself. This results in a distinctive "Fordist commodity aesthetic" in which the values and characteristics of functionality are seen to predominate.

In order to understand how the transformations of the relations of production within the labour process create impulses that play a primordial role in the formation of a mode of consumption, it is necessary not to view consumption empirically as a sum of expenditure functions, nor in terms of the theory of the individual consumer as the source of an axiomatic set of well-organized and stable choices, given certain resources and market conditions. The praxiological conception the theory of the individual consumer forms part of a definition of the object of economic science as a logic of individual choices subject to the constraint of scarcity and the rule of a universal principle of rationality (principle of optimization), which is radically foreign to the conception on which we base ourselves here – that is, a science of the social laws governing the production and distribution of the means of existence by men and women in organized collectivities. Empirical observation of expenditure functions has a completely different status. It is the statistical expression of the subjection of consumption to commodity relations. It is indispensable in order to grasp how an already established mode of consumption evolves over time, because of its location at the point of contact between exchange and consumption proper. What we need here, however, is something more basic – a theory of those practices that make consumption a socially conditioned *activity*,

From *A Theory of Capitalist Regulation: The US Experience*, translated by David Fernbach, (London: Verso, 1987), pp. 155–61. Reprinted by permission of the publishers.

subject to contrary forces of homogenization and differentiation that modify it in a manner favourable to the generalization of wage-labour. . . .

Our point of departure will be a definition of consumption as an activity or more accurately a process, that is, an organized set of activities, which – while predominantly private – are subject to a general logic of the reconstitution of energies expended in social practices and the preservation of abilities and attitudes implied by the social relations of which their subjects are supports. This definition calls for several remarks. First of all, since consumption is a material process, it is located in space; it has a specific geography and object-network. It is also a set of operations in time, an employment of time in the literal sense. The nature of the consumption process and its place in the maintenance cycle of social labour-power are thus strongly conditioned by the importance of labour-time, its intensity as an expenditure of human energy, and the other temporal constraints directly connected with it. Consumption, moreover, is predominantly a private process; its concrete practices take place principally within the household, a site where individuality is protected. They are not directly under the sway of the relations of production. This is why they can give rise to varying ideologies and are susceptible to differentiation. This differentiation is not contingent, for consumption is also the conservation of abilities and attitudes. This aspect of consumption should not be seen in a principally functional sense. It concerns the position of the individuals concerned in social relations, and the representation of this position within the group of individuals who share it, as well as *vis-à-vis* other social groups with whom they maintain relations. The basis of this representation is evidently the exercise of real abilities, not intrinsic to the individual, but inherent in the place occupied in social relations, i.e. the *role* required by society. But this representation is effected in the form of a recognition which involves the perception of definite cultural attitudes. This recognition maintains social relations of an ideological nature, although these possess just as 'material' an existence as economic relations. Such relations, which issue from social stratification and require specific reproduction, actively differentiate the process of consumption. They can be referred to as *status* relations. The concept of status is not merely needed to interpret social differentiations in consumption; it is equally necessary to understand their renewal over time, and the conditions of their stability or distortion which make it possible to speak scientifically of a social process of consumption, or even a mode of consumption. The effect of status on the consumption process is expressed in acquired habits which stabilize the maintenance cycle of labour-power into a routine. These habits are transmitted from one generation to the next. The learning of cultural status codes and the principles of behaviour that follow from them is one of the essential functions of the family; it accompanies the learning of the roles to which families aspire in their inter-generational choices. New individuals thus enter the labour market seeking positions with a status whose ideological features they have already internalized. Only the forces unleashed by capitalist accumulation can dissolve these habits, by generalizing mobility and insecurity of employment.

Given these very summary indications, how should we view the formation and reproduction of the specific mode of consumption of Fordism, which is an essential aspect of the regime of intensive accumulation? For the first time in history, Fordism created a norm of working-class consumption in which individual ownership of commodities governed the concrete practices of consumption. This involved a reversal, both of traditional ways of life and of the initial experience of the working class in an epoch of extreme poverty and total insecurity, which provided no basis for any stabilization of consumption habits. In these circumstances, the consumption process was either totally destructured or else organized in the context of the extended family, with a strict division of domestic labour and a great expenditure of domestic labour-time. With Fordism, on the contrary, the generalization of commodity relations extended to their domination of practices of consumption. This was a mode of consumption restructured by capitalism, because the time devoted to consumption witnessed an increasing density in individual use of commodities and a notable impoverishment of use of non-commodity interpersonal relations. Once the social conditions that enabled this mode of consumption to be reproduced were established, its consumption norm evolved dynamically because its commodity content was directly inscribed in the generalization of the mechanized labour process with semi-automatic control. These conditions were multiple in character and implied so great a change in social practices that it is in no way astonishing that the expansion of Fordism after the Second World War was preceded by a long period of crises and intense class struggles, whose outcome was the establishment of social controls to guarantee the formation of the working-class norm of consumption and to regularize its evolution.

The most immediate of these conditions relate to the influence of transformations of the labour process on the maintenance cycle of labour-power. We have seen how Taylorism, and later Fordism, adapted to the restriction of the working day by sharply increasing the intensity of labour and systematically compressing wasted time. The result was the disappearance of any time for recuperation at the workplace itself. The increased exhaustion of labour-power in the labour process had to be entirely repaired outside the workplace, respecting the new time constraint of a strict separation between working and non-working hours. Since this was overlaid by the further constraint of separation and increased distance between workplace and residence, transport time was considerably prolonged, with the result that the time constraint imposed by labour did not fall despite the limitation of working hours. Individual commodity consumption is the form of consumption that permits the most effective recuperation from physical and nervous fatigue in a compact space of time within the day, and at a single place, the home.

The structure of the consumption norm thus coincides with its conditioning by capitalist relations of production. It is governed by two commodities: the *standardized housing* that is the privileged site of individual consumption; and the *automobile* as the means of transport compatible with the separation of home and workplace.

Whilst remaining commodities for private use, these are durable goods whose acquisition goes far beyond the purchasing power of current wages. The formation of the working-class norm of consumption therefore presupposed a vast socialization of finance, and correlatively a very strict control over workers' resources and expenditures. It was important for the process of individual consumption to be organized and stable, while remaining compatible with the apparently individual and free relationships of commodity exchange. This was achieved by the generalization in the working class of the social structure that was the condition for its cultural integration into the nation, i.e. the small family unit and household. Here the working class received a statute that functioned as the regulator of its norm of consumption, through the formation of its expenditure habits. But it still remained essential to limit the consequences of capitalist insecurity on employment and on the formation of individual wages, so as not to break the continuity of the consumption process, and in order to enable the workers to meet the financial commitments contracted with the acquisition of their consumer goods. This implied legislative arrangements, a homogenization and socialization of wages, and the establishment of social insurance funds against the temporary loss of direct wages. . . .

When the wage relation had been transformed in such a way as to permit the socialization of the conditions for purchasing standardized housing and automobile transport, the production of these complex commodities itself became the central process in the development of the mode of consumption. The production of standardized housing of a chiefly suburban kind had multiple effects. Constructed according to certain basic standards, the new housing put an end to unhygienic and unsafe interiors, and permitted the installation of household appliances that saved domestic labour. Standardized housing is also a symbol of status, once it can be bought rather than simply rented. Its mass production by techniques of prefabrication reduced its costs to a point where, stretched over the overall term of payment, it was less of a burden on the working-class wage of the 1950s than were the rents extorted by the landlords of the interwar years for the unhygienic housing of that time. So far as the automobile was concerned, its mass production coincided with the establishment of the semi-automatic assembly line, in other words the creation of that model of work organization that was later to be extended to the long production runs of means of mass consumption. The general introduction of the assembly line revealed the intimate relationship between the labour process and the mode of consumption that it shapes. For the two basic commodities of the mass consumption process created complementarities which effected a gigantic expansion of commodities, supported by a systematic diversification of use-values. This diversification was inscribed in the very logic of the social norm of consumption, whose evolution was governed by the replacement of direct activity at home by time-saving equipment. It was also sustained by the quest for a status adequate to this norm. But in order for this logic of consumption to be compatible with a labour process oriented towards relative surplus-value, the total of use-values had to be adapted to capitalist mass production.[1] This meant the creation of a *functional aesthetic* ('design'), which acquired fundamental social importance.[2] This aesthetic had firstly to respect the constraints of engineering, and consequently conceive use-values as an assembly of standardized components capable of long production runs. It also had to introduce planned obsolescence, and establish a functional link between use-values to create the need for their complementarity. In this way, consumption activity could be rendered uniform and fully subject to the constraints of its items of equipment. Finally, this functional aesthetic duplicated the real relationship between individuals and objects with an imaginary relation. Not content to create a space of objects for daily life, as supports of a capitalist commodity universe, it provided an image of this space by advertising techniques. This image was presented as an objectification of consumption status which individuals could perceive outside themselves. The process of social recognition was externalized and fetishized. Individuals were not initially interpellated as subjects by one another, in accordance with their social position: they were interpellated by an external power, diffusing a robot portrait of the 'consumer'. Consumption habits were thus already calculated and controlled socially. Yet it cannot be stressed too greatly that the role of the image in consumption, which many sociologists have made into a fundamental explanatory principle of capitalist development, is strictly subordinate to the material and social conditions that we have discussed.

In so far as Fordism increased the rate of surplus-value by developing an overall set of social relations that closely combined the labour process with the social consumption norm, the department producing means of consumption appeared to be endowed with a dynamic arising from consumption itself. Since accumulation managed to preserve a relatively regular rhythm thanks to a certain harmonization of development between the two departments, at the price of a planned obsolescence and a permanent devalorization of capital, the problem of effective demand was not too serious. The 'consumer society' appeared to have definitively resolved the contradictions of capitalism and abolished its crises. Such was the pattern of the two decades after the Second World War . . . : a relatively regular rise in real wages, made possible by a continuing fall in real social wage costs that reflected a rise in the rate of surplus-value.

Notes

1   On this essential point, see A. Granou (1972) *Capitalisme et mode de vie*, Paris.
2   Lapidus and Hoffenberg (1976) *La Société du design*, Paris.

23

Theorizing the Transition

David Harvey

Many recent debates about consumption have been framed by a more general discussion concerning the transition from a Fordist to a so-called post-Fordist economic order. In this chapter the Marxist social geographer David Harvey attempts to summarize and make sense of this period of economic transition which has informed so much of our contemporary thinking about consumption. In doing so Harvey returns to several of the conceptual terms and theoretical principles outlined originally by Marx and later by writers associated with the Regulation School (see chapter 22, this volume).

To the degree that we are witnessing a historical transition, still far from complete and in any case, like Fordism, bound to be partial in certain important respects, so we have encountered a series of theoretical dilemmas. Can we grasp theoretically the logic, if not the necessity, of the transition? To what degree do past and present theoretical formulations of the dynamics of capitalism have to be modified in the light of the radical reorganizations and restructurings taking place in both productive forces and social relations? And can we represent the current regime sufficiently well to get some grip on the probable course and implications of what appears to be an ongoing revolution?

The transition from Fordism to flexible accumulation has, in fact, posed serious difficulties for theories of any sort. Keynesians, monetarists, neo-classical partial equilibrium theorists, appear just as befuddled as everyone else. The transition has also posed serious dilemmas for Marxists. In the face of such difficulties, many commentators have abandoned any pretence of theory, and simply resorted to data-chasing to keep pace with the rapid shifts. But here too there are problems – what data are key indicators rather than contingent series? The only general point of agreement is that something significant has changed in the way capitalism has been working since about 1970.

The first difficulty is to try to encapsulate the nature of the changes we are looking at. In tables 1, 2 and 3 I summarize three recent accounts of the transi-

From *The Condition of Postmodernity* (Oxford: Blackwell Publishers, 1989), pp. 173–88. Reprinted by permission of the publishers.

tion. The first, a rather celebratory account by Halal (1986) of the new capitalism, emphasizes the positive and liberatory elements of the new entrepreneurialism. The second, by Lash and Urry (1987), emphasizes power relations and politics in relation to economy and culture. The third, by Swyngedouw (1986), provides much more detail on the transformations in technology and the labour process while appreciating how the regime of accumulation and its modes of regulation have shifted. In each case, of course, the opposition is used as a didactic tool to emphasize the differences rather than the continuities, and none of the authors argue that matters are anywhere near as cut and dried as these schemas suggest. The schemas indicate, however, some overlaps but also some differences which are instructive, since they suggest rather different mechanisms of causation. Halal appears closer to Schumpeter's theory of entrepreneurial innovation as the driving force of capitalism, and tends to interpret Fordism and Keynesianism as an unfortunate interlude in capitalist progress. Lash and Urry see the evolution in part as the collapse of the material conditions for a powerful collective working-class politics, and attempt to probe the economic, cultural and political roots of that collapse. By the very use of the terms 'organized' and 'disorganized' to characterize the transition, they emphasize more the disintegration than coherence of contemporary capitalism, and therefore avoid confronting the possibility of a transition in the regime of accumulation. Swyngedouw, on the other hand, by emphasizing changes in the mode of production and of industrial organization, locates the transition in the mainstream of Marxian political economy while clearly accepting the regulation school's language.

Table 1 The new capitalism according to Halal

	The old capitalism (industrial paradigm)	The new capitalism (post-industrial paradigm)
Frontier of progress	Hard growth	Smart growth
Organization	Mechanistic structure	Market networks
Decision-making	Authoritarian command	Particioative leadership
Institutional values	Financial goals	Multiple goals
Management focus	Operational management	Strategic management
Economic macro system	Profit-centred big business	Democratic free enterprise
World system	Capitalism versus socialism	Hybrids of capitalism and socialism

Source: Halal (1986)

Table 2 Contrast between organized and disorganized capitalism according to Lash and Urry

Organized capitalism	*Disorganized capitalism*
Concentration and centralization of industrial banking, and commercial capital in regulated national markets	De-concentration of rapidly increasing corporate power away from national markets. Increasing internationalization of capital and in some cases separation of industrial from bank capital
Increasing separation of ownership from control and emergence of complex managerial hierarchies	Continued expansion of managerial strata articulating their own individual and political agendas quite distinct from class politics
Growth of new sectors of managerial, scientific, technological intelligentsia and of middle-class bureaucracy	Relative/absolute decline in blue-collar working class
Growth of collective organizations and bargaining within regions and nation-states	Decline in effectiveness of national collective bargaining
Close articulation of state and large monopoly capital interests and rise of class-based welfare statism	Increasing independence of large monopolies from state regulation and diverse challenges to centralized state bureaucracy and power
Expansion of economic empires and control of overseas production and markets	Industrialization of third world and competitive deindustrialization of core countries which turn to specialization in services
Incorporation of diverse class interests within a national agenda set through negotiated compromises and bureaucratic regulation	Outright decline of class-based politics and institutions
Hegemony of technical–scientific rationality	Cultural fragmentation and pluralism coupled with undermining of traditional class or national identities
Concentration of capitalist relations within relatively few industries and regions	Dispersal of capitalist relations across many sectors and regions
Extractive–manufacturing industries dominant sources of employment	Decline of extractive–manufacturing industries and rise of organizational and service industries
Strong regional concentration and specialization in extractive–manufacturing sectors	Dispersal, diversification of the territorial–spatial division of labour
Search for economies of scale through increasing plant (workforce) size	Decline in plant size through geographical dispersal, increased sub-contracting, global production systems
Growth of large industrial cities dominating regions through provision of centralized services (commercial and financial)	Decline of industrial cities and deconcentration from city centres into peripheral or semi-rural areas resulting in acute inner-city problems
Cultural–ideological configuration of 'modernism'	Cultural–ideological configurations of 'postmodernism'

Source: after Lash and Urry (1987)

Table 3 Contrast between Fordism and flexible accumulation according to Swyngedouw

Fordist production (based on economies of scale)	Just-in-time production (based on economies of scope)
(a) The production process	
Mass production of homogeneous goods	Small batch production
Uniformity and standardization	Flexible and small batch production of a variety of product types
Large buffer stocks and inventory	No stocks
Testing quality ex-post (rejects and errors detected late)	Quality control part of process (immediate detection of errors)
Rejects are concealed in buffer stocks	Immediate reject of defective parts
Loss of production time because of long set-up times, defective parts, inventory bottlenecks, etc.	Reduction of lost time, diminishing 'the porosity of the working day'
Resource driven	Demand driven
Vertical and (in some cases) horizontal integration	(Quasi-) vertical integration sub-contracting
Cost reductions through wage control	Learning-by-doing integrated in long-term planning
(b) Labour	
Single task performance by worker	Multiple tasks
Payment per rate (based on job design criteria)	Personal payment (detailed bonus system)
High degree of job specialization	Elimination of job demarcation
No or only little on-the-job-training	Long on-the-job training
Vertical labour organization	More horizontal labour organization
No learning experience	On-the-job learning
Emphasis on diminishing worker's responsibility (disciplining of labour force)	Emphasis on worker's co-responsibility
No job security	High employment security for core workers (life-time employment). No job security and poor labour conditions for temporary workers
(c) Space	
Functional spatial specialization (centralization/ decentralization)	Spatial clustering and agglomeration
Spatial division of labour	Spatial integration
Homogenization of regional labour markets (spatially segmented labour markets)	Labour market diversification (in-place labour market segmentation)
Worldwide sourcing of components and sub-contractors	Spatial proximity of vertical quasi-integrated firms
(d) State	
Regulation	Deregulative/re-regulation
Rigidity	Flexibility
Collective bargaining	Division/individualization, local or firm-based negotiations
Socialization of welfare (the welfare state)	Privatization of collective needs and social security

Table 3 *contd.*

Fordist production (based on economies of scale)	Just-in-time production (based on economies of scope)
International stability through multilateral agreements	International destabilization; increased geopolitical tensions
Centralization	Decentralization and sharpened inter-regional/ inter-city competition
The 'subsidy' state/city	The 'entrepreneurial' state/city
Indirect intervention in markets through income and price policies	Direct state intervention in markets through procurement
National regional policies	'Territorial' regional policies (third party form)
Firm-financed research and development	State-financed research and development
Industry-led innovation	State-led innovation
(e) Ideology	
Mass consumption of consumer durables: the consumption society	Individualized consumption: 'yuppie'-culture
Modernism	Post- modernism
Totality/structural reform	Specificity/adaptation
Socialization	Individualization: the 'spectacle' society

Source: Swyngedouw (1986)

I am more partial to Swyngedouw's interpretation. But if the language of the regulation school has survived better than most, it is, I suspect, because of its rather more pragmatic orientation. There is, within the regulation school, little or no attempt to provide any detailed understanding of the mechanisms and logic of transitions. This, it seems to me, is a serious lack. To plug the gap requires going back to basics and dealing with the underlying logic of capitalism in general. And it was, of course, Marx's peculiar virtue to have built a theory of capitalism in general through an analysis of capitalism under the broadly competitive and *laissez-faire* mode of regulation to be found in Britain in the mid-nineteenth century. Let us go back, therefore, to Marx's 'invariant elements and relations' of a capitalist mode of production and see to what degree they are omnipresent beneath all the surface froth and evanescence, the fragmentations and disruptions, so characteristic of present political economy.

Since flexible accumulation is still a form of capitalism we can expect a number of basic propositions to hold. I have tried to summarize these propositions elsewhere, and so I shall simply extract some very basic elements of the argument laid out in *The Limits to Capital* (Harvey, 1982). I shall refer, in particular, to three basic features of any capitalist mode of production.

1   Capitalism is growth-orientated. A steady rate of growth is essential for the health of a capitalist economic system, since it is only through growth that profits can be assured and the accumulation of capital be sustained. This implies that capitalism has to prepare the ground for, and actually achieve an expansion of, output and a growth in real values, no matter what the social, political, geopolitical or ecological consequences. To the degree that virtue is made of necessity, it is a corner-stone of capitalism's ideology that growth is both inevitable and good. Crisis is then defined as a lack of growth.

2   Growth in real values rests on the exploitation of living labour in production. This is not to say that labour gets little, but that growth is always predicated on a gap between what labour gets and what it creates. This implies that labour control, both in production and in the market-place, is vital for the perpetuation of capitalism. Capitalism is founded, in short, on a class relation between capital and labour. Since labour control is essential to capitalist profit, so, too, is the dynamic of class struggle over labour control and market wage fundamental to the trajectory of capitalist development.

3   Capitalism is necessarily technologically and organizationally dynamic. This is so in part because the coercive laws of competition push individual capitalists into leap-frogging innovations in their search for profit. But organizational and technological change also play a key role in modifying the dynamics of class struggle, waged from both sides, in the realm of labour markets and labour control. Furthermore, if labour control is fundamental to the production of profits and becomes a broader issue for the mode of regulation, so technological and organizational innovation in the regulatory system (such as the state apparatus, political systems of incorporation and representation, etc.) becomes crucial to the perpetuation of capitalism. The ideology that 'progress' is both inevitable and good derives in part from this necessity.

What Marx was able to show was that these three necessary conditions of a capitalist mode of production were inconsistent and contradictory and that the dynamic of capitalism was necessarily, therefore, crisis-prone. There was, in his analysis, no way in which the combination of these three necessary conditions could produce steady and unproblematic growth. In particular, the crisis tendencies of capitalism would produce periodic phases of over-accumulation, defined as a condition in which idle capital and idle labour supply could exist side by side with no apparent way to bring these idle resources together to accomplish socially useful tasks. A generalized condition of over-accumulation would be indicated by idle productive capacity, a glut of commodities and an excess of inventories, surplus money capital (perhaps held as hoards) and high unemployment. The conditions that prevailed in the 1930s, and have emerged periodically since 1973, have to be regarded as typical manifestations of the tendency towards over-accumulation.

The Marxist argument is, then, that the tendency towards over-accumulation can never be eliminated under capitalism. It is a never-ending and eternal problem for any capitalist mode of production. The only question, therefore, is how the over-accumulation tendency can be expressed, contained, absorbed or managed in ways that do not threaten the capitalist social order. We here encounter the heroic side of bourgeois life and politics, in which real choices have to be made if the social order is not to dissolve into chaos. Let us look at some of these choices.

(1) *Devaluation* of commodities, of productive capacity, of money value, perhaps coupled with outright destruction, provides one way of dealing with surpluses of capital. In simple terms, devaluation means the 'writing down' or 'writing off' of the value of capital equipment (plant and machinery in particular), the cut-rate disposal of surplus stocks and goods (or their outright destruction, such as the famous Brazilian coffee-burning episode in the 1930s), or the inflationary erosion of money power coupled with burgeoning defaults on loan obligations. Labour power can similarly be devalued and even destroyed (rising rates of exploitation, falling real incomes, unemployment, more deaths on the job, poorer health and lower life expectancy, etc.). The great depression saw plenty of devaluation of both capital and labour power, and the Second World War saw even more. There are plenty of examples and abundant evidence for devaluation as a response to over-accumulation since 1973. But devaluation extracts a political price and hurts large segments of the capitalist class as well as workers and the various other social classes comprising modern complex capitalist society. Some shake-out might seem a good thing, but uncontrolled bankruptcies and massive devaluation exposes the irrational side of capitalist rationality in far too brutal a way for it to be sustainable for long without eliciting some kind of revolutionary (right or left) response. Nevertheless, controlled devaluation through managed deflationary policies is one very important and by no means uncommon option for dealing with over-accumulation.

(2) *Macro-economic control*, through institutionalization of some system of regulation, can contain the over-accumulation problem, perhaps for a considerable period of time. It was, of course, the virtue of the Fordist–Keynesian regime that a balance of forces, however tenuous, could be created through which the mechanism causing the over-accumulation problem – the pace of technological and organizational change together with the struggle over labour control – could be kept sufficiently under control so as to assure steady growth. But it took a major crisis of over-accumulation to connect Fordist production with a Keynesian mode of state regulation before some kind of steady macro-economic growth could be assured for any extended period. The rise of a particular regime of accumulation has to be seen, then as now, as the outcome of a whole host of political and economic decisions, by no means always consciously directed towards this or that specific end, provoked by persistent manifestations of the over-accumulation problem.

(3) *Absorption of over-accumulation* through temporal and spatial displacement provides, in my judgement, a much richer and long-lasting, but also much more problematic, terrain upon which to try and control the over-accumulation problem. The argument here is rather complicated in its details, so I shall again draw upon accounts published elsewhere (Harvey, 1982; 1985).

(a) Temporal displacement entails either a switch of resources from meeting current needs to exploring future uses, or an acceleration in turnover time (the speed with which money outlays return profit to the investor) so that speed-up this year absorbs excess capacity from last year. Excess capital and surplus labour can, for example, be absorbed by switching from current consumption to long-term public and private investments in plant, physical and social infrastructures, and the like. Such investments mop up surpluses in the present only to return their value equivalent over a long time period in the future (this was the principle that lay behind the public works programmes used to combat the slump conditions in the 1930s in many advanced capitalist countries). The capacity to make the switch depends, however, upon the availability of credit and the capacity for 'fictitious capital formation'. The latter is defined as capital that has a nominal money value and paper existence, but which at a given moment in time has no backing in terms of real productive activity or physical assets as collateral. Fictitious capital is converted into real capital to the degree that investments are made that lead to an appropriate increase in useful assets (e.g. plant and machinery that can be profitably deployed) or commodities (goods and services which can be profitably sold). For this reason temporal displacement into future uses is a short-run palliative to the over-accumulation problem, that is, there is a continuous displacement via continuously accelerating rates of fictitious capital formation and expanding volumes of longer-term investment. All of this depends upon some continuous and state-backed dynamic growth in indebtedness. Keynesian policies after 1945 in the advanced capitalist countries in part had such an effect.

Absorption of surpluses through accelerations in turnover time – a strong feature in the recent period of flexible accumulation – poses a different kind of theoretical problem. Heightened competition certainly provokes individual firms to speed up their turnover time (those firms with the faster turnover time tend to gain excess profits thereby, and so survive more easily). But only under certain conditions does this produce an aggregate acceleration of turnover time so as to permit aggregate absorption of surpluses. Even then, this is, at best, a short-run palliative, unless it proves possible to accelerate social turnover time continuously year by year (a solution that would surely imply strong write-offs of past assets in any case, since speed-up usually entails new technologies which displace the old).

(b) Spatial displacement entails the absorption of excess capital and labour in geographical expansion. This 'spatial fix' (as I have elsewhere called it) to the over-accumulation problem entails the production of new spaces within which capitalist production can proceed (through infrastructural investments, for example), the growth of trade and direct investments, and the exploration of new possibilities for the exploitation of labour power. Here, too, the credit system and fictitious capital formation, backed by state fiscal, monetary and, where necessary, military power, become vital mediating influences. And it also follows that the manner of prior occupation of the spaces into which capitalism expands, and the degrees of resistance encountered there, can have profound consequences. In some spaces there has been a history of fierce resistance to the implementation of Western capital (e.g. China), whereas in other spaces (e.g. Japan, or the more recent cases of Hong Kong, Singapore or Taiwan), dominant or even subordinate classes have aggressively inserted themselves into what they saw as a superior economic system. If continuous geographical expansion of capitalism were a real possibility, there could be a relatively permanent solution to the over-accumulation problem. But to the degree that the progressive implementation of capitalism across the face of the earth extends the space within which the over-accumulation problem can arise, so geographical expansion can at best be a short-run solution to the over-accumulation problem. The long-run outcome will almost certainly be heightened international and inter-regional competition, with the least advantaged countries and regions suffering the severest consequences.

(c) Time–space displacements, of course, have a double power with respect to absorption of the over-accumulation problem, and in practice, and particularly to the degree that fictitious capital formation (and, usually, state involvement) is essential to both temporal and spatial displacement, it is the combination of the temporal and spatial strategies that counts. Lending money (often raised on, say, London or New York capital markets through fictitious capital formation) to Latin America to build long-term infrastructures or to purchase capital equipment which will help to generate output for many years to come, is a typical and powerful form of absorption of over-accumulation.

How, then, did Fordism solve the inherent over-accumulation tendencies of capitalism? Before the Second World War it lacked the appropriate regulatory apparatus to do very much more than engage in some tentative pursuits of temporal and spatial displacement (mainly *within* countries, though overseas direct investment on the part of US corporations did begin in the 1920s), and was therefore forced, for the most part, into savage devaluation of the sort achieved in the 1930s and 1940s. Since 1945 – and largely as a consequence of detailed wartime planning to stabilize the postwar economic order – there emerged a fairly coherent accumulation strategy built around control of devaluation and the absorption of over-accumulation by other means. Devaluation through violent swings in the business cycle was brought under control and reduced to the kind of steady devaluation through planned obsolescence that posed relatively minor problems. On the other hand, a strong system of macro-economic control was instituted which controlled the pace of technological and organizational change (mainly through corporate monopoly power), kept the class struggle within bounds (through collective bargaining and state intervention), and kept mass production and mass consumption roughly in balance through state management. But this mode of regulation would not have been anywhere near as successful as it evidently was, if it had not been for the strong presence of both temporal and spatial displacements, albeit under the watchful eye of the interventionist state.

By 1972, for example, we find *Business Week* complaining that the US economy was sitting atop a mountain of debt (though from current heights it all looks like a mole-hill now . . .). Keynesian debt financing, initially intended as a short-term management tool to control business cycles, had, predictably, become sucked into an attempt to absorb over-accumulation by continuous expansion of fictitious capital formation and consequent expansion of the debt burden. Steady expansion of long-term investments, orchestrated by the state, proved a useful way, at least up until the mid-1960s, to absorb any excess capital or labour. Spatial displacement (combined, of course, with long-term indebtedness) was an even more powerful influence. Within the United States the radical transformation of metropolitan economies (through the suburbanization of both manufacturing and residences), as well as the expansion into the South and West, absorbed vast quantities of excess capital and labour. Internationally, the reconstruction of the economies of Western Europe and Japan, accelerating flows of foreign direct investment, and the enormous growth in world trade played a critical role in absorbing surpluses. Planning for postwar 'peace with prosperity' in the Second World War emphasized the need for a global strategy for capital accumulation within a world where trade and investment barriers were to be steadily reduced and colonial subservience replaced by an open system of growth, advancement and co-operation within a decolonized capitalist world system. Even though some facets of this programme were to prove ideological and illusory, enough of its content was realized to make a spatial revolution in global trading and investment entirely possible.

It was primarily through spatial and temporal displacement that the Fordist regime of accumulation resolved the over-accumulation problem during the long postwar boom. The crisis of Fordism can to some degree be interpreted, there-fore, as a running out of those options to handle the over-accumulation problem. Temporal displacement was piling debt upon debt to the point where the only viable government strategy was to monetize it away. This was done, in effect, by printing so much money as to trigger an inflationary surge, which radically re-duced the real value of past debts (the thousand dollars borrowed ten years ago has little value after a phase of high inflation). Turnover time could not easily be accelerated without destroying the value of fixed capital assets. New geographical centres of accumulation – the US South and West, Western Europe and Japan, and then a range of newly industrializing countries – were created. As these Fordist production systems came to maturity, they became new and often highly competi-tive centres of over-accumulation. Spatial competition intensified between geo-graphically distinct Fordist systems, with the most efficient regimes (such as the

Japanese) and lower labour-cost regimes (such as those found in the third world countries where notions of a social contract with labour were either lacking or weakly enforced) driving other centres into paroxysms of devaluation through deindustrialization. Spatial competition intensified, particularly after 1973, as the capacity to resolve the over-accumulation problem through geographical displacement ran out. The crisis of Fordism was, therefore, as much a geographical and geopolitical crisis as it was a crisis of indebtedness, class struggle or corporate stagnation within any particular nation-state. It was simply that the mechanisms evolved for controlling crisis tendencies were finally overwhelmed by the power of the underlying contradictions of capitalism. There seemed to be no option except to fall back into devaluation of the sort that occurred in the period 1973–5 or 1980–2 as the primary means of dealing with the tendency towards over-accumulation. Unless, that is, some other and superior regime of capitalist production could be created which would assure a solid basis for further accumulation on a global scale.

Flexible accumulation here seems to fit as a simple recombination of the two basic strategies which Marx defined for procuring profit (surplus value). The first, termed *absolute* surplus value, rests on the extension of the working day relative to the wage needed to guarantee working-class reproduction at a given standard of living. The shift towards longer working hours coupled with an overall reduction in the standard of living either by erosion of the real wage or by the shift of corporate capital from high-wage to low-wage regions captures one facet of flexible capital accumulation.

Many of the standardized production systems built up under Fordism have, for this reason, shifted to the periphery, creating 'peripheral Fordism'. Even the new production systems have tended to shift, once standardized, from their innovative hearths to third world locations (Atari's 1984 move from Silicon Valley to South East Asia's low-wage labour power is a case in point). Under the second strategy, termed *relative* surplus value, organizational and technological change is set in motion to gain temporary profits for innovative firms and more generalized profits as costs of goods that define the standard of living labour are reduced. Here, too, the proliferating violence of investments, which cut employment and labour costs in every industry from coal mining and steel production to banking and financial services, has been a highly visible aspect of capital accumulation in the 1980s. Yet reliance on this strategy brings to the fore the significance of highly skilled labour powers with the capacity to understand, implement and manage the new but much more flexible patterns of technological innovation and market orientation. A highly privileged, and to some degree empowered, stratum with the labour force emerges as capitalism depends more and more on mobilizing the powers of intellectual labour as a vehicle for further accumulation.

In the end, of course, it is the particular manner in which absolute and relative strategies combine and feed off each other that counts. Interestingly, the deployment of new technologies has so freed surpluses of labour power as to make the revival of absolute strategies for procuring surplus value more feasible even in the advanced capitalist countries. What is, perhaps, more unexpected is the way in which new production technologies and co-ordinating forms of organization have permitted the revival of domestic, familial and paternalistic labour systems, which Marx tended to assume would either be driven out of business or reduced to such conditions of gross exploitation and dehumanizing toil as to be intolerable under advanced capitalism. The revival of the sweatshops in New York and Los Angeles, of home work and 'telecommuting', as well as the burgeoning growth of informal sector labour practices throughout the advanced capitalist world, does indeed represent a rather sobering vision of capitalism's supposedly progressive history. Under conditions of flexible accumulation, it seems as if alternative labour systems can exist side by side within the same space in such a way as to enable capitalist entrepreneurs to choose at will between them. . . . The same shirt designs can be produced by large-scale factories in India, co-operative production in the 'Third Italy', sweatshops in New York and London, or family labour systems in Hong Kong. Eclecticism in labour practices seem almost as marked in these times as the eclecticism of postmodern philosophies and tastes.

Yet there is, in spite of the difference of context and the specificities of the example used, something quite compelling and relevant about Marx's account of the logic of capitalist organization and accumulation. Rereading his account in *Capital* strikes home with a certain jolt of recognition. We there read of the ways in which the factory system can intersect with domestic, workshop and artisanal systems of manufacture, of how an industrial reserve army is mobilized as a counter-weight to workers' power with respect to both labour control and wage rates, of the ways in which intellectual powers and new technologies are deployed to disrupt the organized power of the working class, of how capitalists try to foster the spirit of competition among workers, while all the time demanding flexibility of disposition, of location and of approach to tasks. We are also forced to consider how all of this creates opportunities as well as dangers and difficulties for working-class people precisely because education, flexibility and geographical mobility, once acquired, become harder for capitalists to control.

Even though present conditions are very different in many respects, it is not hard to see how the invariant elements and relations that Marx defined as fundamental to any capitalist mode of production still shine through, and in many instances with an even greater luminosity than before, all the surface froth and evanescence so characteristic of flexible accumulation. Is the latter, then, anything more than a jazzed-up version of the same old story of capitalism as usual? That would be too simple a judgement. It treats of capitalism ahistorically, as a non-dynamic mode of production, when all the evidence (including that explicitly laid out by Marx) is that capitalism is a constantly revolutionary force in world history, a force that perpetually reshapes the world into new and often quite unexpected configurations. Flexible accumulation appears, at least, to be a new configuration and, as such, it requires that we scrutinize its manifestations with the requisite care and seriousness, using, nevertheless, the theoretical tools that Marx devised.

References

Halal, W. (1986) *The New Capitalism*, New York.
Harvey, D. (1982) *The Limits to Capital*, Oxford.
Harvey, D. (1985) 'The geopolitics of capitalism', in D. Gregory and J. Urry (eds), *Social Relations and Spatial Structures*, London.
Lash, S. and Urry, J. (1987) *The End of Organized Capitalism*, Oxford.
Swyngedouw, E. (1986) 'The socio-spatial implications of innovations in industrial organisation'. Working Paper No. 20, Johns Hopkins European Center for Regional Planning and Research, Lille.

24

The Politics of Consumption

Frank Mort

The "New Times writers," associated with the now defunct British journal of the Left *Marxism Today*, were, in the late 1980s, concerned that the British Labour Party should "modernize" its ideas in line with the profound social changes that had been initiated in the wake of an emergent "post-Fordist" economic order. In "The Politics of Consumption" Frank Mort argues for the imperative that it should be incumbent on the Left to alter radically its ways of thinking about consumption, in particular to develop political strategies and concrete policies which would accommodate a recognition that, among many things, contemporary consumption represents for ordinary citizens a source of genuine pleasure and a valuable means of articulating a conception of the self and identity.

Take two cultural narratives of consumption.

Spring 1988: the retail boom at its height and the yob and the yuppie are icons of the new materialism. Harry Enfield's[1] bragging London plasterer, Loadsamoney, is working-class affluence personified. A thoroughly modern flash-harry, the tosh with the dosh, Loads is an incarnation of the property-owning democracy. His upmarket soulmate, the yuppie, is hero and heroine of the style manuals and financial markets. A mythical creature of the boom – part agent, part victim – with a lifestyle ruthlessly dedicated to consuming.

Autumn 1989: falling house prices and a sales slump in the shops. The symbolic failure of retailing's Next and advertising's Saatchi and Saatchi. Suddenly, Loads is very much last year's hero: 'I've Lost a Lump in the Slump – Bish, Bosh, I've Spent All Me Dosh'. The rag trade puts it more prosaically: 'Well it had to happen. The bubble had to burst. Like all good things the boom is running out of steam'.[2]

These stories deal not just with material success and failure. Up and downmarket they project profoundly cultural images of economic life. That is why they have stuck in the popular imagination, positively as well as negatively. They condense

From S. Hall and M. Jacques (eds.) *New Times: The Changing Face of Politics in the 1990s* (London: Lawrence and Wishart, 1989), pp. 160–72. Reprinted by permission of the author.

styles of living, forms of identity which demand attention in any political assessment of contemporary consumption.

The politics of consumption lies at the heart of this essay. Indeed, the twin issues of consumerism and the market lie at the heart of the debate over our vision of the future of socialism. Where you stand on them has become a litmus test for the whole question of renewal and realignment. In the redder than red corner stand those for whom markets are the very apogee of capitalist immorality, denying real freedoms and collective decision-making. The reassertion of this version of socialist morality has of course been prompted by the rethink around the issues of collectivism and individualism taking place within the labour movement and elsewhere. Current thinking, certainly in Labour's policy review, is that public provision and the market can be brought into a new relation. But the point of what follows is not simply to endorse 'market socialism' or a new revisionism. It is to argue that thinking through the politics of consumption must be as much a cultural as an economic project. It needs to be about taking our images of the yob and the yuppie (and what lies behind them) seriously. Despite their profound contradictions, ideologies of affluence have had very real effects on large sections of the population. Some of these have been potentially liberating – consuming as a source of power and pleasure. They will need to find a place within our vision of new times.

Economic Populism

Consumption is now centre stage in the political battle over the economy. Its orchestration by the government was a pivotal part of its vaunted economic successes between 1985 and 1988. This was not just the stuff of money supply ratios and macro Treasury forecasts; central to its command of the economic high ground was the ability to deal in popular ideologies of economics – languages which effectively delivered for people's everyday experience.

This is where Thatcherism, in both its first and second phases, scored so dramatically over its rivals. In its skill in embroidering a patchwork of economic common sense which matched so many of our own notions of managing money. If the first term and a half talked of iron times and the political economy of pain, Mr Lawson[3] gave us quite a different tune. Out went the morality of backs to the wall and the handbag mentality of good housekeeping. Britain was booming again: investment up, inflation and unemployment down. And in this revised vision of economic doctrine consumption was cast as a star performer. A retail boom and a bull-market in house prices were flagged up as the most visible signs of recovery. Lawson epitomised it in his own persona – part economic wizard, part *bon viveur*, even a touch sexy. While one-liners from the banks and building societies pushed a brazen regime of consumer pleasure, relaxation and excess. 'Gold Card Service'; 'No Spending Limit'; 'Moneycare: Making It, Spending It, Enjoying It', purred

Nat West seductively.[4] Here was a slap in the face for both the old maxims of save and prosper and the austere morality of the first term.

There were of course deep-seated contradictions in the consumer boom, rooted in the structural weaknesses of the UK economy, which are now coming home to roost. A high street shopping spree was no guide to prolonged economic recovery, for the growing balance of payments deficit pointed up just how many commodities were import-based. While bank give-aways for cars and Amstrads were a timely remainder of finance capital's disinvestment in Britain's industrial base. And at the back of it all lay the accelerating inflationary wage–price spiral.

Underpinning the retail expansion and exacerbating many of the sector's current difficulties has been the expansion in credit. The flexibility and innovations in finance capital have set some of the material conditions here. Britons have taken to charge cards and plastic money like no other EEC country. On 1989 figures we owe a cool £28 million on our personal loans.[5] All of the major high street chains – M & S, Dixons, Next – offer their own financial services with annual interest rates at times topping the 40 per cent mark. Boots, conscious perhaps of its philan-thropic past, withdrew its own in-store card on the grounds that interest charges were excessive. Yet spending on the never-never has never been so acceptable – and for some so necessary. Rising three times faster than annual incomes since 1980, it has thrown up its own growth industries: debt collectors and repossession merchants. We should be cautious, though, in reading this phenomenon over-simply. Some complex patterns are emerging in the *uses* of credit: namely its take-up by sections of the new poor to buy into a vision of prosperity. Students, those in the part-time workforce, as well as the long-term unemployed, may be forced to use plastic to purchase essentials, but it seems that they are also taking up the offer to play the system imaginatively – even to their own advantage.

And despite the current economic downturn these ideologies of buying and selling are still very much in place. The partnership between the financial markets and retailing has thrown up some very late-capitalist images of prosperity. The manic compulsion to consume; the hyper-eroticization of a visit to the shops; economics as a game of chance or wheel of fortune, here today, gone tomorrow – these are now some of the popular representations of material life. Indeed, living with instability is one of the most enduring cultural legacies of the decade. It has replaced the slow but upward gradualism of social democracy (the gold watch for forty years' service and merit rewarded) with icons which are much more precari-ous and fluctuating. Murdoch's popular press in particular has consistently pro-jected economics if not quite as tinsel fairyland, then something unstable and irrational. After all, like bingo or having a flutter, that's what gives it *frisson* and excitement. And while the rhetoric of the popular press is not a direct mirror of real experience, there are resonances here of some very traditional working-class responses to money and success. Fatalism, economic fortunes like the pools' win-ners who blow it all in a fortnight, above all a profound sense that economic forces are 'out there' beyond the control of ordinary people. It is through these cultural maps that many council-house buyers in Basildon or credit debtors in Billericay must be trying to make sense of the present situation.

The general point to come out of all of this is that consumption is as much about the languages and images of economics as about the nuts and bolts of policy. Thus a successful politics in this area needs to be thought through in a vocabulary which matches people's life-chances and experience. This is where theoretical economics (ever since it defined itself as a science) is left floundering. Thatcherism's orchestration of consumption has been adept at channelling perceptions of growing personal prosperity into its own political discourse equating the ring of tinkling cash registers with political and cultural freedoms. What, of course, the government desperately needs now as the third term draws all too rapidly to a close, is a populist package which can 'sell' the current economic situation as effectively as it sold us recession and then the boom.

Labour and the Politics of Austerity

How to challenge Tory economic populism? What languages to draw on to project an alternative economic future which engages with people's desire for their own as well as collective prosperity? One deep-seated response from the opposition is that government policy is so profligate and the economy's weaknesses now so apparent, that there is little need to engage with any sort of populist rhetoric. But if we accept the argument about the centrality of the images which shape material life, Labour will need to find an imaginative way of translating policy into the popular aspirations, desires, even dreams which cluster around common-sense understandings of economics and especially consumption.

Part of the difficulty here lies in the legacy of Keynesianism. For while consumer aggregate demand, along with full employment and public spending, did figure as a cornerstone of postwar consensus politics, it appeared unsung, as an economic abstraction only within Labour's political discourse of those years. There was little attempt to translate Keynesian macroeconomics into a rhetoric which tapped into a burgeoning consumer culture. Again, the Tories had all the best tunes, whether it was Churchill's 'set the people free' slogan to end austerity in 1951, or Macmillan's 'you've never had it so good' slightly later. There were exceptions on Labour's side of course; 'revisionists' (the name says it all) like Crossland and Jenkins did begin to float an expansive scheme for the mixed economy which embraced cultural (albeit tasteful) images of affluence. But Labour never found a way of being easy about prosperity. For the most part when Messrs Wilson and Callaghan did bring economics to the nation we got a lecture about how everything was going wrong – TV graphs of the balance of payments in the red, devaluation and the prices and incomes freeze.

In fact the reasons for that unease, the failure to engage with the politics of affluence, go deeper than failures of policy. They bring us face to face with part of the legacy of socialism's own past – a politics which emerged triumphant in the first half of the twentieth century, and which we continue to inherit. Brutally put, the problem is socialism's over-identification with production. This, fused with the input from an older more explicitly moral and evangelizing Labour tradition, is still engraved in tablets of stone on the hearts and minds of many on the British Left. It effectively acts as a barrier to any more imaginative approach to post-Fordist economics and culture.

Here we need to sketch in the other strand of Labour's postwar history. In the 1940s the Labour Party defined itself as the progressive Fordist party, projecting an economic modernism which identified with large-scale production and the workplace aims of those who ran the plants. Culturally it was, as we now know, a highly gendered modernism, which heroized the butch, macho heavy industries and ranked workers in the new service sector as secondary and inferior. But on the forms of mass consumption which accompanied the Fordist revolution, Labour was always ideologically more wary, more suspicious. The dominance of Fabianism, coupled with an austere Methodism, made large sections of the Left uneasy about the cars, fridges and washing machines that were rolling off the production line. Consuming, as opposed to producing, was at best handled as secondary and trivial, confined to the private, feminized sphere of household duties and personal life. At worst consumption was cast as a moral evil, buying off working people with an orgy of goodies – or so the argument often went. Labour's immediate response to the postwar situation was austerity, rationing, coupons *and* the black market. Austerity may have been a hit with top-down economic planners, but it was a dismal failure for consumer democracy. Labour's austerity Chancellor, Stafford Cripps, aimed to purge consuming passions from the national psyche. Cripps wanted the desire for fashionable clothes and jewellery – and their association with feminine pleasures – eliminated altogether, for good.[6]

The rationale for rehearsing this history is not to castigate past errors, rather to insist that a simple anti-consumerist politics is debilitating in today's economic context. For Labour, growing government disarray on the economic front presents a major political opportunity and we have had some effective performances from Messrs Smith and Brown as the opposition Treasury team. But their negative gloss on the pitfalls of the consumer economy has been laced with more than a hint of Calvinist sadism and 'I told you so' smugness. Labour should beware of deploying consumption as a purely negative symbol of economic performance. To do so is to ignore all those positive aspirations which have jostled for space around Thatcherism's limited market philosophy.

Lifestyles and Market Segments

Arguing for the politics of consumption inside the Left means enlarging and complexifying our map of economic structures and processes. There is nothing innately Thatcherite about consuming, just as there is nothing intrinsically social-ist about the state. A reductionism which collapses the lived experience of con-sumerism with the official version of Tory popular capitalism is blind to the fact that what people actually *do* when they go shopping may be quite different from the official script. Commodities and their images are multi-accented, they can be pushed and pulled into the service of resistant demands and dreams. High-tech in the hands of young blacks or girls making-up are not simply forms of buying into the system. They can be very effectively hijacked for cultures of resistance, reap-pearing as street-style cred or assertive femininity.

But we are already jumping ahead. The first move is to take seriously the indus-tries which fix our experience of buying and selling. Getting to grips with advertis-ing and marketing raises the whole question of the Left's strategy for the service sector in the post-Fordist economy: their functions, forms of knowledge and con-trol and, crucially, their cultural and social effects. But advertising and marketing are not only key institutions in the consumer cycle, they command a higher and higher profile within production as well. The role of these industries has grown qualitatively in tandem with shifts away from standardized mass production to more flexible systems and changes in consumer demand in favour of greater choice and diversity. Key decisions in many sectors have migrated away from the plant and factory to these new captains of industry. In clothing and food retailing, for example, crucial management policy is made largely by marketers and retailers. Marks and Spencers dominate through the backward integration of food process-ing and production, while Benetton have become famous for their flexible franchising systems. Workers in these sectors posses their own reserves of cultural capital – systems of knowledge and training which cannot just be written off as 'Thatcherite'. We are dealing here with fractions of the service class or new petit bourgeoisie whose occupations involve some form of representation in handling symbolic goods and services.[7]

Yet for too many on the Left retailing and advertising provokes a rash of socialist moralism. For these are the ones we really love to hate: personifications of yuppiedom, the docklands interlopers, those who deal in slick images pulled into the service of capital. The whole fall-out over so-called 'designer socialism' has produced a knee-jerk response, branding those who raise its profile as middle-class trendies, hypnotized by the glare of Next and Katherine Hamnett. A more serious look at advertising's dialogue with the market puts paid to the cliché that con-sumption is foisted on gullible populations by hype and the lust for profit. Adver-tisers and marketers are not simply the slaves of capital. They are the intermediaries who construct a dialogue between the market on the one hand and consumer culture on the other. Marketers will tell you that this is a two-way process; it doesn't simply come from above. Product design and innovation, pricing and promotion, are shaped by the noises coming from the street. Market research is in the business of collating these noises and shaping them into consumer profiles. The net result is, of course, contradictory. The industry deals in its own social truisms about 'upward mobility' or 'what women want'. But to fail to recognize that marketing taps something of our pleasures and aspirations as consumers is to ignore the how and why of its success.

The late 1980s have witnessed some major rethinks within the industry about the content and direction of campaigns. The retailing revolution on the high street and the shopping malls has gone hand-in-hand with an intellectual change of direction backstage. *Lifestyling* is the end product, a marketing concept which twins designer-led with shifting patterns of consumer demand. Rodney Fitch of Fitch and Co., the consultants who promoted Next, pinpoints the move quite precisely:

> The consumer is changing. The consumer's ideas, expectations and attitudes towards how they will buy, let alone what they will buy . . . are all in a state of flux. High street shopping simply mirrors changes in our society and demonstrates that you are responsive to them . . . design has become part of these competitive retail strategies. Design is a visual thing and therefore the end result is visual change.[8]

Two basic concepts are at work here: the move to market segmentation, and the input from design and visual communications. The argument goes like this. Traditional market blocs which were the mainstay of the era of postwar mass production (the working-class family, youth, the housewife, etc.), have splintered under the impact of cultural upheavals going on beyond the sales-counter and the supermarket aisle. Consumer profiles have become very sensitive to these social dynamics. They target their audiences with a new precision: Volkswagen for the working woman, Saga Holidays for the young elderly, the pink pound for gay men. In essence it is marketing's bid to come to terms with the cultural agenda of the 1990s. The industry is especially sharp on the new cultures of working-class affluence – in their vocabulary the C1s and C2s in work. *Campaign*[9] deftly rings the changes: traditional Saturday afternoons on the terraces and bingo are out, displaced by saunas, aerobics and eating in with Liebfraumilch and chicken chasseur.

Greater market segmentation demands different methods of communication. This is where the other factors in lifestyling come in – the upbeat stress on design and visual awareness. Advertising theory has long since abandoned the hard-sell technology which worked with simple notions of social or price competitiveness: the 'sell 'em cheap, pile 'em' high campaigns of the 1960s and early 1970s. In a society where large swathes of the population already possess consumer basics like fridges, TVs and washing machines, advertising must find a different language to promote product awareness. The aim is to suggest atmosphere – a style of life – with a message which is 'emotional' rather than rational or informational. Colour, sound and shape are the things which mark out individuality, nudging consumers to identify with commodities through mood and association. As John Hegarty, the consultant responsible for the famous Levi Jeans account, put it, the thing to crack was atmosphere and quality of the image, quite as much as the brand or product.[10] Recent M & S ads, Next Interiors, or the Debenham's refit on the shopfloor all point to lifestyling in action. Of course late 1980s retailing has not itself invented individualism; appeal to the unique *you* has been a staple diet of so many campaigns over the last four decades. But what is currently happening is a hyping of that process, a proliferation of individualities, of the number of 'yous' on offer.

Our argument is that the service sector industries (not on their own but as part of a broader ensemble of post-Fordist practices) are redefining the economic and cultural horizons of contemporary Britain. We may disagree with advertising's conclusions, but we would be foolish to dismiss the insights thrown up about shifting class relations or the redrawn maps of cultural experience going on inside people's heads. And whisper it not too loud, but aren't there some uncanny resemblances between lifestyle market segmentation and the politics of identity which have been argued for by the new social movements? For the fracturing of solid market blocs read the break-up of postwar class certainties and the eruption of quite different political subjects with alternative agendas: women, gays, the elderly, etc. Both the market and formal politics are being forced to adapt to these sea-changes. Moreover, as in the market-place so in the political meeting, postmodern structures of identity are less centred around the certainty of a fixed self. We do not often get the reassurance of a coherent subjectivity these days – politically or culturally. We are not in any simple sense 'black' or 'gay' or 'upwardly mobile'. Rather we carry a bewildering range of different, and at times, conflicting identities around with us in our heads at the same time. There is a continual smudging of personas and lifestyles, depending where we are (at work, on the high street) and the spaces we are moving between. It is the speed, the fluidity with which these identities mingle and overlap which makes any notion of fixed subjects seem more and more anachronistic – distinctly early twentieth century.

Both politics and consumer culture are registering these structural changes. Yet there is one crucial difference between their two fields of vision – a difference which goes to the heart of our argument about the need to take consumption seriously. It is a difference of style, of language, of presentation, but in the profoundest sense. Political language still speaks a vocabulary of power and authority on the one hand or oppression and struggle on the other. By and large it is also a verbal or written discourse which seeks to appeal through rationality. The new consumerism on the other hand is all about floating visual images, pleasures and impossible dreams. To say that these are false dreams, false promises is to miss the point. Formal politics of all persuasions is rigidly self-policing about this uto-pian bundle. It defensively ringfences its boundaries and lets only very particular political subjects in through the door. Needs, rights and demands are OK, but lifestyle, pleasures and aspirations are still out of bounds. Some of the new politics – and notably feminism – have been about breaking down these watertight dis-tinctions between 'politics' and 'life'. In a no less coherent way, and often target-ing the same populations, consumer culture does the same.

The net effect of all of this has been to ask some unanswerable questions of the political culture of Fordism. The collapse of old political certainties, the loss of faith in early twentieth-century forms of organization and identity – public meet-ings, canvassing, party literature and the old-style version of citizenship – are not simply the product of apathy under Thatcherism. 'Depoliticization' registers much more than a pessimism about the political process. It speaks of a growing disen-gagement of 'life', where people choose to put their energies and invest their hopes, from 'politics'. For more and more people it is *outside* work, *outside* the formal political structures, in the world of holidays, home interiors and superstores, that they have a sense of power and freedom to express themselves, to define their sense of self, to mould the good life. Thatcherism has not created that scenario, but the present political culture has certainly capitalized on it. In the current cli-mate the invitation is to 'buy out of politics', to see it as only to do with restrictive bureaucracy and petty nuisance. Life, it seems, lies elsewhere.[11]

So, to put it polemically, should we just sit back and let the marketers get on with it? If we are looking for cultural agendas which energize people and express their sense of self, doesn't consumer capitalism do it better anyway? Is there really nowhere to go but the shops?

There is no one political response to the agenda thrown up by consumption: indeed Politics with a big P may itself be part of the problem. Rather, what are needed are interrelated initiatives which confront issues of economic policy, cul-tural politics and the much-needed modernization of socialist culture in Britain. Some of these are relatively easy to translate into party policy (if the political will is there), while others have a much longer-term future. At the heart of all of them sits the vexed question of the relation between collectivist and individual value systems in any alternative to Thatcherism.

Given the sea-changes in finance capital as well as marketing, consumption is set to remain high priority on the economic front, despite the recent retail slow-down. More important, it is a key point in the popular imagination where eco-nomic policy is judged to succeed or fail – precisely because it touches people where they *feel* active and powerful. Labour's policy needs to take those aspira-tions and forms of common sense seriously. At one level this has to do with pres-entation (not a superficial point by any means), of finding languages which engage with economics on those terms. But there are some tough policy issues here as well. Income tax is certainly one of them. Leaving aside the precise details of the policy review, there will need to be some pretty hard talking about the precise balance to be struck between the collective and individual demands around taxation. Fixing fair *but reasonable* tax levels is about making choices between goods and services directed through public provision and those determined by the private sector. And if that sounds like revisionism, or selling socialism short, it is precisely because the relation between the market and the public sector remains one of the big open-ended questions of socialist strategy.

But thinking needs to go beyond the purely economic, given that consumerism is the point where material and social life collide. One current response here is to take seriously the impact of consumer individualism, but to work for alternative and expanded definitions of choice. Thus Charter 88 returns to the arena of citizen's rights and freedoms, while the rhetoric of consumer choice has become standard practice in many areas of the public sector. And there is everything positive for the Left in striking a new compact between production- and consumption-led values. Yet the programme here is ultimately pragmatic, hoping to bind in the new individualisms to existing ideas of policy and politics. What this of course refuses is the bigger issue of whether leisure and consumption haven't already redefined the terrain.

So our conception of politics must again be prised open. Responding to consumption means recasting our thinking: to begin politically from the pressure points where so many of us invest our energies and life chances. Most of the new politics have been saying much the same thing, yet rarely have they put consumer culture centre stage. Consequently the argument is about sites as well as programmes. Today's consumer culture straddles public and private space, creating blurred areas in between. Privatized car culture, with its collective red nose days and stickers for lead-free petrol; shopping as the quintessential expression of consumer choice now carries social anxieties over eco-politics and food pollution. These are the localized points where consuming meshes with social demands and aspirations in new ways. What they underline is that consumption is not ultimately about individualism *versus* collectivism, but about articulating the two in a new relation which can form the basis for a future common sense.

Notes

1   A popular British comedian [Ed.].
2   *Menswear*, 4 May 1989, p. 2.
3   UK Chancellor of the Exchequer during the boom years of 1985–9 [Ed.].
4   National Westminster Bank, *Moneycare*, Spring 1988, front cover.
5   'The credit boom goes on', *Guardian*, 6 June 1989, p. 11.
6   Sir Stafford Cripps, budget speech, 6 April 1949, in Public Record Office, Treasury Papers, T 171/399.

7   For further analysis of the culture of the new middle class see Pierre Bourdieu, *Distinction: A Social Critique of the Judgement of Taste*, Routledge and Kegan Paul, 1984 [see chapter 7, this volume].

8   'Designs on the new consumer', *Marketing*, 24 October 1985, p. 20.

9   A weekly journal for advertisers and marketing [Ed].

10 'How heritage will be used to launch a Levis classic', *Campaign*, 29 November 1985, pp. 39–43.

11 Zygmunt Bauman, 'Britain's exit from politics', *New Statesman and Society*, 29 July 1988, pp. 34–7.

25
The Commodities of Culture

John Fiske

Originally developed to explain the "active and creative reading practices" of television viewing, John Fiske's theory of "semiotic democracy" was extended in a number of publications in the late 1980s and early 1990s to include an analysis of consumption in the more general sense. Drawing particularly on the ideas expressed by de Certeau in chapter 11, Fiske stresses the oppositional and subversive reading practices of viewers/consumers as they seek to resist the dominant or preferred meanings and ideologies that are inscribed within media texts and consumer goods generally.

Let us take television as the paradigm example of a culture industry, and trace the production and distribution of its commodities (or texts) within two parallel, semiautonomous economies, which we may call the *financial* (which circulates wealth in two subsystems) and the *cultural* (which circulates meanings and pleasures). They can be modeled thus:

	Finacial economy		*Cultural economy*
	I	II	
Producer:	Production studio	Program	Audience
Commodity:	Program	Audience	Meanings/pleasures
Consumer:	Distributor	Advertiser	Itself

The Two Economies of Television

The production studios produce a commodity, a program, and sell it to the distributors, the broadcasting or cable networks, for a profit. This is a simple financial exchange common to all commodities. But this is not the end of the matter, for a television program, or cultural commodity, is not the same sort of commodity as a material one such as a microwave oven or a pair of jeans. The economic function

From "Commodities and Culture" in *Understanding Popular Culture* (London: Unwin Hyman, 1989), pp. 26–32. Reprinted by permission of Routledge.

of a television program is not complete once it has been sold, for in its moment of consumption it changes to become a producer, and what it produces is an audience, which is then sold to advertisers.

For many, the most important product of the culture industries is the commodified audience to be sold to advertisers. Smythe (1977) argues that capitalism has extended its power from the world of work into that of leisure, and so, by watching television and thus participating in the commodification of people, we are working as hard for commodity capitalism as any worker on the assembly lines. This argument is both accurate and incisive as far as it goes, but it remains fixed within the economic base of society, and can explain meanings or ideologies only as mechanistically determined by that base. It can account for the popularity of jeans only in terms of their durability, cheapness, and easy availability, but not in terms of their variety of cultural meanings.

In a consumer society, all commodities have cultural as well as functional values. To model this we need to extend the idea of an economy to include a cultural economy where the circulation is not one of money, but of meanings and pleasures. Here the audience, from being a commodity, now becomes a producer, a producer of meanings and pleasures. The original commodity (be it a television program or a pair of jeans) is, in the cultural economy, a text, a discursive structure of potential meanings and pleasures that constitutes a major resource of popular culture. In this economy there are no consumers, only circulators of meanings, for meanings are the only elements in the process that can be neither commodified nor consumed: meanings can be produced, reproduced, and circulated only in that constant process that we call culture.

We live in an industrial society, so of course our popular culture is an industrialized culture, as are all our resources; by "resources" I mean both semiotic or cultural ones and material ones – the commodities of both the financial and cultural economies. With very few and very marginal exceptions, people cannot and do not produce their own commodities, material or cultural, as they may have done in tribal or folk societies. In capitalist societies there is no so-called authentic folk culture against which to measure the "inauthenticity" of mass culture, so bemoaning the loss of the authentic is a fruitless exercise in romantic nostalgia.

However, the fact that the people cannot produce and circulate their own commodities does not mean that popular culture does not exist. As de Certeau (1984) puts it, people have to make do with what they have, and what they have are the products of the cultural (and other) industries. The creativity of popular culture lies not in the production of commodities so much as in the productive use of industrial commodities. The art of the people is the art of "making do." The culture of everyday life lies in the creative, discriminating use of the resources that capitalism provides.

In order to be popular, then, cultural commodities have to meet quite contradictory needs. On the one hand there are the centralizing, homogenizing needs of the financial economy. The more consumers any one product can reach, and the more any one product can be reproduced by the existing processes within the cultural factory, the greater the economic return on it. It must therefore attempt to appeal to what people have in common, to deny social differences. What people in capitalist societies have in common is the dominant ideology and the experience of subordination or disempowerment. The economic needs of the cultural industries are thus perfectly in line with the disciplinary and ideological requirements of the existing social order, and all cultural commodities must therefore, to a greater or lesser extent, bear the forces that we can call centralizing, disciplinary, hegemonic, massifying, commodifying (the adjectives proliferate almost endlessly).

Opposing these forces, however, are the cultural needs of the people, this shifting matrix of social allegiances that transgress categories of the individual, or class, or gender, or race, or any category that is stable within the social order. These popular forces transform the cultural commodity into a cultural resource, pluralize the meanings and pleasures it offers, evade or resist its disciplinary efforts, fracture its homogeneity and coherence, raid or poach upon its terrain. All popular culture is a process of struggle, a struggle over the meanings of social experience, of one's personhood and its relations to the social order and of the texts and commodities of that order. Reading relations reproduce and reenact social relations, so power, resistance, and evasion are necessarily structured into them.

As Stuart Hall (1981: 238) says,

> The people versus the power-bloc: this, rather than "class-against-class," is the central line of contradiction around which the terrain of culture is polarized. Popular culture, especially, is organized around the contradiction: the popular forces versus the power-bloc.

This leads him to conclude that the study of popular culture should always start with "the double movement of containment and resistance, which is always inevitably inside it' (Hall, 1981: 228).

Tearing or bleaching one's jeans is a tactic of resistance; the industry's incorporation of this into its production system is a strategy of containment. Maintaining the relative autonomy of the cultural economy from the financial opens up cultural commodities to resistant or evasive uses: attempts to close the gap, to decrease the autonomy are further strategies of containment or incorporation. Advertising tries to control the cultural meanings of commodities by mapping them as tightly as possible onto the workings of the financial economy. Advertising works hard to match social differences with cultural differences with product differences.

White patriarchal capitalism has failed to homogenize the thinking and the culture of its subjects, despite nearly two centuries of economic domination (and much longer in the domains of gender and race). Our societies are intransigently diverse, and this diversity is maintained by popular and cultural forces in the face of a variety of strategies of homogenization. Of course capitalism requires diversity, but it requires a controlled diversity, a diversity that is determined and limited by the needs of its mode of production. It requires different forms of social control and different social institutions to reproduce itself and its subjects, so it produces class differences and fractional or sectional differences within those classes. The owners of capital can maintain their social position only because the social order in which they flourish has produced legal, political, educational and cultural systems that, in their own spheres, reproduce the social subjectivities required by the economic system.

But social diversity exceeds that required by capitalism, by patriarchy, by racial dominance. Of course patriarchy requires and thrives off gender differences, but it does not require feminism, it does not require women to opt out of marriage or to decide to raise children with no father figure. Racial dominance does not require black separatism, or that black high school students should opt out of the whitist educational system, to the extent that success in that system can be seen as a betrayal of blackness.

Society is structured around a complex matrix of axes of difference (class, gender, race, age, and so on), each of which has a dimension of power. There is no social difference without power difference, so one way of defining the popular is, as Hall does, to identify it by its oppositionality to "the power-bloc."

The popular can also be characterized by its fluidity. One person may, at different times, form cultural allegiances with different, not to say contradictory, social groups as he or she moves through the social formation. I may forge for myself quite different social allegiances to cope with and make sense of different areas of my everyday life. When, for instance, the age axis appears crucial, my allegiances may contradict those formed when, at other times, those of gender or class or race seem most pertinent.

People watching Archie Bunker, the bigoted male in *All in the Family*, made sense of him quite differently according to how they positioned themselves within the social formation and thus the cultural allegiances they forged. "His" meanings could and did move fluidly along the axes of class, age, gender, and race, to name only the most obvious, as viewers used him as a cultural resource to think through their social experience and the meanings they made out of it. The polysemic openness of popular texts is required by social differences and is used to maintain, question, and think through those differences.

Similarly, product differences are required by social differences, but do not produce them, though they can be used to maintain them. Advertising tries to maintain as close a match as possible between social difference and product difference, and to give the latter some control over the former. The ubiquity of advertising and the amount of resources it requires are evidence of how far social differences exceed the diversity required by the economic system. There is so much advertising only because it can never finally succeed in its tasks – those of containing social diversity within the needs of capitalism and of reducing the relative autonomy of the cultural economy from the financial, that is, of controlling not only what commodities people buy but the cultural uses they put them to. The advertising industry is undoubtedly successful at persuading manufacturers and distributors to buy its services: its success in persuading consumers to buy particular products is much more open to question – between 80 per cent and 90 per cent of new products fail despite extensive advertising. To take another example, many films fail to recover even their promotional costs at the box office.

Information such as the fact that a 30-second television commercial can cost as much to produce as the 50-minute program into which it is inserted can lead to a moral panic about the subliminal manipulation of commercials being in direct proportion to their production values. Collet's report for the IBA in London showed how typical it is for the TV viewer's attention to leave the screen as soon as the commercials appear. And the children who occasionally watch commercials so carefully are not necessarily being turned into helpless consumers. The Sydney children who in 1982 turned a beer commercial into a scatological playground rhyme were neither untypical nor commodified as they sang "How do you feel when you're having a fuck, under a truck, and the truck rolls off? I feel like a Tooheys, I feel like a Tooheys, I feel like a Tooheys or two" (Fiske, 1987). Similarly, the kids who sang jeeringly at a female student of mine as she walked past them in a short skirt and high heels "Razzmatazz, Razzmatazz, enjoy that jazz" (Razzmatazz is a brand of pantyhose, and its jingle accompanied shots of long-legged models wearing the brightly colored products) were using the ad for their own cheeky resistive subcultural purposes: they were far from the helpless victims of any subliminal consumerism, but were able to turn even an advertising text into their popular culture.

Two recent reports add fuel to my optimistic scepticism. One tells us that the average Australian family has 1,100 advertisements aimed at it every day. Of these, 539 are in newspapers and magazines, 374 on TV, 99 on radio, and 22 at the movies. The remainder are flashed on illuminated signs or displayed on billboards, taxis, buses, shop windows, and supermarket checkouts. But, the research concluded, people remember only three or four ads each day (*Daily News*, 15 October 1987). Another survey tested recall of eight popular slogans from TV ads. A total of 300 women between ages 20 and 30 were tested to see if they could add the name of the product to the slogan. The highest score achieved was 14 per cent; the average was 6 per cent (*West Australian*, 2 November 1987). Neither of these surveys evidences a terrifyingly powerful and manipulative industry that is a cause for a moral panic.

Of course, all ads sell consumerism in general as well as a product in particular; their strategy of commodification is not in dispute, only its effectiveness. We all have a lifetime's experience of living in a consumer society and of negotiating our way through the forces of commodification, of which ads are one, but only one, and they are no more immune to subversion, evasion, or resistance than any other strategic force.

If a particular commodity is to be made part of popular culture, it must offer opportunities for resisting or evasive uses or readings, and these opportunities must be accepted. The production of these is beyond the control of the producers of the financial commodity: it lies instead in the popular creativity of the users of that commodity in the cultural economy.

References

de Certeau, M. (1984) *The Practice of Everyday Life*, Berkeley: University of California Press.

Fiske, J. (1987) "British Cultural Studies," in R. Allen, *Channels of Discourse: Television and Contemporary Criticism*, Chapel Hill: University of North Carolina Press.

Hall, S. (1981) "Notes on Deconstructing the Popular," in R. Samuel (ed.) *People's History and Socialist Theory*, London: Routledge & Kegan Paul.

Smythe, D. (1977) "Communications: Blindspot of Western Marxism," *Canadian Journal of Political and Social Theory*, 1 (3), 1–27.

26
Dupes and Guerrillas: The Dialectics of Cultural Consumption

John Clarke

In this chapter John Clarke, a figure strongly associated with the emergence of "British cultural studies" during its formative stages in the 1970s, warns strongly against an overemphasis on the cultural dimensions of consumption at the expense of other, primarily economic, considerations which come into play in the analysis of consumer goods. Clarke suggests that one of the more unfortunate consequences of focusing analysis exclusively on issues connected with the symbolic creativity of reading practices, for example, is a strong temptation to romanticize cultural consumption, to see it almost entirely in terms of some heroic struggle between an oppressed population of consumers and a tyrannical system of production. Such a position, he argues, misses the full complexities involved in consumption itself and vastly oversimplifies the character of production.

At the centre of any analysis of the contradictory place of consumption in modern capitalist societies must be a grasp of the economic relations and processes within which consumption is located. This is not to argue that these economic processes exhaust all the aspects of consumption, but that to separate practices of consumption from these relations means missing crucial dynamics in the way it is shaped. In this context, I want to do no more than to outline the elementary economic forms which underlie the development of mass consumption.

First and foremost are the generic economic tendencies of capitalism towards the concentration of economic power in the form of highly diversified multinational corporations. These forms are the dominant ones in the field of consumption, encompassing production, distribution and exchange in the provision of food, clothing, entertainment, etc. (Clarke and Critcher, 1985: ch. 3). Such concentrations of economic power are not directly reflected in processes of cultural massification or uniformity. On the contrary economic concentration has co-existed with increasing diversity in terms of the objects and services produced for consumption. This mixture of concentration and diversity has a number of different aspects. One is the status of diversity as the residue of the process of concentra-

From "'Mine Eyes Dazzle': Cultures of Consumption" in *New Times and Old Enemies: Essays on Cultural Studies and America* (London: Routledge, 1991), pp. 97–103. Reprinted by permission of the publishers.

tion (take-overs and mergers), leaving behind distinctive brand names, titles and consumer loyalties. These may constitute a set of 'traditions' which may be maintained precisely for the appearance of diversity which they sustain (the car industry and brewing exhibit these tendencies). Such in-house diversity has been enhanced by the development of new production technologies which enable a range of carefully differentiated products to be delivered from the same production process. At the point of distribution, such production-based diversification is mirrored in what Bluestone et al. (1981) have identified as the 'speciality store' within the department store: the internal fragmentation of the store into separate shops corresponding to brand names, designer labels and so forth.

A second aspect of diversity in consumption derives from the self-consciously cultural, or aesthetic, character of many of the products of consumer culture (design, music, entertainment and so on). These processes, in what might be termed the 'cultural industries', often involve a relationship between corporate production and distribution and processes of semi-autonomous or petty commodity production. Music, film and television provide primary examples of this interlocking of the 'creative labour' of cultural production, where creativity is bought in or contracted out, and the corporate structures of mass reproduction and distribution. One distinctive effect of these complex structures of cultural production is the maintenance of a material basis for ideologies of creativity. While it is true that the production of new (or even novel) cultural objects is dependent on sources of creative labour, the material relations of cultural production and distribution are happily ignored in favour of a celebration of creative freedom (for example, 'editorial freedom'), thus losing sight of the structuring powers of corporate capital ranging from agenda setting and selectivity through to direct censorship.

The other economic force which works to maintain diversity in the marketplace is the continuing (though changed) role of the petit bourgeoisie in production and distribution. Traditionally, there has been a strong petit bourgeois role in the distributive and service sectors, often servicing distinctive ethnic–cultural needs, marginalized by Americanizing uniformity of the mass market. The revival of cultural ethnicity in the last twenty years, allied to a more cosmopolitan culture among the professional and managerial classes, has given such cultural diversity a much more visible presence in the culture of consumption. Intersecting with these developments is the post- 'countercultural' revival of arts and crafts in handicraft manufacture of clothing, jewellery, furnishings and so forth. In addition, and perhaps the most distinctive innovation in the petit bourgeois sector, there are the implications of some of the new information technologies which have allowed the development of so-called 'garage industries' in such fields as computer software, video-making and music production. Such developments feed the constant revitalization of cultural production both within the petit bourgeois sector and through their potential incorporation into the corporate industries.

These expansionary tendencies of the culture of consumption undercut the assumptions of 'cultural pessimism' about the unity of economic interests and ideological domination. The pessimistic view of the incorporation of passive subordinate groups into a bourgeois hegemony through the process of consumption fails to take account of the contradictions that the creation and constant recreation of a popular culture involves. The economic impulse of the culture of consumption, its search for new markets and profits, has always involved the revitalization of popular culture through the use of subordinate, oppositional and alternative cultural forms and practices. This poses a tension between the logic of the economic impulse and the ideological drive towards hegemony: innovation versus conventionalization. The cultural industries need to be seen both as exploratory and responsive (to social and cultural changes) and as conventionalizing and containing (reconciling the new to existing cultural expectations).

This process of cultural revitalization can be characterized as 'the appropriation of the vernacular': expansion through the use of pre-existing popular or subordinate culture. It raises a number of problems about the relationship between hegemony and popular culture. First, it means that it is important to recognize that hegemony is not a process of supplanting an 'indigenous' or 'authentic' popular culture by the imposition of an 'alien' or 'bourgeois' culture. Rather, it is the creation of a national–popular culture which reworks popular forms and content through a process of translation into the themes, forms and conventions of hegemony. To put it metaphorically, we might view the passage of the popular/vernacular elements into a national–popular culture as a process which requires popular forms to lose their rough edges, to become 'respectable' and capable of being generalized well beyond their point of origin.

Unless we subscribe to a view of culture that distinguishes between 'authentic' and 'false' cultural symbols, the significance of this appropriation of 'vernacular forms' for analysing popular culture is considerable. Most importantly, it suggests that we should view the cultural content of mass consumption not as the product or effect of a 'bourgeois culture' or ideology, but as a highly contradictory *ensemble* of diverse cultural elements.[1] This includes appropriations from the cultures of subordinate groups, which find themselves nationalized (and in some cases, internationalized) beyond their local origins. Dashiell Hammett, and the genre of hard-boiled writing, offer a very sharp example of this process in which the vernacular is used to revitalize cultural production, at one and the same time opening up the world of the vernacular to a respectable readership, and also making reading a practice of consumption for a wider audience, undermining its cultural exclusivity. It is important to remember that . . . this process is one of transformation rather than reproduction – things happen to the vernacular in the process of appropriation. The original popular forms may be 'cleaned up' (as in the lyrics of 'Rock around the Clock'), sanitized or sentimentalized (as in many instances of populism in the American film), but even allowing for such changes, what is at stake is the use of popular forms to sustain the cultural content of mass production and consumption.

These arguments may seem to sustain the conclusions of the 'cultural pessimists': an absence of authenticity, the power of cultural ventriloquism and a popular culture saturated in hegemonic connections. But that would be to stop the dialectics of cultural production and consumption before they are complete. Once again, it would mean returning to a view of consumption which sees people only as consumers – linked only to a mediated national–popular culture. However, we are always more than consumers, always located in other sets of social relations and social identities (of class, gender, race, age, locality and so on). Each of these carries with it a series of cultural practices and resources with which the national–popular culture strives to intersect, by addressing us and inviting us to recognize ourselves in its imagery. But the emphasis here must be placed on the words 'strives to', rather than presuming that such addresses and intersections are monolithically successful. Indeed, many of the struggles of cultural politics over the last twenty years, concerning the representations in the popular media of gender, race, sexuality and disability, for example, point precisely to the *failure* of the national–popular to construct such intersections.

To this needs to be added the consideration of the polysemic character of signs: their ability to carry more than one meaning, and thus to be available for different readings. (A character perfectly expressed in the diverse readings of Bruce Springsteen's track 'Born in the USA', which has been read as both celebratory and condemnatory of the contemporary state of the nation.) This potential diversity of meaning in the sign allied to the differentiated social positions in which consumers are socially located suggests that the 'insertion' of consumers into the hegemonic domain of a national–popular culture is profoundly uneven. Signs may be absorbed according to their stabilized (preferred or dominant meaning), that is, consumers may behave like the ideal consumer. Signs may be appropriated partially or selectively; treated ironically, or with indifference or hostility. They may also be reworked, transposed and have alternative meanings imposed on them. Cora Kaplan has argued this in relation to the consumption of the American soap opera *Dallas*:

> *Dallas* may, in part, be pleasurable to watch not because the fantasy it engenders fulfils our most unprogressive social and psychic desires, but rather because it allows us to make fun of them. Which is surely one way its makers intended it to grab us. Most of the mass popular narrative made today for an international viewing or reading audience has a deliberately ambiguous, even unstable tone. Enjoy it as melodrama or as satire, *or both*, the texts seem to say. Make it part of whatever political paradigm you like, only enjoy.
>
> Yet that instability of tone exposes, deliberately again, the narrative conventions, encouraging viewers of all kinds to discuss the form and limits of serial soap as part of the pleasure of consumption. This self-aware element of soaps does not make the product radical, but it does tend to make its effects quite complicated and contradictory, harder to pin down for all or every class, gender, age and race of viewer. Into

291

that gap between plot and presentation . . . the social and political context in which *Dallas* is seen by different cultural, class and national constituencies is inserted, and determines how it will, in the end, be understood. (Kaplan, 1986: 39; emphasis in original)

It is this 'field of possibilities' that constitutes cultural consumption as a social and cultural practice – as opposed to seeing it collapsed into the economic and ideological domination of the exchange relationship. It is also the idea of active cultural practice which cultural studies in its various forms has sought to stress: the bending of received cultures to a role in a 'lived' cultural project; the making sense of the social relations which people inhabit, and the construction of cultural strategies for surviving those processes. Even so, there are some difficulties surrounding these arguments.

One problem is that the types of readings of popular culture offered by Kaplan and others have tended towards a radical culturalism, emphasizing the volatility of meaning at the expense of two other considerations. On the one hand, the emphasis on volatility of meaning has displaced a concern with the economic conditions of cultural production and consumption. Like the 'resistances' which they analyse, many of the studies of the cultural creativity of consumers tend to take the conditions of production and exchange for granted, leaving them as the unexamined background to the cultural projects of subordinated groups. In that sense, these approaches miss the structured secondariness of consumption. On the other hand, this disconnection of cultural texts from their conditions of production is reflected in the overestimation of the polysemic character of the sign. While signs may carry multiple meanings, their insertion into the field of hegemony also involves efforts to fix or stabilize preferred or dominant meanings: to inflect the sign in one particular direction. This suggests that reading (that is the signifying practice of consumption) is not a free-floating process, but a process of cultural struggle in which alternative or oppositional meanings have to be worked for and won against hegemonic meanings (Ellsworth, 1988).

It is also important to register the cultural, as well as economic, limitations of this relativization of meaning. It is not sufficient to point to the existence of social difference (as Kaplan does) as the basis for cultural diversity: positions of social difference merely constitute the possibility of cultural diversity, and do not guarantee its realization. The creation of alternative meanings requires the use of alternative cultural resources: vocabularies of difference that can articulate social divisions. One of the effects of a nationalizing popular culture may be to rework positions of social division and antagonism as mere difference, and to circumscribe vocabularies of division (as in the naturalization of gender divisions, for example).

A further difficulty is how to avoid romanticizing the political character of cultural resistances. While this approach correctly gets rid of the pessimism of seeing subordinate groups as 'cultural dupes', the alternative vision of guerrilla armies of cultural activists seems excessively celebratory, and contains few means for assessing the political direction of such resistances. A variety of subcultural studies have revealed – either implicitly or explicitly – the potentially regressive character of resistance, constructing cultural projects which have as their dynamics the reproduction of the 'bad sense' of 'common sense': its racism, its sexism or its homophobia (for example, Hall and Jefferson, 1976, and Willis, 1979). Since the social positions and relations on which they rest are contradictory and potentially antagonistic, splitting the social subject through race, class, gender and other social identities, there is no guarantee that cultural diversity does not reproduce or reinforce these divisions.

The distance which social divisions may create between cultural commodities and their consumption can also take the form of cynicism. Although the repertoire of cynicism ('well, they would say that, wouldn't they?' or 'you can't take it seriously') involves a form of refusal, it is nevertheless demobilizing: a state of *passive* dissent. The playfulness of postmodernism evokes precisely this state of emotional and/or political disinvestment: a refusal to be engaged (see Grossberg, 1989). There is, then, nothing intrinsic in the practice of alternative readings that requires them to promote the forging of larger collective identities of opposition. The dilemmas of the split between structural pessimism and cultural radicalism are nowhere more sharply visible than in responses to the changing shape of consumption in the 1980s.

Note

1   Stuart Hall's 'Notes on deconstructing "the popular"' (1981) remains the best starting point for this sort of analysis.

References

Bluestone, B. et al. (1981) *The Retail Revolution*, Boston, Mass.: Auburn House Publishing.

Clarke, J. and Critcher, C. (1985) *The Devil Makes Work: Leisure in Capitalist Britain*, Basingstoke: Macmillan; Chicago and Urbana, Ill.: University of Illinois Press.

Ellsworth, E. (1988) 'Illicit pleasures, feminist spectators and *Personal Best*', in Roman et al., *Becoming Feminine*.

Grossberg, L. (1989) *It's a Sin: Postmodernism, Politics and Popular Culture*, Sydney: Power Publications.

Hall, S. (1981) 'Notes on deconstructing "the popular"', in R. Samuel (ed.) *People's History and Socialist Theory*, London: Routledge and Kegan Paul.

Hall, S. and Jefferson, T. (eds) (1976) *Resistance through Rituals*, London: Hutchinson.

Kaplan, C. (1986) 'The culture cross-over', *New Socialist*, November, pp. 38–40.

Willis, P. (1979) *Learning to Labour*, London: Saxon House.

27

Sovereign Consumption

Jim McGuigan

In this extract from his essay "Cultural Populism Revisited" Jim McGuigan launches an attack on those cultural populist writers, such as John Fiske and Paul Willis, who emphasize the symbolic creativity of ordinary people in their consumption of mass-produced commodities. That Fiske's ideas should be attacked is not in itself surprising (the critique of Fiske's concept of "semiotic democracy" became something of a growth industry in cultural studies during the early 1990s). What is surprising, however, is the form of the critique made by McGuigan, who concludes that the cultural populism of writers like Fiske and Willis actually amounts to little more than a restatement of the neo-conservative philosophy of "sovereign consumption." This new twist in the assault on the concept of semiotic democracy is all the more savage for a writer such as Fiske, who is always keen to frame his arguments within a strongly Leftist rhetoric.

The repressed has a habit of returning in symptoms opaque to the subject's own self-consciousness, as Freudian theory has always insisted. Take, for instance, John Fiske's (1987) claim concerning an actual existing 'semiotic democracy', originally stated with regard to television-viewing as 'producerly' and which was subsequently expanded into a generalized account of popular subversion of what he calls the 'dominant culture' (Fiske, 1989a; 1989b). For Fiske (1991) the 'dominant culture' is one and the same with the approved canon of great works and their supposedly inherent values that are taught in the traditional university curriculum. By contrast, contemporary sources of resistance and opposition somehow derive, according to Fiske, from the popular consumption and meaningful transformation of mass-distributed cultural products in the market-place. Quite apart from the persistently simplistic binary opposition of dominant and subordinate cultures, with nothing much in-between, Fiske's model, similarly to many academic conceptions of knowledge, vastly overestimates the role of the higher education curriculum in securing cultural power. It is a good deal more plausible to argue, alternatively, that the 'dominant culture', if there is indeed such a phe-

From M. Ferguson and P. Golding (eds.) *Cultural Studies in Question* (London: Sage, 1998), pp. 140–5. Reprinted by permission of the author and Sage Publications Ltd.

nomenon, is formed most profoundly by prevailing market forces and their legitimating ideologies.

Fiske's semiotic democracy is very similar to Paul Willis's (1990) actually existing 'common culture'. Willis argues that the market has delivered the goods to everyone's satisfaction and especially to the satisfaction of young people, who are making utopian use of cultural commodities here and now in Britain and, when he was writing, before Margaret Thatcher had been deposed due to the failing popularity of her 'authoritarian populism'. The main target of disapprobation for Willis is not so much the university curriculum but, instead, the British system of public arts patronage, which he claims has no relevance at all for the vast majority of people and particularly for the young, although he pays no attention to the universal role of arts and cultural education in the state's schooling system. Rather than the state seeking to enculture youth with community arts projects and the like, Willis calls for an appreciation of the 'symbolic creativity' and 'grounded aesthetics' involved in watching television advertisements, reading mass-market magazines, listening to and remixing popular music, fashion *bricolage*, and drinking and fighting in pubs.

'Common culture' in the social-democratic tradition was an 'ought' concept which was given a radical and 'productionist' inflection by the New Left (Williams, 1968). Although of more recent provenance, 'semiotic democracy' would also seem to be a normative ideal, identifying a desirable condition for which to strive rather than an achieved reality. It is conservative theoretically to claim that a condition that, arguably, ought to exist already is; but more than this, in spite of the manifest avoidance, and indeed repression, of political economy in the work of exemplary populist writers such as Fiske and Willis, it is strangely homologous, albeit latently so, in the sense of a homology of structures (Goldmann, 1969), with the right-wing political economy that is founded upon the concept of the 'sovereign consumer'. Before proceeding with this hypothesis, two qualifications need to be made: first, with regard to the potential disjunction between the professed politics of a theoretical position and the underlying logic of that position; and, secondly, with regard to the clearly observable disjunction between conservative cultural theory and right-wing political economy.

There is no doubt that Fiske is on the side of the angels, as his *Power Plays, Power Works* (1993) would readily attest. His sympathies are evidently with the oppressed and their struggles against the powers that be, yet his theorizing, focused so narrowly as it is on the micro-politics of consumption and the local victories and defeats of everyday life, provides little space for transformative struggle of any kind. Willis is also well aware of the material inequalities that obstruct the equitability of consuming pleasures. In his contribution to the 1991 British Arts and Media Strategy debate, while reiterating the critique of publicly subsidized culture, Willis recommended the Dutch idea of a 'culture card' for the poor and unemployed. The problem with local authority 'leisure cards' is that they only provide concessionary access to public facilities, for instance, swimming pools and theatres. However, most people's preferences are for the products of the private sector. Hence, the 'culture card', 'cheapening access to and purchase of the products and services of the cultural industries on a very wide definition: body culture; photo culture; youth culture; home culture; music culture, and so on' (Willis, 1991: 54). Although commercial cinemas, for instance, do quite commonly offer concessionary entrance to the unemployed, pensioners and students to boost box-office takings where audience attendance is flagging, it seems implausible to expect capitalist enterprises to suddenly become genuinely philanthropic on a significant scale of their own volition. Businesses may be forced by local governments to pay a 'percentage for art' when relocating, and companies like McDonald's contribute to charitable activities in the interest of public relations, but more comprehensive voluntary contributions to equitable cultural consumption are less than likely. On reading Willis, I conjure up an image of long queues of unemployed youth snaking into the local music store on a Saturday morning, each member of which, when reaching the counter inside, declares 'I am an unemployed young person. This is my culture card. I claim this week's free chart-topping CD!'

No ideology is ever entirely consistent but it is striking how the neo-classical economics of contemporary conservative parties is diametrically opposed to the traditional forms of conservative cultural thought. The latter tends to be authoritarian, stressing eternal truths and absolute values, while seeing the social value of culture as one of a moral education that abhors relativism of all kinds. In comparison with such cultural authoritarianism, right-wing thought in political economy is downright libertarian and populist. And, when applied to culture, it is cultural populist, rather like Fiske and Willis, in fact. It is hard to see quite how the position represented by Fiske and Willis differs materially on cultural issues from right-wing think-tanks such as the Centre for Policy Studies, the Institute of Economic Affairs and the Adam Smith Institute, the very think-tanks that provided a steady flow of policy ideas, including cultural policy ideas, for strategic implementation over the past decade and a half of Conservative governmental hegemony in Britain (Desai, 1994). In a North American context, one might similarly refer to the Heritage Foundation, the Cato Institute and the American Enterprise Institute. One has to read beneath the Leftist rhetoric, to which Fiske is especially prone, in order to perceive this theoretical convergence of an exclusively consumptionist cultural populism with right-wing political economy.

As Russell Keat has noted accurately of 'consumer sovereignty', at least in my experience of trying to locate a satisfactory theoretical statement of it, 'one is unlikely to find much explicit discussion of this concept in standard textbook accounts of a market economy' (Keat, 1994: 27). It is, none the less, the ideological linchpin of the neo-classical economics that was so successfully revived politically, if not economically, during the 1980s. That it is not always stated explicitly is perhaps symptomatic of its totemic function in contemporary culture and New Right politics.

The concept of consumer sovereignty and its implications for cultural policy were, however, expressed succinctly in the 1986 *Report of the Committee on Financing the BBC* (known as the Peacock Report) on broadcasting, which was originally set up by the second Thatcher government in order to produce a rationale for introducing advertising to the BBC. It did not eventually fulfil the implicit governmental brief because of a fear that this would reduce the advertising revenue of commercial television. None the less, the Peacock Committee did produce a useful articulation of free-market ideology in relation to a broadcasting system which had hitherto been regulated according to principles of public service:

> British broadcasting should move towards a sophisticated market system based on consumer sovereignty. That is a system which recognizes that viewers and listeners are the best ultimate judges of their own interests, which they can best satisfy if they have the option of purchasing the broadcasting services they require from as many sources of supply as possible. (*Report of the Committee on Financing the BBC*, 1986: para. 592)

In such neo-classical economics, the sovereign consumer is a necessary fiction, a construction of an all-rational, calculating subject, forever seeking to maximize marginal utility in consumption choices. Rational consumer decisions, aggregated as demand, are said to trigger supply or, rather, result in success or failure on the supply side in the free market. Nothing should be permitted to interfere with this magical process.

There are two basic criticisms of the ideology of consumer sovereignty that should be mentioned. First, sovereign consumption ideally depends upon perfect knowledge of what is actually or potentially available to consume, in order to facilitate rational choice, since consumption is said to determine production. The counter-argument is that perfect knowledge of what could be consumed is impossible and that demand is not simply aggregated from the sum of rational choices made by consumers, in any case, but is at least partly cultivated by suppliers through advertising and marketing. Thus, production has some determinancy over consumption and the consumer may not be very knowledgeable of how the process actually works in practice. This argument holds, I would suggest, in spite of the selective accounts of production that are now frequently included in the marketing packages of, say, blockbuster movies. The main implication of such an argument for cultural studies is that actually existing consumption patterns are not necessarily a wholly reliable guide to what people might want if they could have it.

The second criticism is similarly well known but is rarely stated with much conviction nowadays. This is that there is a false equalization in the claim that we are all sovereign consumers. Some consumers are more sovereign than others. In effect, it is still a minority of people, according to any universal standards of comparison, who are in a privileged position, by sheer virtue of material advantage, to exercise freedom of choice in consumption and to consume exactly what they want or need. There is also symbolic advantage, resulting from familial habitus and education, which is only partially separable from possession of wealth in shaping the distribution and the various combinations of cultural competence and taste. Fundamentally, if you do not have the money or an appropriately cultivated range of competences, which in the 1990s includes a postmodernist picking and mixing of tastes, high and low, then your potential choices in consumption are thereby limited.

Two further considerations in connecting this critique of consumer sovereignty to consumptionist cultural populism should be taken into account. These considerations cover both a 'post-Marxist' accommodation to capitalism and the irrationalism of 'postmodern' capitalism. The first consideration is the possibility that a critical view of the symbolic and material economies might still be sustained alongside a commitment to rational choice, which does, after all, attribute a dignified sentience to the human subject, as in 'rational choice Marxism'. However, as Ellen Meiksins Wood has demonstrated powerfully, it is very difficult to produce a convincing critique of the prevailing economic, social and cultural orders out of a mixture of 'neo-classical economics, game theory, methodological individualism, and neo-contractarian philosophy' (Meiksins Wood, 1989: 87), which were such vital ingredients of Reagonomics and Thatcherism. And, as Joan Robinson remarked many years ago in her commentary on the original marginalist economics of Jevons and Alfred Marshall, 'This is an ideology to end ideology, for it has abolished the moral problem' (Robinson, 1964: 53). We are in the presence here of that 'value-free' economics which claims merely to describe positivistically how the ineluctable forces of the unfettered market work and, when challenged for its inegalitarianism, is forced to acknowledge the 'naturalness' of inequality and to plead that with the growth brought about by the proper operation of market forces the 'trickle down' effect will, thence, occur.

Secondly, there is the refusal to accept a rationalistic model of the consuming subject and to conceptualize consumption in more visceral and situated ways, which may well be the position that Fiske and Willis would actually subscribe to, although it is difficult to tell for sure from their writings. It is a position which squares quite neatly with the prevalent forms of irrationalist theorizing (Larrain, 1994). Here agin, there is also a notable correspondence with right-wing political economy, to whit that of Frederick Hayek, whose *The Road to Serfdom* (1994) and his own personal tutoring provided such inspiration for the Thatcherite project which promised to eliminate socialism once and for all from Britain. Hilary Wainwright (1994) has shown how Hayek's version of free-market theory differs not only from socialist regulatory rationalism, but also from the rational fictions of neo-classical economics. For Hayek, the consumer does not choose on the basis of rational knowledge of what would maximize utility but, instead, makes decisions purely subjectively without recourse to reason and reliable information since knowledge, for both consumers and economists, is inherently fallible. In a sense, one might argue, Hayek was a postmodernist *avant la lettre* and his belief in the beneficence of freely chosen consumption shorn of rationalist illusions is uncomfortably close to consumptionist cultural populism.

During the recent period of New Right hegemony it was only to be expected that the ideologues of the free market would claim, along with Francis Fukuyama (1989), that an ideal cultural polity had virtually been achieved or was in the immediate grasp of right-wing governments. That leading proponents of cultural studies should say something similar is rather more surprising. It is one thing to claim that people make the best use of the cultural products available to them and, therefore, appreciate the ordinary semiotic and symbolic work that this entails, but it is quite another thing to claim that we live in an actually existing 'semiotic democracy' or 'common culture'. If such concepts serve any useful purpose, surely it is to function as a standard of principled criticism by which to measure and find wanting actually existing conditions, not, unwittingly, to endorse the powerful ideologies of think-tanks like the Adam Smith Institute.

References

Desai, R. (1994) 'Second-hand dealers in ideas – think-tanks and Thatcherite hegemony', *New Left Review*, 203 (January–February): 27–64.

Fiske, J. (1987) *Television Culture*, London: Methuen.

Fiske, J. (1989a) *Reading the Popular*, Boston, MA: Unwin Hyman.

Fiske, J. (1989b) *Understanding Popular Culture*, Boston, MA: Unwin Hyman.

Fiske, J. (1991) 'Popular discrimination', pp. 103–16 in J. Naremore and P. Brantlinger (eds.) *Modernity and Mass Culture*, Bloomington, IN: Indiana University Press.

Fiske, J. (1993) *Power Plays, Power Works*, New York and London: Verso.

Fukuyama, F. (1989) 'The end of history?', *National Interest* 16 (summer): 3–18.

Goldmann, L. (1969) *The Human Sciences and Philosophy*, London: Jonathan Cape.

Hayek, F. (1944) *The Road to Serfdom*, Chicago: University of Chicago Press.

Keat, R. (1994) 'Scepticism, authority and the market', pp. 23–42, in R. Keat, N. Whiteley and N. Abercrombie (eds), *The Authority of the Consumer*, London: Routledge.

Larrain, G. (1994) *Ideology and Cultural Identity*, Cambridge: Polity Press.

Meiksins Wood, E. (1989) 'Rational choice Marxism – is the game worth a candle?', *New Left Review*, 177 (September–October): 41–88.

Robinson, J. (1964) *Economic Philosophy*, London: Penguin Books.

Wainwright, H. (1994) *Arguments for a New Left*, Oxford: Blackwell Publishers.

Williams, R. (1968) 'The idea of a common culture', reprinted in R. Gable (ed.) (1989) *Resources of Hope: Culture, Democracy, Socialism*, London: Verso.

Willis, P. (1990) *Common Culture*, Milton Keynes: Open University Press.

Willis, P. (1991) 'Towards a new cultural map', *National Arts and Media Strategy*, London: Arts Council of Great Britain.

28
The Promotional Condition of Contemporary Culture

Andrew Wernick

In this, the concluding chapter to his book *Promotional Culture* published in 1991, Andrew Wernick makes explicit his bold thesis that the "condition" which best characterizes contemporary culture is that formed by the logic of promotion as an all-pervasive and irresistible force. All our contemporary discourse, at least in our professional and public lives, argues Wernick, is saturated in the rhetoric of promotion, which now exists as a generalized social category. Where once we might have distinguished between, say, advertising, marketing, and public relations as discrete promotional categories, today these forms merge and become interlocked in a self-referential nexus of signification. It is virtually impossible, concludes Wernick, to think beyond or outside such promotional discourse; we are all drawn, voluntarily or otherwise, to play the "game" of promotion.

'There must be some way out of here', said the Joker to the Thief. (Bob Dylan)

The Category of Promotion

In the same breath that cultural theorists, from Adorno to Jameson, have acknowledged the pervasiveness of advertising in the culture of late capitalism, they have limited the force of that insight by assimilating it to a critique of commercialism in general, and by circumscribing what advertising refers to precisely by using that term.

Advertising is commonly taken to mean *advertisements*, paid for and recognizable as such, together with the process of their production and dissemination. In that restricted sense, however vast and ubiquitous a phenomenon, advertising is certainly one aspect of a wider process of cultural commodification: institutionally, a sub-sector of the culture industry; textually, a delimited sub-field within the larger field of commercially produced signs. At the same time, the word has a

From *Promotional Culture* (London: Sage, 1991), pp. 181–98. Reprinted by permission of the author and Sage Publications Ltd.

more general meaning. Originally, to animadvert to something was just to draw attention to it; whence to advertise came to mean to publicize, especially in a favourable light. By extension, then, the word refers us not only to a type of message but to a type of speech and, beyond that, to a whole communicative function which is associated with a much broader range of signifying materials than just advertisements *stricto sensu*. Whether as senders, receivers or analysts of cultural messages we all recognize that advertising in this second, generic, sense exceeds advertising in the first. But it is hard to grasp the full significance of advertising for contemporary culture unless these meanings are clearly separated. A starting point for the present study, then, has been to give the functional or expanded sense of advertising a name of its own: *promotion*.

The term has two semantic advantages. The first, reflecting its colloquial usage, is its generality, which directs our attention to the way in which all manner of communicative acts have, as one of their dimensions, and often only tacitly, the function of advancing some kind of self-advantaging exchange. *Promotion* crosses the line between advertising, packaging and design, and is applicable, as well, to activities beyond the immediately commercial. It can even (as in 'promoting public health') be used in a way which takes us beyond the domain of competitive exchange altogether. For current purposes, though, I have confined it to cases where something, though not necessarily for money, is being promoted for sale – while recognizing that the metaphorical diffusion of the word, wherein it has come to mean any kind of propagation (including that of ideas, causes and programmes), reflects a real historical tendency for all such discourse to acquire an advertising character. The second advantage stems from the word's derivation. Promotion (as a noun) is a type of sign, and the promoted entity is its referent. From this angle, the triple meaning of the Latin prefix 'pro' usefully highlights the compound and dynamic character of the relationship between promotion and what it promotes. A promotional message is a complex of significations which at once represents (moves in place of), advocates (moves on behalf of) and anticipates (moves ahead of) the circulating entity or entities to which it refers.

Given that definition, the thesis I have been exploring can be simply stated: that the range of cultural phenomena which, at least as one of their functions, serve to communicate a promotional message has become, today, virtually, co-extensive with our produced symbolic world.

This may seem hyperbolic, until we start to enumerate the sorts of promotional message, and, associate with them, the circuits of competitive exchange, which are actually swirling about. As we have seen, these include not only advertising in the specific and restricted sense, that of clearly posted 'promotional signs'. They also include the whole universe of commercially manufactured objects (and services), in so far as these are imaged to sell, and are thus constructed as advertisements for themselves. A special case of the latter (in my terminology: 'commodity-signs') is cultural goods. These, indeed, are typically cast in a doubly promotional role. For not only are cultural goods peculiarly freighted with the need and capacity to promote themselves. Wherever they are distributed by a commercial medium whose profitability depends on selling audiences to advertisers they are also designed to function as attractors of audiences towards the advertising material with which they are intercut. In the organs of print and broadcasting, information and entertainment are the flowers which attract the bee. In this sense, too, the non-advertising content of such media can be considered, even semiotically, as an extension of their ads.

But this is not all. The multiply promotional communicative organs constituted by the commercial mass media (and even, via sports sponsorships and the like, by the organs of 'public broadcasting') are also transmissive vehicles for public information and discussion in general. Through that common siting, non-promotional discourses, including those surrounding the political process, have become linked (Bush in Disneyland on prime time news) to promotional ones. It is this complex of promotional media, too, which mediates the communicative activity of all secondary public institutions – aesthetic, intellectual, educational, religious, etc. – to what used to be called 'the general public'. Furthermore, even if not directly commercial themselves, these secondary institutions also generate their own forms of promotional discourse, whether, as in the case of university recruitment campaigns, because they have become indirectly commodified, or, as in the case of electoral politics, because they have a market form which is analogous to the one which operates in the money economy.

There are several respects, finally, in which competition at the level of individuals generates yet a further complex of promotional practices. In part this is an outgrowth of the commodification of labour power, and more particularly, in the professional and quasi-professional sectors of the labour market, of the way in which differentially qualified labour power commands a differential price. Hence the dramaturgical aspects of careers and careerism. In addition, however, as Veblen [see chapter 4, this volume], and many others have described, the promotion-alization of the individual also extends into the sphere of consumption, both through fashion and more generally through the way in which status competition is conducted through the private theatre of projected style. At a quite different level of social practice (though, as in the TV ads for Towers department stores, 'everything connects'), the entry, on increasingly symmetrical terms, of (unattached) women and men into free (or non-parentally supervised) socio-sexual circulation has also created a mate/companion/friendship market which generates its own forms of competitive self-presentation. Lastly, when any instance of individual self-promotion spills over from the private realm to become a topic of public communication, whether unintentionally, as a personal drama that makes the news, or deliberately, as the amplified staging of a career (sporting, political, artistic, intellectual, etc.), inter-individual competition gives rise to yet a further form of promotional practice: the construction of celebrityhood. This itself enters into the realm of public promotion not just as self-advertising, but as an exchangeable (and promotable) promotional resource both for the individual involved and for other advertisers.

It is tempting to summarize these developments by saying that in late capitalism promotion has become, as Frederic Jameson (appropriating the term from Raymond Williams) has argued of postmodernism (Jameson, 1984: 57), a 'cultural dominant'. Given the provenance of that term, however, and the peculiarity of promotion itself as a cultural category, such a formulation will only do if carefully qualified.

Raymond Williams (1982: 204–5) originally developed his distinction between 'dominant', 'residual', 'oppositional' and 'emergent' culture in the context of class–cultural analysis. For him, the interplay of these complexes was conditioned by (and in turn conditioned) that of the emergent, dominant and oppositional classes whose positions and sensibilities were expressed in them. In taking over this terminology Jameson gave it a different sociological spin. His problematization of postmodernism focused not on class dynamics, but on the structuring effects of 'third stage' capital on social relations as a whole. This has evident parallels with the approach to the rise of promotion being taken here. Still, in Jameson's hand, as in Williams's, the notion of 'cultural dominant' remains linked to a notion of culture as (collective) expression. It refers us to the impact of (ascendant) cultural values on the styles, themes and inflections of artistic, pop cultural, architectural, etc., symbolic domains. In late capitalism, he writes (Jameson, 1984: 57), postmodernism has replaced modernism as 'a new systematic cultural norm'.

The problem is that promotion – unlike any cultural movement – is not only a class phenomenon, it is not an expressive one either. To be sure, it is embodied in significations, and it is ramified by socialization practices, psychological strategies and habits, and cultural/aesthetic norms and values. But in the first instance, promotion is a mode of communication, a species of rhetoric. It is defined not by what it says but by what it does, with respect to which its stylistic and semantic contents are purely secondary and derived.

I can put the matter more precisely, perhaps, by saying that promotion has become a key, structuring element of what Scott Lash (1990: 4–5 and *passim*) has termed contemporary society's 'regime of signification'. He defines this as a combinatory structure, parallel to the material economy (conceived as a 'regime of accumulation'), which comprises two sub-formations. The first is the 'cultural economy', which itself consists of a combination of four elements: (a) the relations of symbolic production (its property regime), (b) conditions of reception, (c) a mediating institutional framework, and (d) the means of symbolic circulation. The second is the 'mode of signification', involving a determinate set of relations (for example, the realist model of representation) between the signifier, and the signified, and referent and symbolic objects. In general, while allowing for a certain 'relative autonomy', the causal assumption is that the second complex of relations is shaped by the first.

The case of promotion fits the model well. In a promotional message the relation between sign and referent has been (re)arranged in such a way that, first, the former is an anticipatory advocate of the second, and second, within the construction of a promotional image, the boundary between sign and object is blurred. What the suffusion of promotion throughout all levels of social communication has amounted to, then, is a change in the prevalent mode of signification. Moreover, this transformation has itself been associated with changes in the mode of production and circulation of signs (commodification, the rise of the culture industry, and the commercial mass media), that is, with changes in the cultural economy. Indeed, while Lash's model (which he deploys in a fresh attempt to account for the rise of postmodernism) allows for a certain degree of autonomy of the mode of signification from the cultural economy, the causal relation in the case of the late capitalist rise of promotion is direct and virtually unmediated.

But here, the notion of a 'regime of signification', a structure of structures, definable in itself, which can enter into interactive relations with the (capitalist) economy proper, reveals a limitation. For the rise of commercialized culture, in symbolic relation with mass-media advertising, has itself been intrinsic to a more general process of capitalist development. Not only has culture become a sector of consumer goods production just like any other produced object of human use. Industrialization and mass production have also, and again for purely economic reasons, led to an expansion of the sphere of commodity circulation, of which the culture industry, via advertising, has itself become a heavily subsidized adjunct. In addition, and further complicating the picture, the rise of inter-individual and non-commercial promotion has registered the effects of a parallel, and only indirectly related, socio-cultural process in which social life in every dimension has increasingly come to assume a commodity or quasi-commodity form.

In trying to locate the place of promotion on the sociological map, in other words, the very distinction between the symbolic and material economies, between the regime of accumulation and the regime of signification, cannot be clearly drawn. And for good reason. Promotional practice is generated exactly on the boundary, a locus which implies the dissolution of the boundary itself.

What the rise of promotion as a cultural force signals, in fact, is not simply a shift to a new mode of producing and circulating signs (cultural commodification), but an alteration in the very relation between culture and economy. Baudrillard (1981) [see chapter 3, this volume], following Debord (1977), has depicted this movement ('the union of sign and commodity')[1] as a merger, although it might be more accurate to depict it as a take-over, since culture has lost its autonomy thereby, while the (market) economy has hypostatized into an engulfing dynamic. The result is a mutation: still capitalism, but a capitalism transformed. In effect, during the course of advanced capitalist development the globalization and intensification of commodity production have led to a crucial economic modification in which (a) with mass production and mass marketing the moments of distribution, circulation and exchange have become as strategic as technical improvements in production for profitability and growth and (b) through commodity imaging the circulation and production processes have come to overlap. In which context (with disturbing implications for even an updated Marxism) it has further come about that the ('superstructural') domain of expressive communication has been more and more absorbed, not just as an industry but as a direct aspect of the sale of everything, into the integral workings of the commodified economic 'base'.

This has been a complex transformation, and it did evidently not occur all at once. There have been many phases and stages: from industrialism and the first consumer-oriented urban centres to the radio/film age, coca-colonization and the electronic malls of commercial TV.[2] Whence a further caveat. Besides eschewing an expressionist view of its object, any thesis about the changed weight of promotion within 'late' capitalist culture must also be careful to avoid too sharp a sense of periodization.

Promotion as culturally generalized as commodification has spread, as consumer goods production has industrialized, leading to the massive expansion of the sphere of circulation, and as competitive exchange relations have generally established themselves as an axial principle of social life. But there has been no catastrophe point, no single historical juncture (for example, in the 1950s and 1960s) at which we can say that promotion, having previously been 'emergent', finally became a 'dominant' structuring principle of our culture. It is a question, rather, of a cumulative tendency; a tendency, indeed, of very long standing, since, as Bourdieu (1977: 177) has reminded us, the market as a principle of socio-cultural organization predates capitalism and, even in 'primitive' societies, the symbolic and material economies are to some degree 'interconvertible'. Nor can the process of promotionalization be said to be complete. As with commodification as a whole, the advance of promotion has been uneven, both internationally and also within leading capitalist countries themselves. Even in Baudrillard's America, the mirage runs out at the desert and there are low-intensity zones.

Both for the present and historically, then, all that can be safely asserted is that *parri passu* with the development of the market, promotion is a condition which has increasingly befallen discourses of all kinds; and the more it has done so, the more its modalities and relations have come to shape the formation of culture as a whole. But what condition? What are the characteristics of a culture whose communicative processes have come to be saturated in the medium of promotion? What qualities does it exhibit, more precisely, just by virtue of that fact?

Promotion as a Cultural Condition

The guiding thesis of Horkheimer and Adorno's essay on the culture industry in *The Dialectic of Enlightenment* was that 'culture now impresses the same stamp on everything' (Horkheimer and Adorno, 1972: 120). In support, they cited such tendencies as the monopolistic centralization of cultural production, the stand-ardization of cultural produce (which reflects and transmits the rhythms of indus-trial mass production), the classification of goods and consumers ('Something is provided for all so that none may escape'), the sensate emphasis of style over work, and the promiscuous, mid-market merging of serious art and distractive entertain-ment.

In the first instance, their thesis was ironically aimed against conservative la-ments about the cultural chaos that would ensue from specialization and the de-cline of organized religion and other ideologically unifying remnants of pre-capitalist society. But it also ran dialectically counter to the analysis of classical sociology. For if, as Durkheim and Weber had asserted, cultural modernity entailed the ra-tional differentiation of social activities and sectors, including, within the cultural sphere, those of art, science, ethics and religion, then, through the homogenizing impact of commodification, that same movement could be shown to contain the seeds of its own reversal.[3]

Now, implicit in Horkheimer and Adorno's account, though they do not con-sider it as an independent factor, is that one of the ways in which commodification has been a culturally homogenizing force is through the similar ways in which, whatever the medium and genre, the products of the culture industry present themselves to us as objects and sites of a promotional practice.[4] The point is worth drawing out. It is not just that such diverse vehicles of symbolic expression as pop records, political candidates, philosophical texts, art galleries, news magazines, and sporting events, are all intensely advertised, and that this draws attention to what, as promotables, they all share: the de-sacralized status of publicly circulating, and privately appropriable, items of commercial exchange. The marketing imperative feeds back into their actual construction; so that, for example, the use and build-up of promotional names and the adoption of majoritarian entertainment values have become a common feature of all marketed discourse, regardless of whether its manifest function is to inform, inspire, solidarize or just to entertain. Moreover, this homologous proliferation of self-promotional forms goes beyond the cultural sphere. Not only are the same forms – imaged commodities as advertisements for themselves – to be found throughout the whole world of commercially produced goods. From the clothes we wear, to the parties we vote for at election time, wherever in fact a market of some kind operates, everything mirrors back the same basic signifying mode.

However, the rise of promotion has entailed more than just the boundary-crossing spread of similar rhetorical forms. In a multitude of instances, promotion in one sector has come to dovetail with promotion in another. Bush's campaign appear-ance at Disneyland advertised that company, just as Disney's $13 million hyping of *Dick Tracy* two years later incidentally boosted the sales of ('Breathless') Ma-donna's latest album, not to mention audience receipts from the world tour which launched it. In addition, promotional messages borrow their imaging ideas and techniques from one another, whether through direct quotes (in the cola wars), through the logic of positioning wherein a market is segmented into differentially imaged niches, or, more diffusely, by circulating the same stock of promotionally tried-and-tested motifs and social types.

Promotion in different spheres, then, multiply interconnects – both in terms of the common pool of myths, symbols, tropes and values which it employs, and through the way in which each of the objects to which a promotional message is attached is itself a promotional sign, and so on in an endless chain of mutual reference and implication. Following McLuhan's (1967: v) reference to Poe's sailor, I have described the symbolic world which results as a giant vortex in which, for producers and receivers of culture alike, all signifying gestures are swallowed up. But having in mind the *promesse de bonheur* which the discourses of promotion continually proffer, and defer, that vortex can also be thought of as a maze. In fact, an infinite maze: in which there is no final destination, no final reward, and where the walls are pictures (and pictures of pictures) of ever multiplying varieties of cheese.

Thus, and this is my first point, we can say that the extension of promotion through all the circuits of social life is indeed a force for cultural homogenization, but only if we add the rider that the outcome is not a mere repetition everywhere of the same. For it brings into being a vast web of discourse which is at once continuous from one part to the next, yet asymmetrical with regard to what (and how many) purchasable entities are being aided thereby in their competitive circulation. Overall, then, the sameness of rhetorical form which promotion everywhere installs is counter-balanced by a semiological complexity which makes every point in the flow as intriguing in its formal construction as it is boringly void of deeper content. As Daniel Boorstin has noted, this seductive quality frustrates any merely demystifying critique. 'Information about the staging of a pseudo-event simply adds to its fascination' (Boorstin, 1961: 38).[5]

A second respect in which promotion shapes the signifying materials of a culture in which that mode has generalized is that these materials become pervasively instrumental in character. The point of promotion is to effect a valorizing exchange, and its whole communicative substance is directed to that end.

Again, instrumentalism is a trend about which traditional social theory has had much to say. The notion that in the transition to modernity means–ends rationality became an end in itself, both in the economy, through science-based production, and in the state, through law and bureaucracy, passed from Weber and Heidegger to the Frankfurt thinkers, and thence to Habermas, through whom it has remained a central preoccupation of contemporary thought. For postwar critics of consumer culture, particularly in the United States, the same problematic has framed a corresponding interest in how, through the applications of behavioural psychology, psychoanalysis and the like, the needs and purchasing decisions of consumers are manipulated from above. In that spirit popular writes from Vance Packard [see chapter 17, this volume] to Brian Key have joined with philosophical ones like Marcuse to generate a picture of advertising as the cultural arm of a totally administered society. Such analysis falters, however, when it comes to demonstrating, whether in the case of selling soap or selling politicians, that such manipulation is really scientific, and, more to the point, that it actually works. As Schudson (1986: 210) notes: 'Advertising may shape our sense of values even where it does not greatly corrupt our buying habits.'

In any case, the cultural problem presented by the instrumental character of advertising, or indeed of promotion in any of its forms, is not just a question of the freedom-violating devices through which goods are sold, needs are shaped, or political order maintained. Beyond this external instrumentality, the discourse of promotion is instrumental *vis-à-vis* itself. If we consider that speech acts have two functions, the performative (aiming at an external change of state in the listener) and the referential (aiming at the communication of a meaning), then what characterizes promotional speech is the thoroughness with which the former is subordinated to the latter. The case is similar to propaganda, though there is a difference. The effectiveness of promotion is not measured by the extent to which its claims and perspectives are actually believed. What matters is simply the willingness of its audience to complete the transaction promotion aims to initiate. And in this, the causality is not so much 'truth' as the very meaningfulness of the language material (whether verbal, visual or auditory) which promotional messages mobilize to that end.

Because of their calculatedly supporting role, in other words, the ideals and myths conjured up by the words and symbols used to endow a product, institution or personality with imagistic appeal are emotionally, and existentially, devalued. The effect is complementary to the one Roland Barthes (1972) focused on in his analysis of myth. There – for example, in the French *lycee* teacher's use of the Latin tag 'ego nominor leo' (my name is lion) to indicate a grammatical rule – a first-order meaning (who cares about the lion?) is effaced before a second-order one (grammatical correctness) conjured up by the first-order sign as a whole. In promotion, these second-order meanings themselves fade in the extrinsic (and profaning) use to which they are put. The Paradise myth evidently packs less of a spiritual punch in a cigarette ad than in an act of worship. In turn, because of the associative responses which advertising itself engenders, this cheapening of the symbolic currency becomes general and feeds back. Even in a church, it is hard to hear 'paradise' without thinking of the multitude of goods – starting with song and film titles – to which that idea, and the many ways of rendering it, have been promotionally linked.

Such devaluation applies, moreover, not only to the plane of the signified, but also to that of the signifier. When Billie Holiday's poignant rendition of 'Summertime' is played as the voice-over for a VW ad, its own mystique as a 'classic' performance, which is inextricable from her own as a tragic figure, is diminished in the very act wherein that of the car is associatively enhanced. Fear of a similar effect has led to the banning in British commercials to direct references to royalty. Paradoxically, then, while the vast apparatus of selling uses established social and psychological values to move the merchandise, and thus incidentally serves as an ideological transmitter as well, that very linkage, which makes the rhetoric of ideology itself rhetorical, dis-cathects the moral, political, etc., categories and symbologies of ideological discourse as such.

I have been speaking, so far, about the way that the rise of promotion has been associated with the generation and diffusion of a certain kind of language material. But it is important to consider as well the effect of promotion on the things it promotes. At first sight, promotion stands apart from its object as an external instrument in that object's circulation. However, the (self-interested) exchange of buyer–seller information is an intrinsic aspect of any market. Promotion of some kind – even if it is only a matter of heaping apples on a road-side table to indicate that they are for sale – is necessary to complete an object's instantiation as an item of exchange. In the developed state, moreover, where commodities are designed to have symbolic appeal as part of their own selling operation, the unity of this process is replicated in the very form of the object. There, what is promoted, cannot be disentangled from what it promotes, even in principle.

Haug (1986) [see chapter 20, this volume] has coined the term 'commodity aesthetics' to describe this reflexive effect. But, adopting Marx's language of prostitutes and pimps, he still sees the promotional dressing-up of commodities as an externality; indeed, as an unnatural embellishment which both mystifies what circulating objects really are – items of human use – and distorts our needing/desiring relation to them. However, for things implicated in a competitive market to be given a self-promotional form is not merely a decorative – and dissimulating – addition. It changes their very being. An object which happens to circulate is converted into one which is designed to do so, and so is materially stamped with that character. In the case, say, of a Morphy-Richards iron, or even of a Wedgewood vase or a GM car, the distinction between a commodity – only marked as such by its invisible price – and a (self-advertising) commodity-sign may not seem to be of great consequence. For it is only the outward appearance of the latter which is semiotically inscribed, while the bundle of performance characteristics which define what such objects 'really' are remains the same. This cannot be said, though, when the imaged commodity (or quasi-commodity) is already, at the level of its actual use, a complex of signs. When a piece of music, or a newspaper article, or even an academically written book about promotional culture, is fashioned with an eye to how it will promote itself – and, indeed, how it will promote its author and distributor, together with all the other produce these named agencies may be identified with – such goods are affected by this circumstance in every detail of their production.

The necessary and determinate extension of a commodity or quasi-commodity into a promotional sign, and the reincorporation of this into the constitution of the promoted entity itself, manifests, in the clearest fashion, what Derrida has called the logic of the supplement. Promotion is the significative supplement of the commodity. It transforms what it doubles and extends. Furthermore, just as (in Derrida's account) the transformative supplement of writing has been part of language since its oral origins, so too has promotion always been an aspect of even the most undeveloped form of market. The absorption of the circulating object into the circulating sign through 'commodity aesthetics', for all that it has been a real historical process, builds on, develops and extends a characteristic of the commodity form which is inscribed in its very origin.

Beyond the impact of generalized impact of promotion on the discourses and objects that make up the external aspects of our symbolic world, a few words are needed, finally, on what this development has implied for the subjectivity of those whose communicative activity is mediated by it.

No reflection on the contemporary situation of 'the subject' can avoid reference to the debate which has raged for the last three decades about that category. The initial challenges of structuralism and deconstruction were aimed against radical currents of thought which deployed a vocabulary of history, praxis and freedom against the alienating and reifying tendencies of a developed capitalism.[6] However, the critique of that humanist vocabulary by Barthes, Althusser, Foucault and Derrida joined forces with those who used it (against the system) in questioning the inflated individualism which they all took to be an ideological foundation of the established order. As a result, two different kinds of theses about the 'death of the subject' have tended to get confused. The first is a historical thesis, advanced by the early Frankfurt thinkers,[7] to the effect that the (industrial capitalist) organization of production has led to the disorganization of the (classical liberal) subject. At issue, here, is the actual decline, fragmentation and alienation of the producing and consuming individual in the face of a market-orientated socio-economic development whose justifying rhetoric falsely promised a moral and political progress predicated on the individual's emancipation as a (responsibly) free being. The second is a philosophical thesis deriving from Nietzsche's reflections on the Cartesian ego. This has questioned whether it is meaningful to talk about the subject at all – especially as an integrated entity which is the real author of its own thought and practice – since, in whatever social and historical situation, the thinking, believing, acting, self, both actually and as a concept, is constituted by, and in the medium of, language.

To propose that contemporary subjectivity is shaped by the cultural determinations I have been describing is evidently to place oneself in the register of the former, that is within the narrative of the (male/bourgeois/Protestant) individual's disautonomizing decline. To which it should be added, however, that the second, poststructuralist, thesis is not irrelevant to the question of how to factor in the mediating implications of promotion, since promotion itself is a communicative phenomenon. Thus the question of what has happened to the subject as a result of the spread of promotion turns, at least in part, on what has happened to the signifying practices and materials by which the individual subject has come to be enveloped.

The literature on advertising has tended to focus on this question from the side of reception, in which the most highlighted effects have been those which derive from the continual interpellation of subjects as consumers. That is: the growing prevalence of an anomic, feed-me, orientation to the world, and a psycho-economy of needs, desires and beliefs which is expressed in a totemic and fetishizing attitude towards branded goods.[8] As many commentators (Reisman, 1950; Reiche, 1970; Lasch, 1976) have noted, the ideological complex represented by consumerism has also been associated with the emergence of a modal character type – anxious, schizoidal, other-directed, oral-dependent, etc. – which exhibits the psycho-pathological features of what Freud dubbed the 'narcissistic personality'.

To catalogue, I would add only one further point. It concerns not the psychology or anthropology of consumption but the impact on individual consciousness of promotional culture as a whole. If we accept that the symbolic universe reconstituted by the rise of promotion has been de-referentialized – a quality which stems, on the one hand, from promotion's instrumentalization of values and symbols, and on the other from its perpetual deferral of the promoted object, together with any closure of the gap of desire which that object's final arrival might bring – then the promotionally addressed subject has been placed in a novel cultural predicament: how to build an identity and an orientation from the materials of a culture whose meanings are unstable and behind which , for all the personalized manner in which its multitudinous messages are delivered, no genuinely expressive intention can be read. Schizophrenic disintegration and the consumerized conformism of the Pepsi Generation are only the most extreme poles of possible response. More common is a sensibility which oscillates between a playful willingness to be temporarily seduced and a hardened scepticism about every kind of communication in view of the selling job it is probably doing. In that light, cynical privatism and mass apathy – an index of which is falling participation rate in American elections – can even be construed as a sign of resistance: for Baudrillard (1983), the only form of resistance still open to the media-bombarded 'silent majority'.

But the envelopment of the individual by promotion must be grasped from both sides of the promotional sign. It is not enough to look at this question only from the side of reception, that is to look at subjects only as readers/listeners addressed only by a certain kind of speech. We must also take account of the way in which the contemporary subject has become implicated in promotional culture as a writer/performer of its texts.

Of course, only a minority play a directly authorial role in the imaging and marketing of commercial produce. Fewer still are the named creators or performers of cultural goods, though these have an exemplary importance since media stars are our equivalent of mythic heroes, providing the most salient paradigms of how individual praxis contributes to the shaping of our world. But the list grows if we also include all those playing a more specialist or subordinate role in commercial promotion, as well as those engaged in non- or quasi-commercial forms of promotional practice like electoral politics, or the public relations side of hospitals, schools and churches. In any case, from dating and clothing shopping to attending a job interview, virtually everyone is involved in the self-promotionalism which overlays such practices in the micro-sphere of everyday life.

At one level or another, then, and often at several levels at once, we are all promotional subjects. Nor can we practically choose not to be. The penalty of not playing the game is to play it badly; or even, inadvertently, to play it well. Sincerity has become a prized virtue in a society where phoniness is a universal condition. Hence the cult of the natural and unaffected – a cult which is catered to even in the transparently artificial world of show business when, for example, David Bowie in the early 1980s put Ziggy Stardust and the Thin White Duke behind him and reincarnated as himself.

This example illustrates an even more fundamental point. Individuals who self-advertise are doubly implicated in such practice. They are, that is, not only promotional authors but promotional products. The subject that promotes itself constructs itself for others in line with the competitive imaging needs of its market. Just like any other artificially imaged commodity, then, the resultant construct – a persona produced for public consumption – is marked by the transformative effects of the promotional supplement. The outcome is not just the socially adapted self of mainstream social psychology, a panoply of self-identified roles attuned to the requirements of the social position(s) which a person has come to occupy. It is a self which continually produces itself for competitive circulation: an enacted projection, which includes not only dress, speech, gestures and actions, but also, through health and beauty practices, the cultivated body of the actor; a projection which is itself, moreover, an inextricable mixture of what its author/object actually has to offer, the signs by which this might be recognized, and the symbolic appeal this is given in order to enhance the advantages which can be obtained from its trade.

While in other respects their writings are now dated, the social phenomenologists, from Sartre to Goffman, who pondered these matters in the late 1950s (against a drum-beat of concerns about conformism, alienation and anxiety), drew attention to a real issue. The contemporary subject, and nowhere more than in the competitively mediated zones of work and play where our personal self-presentations directly affect our inter-individual rates of exchange, is faced with a profound problem of authenticity. If social survival, let alone competitive success, depends on continual, audience-orientated, self-staging, what are we behind the mask? If the answer points to a second identity (a puppeteer?) how are we to negotiate the split sense of self this implies?[9]

Intersubjectivity, too, is infected by doubt. Knowing how our own promotional moves will be read, how can we make credible to others the imaged egos we want to project as truly our own? And conversely: how can we decipher aright the self-stagings which are similarly projects towards us? To be sure, the result need not be total moral chaos. An ironic distantiation is always possible, and signalling this, or just mutually acknowledging it to be the case, enables us, despite the promotional enactments normally dissimulated on the surface of our discourse, to preserve dialogical respect. None the less, public acts of communication will always be distorted, and properly distrusted, in a social universe in which market forms, and the promotional dynamics to which they give rise, are universally operative. Inauthentic writers are constantly being counterposed to cynical readers: a relationship in which the latter always need to be convinced, while the former must find ways to obviate that resistance when crafting messages for release.

From top to bottom, in short, promotional culture is radically deficient in good faith. For those with sensitive moral digestions, this description will seem too weak. Considering the sugar coating which pastes a personal smile, and a patina of conformist values, over the pervasively self-interested motives which underlie virtually all publicly communicated words and images, the total impression it makes (against which, of course, we screen ourselves through wise inattention) is not merely vacuous, but emetic in its perpetual untruth.

Exit?

The transformist impulse within the tradition of critical social theory from which I have drawn joins with the affirmative conventions of promotional culture itself to direct me to close these reflections on a note, if not of optimism, then at least of openness to what a better future might bring. In doing so, I will not disavow the bleakness of the diagnosis. The spectre of totalitarianism has evidently receded in advanced industrial societies. In two respects, though, a meditation on the place of promotion in contemporary society faces even more difficulties when it comes to thinking our way towards a more liberated, civilized and organic path of cultural development than was the case for Horkheimer and Adorno when they wrote their gloomy analysis of the culture industry under the shadow of Auschwitz and Mickey Mouse in the early 1940s.

The first is bound up with what both opponents and celebrants of the Thatcher–Reagan era have concurred in describing as the global triumph of liberal capitalism. Not only have the Stalinist regimes of the East collapsed, but also state socialism as a credible project for the Western left. As well, even proponents of a 'third way' – whether cast in the form of socialist democracy, or of a mixed economy with a devolved public sector – have come to seem hopelessly out of touch with a march of events dominated by free trade, the privatization of state enterprise, and the globalization of corporate capital. With markets as with procreation, it seems, you can't be a little bit pregnant.

The correlative development of a culture increasingly made up of endless ads, and driven throughout by the dynamics of commodities and their competitive circulation, has also established itself on a world scale. And to this, the only alternative which currently presents itself is the type of solution represented, most dramatically, by the revival of Islam. That is: the renewed imposition, in a developmental crisis of modernization, of those traditional/authoritarian blockages to market circulation which a colleague of mine has aptly (and approvingly) characterized as 'atavisms'.[10] It is hard to think of this as more than a temporary (and terroristic) halt. In any case, a reactive fundamentalism, which has its weak First World echoes in born-again Christianity, can have little appeal for those whose vision of social progress has itself emerged from the expectations generated out of the partial freedoms delivered by the market, for example in a more egalitarian and emancipated relation between the sexes.

The second difficulty stems from the very character of the phenomenon under discussion. The way in which the promotional mode has extended to all facets of social communication suggests that commercialism, and the market principle more generally, is an even more engulfing cultural force than was supposed by the Frankfurt thinkers. I can illustrate this with a trivial incident from a recent late night chat show on British TV.[11] The interviewee was a member of the fictional heavy metal band Spinal Tap, as featured in the satirical movie of that name. The first half of the interview was 'in character', like an episode from the movie itself. The second half, after a chuckle, got down to the serious business of trade talk. It transpired that Spinal Tap (one of the songs from the movie's soundtrack had already been a minor hit) were now really on tour, lip-synching their numbers to live audiences in the midst of the same preposterously exaggerated gothic sets has had graced their equally simulated performances on screen. Having performed in Seattle, they were about to try their hand in London. (The fact that they were not a great success can be attributed to the fact that by the late 1980s heavy metal had been eclipsed by rap as the music of choice for working-class youth, so that the parodic effects were blunted.)

Retroactively, then, the original movie's (pseudo-promotional) savaging of the music business had been turned into actual promotion for an 'act' which was itself designed to promote the re-released video and accompanying record. Echoing this, the interview's mid-point switch from a fake conversation registered only the transition from the promotional satirization of promotion to promotion itself. Not even satire, then, is immune from a process it may seek to destroy through laughter. And the same can be said of other forms of critique as well. Once we are communicating at all, and especially in public, and therefore in a medium which is promotional through and through, there is no going outside promotional discourse. These very words are continuous with what they are seeking to distance themselves from. To paraphrase what Derrida remarked of textuality in general: there is no *hors-promotion*.

That said, discourse is not the whole of being. And when we look at things in wider perspective, we can see that the extensive and intensive penetration of culture by promotion has not been without its elements of tension and conflict.

Two levels of contradiction can be identified. The first involves what may be termed contradictions of circulation. Here, there is a clash between the promotional imperative inherent in the market's lust-to-expand, and the resistance exercised by the moral, aesthetic or religious mechanisms which, in the interests of the current order, surround certain symbols, entities or sites of potential publicity so as to secure their exclusion from profane processes of circulation. Contradictions of this kind are evident in the uneasiness which, since John Stuart Mill, has attended the development of electioneering, in the clash of campaigns for and against legalizing street prostitution, and in the controversies which break out (though I am not remotely suggesting that this was Rushdie's motive) when an author enhances his name by dancing pirouettes through the revealed truths of a militant world religion. The second type of contradiction is at the level of mass psychology. This concerns the tendency of a promotionalized culture to become depleted of the (existential and cosmological) meaningfulness which those implicated in it, just because it is a culture, seek to derive from its symbolic material. In this direction lie the worried hunches not only of conservative thinkers like Daniel Bell or Robert Nisbet, but also of more liberal ones like Anthony Giddens (1990), that late capitalism is drifting towards a fully-fledged spiritual-cum-ideological crisis.

These two sources of tension generate the space and energy for a kind of politics. Normally, as in the instances cited, it is localized and intermittent. However, and without wishing to reduce very complex events and processes to a simple formula, modern history has also shown us, as in interwar Europe and in North America during the 1960s, that a condensation of the contradictions of circulation of a depleted ideological meaning can create the conditions for a massive cultural revolt. All of which implies that, while history never repeats itself, the spread of commodification is associated with ongoing cultural contradictions which go to the roots of capitalism's processes of social reproduction, and that the activization of these provides a certain room to manoeuvre for those wishing to influence, against the grain of the advancing market, the larger drift of events.

But manoeuvre how? The long-range goal that suggests itself is to enlarge the sphere in which promotion is circumscribed. Even as a gradualist project, it should be emphasized, this is not just a question of restricting bad symbols, but of restricting a bad kind of circulation. At the same time, to speak of restriction alone is not enough. There is an evident danger that any politics of inhibiting promotional circulation can get tangled up in rearguard struggles in which pre-market unfreedoms, associated with repressive–hierarchical definitions of the sacred, are reactively defended or restored. A more radical objective would therefore involve not just rolling back the area of cultural life colonized by competitive exchange, but doing so at the same time as the sacralized categories marking out the boundaries

315

of permissible, competitive circulation were themselves humanistically redefined. This possibility can already be glimpsed in situations of familial or affective intimacy where, against the weight of convention and habit, the creative power of symbolic exchange, and the new forms it can create, can be commonsensically acknowledged and given their due. In the public realm, hemmed in by economic interests, state regulation and institutional rigidity, a similar recognition would require a transformed consciousness on the part of those who are stewards of socially important institutions and resources, and the translation of such recognition into a transformed practice.

In the long term, any strategy of promotional limitation evidently depends on releasing cultural production from its currently overwhelming commercial imperative. In turn, this implies greater subsidies from taxation for all forms of cultural activity, whether popular, mass or minority, so as to reduce reliance both on advertising revenue and on corporate sponsorships. As well, it implies a sustained effort to revalorize the public realm itself as a space for disinterested expression and communication. That all this is intimately connected to a larger project of restricting the market in favour of co-operation, rehabilitating the public sphere, and dis-alienating secondary institutions, both internally, and *vis-à-vis* their clients and constituencies, also goes without saying.

At a time of sustained neo-conservative retrenchment, such sentiments will seem dismissibly utopian. If so, I offer no counter-prognoses about when, or whether, contemporary civilization will reopen to buried dreams. Proving the this-sidedness of our (social) thinking is a matter for (political) practice, not theoretical speculation – and who would dare to predict? Meanwhile, in an exercise which has sought merely to depict some of the consequences of blindly pursuing the current market-oriented path, the most that can be hoped for is as modest as the horizons of the time to which it belongs: that while history spins its wheels some hint of what the present dispensation blocks can be kept, at least negatively, alive.

Notes

1 For Baudrillard, however, the crux of the sign-commodity conjunction lies in the totemic and status-differential 'system of object' which mass-produced consumer goods represent at the point of consumption. Sign-exchange-value doubles exchange-value in the constitution of the commodity, constituting a new term (the commodity-sign) within an expanded, and infinitely commutable, field of 'general exchange'. This model is elaborated throughout Baudrillard's early writings, and receives its most formal treatment in Baudrillard 1981, especially pp. 123–9 and 143–63.

2 To which we might now add the promotional conquest of outer space. In saying this I am not just referring to the superpower boosterism of the space race, but to its actual commercialization as a spectacle (logos on spaceships, etc.) which the post-Cold War Soviet programme, suddenly starved for cash, has pioneered.

3 Lash, Featherstone, and others have recently taken this argument up again in the context of contemporary discussion about postmodernity and postmodern culture. See Featherstone (1988) and Lash (1990).

4 'The prevailing taste takes its ideal from advertising, the beauty in consumption. Hence the Socratic saying that the beautiful is the useful has been fulfilled – ironically. The cinema makes propaganda for the culture combine as a whole; on radio, goods for whose sake the cultural commodity exists are also recommended individually' (Horkheimer and Adorno, 1972: 156).

5 That advertisements are creative and can be enjoyed, and judged, in aesthetic terms beyond utilitarian criteria about sales effectiveness, has occurred to many, inside and outside the advertising industry. In a recent article, Nava and Nava (1990) highlight the 'interconnections and overlap between commercial and other forms of art in order to expand our understanding of the ways in which young people exercise critical abilities as audience'. The Cannes Film Festival (whose promotional function is self-evident) includes a competitive section on TV ads. Of course, whether or not advertising has to be regarded (properly speaking) as 'art' depends on whether that category is descriptively and normatively identified with autonomous art, an ideal that rose and fell between the Renaissance and the beginning of this century.

6 For Althusser's decentring assault on humanism and existentialism as the basis for a 'scientific' revolutionary theory, see especially 'Marxism is not a humanism' in Althusser (1969). In a parallel (though not of course identically inspired move) Derrida was equally concerned to rescue Husserl and Heidegger from the left-existentialism to which, through Sartre, especially, their work had become linked. See 'The ends of man' in Derrida (1986: 109–36).

7 See, for example, Horkheimer (1972: 235–7)

8 For a discussion of totemism and consumer goods see Leiss et al. (1986) [chapter 21, this volume], Jhally (1987) and Douglas and Isherwood (1979) [chapter 6, this volume].

9 The work of Irving Goffman (especially 1959) can be read, in this context, as an interactionist exploration of the promotional self, while that of R. D. Laing and associates can be read as an exploration of the schizophrenogenic consequences.

10 I owe this phrase to my colleague Pradeep Bandyopadhyay, for whom the 'atavisms' however are to be viewed positively, i.e. as a way for non-Western civilizations to assert themselves against the West.

11 The clip was shown shortly after midnight, 22 October 1990, on channel 3.

References

Althusser, L. (1969) *For Marx*, London: Allen Lane.
Barthes, R. (1972) *Mythologies*, New York: Hill and Wang.
Baudrillard, J. (1981) *Towards a Critique of the Political Economy of the Sign*, Paris: Gallimard.
Baudrillard, J. (1983) *In the Shadow of the Silent Majority*, New York: Semiotext(e).
Boorstin, D. (1961) *The Image: or What Happened to the American Dream*, London: Weidenfeld and Nicolson.

Bourdieu, P. (1977) *Outline of a Theory of Practice*, translated by R. Nice, Cambridge: Cambridge University Press.

Debord, G. (1977) *The Society of the Spectacle*, Detroit: Black and Red.

Derrida, J. (1986) *The Margins of Philosophy*, Brighton: Harvester.

Douglas, M. and Isherwood, B. (1979) *The World of Goods*, New York: Basic Books.

Featherstone, M. (1988) 'In pursuit of the postmodern: an introduction', *Theory, Culture and Society*, 5: 195–215.

Giddens, A. (1990) *The Consequences of Modernity*, Cambridge: Polity Press.

Goffman, E. (1959) *The Presentation of Self in Everyday Life*, Garden City, NY: Anchor.

Horkheimer, M. and Adorno, T. (1972) *Dialectic of Enlightenment*, New York: Herder and Herder.

Horkheimer, T. (1972) *Critical Theory: Selected Essays*, New York: Seabury.

Jameson, F. (1984) 'Postmodernism, or the cultural logic of capital', *New Left Review*, 146: 55–92.

Jhally, S. (1987) *The Codes of Advertising: Fetishism and the Political Economy of Meaning in the Consumer Society*, London: Frances Pinter.

Lasch, C. (1976) *The Culture of Narcissism: American Life in the Age of Diminishing Expectations*, New York: Norton.

Lash, S. (1990) *The Sociology of Postmodernism*, London: Routledge.

Leiss, W., Kline, S. and Jhally, S. (1986) *Social Communication in Advertising: Persons, Products and Images of Well-Being*, Toronto: Methuen.

McLuhan, M. (1967) *The Mechanical Bride: Folklaw of Industrial Man*, Boston: Beacon.

Nava, M. and Nava, O. (1990) *MOCS* No. 1, March 1990.

Reiche, R. (1970) *Sexuality and Class Struggle*, London: New Left Books.

Reisman, D. (1950) *The Lonely Crowd: A Study of the Changing American Character*, Garden City, NY: Doubleday.

Schudson, M. (1986) *Advertising: The Uneasy Persuasion. Its Dubious Impact on American Society*, New York: Basic Books.

Williams, R. (1982) *The Sociology of Culture*, New York: Schocken.

Name Index

Subject Index